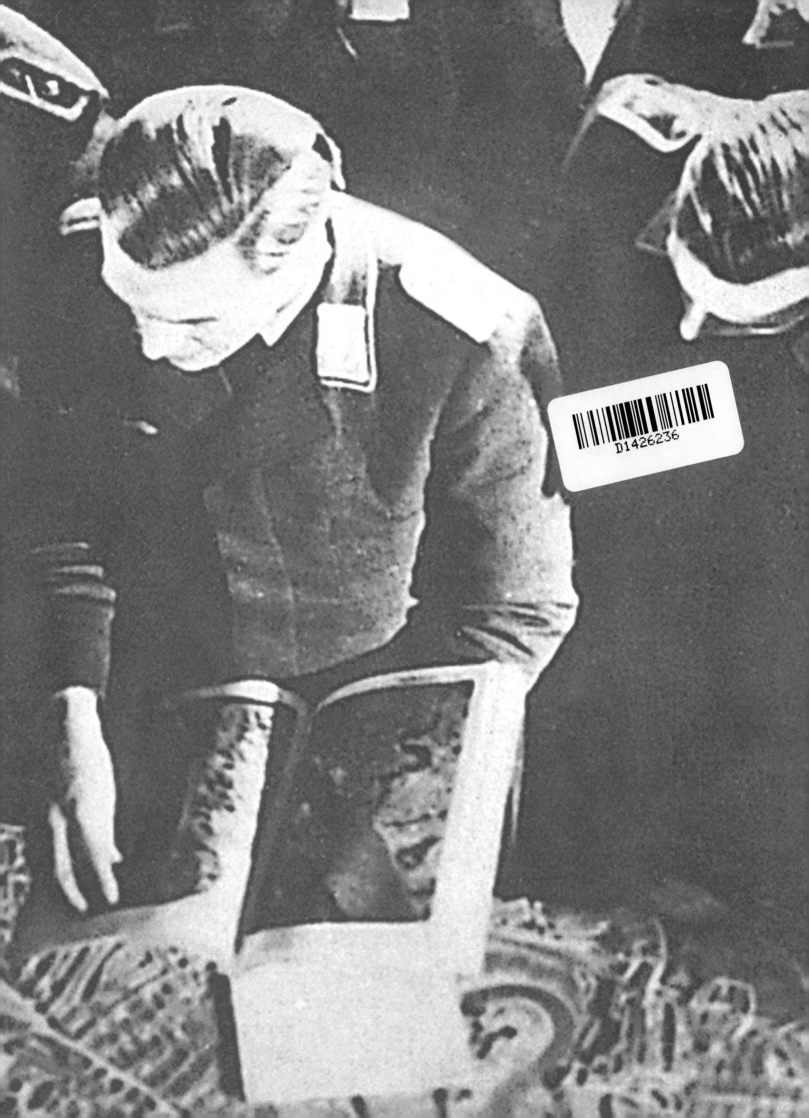

ATLAS
OF WORLD WAR II

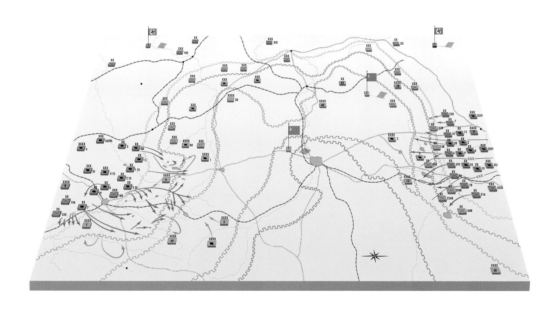

ATLAS
OF WORLD WAR II

OVER 160 DETAILED BATTLE & CAMPAIGN MAPS

DAVID JORDAN AND ANDREW WIEST

Published in 2004 by Silverdale Books
an imprint of Bookmart Ltd
Registered Number 2372865
Trading as Bookmart Ltd
Blaby Road
Wigston
Leicester LE18 4SE

Editorial and design by
Amber Books Ltd
Bradley's Close
74-77 White Lion Street
London N1 9PF
www.amberbooks.co.uk

ISBN: 1-84509-035-7

Project Editors: Charles Catton, Charlotte Judet and Tom Broder
Design: Jerry Williams

Printed in Dubai, U.A.E.

Photo credits: TRH Pictures Ltd and Art-Tech Ltd
All maps drawn by Cartographica Ltd

CONTENTS

LIST OF MAPS

The Background to War

The old world order which had lasted since 1815 may have disappeared in the aftermath of World War I, but the treaties signed at Versailles and elsewhere failed to reflect a shift in the balance of power and the emergence of Germany, the Soviet Union, Japan and, to some extent, Italy as great powers. Each felt cheated by its peace settlement and looked for opportunities to claim its rightful due.

The cataclysm that was World War I left Europe battered, transformed and in desperate danger of renewed conflict. The battles of 1914–18 had been ghastly, yet indecisive. Germany, seen by many as the culprit in the coming of the war, had been defeated – but never invaded and destroyed. The closing act to the war, the Treaty of Versailles, proved to be a bizarre and fatally flawed compromise between two extremes. The French, who had suffered grievous losses during the war, wanted finally to destroy Germany and ensure that it could never threaten them again. The United States, on the other hand, sought a more magnanimous peace based on President Wilson's famous Fourteen Points. The results of the compromise peace proved dangerous indeed.

Russia, driven to defeat by the Germans in 1917, had collapsed into revolution, and the spectre of worldwide Communist revolution was unleashed – at least for a few years. In addition, the former ally of the winning side lost much territory in eastern Europe, notably to the newly formed Baltic states and to Poland. The Austro-Hungarian Empire, long a front-rank power, disappeared overnight, shattering into its component national parts, creating a host of new nations and forever altering the balance of power in Europe. Of the greatest importance, though, was the fate of Germany. Blamed for the conflict, Germany was to pay reparations for the entire war, faced severe military restrictions and lost nearly one-third of its land. The Treaty of Versailles left Germany humiliated and near societal breakdown; however, Versailles also left Germany with the seeds of great strength. Germany remained the most populous nation in western Europe with the potential for a massive economy and plenty of natural resources.

Amid the chaos in the wake of World War I, several European nations saw the rise of radical political parties dedicated to the destruction of the existing system. Communists, drawing strength from the revolution in Russia, gained political support and led strikes across the continent. In many nations, parties of the far right arose to counter what they saw as the Communist threat. In 1923 the proponents of the right scored a startling success with Benito Mussolini's Fascist takeover in Italy. An era of political extremism and social revolution had been created by the war and now swept across Europe.

GERMAN CHAOS

In Germany, the political situation was dire. Although the democratic but chaotic Weimar Republic attempted to steer a middle course during the troubled times, the very existence of a democratic Germany would be thrown into doubt by a series of economic disasters. In 1923 the French occupied the German industrial area of the Ruhr over a reparations dispute. During the occupation, the rate of inflation in Germany spiralled out of control. Before World War I, the exchange rate was 4.2 German marks to one US dollar. At the height of the inflation, it took 4.2 *trillion* marks to equal a dollar. The economic crisis simply wiped out Germany's middle class and drove ever-greater numbers of Germans into the ranks of the radical political parties.

A rather small but energetic group known as the National Socialist German Workers' Party (NSDAP), commonly called the Nazis, worked tirelessly to gain support during the difficult times under its charismatic leader Adolf Hitler. Through a combination

Left: Dornier Do 17 bombers overfly a Nazi Party rally in the late 1930s. The military successes of the German army in World War I and the fact that it remained ultimately undefeated at the end of the war – the war was ended by an armistice, not a general surrender – led to the rise in popularity of a theory that Germany's soldiers had been 'stabbed in the back' by a lack of support at home or, worse still, a 'Jewish conspiracy'. Hitler and the Nazis deliberately fed such theories, and they undoubtedly helped to draw in supporters for the extremist political parties.

of oratory and pageantry, Hitler brought a powerful message to the German people. The Nazis promised to make Germany great again through the destruction of the Treaty of Versailles and the reconstruction of the German economy. The Nazis also told Germans exactly whom to blame for their current misfortunes – Communists and Jews.

As the Weimar Republic slowly put its economic house in order, disaster struck again in 1929 with the onset of the Great Depression. Once again the resurgent German middle class was destroyed, resulting in an upsurge of support for the Nazis, transforming them into the largest political party in Germany. After a sea of riots and political street fighting, on 30 January 1933 Adolf Hitler took over the position of Chancellor of Germany, and the Nazi era had begun.

The economic and political chaos of Europe in the wake of the Great Depression led to a series of major foreign policy developments that would set the sides for the coming conflict. In Germany, Hitler quickly acted on his ambition to scrap the Treaty of Versailles by announcing the expansion of the German military. At the same time, Hitler, something of an international pariah, announced his first major international agreement, a non-aggression pact with Poland. Ever ambitious, Hitler next began to look towards *Anschluss*, or union with Austria.

REDRAWING EUROPE

The harsh terms of the 1919 Treaty of Versailles, which brought World War I to its conclusion, ensured a lasting sense of resentment in Germany. The treaty altered the map of central Europe dramatically. Alsace and Lorraine (gained by Germany in 1871) were ceded back to France, and an important German coalmining area, the Saar, fell under League of Nations' supervision for 15 years. The Rhineland, too, was to be occupied by Allied troops for 15 years before becoming permanently demilitarized.

The most significant territorial changes, however, came in the east: Poland reappeared on the map of Europe, rebuilt from land taken from both Germany and the Soviet Union. The most controversial loss to Germany was the 'Polish corridor', a strip of ethnically-German land awarded to Poland to allow access to the Baltic Sea, which was deemed necessary for the new state's survival. The port of Danzig became a free city under the control of the League of Nations, but Poland could use its facilities. Germany had thus lost a significant amount of territory; however, much of Germany's core population and economic potential remained untouched. Germany was still the largest economic power on the continent and second only to the Soviet Union in terms of population size. The country's latent power remained, ready to be tapped by Hitler's aggressive drive for growth in the 1930s.

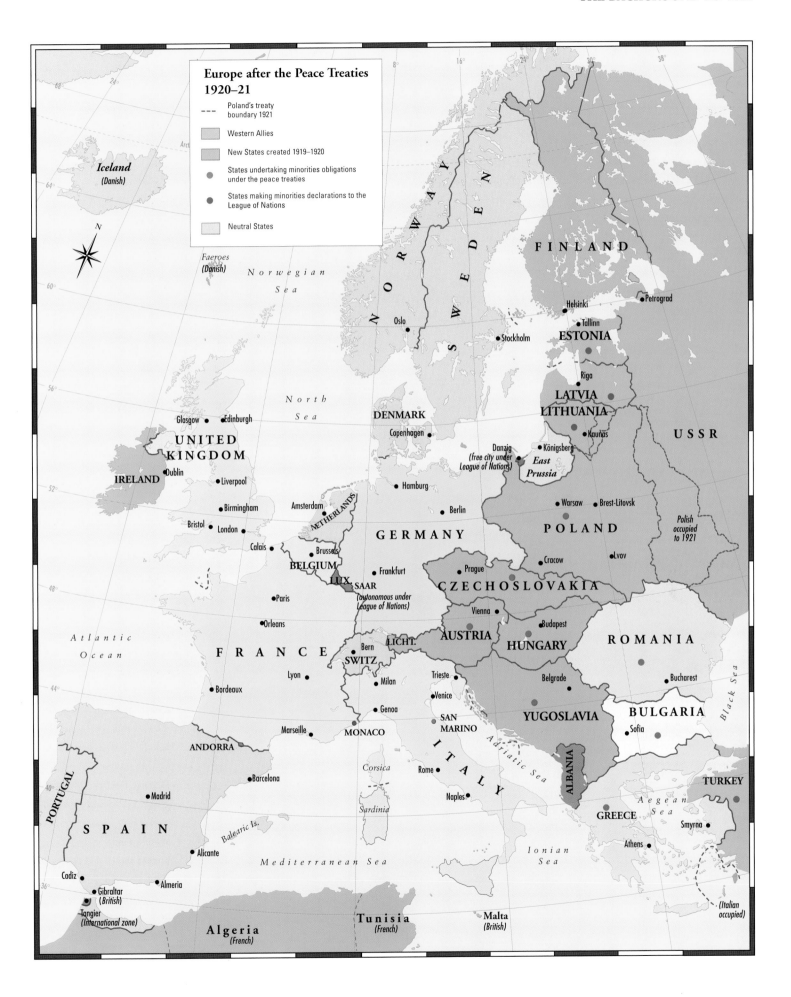

**Europe after the Peace Treaties
1920–21**

- - - - Poland's treaty
boundary 1921

Western Allies

New States created 1919–1920

States undertaking minorities obligations
under the peace treaties

States making minorities declarations to the
League of Nations

Neutral States

Iceland
(Danish)

Arch

Faeroes
(Danish)

*Norwegian
Sea*

N O R W A Y

S W E D E N

F I N L A N D

•Helsinki

•Petrograd

Oslo•

•Tallinn

ESTONIA

•Stockholm

*North
Sea*

DENMARK

Copenhagen•

•Riga

LATVIA

LITHUANIA

•Kaunas

U S S R

Glasgow• •Edinburgh

**UNITED
KINGDOM**

Danzig
(free city under
League of Nations)

•Königsberg

*East
Prussia*

IRELAND

•Dublin

•Liverpool

•Hamburg

•Warsaw   •Brest-Litovsk

*Polish
occupied
to 1921*

Amsterdam•

•Berlin

P O L A N D

Bristol• •London

NETHERLANDS

G E R M A N Y

•Birmingham

Calais•

Brussels•

•Frankfurt

Cracow•

•Lvov

BELGIUM

LUX.

CZECHOSLOVAKIA

SAAR
*(autonomous under
League of Nations)*

•Prague

•Paris

Vienna•

Orleans•

LICHT.

AUSTRIA

•Budapest

R O M A N I A

*Atlantic
Ocean*

F R A N C E

Bern•

SWITZ.

HUNGARY

Lyon•

•Milan

Trieste•

Belgrade•

•Bucharest

Black Sea

•Bordeaux

•Genoa

•Venice

Marseille•

MONACO

SAN
MARINO

YUGOSLAVIA

BULGARIA

*Adriatic
Sea*

ANDORRA

I T A L Y

Sofia•

•Barcelona

Corsica

Rome•

ALBANIA

TURKEY

•Madrid

•Naples

*Aegean
Sea*

GREECE

•Smyrna

S P A I N

Sardinia

•Alicante

Balearic Is.

*Ionian
Sea*

Athens•

PORTUGAL

Mediterranean Sea

Cadiz•

•Almeria

•Gibraltar
(British)

Tangier
(International zone)

Algeria
(French)

Tunisia
(French)

Malta
(British)

*(Italian
occupied)*

THE GREAT DEPRESSION

Despite the fact that the nations of the world – most notably the United States – struggled to salvage the post-war economic situation in Europe, the damage done by World War I was seemingly too great. Weakened further by the German hyper-inflation of 1923, the world's economy had never truly recovered from the privations imposed by the Great War.

In October 1929, the crash of the American stock market began a cascade of events that caused the Great Depression. Unemployment, poverty and hunger swept across the world. In Europe, the economic collapse caused a surge in support for radical parties at both extremes of the political spectrum, including both the Fascists and the Communists.

In the resulting turmoil, Germany and Spain joined Italy in the Fascist camp. In eastern Europe, regimes from Estonia in the north to Greece in the south walked a tightrope of repression, situated as they were between the Communist Soviet Union to the west and Nazi Germany to the east. Only Czechoslovakia persevered as a liberal democracy – joining France, Britain, the Low Countries and Scandinavia. Dictatorships and repressive governments with aggressive agendas now outnumbered democracies in Europe, setting the stage for war to break out in the region once more.

Above: At a *Parteitag* (Party Day) rally held at Nuremberg in southern Germany, the *Führer* Adolf Hitler surveys the massed ranks of the SA (*Sturmabteilung*, or 'Storm Detachment') in their distinctive brown uniforms. The SA helped him to power in 1933, but afterwards its leaders – perhaps the only potential rivals for Hitler's position – were removed in the bloody purge known as the 'Night of the Long Knives'. Having secured complete control of Germany, Hitler then decided to challenge the dominant powers in Europe.

Increasing German strength caused great consternation in both Italy and the Soviet Union. Mussolini ordered troops to the Austrian border to forestall *Anschluss*, and in 1935 representatives of Britain, France and Italy met in Stresa, Italy, to form the so-called 'Stresa Front' against German aggression. The Soviets, for their part, began to fear German power and signed a defensive military alliance with both France and Czechoslovakia in 1935. Thus it seemed that Hitler had been, in the main, diplomatically isolated and that both Communist and Fascist dictatorships had found common cause with democracies.

Unfortunately for the cause of peace, Italian ambitions in Africa would doom the Stresa Front. In late 1935 Mussolini sent his forces to invade Ethiopia. Britain and France, the leading colonial powers in Africa, were forced to respond and, through the League of Nations, placed economic sanctions on Italy, leaving Mussolini furious. For his part, Hitler saw the squabble over Africa as an opportunity. Hoping that France and Britain were too preoccupied to react, Hitler sent his fledgling armed forces into the Rhineland on 7 March 1936. The French and British chose not to risk war over German troops moving into what was, after all, German territory. Appeasement was born, and Mussolini did not fail to take notice of Germany's continued growing strength.

THE SPANISH CIVIL WAR
Shortly after the occupation of the Rhineland, simmering political problems erupted into open civil war in Spain. The Spanish Civil War pitted Fascist forces under the command of General Francisco Franco against troops loyal to the Socialist-Communist coalition government. During the conflict, both Italy and Germany made common cause with Franco and sent aid to the Fascist forces. The Soviet Union, in turn, sent aid and volunteers to the forces of the Spanish government. The vicious war in Spain dragged on until 1939, ending in a victory for Franco. It was during the war, however, that Italy and Germany moved closer together, while the Soviet Union drifted apart from its western alliance partners.

Impressed with the rising power of Germany, the Italians exited the Stresa Front in 1936 in favour of closer relations with the Third Reich. At the same time, tiny Belgium entered the diplomatic fray. Involved in a close military alliance with France, the Belgians would play a major role in any upcoming war with Germany. A Belgian system of defensive works, based on the mighty fortress of Eben Emael, was a buttress upon which a great deal of Allied planning depended. Disturbed, though, by the course of diplomatic events and perceived Allied weakness, in 1936 the Belgians opted instead for a declaration of neutrality – a move that threw French military planning into a state of disarray.

THE AXIS POWERS

The rapid development of events, which strengthened the German position in Europe, served to convince Mussolini that his future lay in an alliance with Germany. In November 1936 Germany and Italy signed an agreement that promised only a general cooperation between the two nations for the foreseeable future. In the rather vague treaty, termed the Rome–Berlin Axis, Mussolini technically retained options in time of war. Still, although he would often question German military adventures, the Italian dictator would honour the Axis agreement until the bitter end.

In the Far East, the coming of World War II was dominated by the collapse of the historical great power of the region, China, and the rise of a new world power, Japan. Possessing an advanced

Below: By the time World War II broke out, a number of the German armed forces had already seen action in the Spanish Civil War. Serving in the Condor Legion, supposedly a volunteer body, German soldiers and airmen fought for the Republican (pro-Franco) cause and gained valuable experience in combat. Such experience was to stand men, such as these crewmen of a Junkers Ju 88, in good stead during the opening years of World War II.

TREATIES AND AGREEMENTS

Adroit diplomatic manoeuvring on the part of Germany and a litany of diplomatic failures on the part of the Allies between 1934 and 1939 not only ended Germany's isolation, but also left the Third Reich in a position to launch a military effort aimed at world domination. In 1934 the Third Reich, desperate to break its isolation, made common cause with Poland – in fear of the might of the Soviet Union. German weakness was further demonstrated by a failed attempt at union with Austria. As a result, both Austria and Hungary signed protocols with their Italian protectors.

Of greatest importance, though, was the onset of the Franco–Soviet–Czech Pact. The alliance placed Germany in an untenable strategic situation and might well have halted the onset of World War II; however, the alliance was doomed by the onset of appeasement in the west. Within a single year, the diplomatic situation would change significantly.

Impressed with the rise in German power, Italy signed the Rome–Berlin Axis in November 1936, shortly after Belgium had complicated the military planning of France by declaring neutrality. During 1938 and 1939, German expansion was to shatter the Franco–Soviet–Czech Pact and finally convince the nations of Europe of Hitler's massive military ambitions and the threat to their sovereignty.

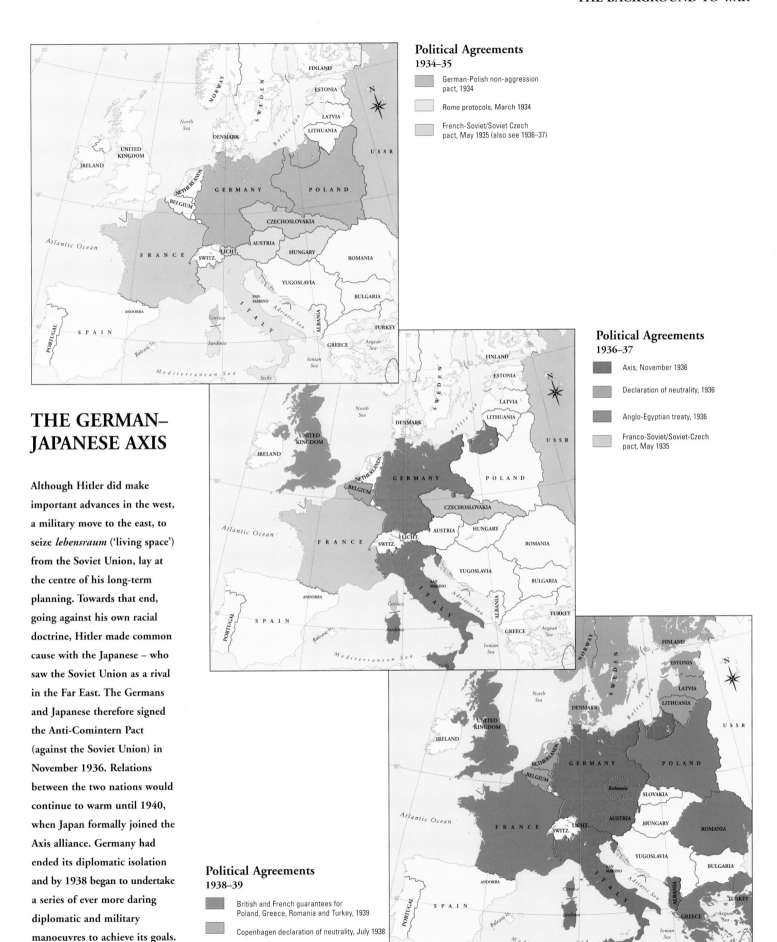

Political Agreements
1934–35

German-Polish non-aggression pact, 1934

Rome protocols, March 1934

French-Soviet/Soviet Czech pact, May 1935 (also see 1936–37)

Political Agreements
1936–37

Axis, November 1936

Declaration of neutrality, 1936

Anglo-Egyptian treaty, 1936

Franco-Soviet/Soviet-Czech pact, May 1935

Political Agreements
1938–39

British and French guarantees for Poland, Greece, Romania and Turkey, 1939

Copenhagen declaration of neutrality, July 1938

Axis, May 1939

THE GERMAN–JAPANESE AXIS

Although Hitler did make important advances in the west, a military move to the east, to seize *lebensraum* ('living space') from the Soviet Union, lay at the centre of his long-term planning. Towards that end, going against his own racial doctrine, Hitler made common cause with the Japanese – who saw the Soviet Union as a rival in the Far East. The Germans and Japanese therefore signed the Anti-Comintern Pact (against the Soviet Union) in November 1936. Relations between the two nations would continue to warm until 1940, when Japan formally joined the Axis alliance. Germany had ended its diplomatic isolation and by 1938 began to undertake a series of ever more daring diplomatic and military manoeuvres to achieve its goals.

Revolution in China
1912–35

Areas of China under warlord control, 1920s

Chang Tsao-lin

Feng Yu-hsiang } Chihli faction

Sun Ch'uan-fang

Wu Pei-fu

Kwangsi clique (group of local warlords)

T'ang Chi-yao

Kuomintang control

Under Kuomintang control, 1926

Under Kuomintang control. 1928

1937 Date providence brought under Kuomintang control or influence

Communist activities

Communist self-governed area, 1927–35

The Long March, 1934–35

Japanese Intervention and Invasions 1927–41

Japanese Empire c. 1930

Japanese troops advance and occupy, 1927–29

Invaded, 1931

Invaded, 1933

Attempt to set up North China state, 1935

Major lines of Japanese advances 1937–41

Approx. Japanese front line in China December 1941

Japanese–Soviet border clashes

THE STRUGGLE FOR CHINA

After the fall of the Manchu Dynasty, General Chiang Kai-shek and the Kuomintang Party began their campaign to take control of China from the single southern province of Guangdon. Winning consistent victories over the other important Chinese warlords, notably the powerful Chihli faction, by 1928 Chiang had taken control of most of central China. Fighting, though, continued against the Chinese Communists under the leadership of Mao Tse-tung.

Kuomintang military pressure forced the Communists to flee their bases of support in Jiangsi and Hunan provinces. The Long March took Mao's followers through remote Sichuan province before reaching relative safety in Shaanxi province, far from the areas controlled by the Kuomintang. Chiang initially also failed in his efforts to stem the rise of Japanese colonialism in the area. Japan met with its greatest success in the distant north, conquering Manchuria in 1933 and much of Hopeh and Shaanxi provinces by 1935.

Frustrated by continued Chinese resistance, the Japanese launched a punitive campaign in the heartland of China, culminating in the Rape of Nanking in 1937. Although much of central and coastal China had fallen, both Kuomintang and Communist forces would continue to resist Japanese rule for the remainder of World War II.

army and navy, and determined to compete with the nations of the West, the Japanese sought a colonial empire at the expense of a tottering China under warlord and Kuomintang control. Japan's territorial ambitions brought conflict with Russia, which also coveted gains at China's expense. Following a stunning victory in the Russo–Japanese War in 1905, the Japanese went on to solidify their power over Korea and gained special rights in the Chinese northern province of Manchuria. Fighting on the Allied side in World War I, Japan seized further territory in China on the Shantung Peninsula. The series of Japanese successes in China, though, placed the island nation on a collision course with the other great power of the Pacific Ocean, the United States.

THE CHANGING FACE OF CHINA

Events in China also served to raise tensions in the area. After the overthrow of the Manchu Dynasty in 1911, China had suffered through a period of anarchy as local warlords vied for control of a fledgling republic. Finally in 1928 General Chiang Kai-shek, leader of the Kuomintang Party, emerged victorious. Chiang, a ruthless military dictator in his own right, sought to reclaim sovereignty over all of China's territory and as a result posed an imminent threat to Japanese ambitions in the region.

Mao Tse-tung, the leader of the small Chinese Communist Party, had been a nominal ally of the Kuomintang until open war erupted between the two groups in 1927. Immediately forced on to the defensive due to the size of the Kuomintang's army, Communist forces fled to the province of Jiangsi. Here the Communist forces would remain, their civil war with Chiang Kai-shek still simmering even as the Kuomintang found itself preoccupied with the ever-present threat from Japan. In 1934, though, a renewed government offensive forced Mao's followers to flee further into the hinterlands of China. In the fabled Long March, the Communists and their supporters trekked some 10,000km (6000 miles) to the distant Shaanxi province. From this new

Below: Japanese tanks cross a river in China in 1937, during the prolonged war which took place in China as Japan sought to expand its territory and its stock of raw materials. Unfortunately for the Japanese, the Chinese military put up significant resistance, and American–Japanese relations were reduced to a low point. The Japanese intervention in China lasted until 1945, tying up large numbers of men and significant resources.

base the Communists would continue to prosecute their war against the Kuomintang, even as China struggled for its very survival against the rapacious Japanese invaders.

The Japanese viewed the rise of Chiang Kai-shek with considerable alarm. When the nominal leader of Manchuria, Chang Hsueh-liang, recognized Kuomintang authority in his province, the Japanese reacted with force. Japanese military firebrands in the area staged a bomb blast on the South Manchuria Railway near Mukden on 18 September 1931. Japanese ground forces quickly moved in to provide 'protection', and the province of Manchuria had soon fallen under direct Japanese control.

The Kuomintang reacted to the Japanese aggression by staging a massive boycott of Japanese goods. Unwilling to accept such an open defiance of their will, in 1933 Japanese military forces invaded the Jehol and Hopeh provinces of northern China. Again realizing that military resistance would be futile, Chiang Kai-shek entered into negotiations with the Japanese. In the resulting treaty, the Kuomintang not only recognized Japanese control over Manchuria and Jehol, but granted Japan

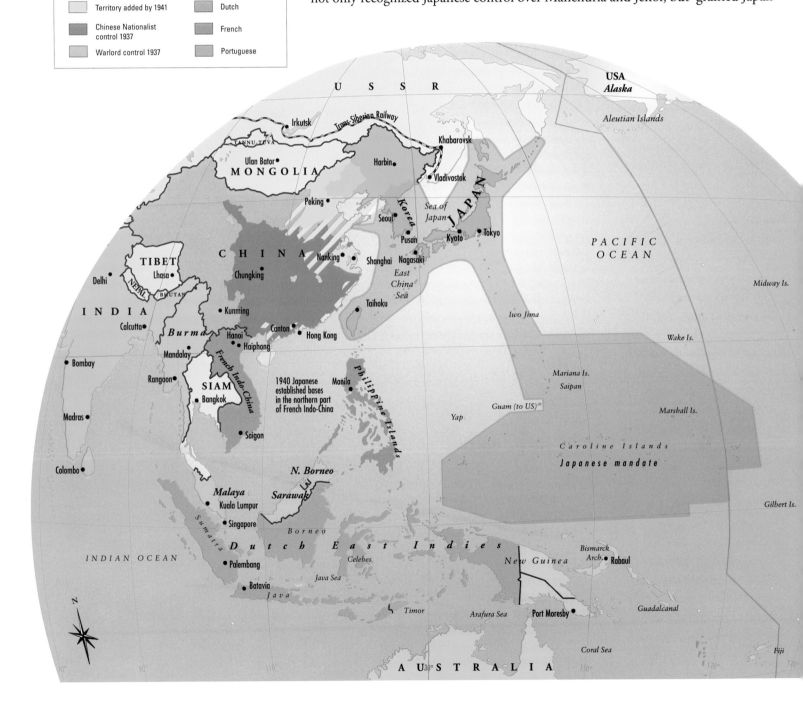

The Expansion of Japan 1920–41

- Japanese Empire 1920
- Territory added by 1931
- Territory added by 1933
- Territory added by 1937
- Territory added by 1941
- Chinese Nationalist control 1937
- Warlord control 1937

Colonial possessions 1941
- British
- United States
- Dutch
- French
- Portuguese

'exclusive rights' over Hopeh as well. Japanese aggression had met with very subdued reactions across the globe. Even the mighty United States, which coveted continued open trade with China, did nothing. As in Europe, then, the aggression of an autocratic state was ignored. Like Hitler, the Japanese would be encouraged to ever more reckless aggression by the world's silence.

Disgusted with the uneasy peace that had settled on the region, military extremists seized effective power in Japan in 1936. Resulting national policy called for renewed expansion in China and for a repudiation of all treaties that limited Japanese power. On 7 July 1937, tensions in China flared into battle near the Marco Polo Bridge only about 30km (20 miles) from Beijing. Japanese extremists were quick to use the clash as a pretext for the overt invasion of China. By August, the city of Beijing had fallen, and shortly thereafter Japanese forces captured the pivotal port city of Shanghai. At this point, the Japanese had expected that Chiang Kai-shek would recognize the inevitability of his defeat and surrender; however, the Kuomintang decided to fight on even in the face of unquestioned Japanese military superiority.

THE RAPE OF NANKING

Shocked by the continued Chinese resistance, the Japanese decided to drive up the Yangtze River to the Chinese capital of Nanking. Realizing that his forces could not face the Japanese in pitched battle, Chiang opted for a strategy of irregular warfare. The Japanese advance was slow and costly, but Nanking finally fell in December 1937. Intensely frustrated that the Chinese continued to resist, and possessed of a racial animus towards their enemy, Japanese forces ran riot in an orgy of slaughter and lawlessness following the fall of Nanking. During a month of looting and murder, Japanese forces killed some 200,000 men, women and children. Once again, though, the renewed Japanese aggression was met by only feeble diplomatic protests from the west. Abandoned, Chiang and his government fled to remote Chungking hoping to outlast the Japanese in a long war – but without allies China's hopes for the future were dim.

Again outraged that the Chinese had not capitulated, Japanese forces remained on the offensive and in 1938 seized all remaining major Chinese seaports. Much of China was now in Japanese hands, but the Japanese military was simply not large enough to conquer and rule the seeming countless millions of inhabitants of the massive Chinese hinterlands. Thus the war in China devolved into a long war of attrition, tying down some 1.6 million Japanese troops. The prosecution of such a war placed great strain on Japan, causing many in the military elite to favor continued expansion in other parts of Asia in search of the vital natural resources needed to prosecute continued war.

One favoured route of expansion was northward to the Soviet Union. In July 1939 Japanese and Soviet forces engaged in a bitter, undeclared war along the Mongolian border. The Japanese, lacking in armour, fared extremely poorly against the Soviets, losing nearly the entire 23rd Division in battle. The humiliating defeat demonstrated clearly to the Japanese leadership that the most favourable opportunity for further territorial expansion lay to the south.

Finally the United States could no longer ignore Japanese expansionism. President Franklin Roosevelt opted to send increasing aid to the Chinese war effort, mainly through the French colony of Indo-China. The United States also began to consider taking economic action to stem Japanese aggression. In 1940 matters worsened immeasurably after the successful German campaigns in western Europe. The fall of the Netherlands and France, and the assault on Britain left the Asian colonies of those nations in dire peril. In 1940 and 1941 the Japanese established military bases in French Indo-China, cutting a valuable American aid route into China. Roosevelt was now convinced that the Japanese were preparing for a major offensive aimed at Malaya, the Dutch East Indies and possibly even the US

JAPAN'S EXPANSION

Japan had been dissatisfied with the settlement it received after its victories in World War I, which established it as a key player in the Pacific region, joining the Americans and the British. Its acquisition of Korea had given Japan a foothold on the Asian continent, and the takeover of Manchuria, the easternmost province of China, offered both room to expand and precious raw materials.

The staged Mukden incident in 1931 gave the Japanese an excuse to seize and annex Manchuria, while a similar false 'Shanghai Incident' saw Japan occupy the southern port. The ineffectually mild protests of Britain, the United States and the Soviet Union and their lack of military response did nothing to dissuade Japan, but rather encouraged the expansionists.

In 1933 the province of Hopeh was invaded by the Japanese Kwantung Army, but Chiang Kai-shek was more concerned about the success of the Communists and agreed a treaty with the Japanese which recognized Japan's control of its territories in China.

In 1937 a clash near Beijing prompted a full-scale invasion of China by the Kwantung Army. Beijing and Shanghai quickly fell, before Nanking, the Nationalist capital, was captured. Japanese troops raped and looted their way through the city. Although the war in China settled into a stalemate, Japan now had ambitions to intervene in French Indo-China.

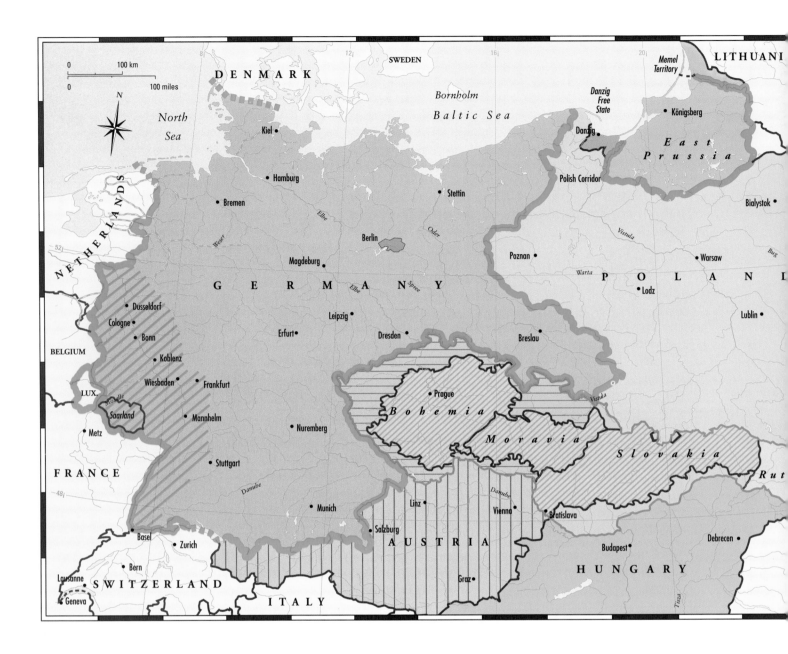

protectorate in the Philippines. In a bid to stem the continuing aggression, Roosevelt made the fateful decision to cut off all oil exports to Japan. The move was a very provocative one, for the Japanese depended on the United States for nearly 88 per cent of their oil. Indeed, without US oil, the Japanese military would grind to a halt. Facing such a cataclysm, the Japanese made ready to seize the oil-rich Dutch East Indies – and war in the Pacific loomed.

Meanwhile, confident that Britain and France would not stand in the way of his territorial ambitions in Europe, Hitler again turned his eyes towards *Anschluss* (union) with Austria. In February 1938 Hitler succeeded in cowing the Austrian chancellor, Schuschnigg, into submission during a meeting in Bavaria. On his return to Vienna, though, Schuschnigg decided to put the matter of *Anschluss* to a popular vote. Fearful of the outcome, Hitler threatened imminent invasion. Even though Schuschnigg backed down, the German military crossed the border into Austria on 12 March and annexed the nation the following day. Somewhat surprised by the speed of German actions, neither Britain nor France chose to risk war over Austria, further emboldening Hitler.

Next Hitler turned his attention to Czechoslovakia and the German ethnic minority that lived in the border area known as the Sudetenland. The coming crisis over the Sudetenland presented a situation quite different to that of the annexation of Austria. Czechoslovakia seemed more than capable of standing against any German aggression, with a strong army and alliances with both the Soviet Union and France. In addition, the German claims to the Sudetenland were quite sketchy. It seemed an obvious time to stand up to Hitler's ongoing aggression.

Even though the case for defending Czechoslovakia seemed strong, the French remained wary of going to war against Germany

Hitler's Annexations
1936–39

Germany after 1919

Troops into demilitarized Rhineland March 1936

Anschluss (union with Austria), March 1938

Occupation of Sudetenland October 1938

Original Czechoslovakian border

Formerly Czechoslovakia occupied March 1939

Moravian territory to Poland October 1938

Memel territory to Germany March 1939

Protectorate of Slovakia territory to Hungary Nov. 1938

Czechosovakian territory to Hungary March 1939

Vilna Strip

Annexed by Lithuania October 1939

tovsk

Lvov

Dneister

O M A N I A

without British aid. For his part, the new British Prime Minister, Neville Chamberlain, was keen to avoid war and was, indeed, the chief architect of the policy of appeasement towards Hitler. Although the German army was quite concerned by the prospect of war, Hitler raised the stakes in the ongoing crisis by threatening war as the only way to settle the Sudeten issue. Eager to avoid conflict, Chamberlain flew to Germany for two rounds of personal diplomacy. His efforts at conciliation failed, however, and Europe seemed poised on the brink of a second world war.

After frantic diplomacy, a conference convened in Munich on 30 September to solve the Sudeten crisis. With neither the Soviet Union nor Czechoslovakia in attendance, Britain and France agreed that Germany would occupy the entire Sudetenland, complete with its powerful defensive works and armament factories, while other portions of Czechoslovakia were ceded to Poland and Hungary. What Chamberlain got for his trouble was a worthless promise by Hitler to refrain from further aggression. The British Prime Minister returned to London to an enthusiastic greeting, at which he brandished papers signed by Hitler and proclaimed 'peace in our time'.

Far from being appeased, in March 1939 Hitler broke his promise to Chamberlain as the German military moved in to occupy the remainder of Czechoslovakia without opposition. At this point, Britain and France came to the belated conclusion that Hitler could not be trusted and resolved not to yield any more territory to him. Both nations subsequently guaranteed the borders of Poland – Hitler's next target. In addition, Britain and France made clumsy diplomatic overtures to the one nation that could stand in the way of Hitler's ambitions in the east: the Soviet Union.

THE POLISH CORRIDOR

The lost German lands in the east had long been contentious, in particular the 'Polish Corridor' and the port city of Danzig. The issue had simmered for years, but only broke into a crisis in the summer of 1939. Poland refused German demands in the area, in part due to fear of Soviet reaction to concessions to Germany – walking a fine path of neutrality between the two great powers. Convinced that Britain and France would not intervene, Hitler began making plans to invade Poland. Only the possible reaction of the Soviet Union to an invasion remained a stumbling block. For their part, the Soviet premier Stalin and his new foreign minister, Molotov, began to believe that working with Hitler was superior to relying on the western Allies for support.

Ever opportunistic, Hitler and Stalin signed the Nazi–Soviet Non-Aggression pact in August 1939. The pact, which shocked Britain and France, publicly stated that Germany and the Soviet Union would remain neutral if the other found itself at war. Privately the pact made ready to divide much of eastern Europe between the two powers. Germany would claim western Poland and parts of Lithuania, while the Soviet Union would seize Finland, Latvia, Estonia and parts of Romania. With the Soviet Union as a benevolent neutral – and certain that Britain and France would revert to appeasement without Stalin as their ally – Germany invaded Poland on 1 September 1939. Two days later, to Hitler's surprise and considerable annoyance, Britain and France declared war, marking the start of World War II in Europe.

HITLER'S ANNEXATIONS

Between 1935 and 1939, Hitler's string of foreign policy successes not only solidified his power in Germany, but also drove Europe to the brink of a second world war. Germany's rise from the ashes was first seen when the Saarland voted in 1935 to return to German rule by plebiscite. In 1936 Hitler sent his newly created military into the Rhineland.

With his power still tenuous and his army small, it was the opportune time for France and Britain to stand firm against Hitler, yet they did not. Now with the support of Italy, Hitler moved with rapid speed into a union with Austria in 1938. Later during the same year, Hitler created a crisis over the borderlands in Czechoslovakia known as the Sudetenland. Despite being vital to the defence of Czechoslovakia, the Sudetenland was ceded to Germany after the Munich Conference in September 1938.

Early the following year, Hitler moved to occupy the remainder of the Czech state. The diplomatic momentum was with Germany, which had conquered two nations without bloodshed, while Britain and France remained passive. And even though the western Allies guaranteed Poland's borders, Hitler thought they would not fight. After signing the Nazi–Soviet Nonaggression Pact, Hitler was certain that retaking lands lost to Poland in the Treaty of Versailles would not be opposed by the great powers.

The Blitzkrieg

In September 1939 Adolf Hitler stood poised on the threshold of war, with the newly re-created nation of Poland as his intended victim. Having already bought off the Soviet Union with promises of a partition of Poland, Hitler was certain that the French and British guarantee of the Polish borders was merely a bluff. Poland was to be the stage for an exhibition to the world of German might.

In the wake of World War I, the nations of the world and their military forces struggled to make sense of the conflict. In the main, the victorious powers dabbled little in true military innovation, seeking simply to avoid future war. If war did come again, many in the West believed that the conflict would bear a close resemblance to World War I and would be both defensive and static in nature. Even so, some military thinkers in the West did manage to look forward rather than backward.

Building on the theories of Giulio Douhet in Italy, General Hugh Trenchard in Britain and General Billy Mitchell in the United States turned to air power as the answer to modern war. Airpower proponents believed that massed bomber formations, by striking either industrial or civilian targets, could bring a nation to its knees. Protected from an invasion as their nations were by significant water barriers, the leadership of the United States and Britain naturally found these theories appealing. The concept of 'strategic bombing' was thus born. Although others, such as J.F.C. Fuller in Britain, saw armoured formations as the way forward, the armed forces of the West in the main would find themselves at a distinct disadvantage on the battlefield due in part to the national emphasis on air power.

The defeated nations of World War I, especially Germany and the Soviet Union, made much more serious and systematic attempts to rethink the nature of warfare. The Germans, under the inspired leadership of young military men such as General Heinz Guderian, began to codify an armoured theory of warfare. It was Guderian's belief that tanks should be massed together into panzer divisions. These formations, with integral all-arms capability, would be the mailed fist that restored mobility to modern warfare and avoided the stalemate of the trenches of World War I. Tanks, working in conjunction with infantry, engineers and tactical air power, would mass at the enemy's weakest point and use their combined weight of fire to punch through enemy lines. Once through the tanks would use one of their main assets, speed, to keep the enemy off balance – eventually encircling enemy forces in a 'cauldron' and defeating them in decisive battle. Hitler was quite enamoured of the new theories and hoped that they could catapult him to domination of the continent.

SOVIET MILITARY THOUGHT

Further east, the Soviet armed forces, led by Marshal M.N. Tukhachevsky and V.K. Triandafillov, had developed their own theories of modern warfare. Also reliant on massed armour and all-arms coordination, the Soviet theory of tank warfare was termed 'deep battle'. Recognizing the enemy army as a system, the Soviets planned their armour to strike deep into the enemy formation, crippling its command structure and causing its collapse – rather than aiming for an effort to surround and destroy an enemy force. The Soviets also believed that one such victory in battle could not be decisive and opted to depend on 'operational art', stringing together numerous, integral tactical victories to achieve their strategic aim. Although Stalin's purge of the Soviet military in the 1930s did great damage to the climate of innovation, the ideas of deep battle and operational art would remain.

Left: German paratroopers, or *Fallschirmjäger*, seen during the invasion of Norway in 1940. Initially paratroops played a key role in Germany's swift victories, seizing key bridges or strongpoints to allow the momentum of the German advance to continue unchecked. For many Germans, the rapid gains of 1939–40 seemed to wipe clean the slate of memories of defeat in 1914–18. Most had expected victory over Poland, perhaps even France – but certainly not so swiftly and at so little cost to Germany.

Invasion of Poland
1–28 September 1939

German advance
Russian advance
Polish retreat
German field work
Polish defensive lines
Polish positions
German-Russian demarcation line

INVASION OF POLAND

On 1 September 1939, the German blitzkrieg thundered into Poland. The XIX Panzer Corps, led by Heinz Guderian, served as the mailed fist of Army Group North, slicing across the Polish Corridor in only two days. Army Group South flanked Polish resistance from the remains of Czechoslovakia. The XI Panzer Corps reached the outskirts of Warsaw on 8 September, encircling several Polish pockets of resistance. Still the panzers rolled on, Guderian attacking southwards from East Prussia on 9 September, later to meet with panzers under the command of Kleist attacking from the south. The pincers closed at Brest-Litovsk, as Soviet forces moved in from the east.

THE WINTER WAR

On 30 November 1939, the Soviet Union invaded Finland. Initially the Soviet Seventh Army and Thirteenth Army failed to break the Mannerheim Line on the Karelian Isthmus. Further north, elements of two other Soviet armies, the Eighth and the Fourteenth, advanced into Finland – fighting above the Arctic Circle – only to be cut off. After suffering disastrous losses at Suomussalmi and Kemiträsk, in early March the reorganized and rested Soviet troops, aided by lavish fire support, burst through the Mannerheim Line, forcing the Finns to sue for peace.

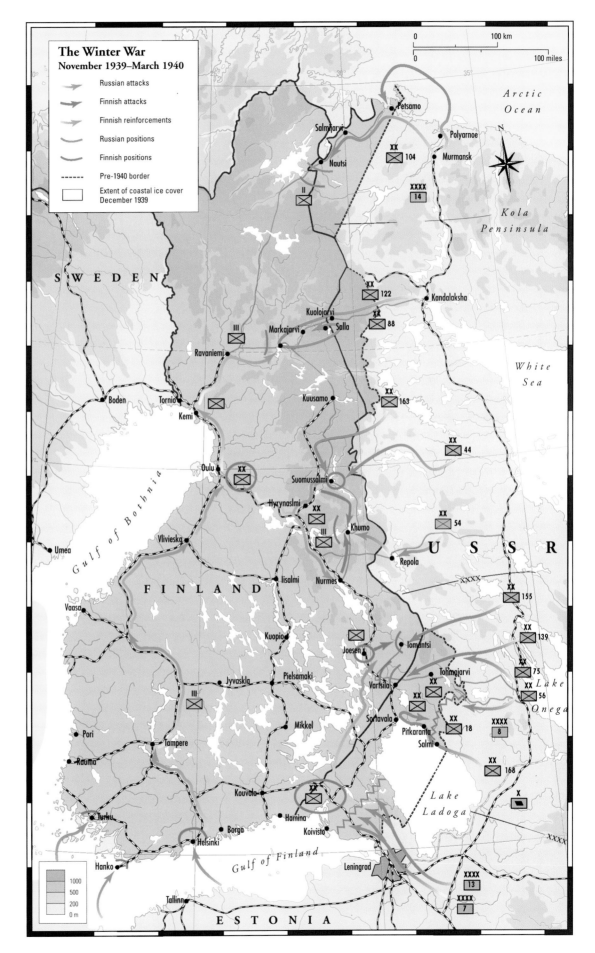

The Winter War
November 1939–March 1940

- Russian attacks
- Finnish attacks
- Finnish reinforcements
- Russian positions
- Finnish positions
- Pre-1940 border
- Extent of coastal ice cover December 1939

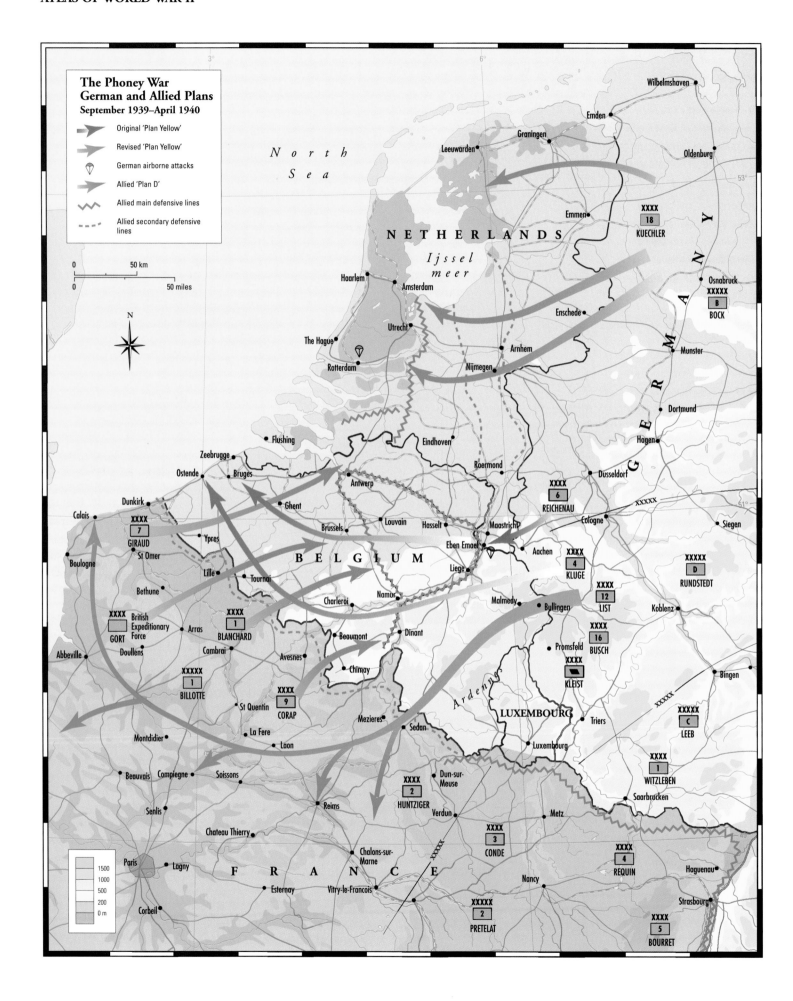

**The Phoney War
German and Allied Plans**
September 1939–April 1940

- Original 'Plan Yellow'
- Revised 'Plan Yellow'
- German airborne attacks
- Allied 'Plan D'
- Allied main defensive lines
- Allied secondary defensive lines

0   50 km

0   50 miles

N

*North
Sea*

NETHERLANDS

*Ijssel
meer*

GERMANY

Wilbelmshaven

Emden

Graningen

Leeuwarden

Oldenburg

Emmen

XXXX
18
KUECHLER

Osnabruck

XXXXX
B
BOCK

Haarlem

Amsterdam

Enschede

Munster

The Hague

Utrecht

Arnhem

Nijmegen

Dortmund

Rotterdam

Dusseldorf

Hagen

Flushing

Eindhoven

Roermond

XXXX
6
REICHENAU

Cologne

Siegen

Zeebrugge

Ostende

Bruges

Antwerp

Ghent

XXXXX
51°

Dunkirk

Calais

XXXX
7
GIRAUD

Ypres

St Omer

Brussels

Louvain

Hasselt

Maastricht

Eben Emael

Aachen

XXXX
4
KLUGE

XXXXX
D
RUNDSTEDT

Boulogne

Lille

Tournai

BELGIUM

Namur

Liege

Malmedy

Bullingen

XXXX
12
LIST

Koblenz

Bethune

XXXX
British
Expeditionary
Force
GORT

Arras

Cambrai

XXXX
1
BLANCHARD

Charleroi

Beaumont

Dinant

Promsfeld

XXXX
16
BUSCH

Bingen

Abbeville

Doullens

Avesnes

Chimay

XXXX
KLEIST

XXXXX
1
BILLOTTE

St Quentin

XXXX
9
CORAP

Mezieres

Ardennes

LUXEMBOURG

Triers

XXXXX
C
LEEB

Montdidier

La Fere

Sedan

Luxembourg

XXXX
1
WITZLEBEN

Beauvais

Compiegne

Soissons

Laon

Dun-sur-
Meuse

Saarbrucken

Senlis

Reims

XXXX
2
HUNTZIGER

Verdun

Metz

Chateau Thierry

Chalons-sur-
Marne

XXXX
3
CONDE

XXXX
4
REQUIN

Haguenau

Paris

Lagny

Esternay

Vitry-le-Francois

Nancy

1500
1000
500
200
0 m

FRANCE

XXXXX
2
PRETELAT

Strasbourg

XXXX
5
BOURRET

Corbeil

THE PHONEY WAR

Knowing that the Germans would not strike the Maginot Line or advance through the supposedly impassable forest of the Ardennes, the western Allies developed 'Plan D'. French and British forces would advance into Belgium to meet the Germans near the Rive Dyle. Although the Belgian declaration of neutrality had complicated Allied planning, it was hoped that Belgian resistance at fortresses such as Eben Emael would allow the Allies time to move up into position.

The original German 'Plan Yellow' called for just such an offensive, striking the prepared defensive positions of the Allies head on. However, the Germans altered the plan, opting for a surprise advance through the 'impassable' Ardennes. Spearheaded by panzer divisions, the plan called for a rapid advance to the English Channel to cut off and destroy the Allied forces in Belgium.

BATTLE OF SUOMUSSALMI

In November 1939, the Soviet 163rd Division advanced across frozen Lake Kianta towards Suomussalmi. The Finns managed to surround the division, cutting off its supplies. By 30 December, it had been destroyed. Other Finns, utilizing a traditional ice road, struck the newly arrived Soviet 44th Division along the Raate road, destroying several isolated Soviet formations.

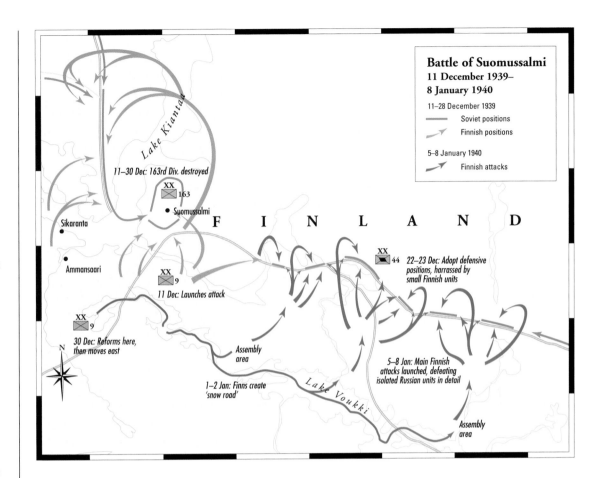

Battle of Suomussalmi
11 December 1939–
8 January 1940

11–28 December 1939

—— Soviet positions

⟿ Finnish positions

5–8 January 1940

⟹ Finnish attacks

WAR BREAKS OUT IN THE EAST

On 1 September 1939, nearly one million German soldiers crossed the Polish border – beginning the European phase of World War II. The antiquated Polish army, which had mobilized only 600,000 men, found itself stretched very thin in forward defensive positions. It was the perfect situation for blitzkrieg. First the German Luftwaffe struck the stunned Polish Air Force, destroying many of its aircraft on the ground and thus seizing control of the skies over the battlefront. The German forces, Army Group North under the command of General Fedor von Bock and Army Group South under the command of General Gerd von Rundstedt, made furious progress against their outmatched opponents. Most successful were the mighty German panzer divisions. Even though the Germans often relied on the outdated Panzer Mark I, the tank units brushed aside valiant resistance on the part of Polish infantry and cavalry units. By 3 September, panzers commanded by Guderian had closed the Polish Corridor. Further to the south, armour under the command of General Erich Höpner broke through the Polish defences and by 8 September had reached the outskirts of Warsaw. Even as events in Poland rushed forwards, Hitler received a surprise when both Britain and France honoured their guarantee of Poland's borders by declaring war on Germany. Despite this outward show of support, the Poles quickly realized that they could expect little in the way of aid from the West.

Inexorably the German pincers closed on Warsaw – and still the panzers surged ever forward, encircling another major Polish force outside Brest-Litovsk. At the same time, Soviet forces were striking into Poland from the east, effectively ending Poland's existence. Despite facing two world superpowers, Poles in the capital of Warsaw fought on, even in the face of German aerial assault. The end finally came on 28 September 1939 when Germany and the Soviet Union partitioned a defeated Poland. Blitzkrieg had proven its worth, winning a shockingly quick victory. Britain and France should have taken heed, but instead chose to blame much of the outcome on Polish incompetence.

Above: Soldiers of the German Wehrmacht pose for a war correspondent's camera during the invasion of Poland. The swift victory in the East, followed by the rapid conquest of Norway, helped to unnerve the Allied soldiers and build a myth of invincibility around the German soldier. Magazines such as *Signal* were quick to burnish this reputation, showing pictures of triumphant Germans taking dejected Allied soldiers prisoner. For the British, the myth of German superiority and its detrimental effect on morale would last until the end of 1942.

THE WINTER WAR

Further north, the Soviets went about claiming the remainder of the sphere of influence allotted them by the Nazi–Soviet Pact. From the tiny nation of Finland the Soviets demanded much of the Karelian Isthmus near Leningrad, as well as territory north of Lake Ladoga. The Finns, a nation of only four million, refused. On 30 November 1939, some 30 Soviet divisions attacked the minuscule Finnish army, which initially only fielded nine divisions. The war seemed destined to be a classic mismatch. However, the Soviets bungled their offensive against the Finnish defences on the Karelian Isthmus, dubbed the Mannerheim Line, and the attack failed miserably. Further north, Soviet incompetence led to outright disaster. Soviet forces, straying dangerously far from their supply lines, moved ponderously through the broken terrain amid the dead of winter. The Finns, fighting on home soil and therefore familiar with the terrain and prepared for the bitter cold – even to the point of wearing skis – used speed and mobility to ambush and destroy several isolated Soviet units.

By January it was clear that the massive Soviet offensive had failed; however, an enraged Stalin appointed a new commander, Marshal Semyon Timoshenko, and poured more men and resources into the struggle, refusing to accept defeat. The new commander concentrated his efforts against the sorely pressed Mannerheim Line and finally broke through in early March. The stubborn Finns, outnumbered nearly 50:1 on the battlefield, finally chose to seek peace. The Winter War ended in an armistice in which the Soviets gained all of the critical territory around Lake Ladoga.

DENMARK AND NORWAY

After quickly overrunning
Denmark, on 9 April 1940 six
separate German naval groups
made a daring dash to seize all
of the major ports of Norway.
Though the Germans lost three
cruisers, the British Home Fleet
was slow to react from its home
port of Scapa Flow in the
Shetland Islands.

The German landings,
augmented by daring airborne
assaults near Stavanger and
Oslo, met with great success.
Only at Narvik, in the far
north, did British seapower
severely disrupt German
planning by destroying 10
German destroyers and taking
control of the area's waters.
Britain struck back by landing
some 12,000 men at Namsos
and Andalsnes in an effort to
recapture Trondheim.

Fearing for their isolated
garrison, German forces
advanced from Oslo. Utilizing
air superiority the Germans
defeated the Allied effort,
forcing the evacuation of Allied
forces at both Namsos and
Andalsnes. At Narvik a tiny
German force of only some
4000 men, under the command
of General Eduard Dietl, were
besieged by nearly 25,000
Allied troops.

In desperate straits, the
German force fought its way
out of Narvik and sought refuge
on the Swedish border. By June,
though, due to impending
disaster in France, Allied units
left Narvik, allowing the
Germans to move in and
occupy the port unchallenged.

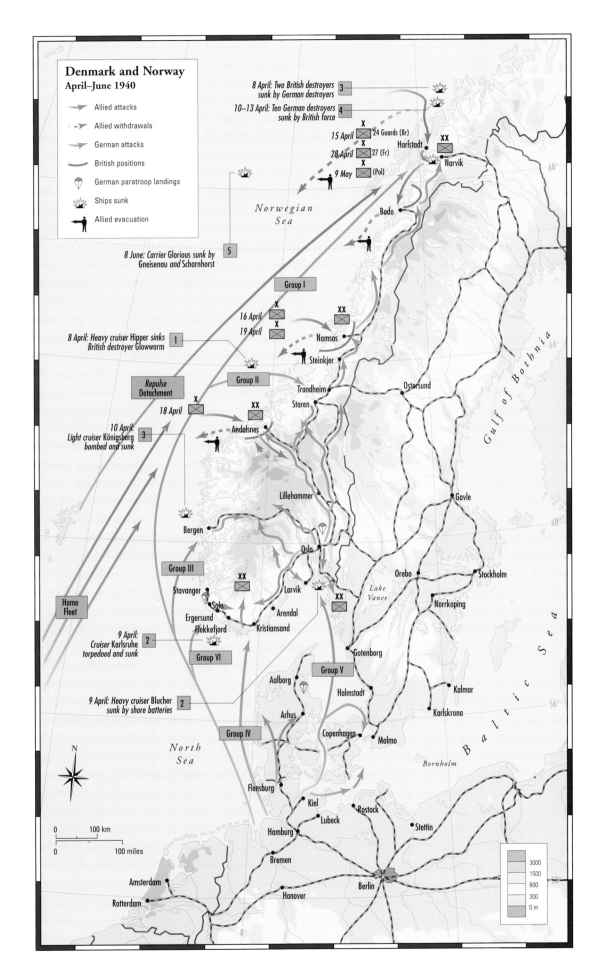

Although the Soviets had eventually been successful, their poor showing against a nation with such slim resources as Finland did much to convince both Hitler and the West of Soviet military weakness.

BLITZKRIEG IN THE WEST

After the defeat of Poland, Hitler was anxious to attack in the west. Originally the German plan, dubbed 'Plan Yellow', called for a strike through the centre of the Belgian defences, something expected and welcomed by Allied planners. Some within the

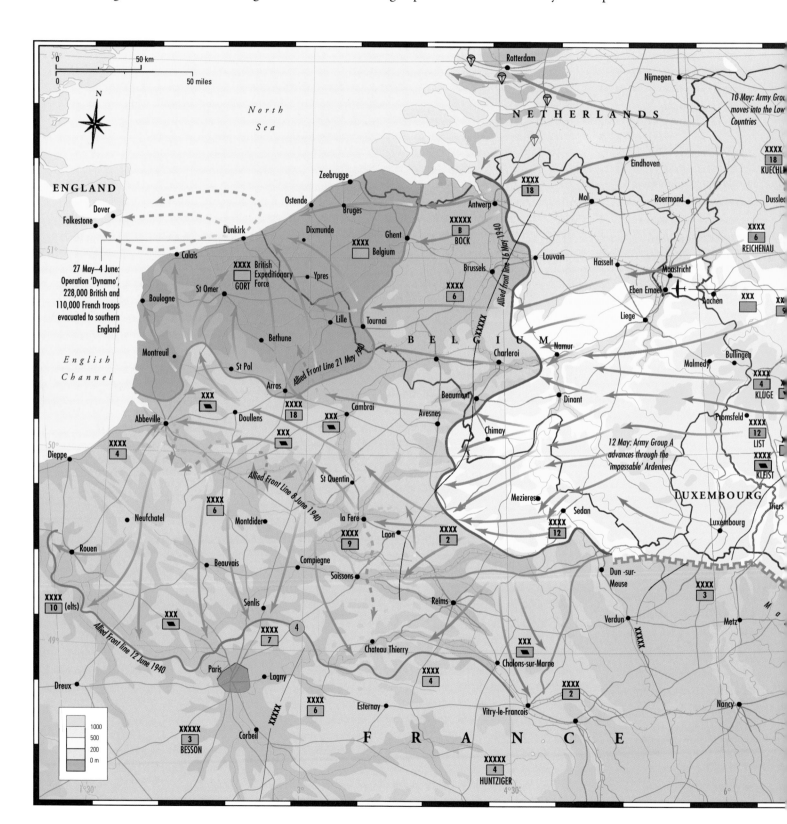

Wehrmacht, though, including General Erich von Manstein, did not favour the plan. Matters came to a head in January 1940 when a German courier plane, carrying plans for the offensive, was forced to make an emergency landing in Belgium – thus compromising Plan Yellow. Led by Manstein, and with the approval of Hitler, the Wehrmacht made fundamental and brilliant alterations to the plan. The new plan called for Army Group B, under the command of Bock, to advance into central Belgium as a diversion. Further south, Army Group A, under the command of Rundstedt and with the preponderance of German armoured strength, would attack through the supposedly impenetrable Ardennes, hoping to catch the Allies off-guard. After achieving a breakthrough, the panzers would then advance to the English Channel, thus cutting off Allied forces in Belgium. It was an audacious and risky plan.

British and French forces, under the command of Lord Gort and General Maurice Gamelin respectively, awaited any German attack with confidence. The balance of forces in the west was even, and it seemed that the Germans would do exactly as the Allies expected. However, the Allies had a number of critical weaknesses. Gamelin was aged and inflexible, and remained distant and detached in his chateau headquarters as events ran their course. In addition, so sure was Gamelin that his planning was correct that only rather weak elements of two French armies, mainly made up of reserve divisions, defended the Ardennes area. These men would soon face the brunt of the German attack, led by 1800 tanks.

The German blitzkrieg rolled into the Low Countries on 10 May 1940. Bock's Army Group B had to advance quickly to make good the ruse. The Germans made extensive use of airborne forces to seize critical bridges intact in order to maintain the tempo of advance. Overmatched, the Dutch surrendered quickly, but the Allies expected and planned on the fact that the Belgians would put up a more spirited resistance. The impregnable fortress of Eben Emael was to form the linchpin of the Belgian defensive line. The imposing defensive works were supposed to hold up the German advance for weeks; however, a German airborne force of only 85 men landed atop the fortress in gliders. Using special shaped charges, the Germans were quickly able to penetrate the fortress and subdue its 750 defenders. Partly due to this *coup de main*, Bock's forces were able to advance quickly. As a result, the British and French forces rushed into position along the River Dyle – only to walk directly into a trap.

While engaging Bock's forces, the British and French were not aware that at that very moment the German panzer units were struggling through the broken terrain of the Ardennes. It was one of the most critical moments of the battle. Army Group A was enmeshed in a traffic jam

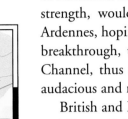

10–11 May: Air assault by special troops neutralizes the fortress of Eben Emael

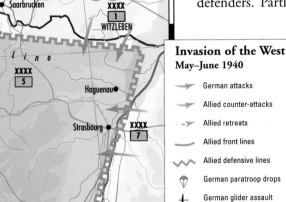

Invasion of the West
May–June 1940

→ German attacks
→ Allied counter-attacks
⇢ Allied retreats
— Allied front lines
〜 Allied defensive lines
⏀ German paratroop drops
✝ German glider assault

INVASION OF THE WEST

On 10 May 1940, Army Group B began its diversionary assault into central Belgium. Aided by the quick seizure of the Belgian fortress of Eben Emael, Bock's forces moved so quickly that they disrupted the Allied defensive positions situated along the River Dyle.

To the Allies, it seemed that Bock led the main strike force of the German army. To the south, though, Army Group A, containing seven panzer divisions, emerged from the Ardennes on 12 May. Utilizing superior armoured tactics and all-arms coordination, the panzers of generals Guderian and Rommel quickly brushed aside French resistance and crossed the River Meuse, breaking out into the open country beyond.

Instead of driving for Paris, as the French expected, the panzers thundered northwards towards the English Channel – hoping to cut off Allied units enmeshed in battle in Belgium. The French, lacking a reserve, were unable to react to events. A French armoured counter-attack near Laon on 17 May, led by Colonel Charles de Gaulle, was rebuffed by the German 1st Panzer Division. A British armoured counterattack at Arras on 21 May also failed due to the presence of German anti-tank guns. In fact, it was far too late for the Allied cause, for Guderian's panzers had reached the English Channel the day before – cutting off the Allied forces in Belgium.

THE PANZERS BREAK THROUGH

On 12 May 1940, the XIX Panzer Corps under Guderian broke out of the Ardennes and made for the River Meuse near Sedan. The French forces from X Corps defended the significant river barrier, thinking that they would be able to hold firm against any German attack.

However, the crossing of the Meuse at Sedan proved to be a model of German tactical proficiency. Using his initiative, Guderian struck the Meuse defences on 13 May, under the cover of lavish air support provided by the Luftwaffe. With the guns of the French defenders silenced by air and artillery assault, German infantry quickly crossed the Meuse in rubber boats. Combat engineers followed in their wake, constructing pontoon bridges. Within 10 hours, the panzers began to cross the completed bridges, instantly compromising the French defensive positions.

With his force now divided on both sides of the river, Guderian found himself in a very vulnerable position. On 14 May, elements of the French XVI Corps struck Guderian's flank. Although many German tanks had not yet crossed the Meuse, air support and anti-tank fire thwarted the French counterattack. Thus the vital crossing of the Meuse succeeded in large part due to German tactical prowess and all-arms coordination, rather than the might of their vaunted armour.

nearly 160km (100 miles) long. Had the Allies not been fully occupied by Army Group B, a diversion of air power to the Ardennes might have stopped the German offensive in its tracks. However, secrecy held – and the German tanks began to emerge from the Ardennes on the 11th and 12th of May. Still, the Allies had an advantage. The French units in the area, part of X Corps, stood behind the powerful defensive obstacle of the River Meuse.

CROSSING THE RIVER MEUSE

The Germans now faced the moment of decision in the Battle of France – the crossing of the River Meuse outside Sedan. If the French held firm behind the river barrier, the Germans would lose their forward momentum, possibly spelling doom for their innovative plan. In the end, victory at the Meuse was won by the speed and flexibility of the German panzer divisions. Unlike Gamelin, ensconced at his distant headquarters, the Germans employed a more lithe system of command. Guderian was with the German spearhead as it neared the river barrier. Given great initiative by Rundstedt, Guderian would have the latitude to react to the situation as it unfolded, rather than being forced to wait for orders even as opportunity slipped past.

The panzer divisions, far from being tank units, were all-arms formations, including infantry, artillery, anti-tank, anti-aircraft and engineer formations that would make victory possible. Upon reaching the Meuse, Guderian was able to call upon the close air support of the Luftwaffe to provide cover as infantry formations crossed the river in rubber boats – seizing tiny bridgeheads on the far bank. Next combat engineers rushed forwards and within 10 hours had constructed a pontoon bridge that would enable the German tanks to cross the river. Noting disaster looming in the south, the Allies launched air attacks on the new German bridges; however, German air support and integral anti-aircraft batteries dealt the Allies a harsh blow, downing 40 of the 71 Royal Air Force aircraft involved in the attacks.

Thus on 13 May the Germans had crossed the Meuse at Sedan, surprising the understrength French X Corps. Even so, Guderian remained in a vulnerable position as his units slowly crossed the Meuse. On 14–15 May, elements of the French 3rd Armoured Division struck Guderian's flank, endangering the entire German operation. By utilizing 88mm (3.46in) anti-aircraft guns in an anti-tank role, however, the Germans were able to rebuff the rather disorganized attack and destroy 33 French tanks. With the counterattack defeated, the Germans had been successful in blowing open an 80km (50-mile) wide hole in the French lines, and German armour began the advance northwards.

The French, thoroughly surprised and dispirited, attempted to form lines of defence in the paths of the onrushing panzers – only to find that the Germans had already captured the area and continued their advance. On 17 May, the hastily organized French 4th Armoured Division, under the command of Colonel Charles de Gaulle, attacked the advancing German panzers at Laon, but failed. Nonetheless, the German command began to fret about the vulnerability of their flanks as the panzers moved ever northwards through enemy territory. The Germans need not have worried, though, for the outmatched Gamelin had lost control of events and had no armoured reserve with which to attack the German flanks.

After a brief pause, the leading elements of German armour reached the English Channel on 20 May – surrounding Allied forces in Belgium. Still, the German encirclement was as yet weak, allowing

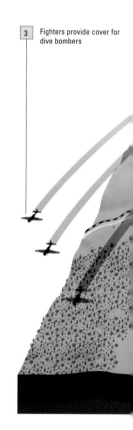

3 Fighters provide cover for dive bombers

the Allies a breakout attempt. On 21 May, two British divisions, supported by two tank battalions, struck the Germans at Arras. Without much-needed reserve forces, though, the attack was far too weak and only succeeded in denting the German lines. Allied forces in Belgium were irrevocably surrounded, and disaster was at hand.

THE FALL OF FRANCE AND OPERATION DYNAMO

The new British Prime Minister, Winston Churchill – who had only taken office on 10 May – faced a very difficult decision, for British and French forces in Belgium faced annihilation at the hands of the advancing German panzers. There was to be a brief respite, though, when the German spearhead halted on 24 May only 24km (15 miles) from Dunkirk, allowing time for the non-mechanized infantry to close a vulnerable gap in the German lines. With Allied forces caught in a shrinking pocket, on 26 May Churchill made the fateful decision to rescue as much of the Allied force as possible through a seaborne evacuation mission dubbed 'Operation Dynamo'.

British and French soldiers made their way to the beaches where hundreds of small British civilian craft were on hand to take them to larger ships waiting in deeper water. Ships of all shapes and sizes answered the call to rescue the stranded Allied force. Exhausted men waded out to the ships, while their comrades fought a stubborn holding action against the attacking Germans. By the conclusion of Operation Dynamo on 4 June 1940, the flotilla had rescued some 338,000 Allied soldiers. Nevertheless, disaster still loomed, and the men returned to Britain without their heavy weaponry even as the fall of France proceeded apace.

Having destroyed Allied resistance in Belgium, the Wehrmacht now turned southwards towards Paris. An air of defeatism permeated the French Government, with French Prime Minister Reynaud declaring as early as 13 May: 'We are beaten. We have lost the battle.' On 5 June, 95 German divisions slammed into 61 French divisions along the River Aisne and

Panzer strike through the Ardennes
12–14 May, 1940

- Armoured advance
- Air support
- Artillery support
- French retreat

2 13 May: Guderian launches four attacks across the Meuse river, covered by Stuka dive bombers. Three attacks succeed.

1 12 May: XIX Panzer Corps Commanded by Gen. Guderian advances using country lanes and tracks through the lightly defended Ardennes forest. It quickly brushes aside the French forces.

4 14 May: French forces harassed by armoured and air attacks fall back, unable to reorganize. Efforts by Ravigny's XXI Corps to mount an armoured counterstroke are defeated by the power of Guderian's Corps.

GUDERIAN

Montherme

Bohan • Membre

Alle

Sugny

Pussemange

Bouillon

Charleville

Sedan

PART OF FRENCH
X CORPS

OPERATION DYNAMO

Given a respite by Guderian's halt on the Channel coast, the British launched Operation Dynamo, a seaborne rescue operation of the Allied forces in Belgium and northern France. The vast British armada set sail from the south coast of England, mainly from the Dover area. The larger ships were unable to navigate the complicated, shallow shoals surrounding Dunkirk, leaving the actual evacuation from the beaches to a motley assortment of civilian pleasure craft and lifeboats crewed by civilian volunteers. The civilian vessels entered Dunkirk Road to pluck soldiers from the water under a hail of attacks from the Luftwaffe. Miraculously, Operation Dynamo succeeded in rescuing some 338,000 Allied soldiers before the end of the operation on 4 June 1940.

THE FALL OF FRANCE

Following the Allied defeat in Belgium, the Wehrmacht rushed southwards against minimal resistance, seizing Paris without a struggle on 14 June. In the east, the Germans struck the Maginot Line. The French forces there fought hard, only surrendering nearly a week after the fall of their country. On 16 June, the French Government surrendered. The Germans occupied northern and western France, leaving southern France under the control of a pliant French government in Vichy.

quickly broke through. As the panzers rushed forwards, the French declared Paris an open city, and on 14 June it fell without a fight. On 16 June, the French Government, now under the control of the ageing Marshal Pétain, chose to sue for peace. The Germans imposed a strict treaty upon the French, leaving only the southern portion of France, dubbed 'Vichy France', even nominally independent. In the space of just 35 days, France had fallen, leaving Britain isolated in the war against Germany.

THE BATTLE OF BRITAIN

After the fall of France, Churchill chose to fight on against all odds. As a result, the Germans cobbled together an invasion scheme, dubbed 'Operation Sea Lion', designed to land a force of some 400,000 in southern England. Admiral Erich Raeder, the Commander of the German Navy, thought the plan to be very dangerous against the strength of both the British Navy and the Royal Air Force (RAF). Thus Hitler chose to launch an air campaign to destroy the RAF in preparation for the invasion of England.

Although Hermann Göring, the Commander of the German Luftwaffe, was confident of success, the Luftwaffe had been designed for close air support of ground campaigns, and thus lacked the heavy bombers required for such a strategic mission. The main Luftwaffe strike force, based in two air fleets in northern France, consisted of 1000 medium bombers. As the bombers were poorly armed, they required the fighter protection of some 750 Messerschmitt 109s. Defending against the coming onslaught were the 650 fighter aircraft (mainly Hurricanes and Spitfires) of RAF Fighter Command under Air Marshal Hugh Dowding. Helping to offset the disparity in numbers was a new, critical British development. Radar stations dotted along the British coast would give Fighter Command advance warning of impending German strikes.

OPERATION EAGLE

After some preliminary bombing of British coastal targets, the Germans launched their effort to destroy the RAF – dubbed 'Operation Eagle' – in August 1940. This most important stage of the Battle of Britain saw German bombers striking RAF bases and radar stations. Across southern England, dogfights raged daily between British and German aircraft as outnumbered RAF pilots pushed themselves to breaking point. It was not uncommon for a pilot to be shot down,

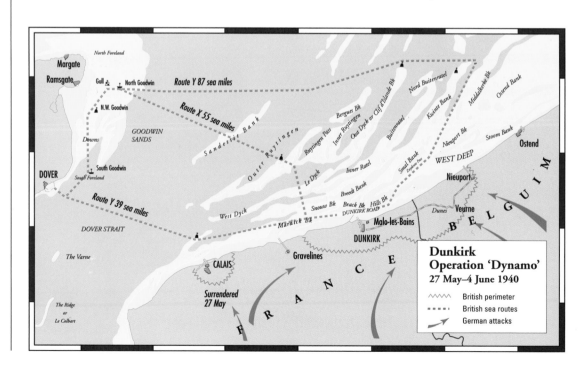

Dunkirk
Operation 'Dynamo'
27 May–4 June 1940

~~~~~ British perimeter
┄┄┄┄ British sea routes
➤ German attacks

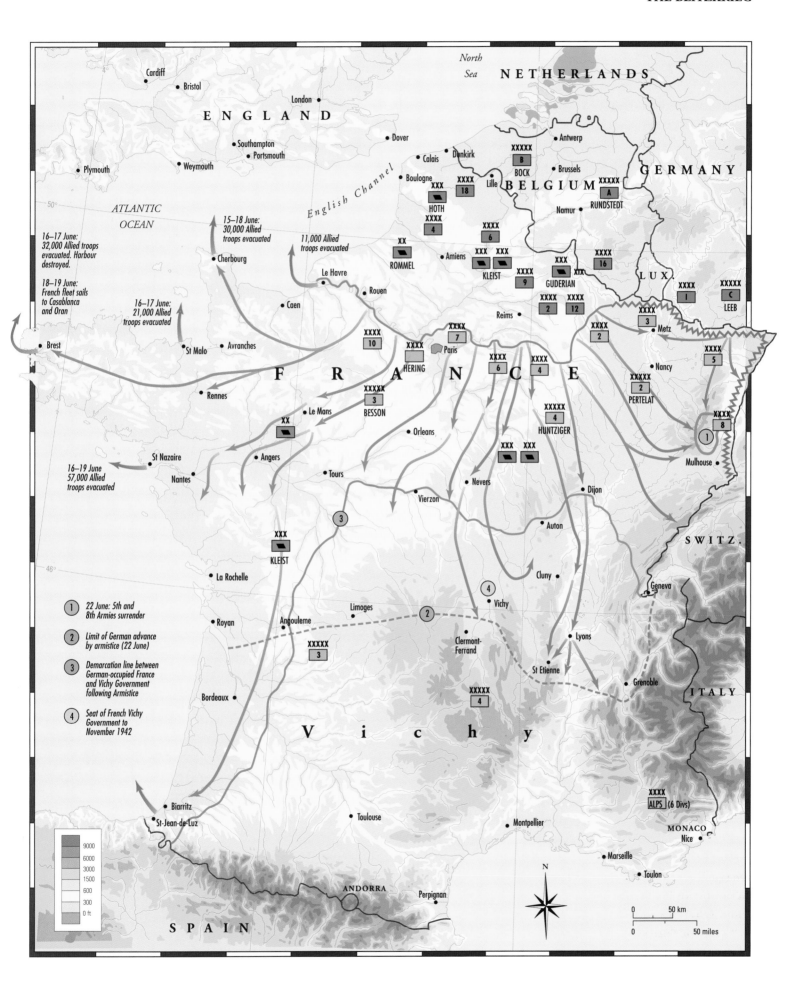

North
Sea

NETHERLANDS

Cardiff

Bristol

London

ENGLAND

Dover

Southampton

Portsmouth

Weymouth

Antwerp

Calais   Dunkirk

Boulogne

English Channel

Brussels

Namur

GERMANY

B
BOCK

18

XXXX
HOTH

Lille

BELGIUM

A
RUNDSTEDT

LUX.

Plymouth

*ATLANTIC
OCEAN*

*16–17 June:
32,000 Allied troops
evacuated. Harbour
destroyed.*

*18–19 June:
French fleet sails
to Casablanca
and Oran*

Cherbourg

*15–18 June:
30,000 Allied
troops evacuated*

*11,000 Allied
troops evacuated*

Le Havre

Rouen

ROMMEL

Amiens

4

6

KLEIST

9

GUDERIAN

Reims

2   **12**

16

C
LEEB

1

3

2

Metz

Nancy

5

Brest

St Malo

Avranches

Caen

*16–17 June:
21,000 Allied
troops evacuated*

10

HERING

Paris

7

F   R   A   N   C   E

6   **4**

PERTELAT

2

8

Rennes

Le Mans

BESSON
3

HUNTZIGER

4

Mulhouse

*16–19 June
57,000 Allied
troops evacuated*

St Nazaire

Angers

Nantes

Orleans

Tours

Vierzon

Nevers

KLEIST

Auton

SWITZ.

Cluny

Dijon

La Rochelle

①
22 June: 5th and
8th Armies surrender

Limoges

②
Limit of German advance
by armistice (22 June)

③
Demarcation line between
German-occupied France
and Vichy Government
following Armistice

④
Seat of French Vichy
Government to
November 1942

Royan

Angouleme

3

Clermont-
Ferrand

4
Vichy

Lyons

St Etienne

Grenoble

Geneva

ITALY

Bordeaux

V   i   c   h   y

4

ALPS (6 Divs)

Biarritz

St-Jean-de-Luz

Toulouse

Montpellier

MONACO
Nice

Marseille

Toulon

9000
6000
3000
1500
600
300
0 ft

SPAIN

ANDORRA

Perpignan

N

0   50 km

0   50 miles

THE BATTLE OF BRITAIN

In the Battle of Britain, three *Luftflotte*, or 'air fleets', struck at the RAF from bases in northern France and Norway. Utilizing lightly armed medium bombers, such as the Heinkel 111, the Luftwaffe was reliant upon fighter support, mainly of its Me 109s.

British Fighter Command, receiving early warning of German attacks from a string of 21 radar bases along the coast and a network of observers, relied on the Hurricane and newer Spitfire fighters for defence. Much of the fighting in the Battle of Britain fell to Fighter Command's 11 Group, under the command of Air Marshal Keith Park. The fighting was especially heavy in southeast England, due in part to the limited range of the Me 109. In combat, the Me 109 proved slightly superior to the Hurricane, but it met its match in the Spitfire.

For two months, aided by heavy anti-aircraft fire that would become increasingly important in the Blitz, the RAF fought on – seemingly surviving by the slimmest of margins as pilot attrition took its toll on the force.

By 17 September, the valiant resistance of the RAF forced Hitler effectively to call off the invasion of southern England, although it was technically only postponed. The German Luftwaffe had been defeated in the Battle of Britain.

parachute to safety and return to the sky in another aircraft the same day. Göring was somewhat surprised by the effectiveness of RAF resistance, and on 24 August the Luftwaffe redoubled its attacks on Fighter Command. For the first time in the struggle, RAF losses exceeded new aircraft production – it seemed that disaster loomed.

Concerned that the Battle of Britain was lingering on too long, Göring changed strategy and on 7 September began to concentrate on the daylight bombing of London. Göring hoped that the threat to the capital city would draw even more of the RAF into battle, whereas before Dowding had been able to husband his resources closely. The shift to the bombing of London was, instead, a blessing for beleaguered Fighter Command – even if the people of London would not have seen it that way – as it granted the RAF the necessary time to recover from the continued strikes on its bases. Frustrated that the RAF struggled on regardless, on 17 September Hitler effectively called off Operation Sea Lion, although it was not formally cancelled until the following year. The RAF had survived its sternest test.

THE BLITZ

Unwilling to admit defeat, in late September Göring ordered the Luftwaffe to shift to night bombings of London – beginning a period that would become known as 'the Blitz'. Bombers, now free of the need for fighter escorts, could penetrate further into Britain; however, at first the new wave of bombing concentrated on the densely populated East End of London. Göring hoped that the continued pounding of the capital city would cause a collapse of British morale. Although the continuing attacks were deadly and disruptive, Londoners soldiered on. Lacking in adequate air raid shelters, many Londoners sought refuge by spending the night in Underground stations. Morale did not crumble; in fact, quite the opposite. As their city blew apart around them Londoners developed a spirit of grim determination and togetherness. By night, the air raid sirens would wail, the anti-aircraft batteries would boom and the bombs would wreak havoc. By day, Londoners would count their losses and get down to the work of winning the war.

In November, the Germans widened their assault by striking hard at cities across Britain when some 400 German bombers struck the unsuspecting city of Coventry. Dropping high-explosive and incendiary bombs, the Germans killed some 500 people and destroyed much of the centre of the city. Although attacks slackened somewhat in the winter, on 29 December bombers struck the area around St Paul's Cathedral in London. Several incendiary bombs struck the famed cathedral, but it remained standing and became a

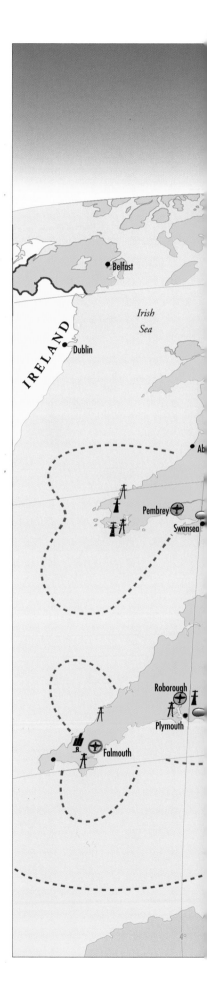

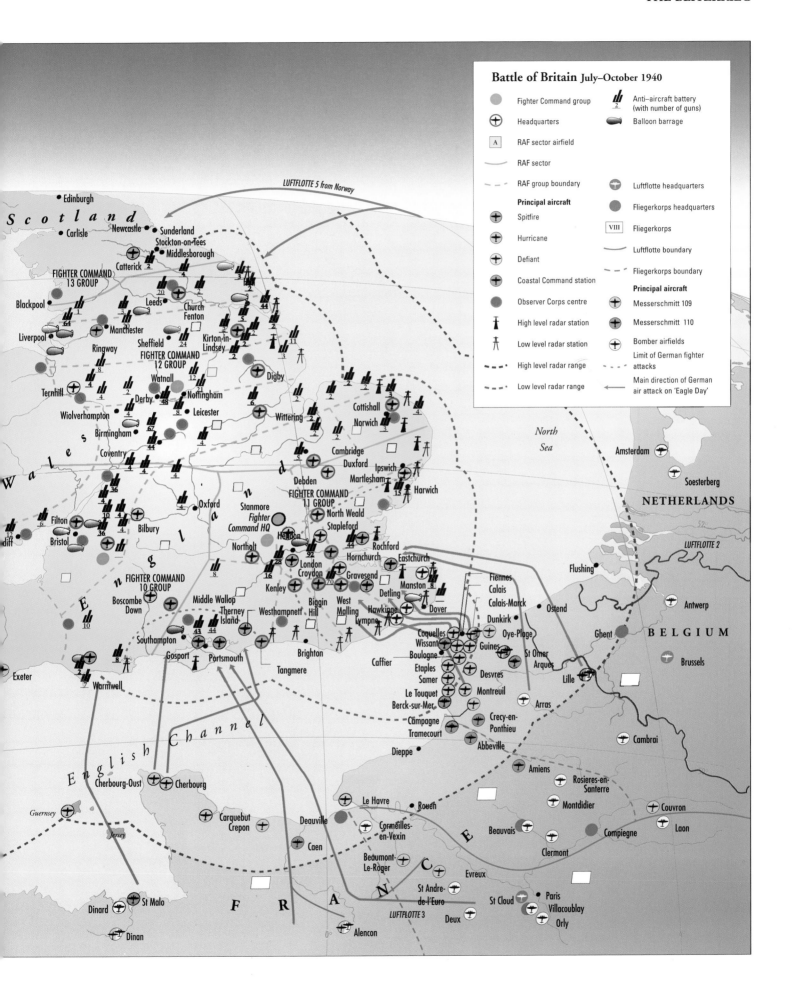

Battle of Britain July–October 1940

⬤ Fighter Command group	Anti–aircraft battery (with number of guns)
⊕ Headquarters	Balloon barrage
A RAF sector airfield	
RAF sector	
RAF group boundary	Luftflotte headquarters
Principal aircraft	Fliegerkorps headquarters
Spitfire	VIII Fliegerkorps
Hurricane	Luftflotte boundary
Defiant	Fliegerkorps boundary
Coastal Command station	**Principal aircraft**
Observer Corps centre	Messerschmitt 109
High level radar station	Messerschmitt 110
Low level radar station	Bomber airfields
High level radar range	Limit of German fighter attacks
Low level radar range	Main direction of German air attack on 'Eagle Day'

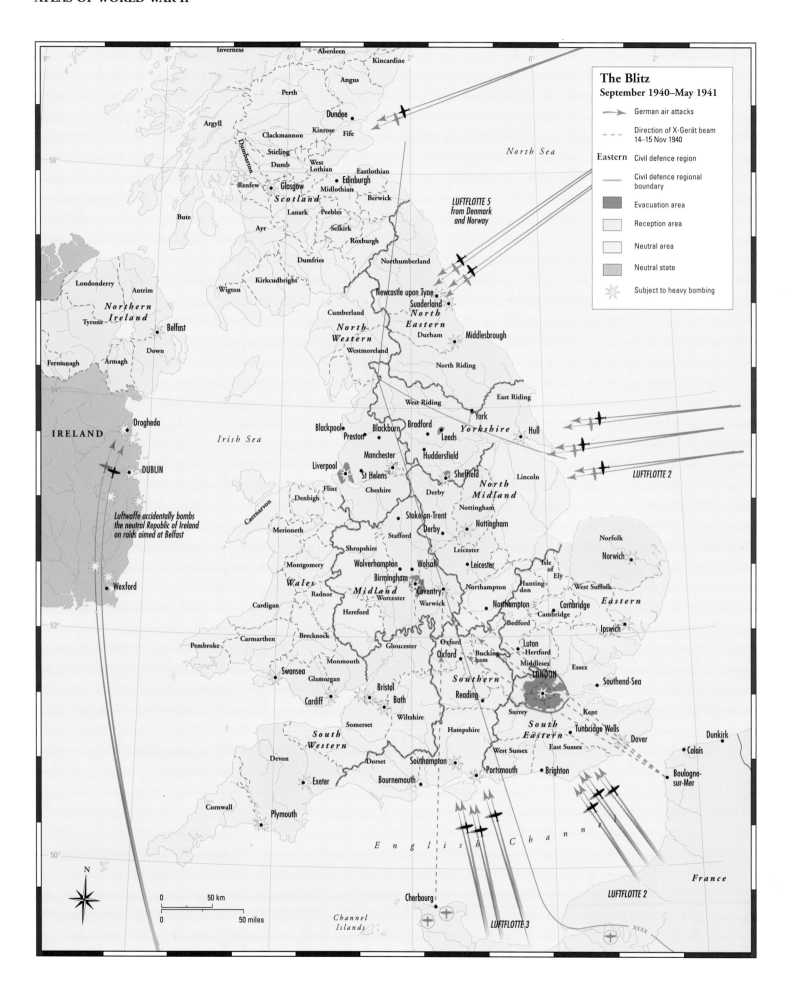

The Blitz
September 1940–May 1941

→ German air attacks

Direction of X-Gerät beam
14–15 Nov 1940

Eastern Civil defence region

Civil defence regional boundary

Evacuation area

Reception area

Neutral area

Neutral state

Subject to heavy bombing

Inverness
Aberdeen
Kincardine
Angus
Perth
Dundee
Argyll
Kinrose Fife
Clackmannon
Stirling
Dumbarton
Dumb West Lothian
Renfew Glasgow Midlothian Edinburgh Eastlothian
Scotland Berwick
Bute
Lanark Peebles
Ayr Selkirk
Roxburgh
Dumfries
Northumberland
Kirkcudbright
Wigton
LUFTFLOTTE 5
from Denmark
and Norway

North Sea

Londonderry
Antrim
Northern Ireland
Tyrone
Belfast
Fermanagh Down
Armagh

Cumberland
Newcastle upon Tyne
Sunderland
North Eastern
Durham
North Western
Westmoreland
Middlesbrough
North Riding

East Riding
West Riding
York
Yorkshire Hull

Drogheda
IRELAND
DUBLIN
Irish Sea
Blackpool Bradford
Preston Blackburn Leeds
Manchester Huddersfield
Liverpool
St Helens Sheffield
Flint Cheshire Derby Lincoln
North Midland
Denbigh
Caernarvon
Nottingham
Stoke-on-Trent
Derby
Nottingham
Stafford
Shropshire Leicester
Merioneth Leicester
Montgomery Wolverhampton Walsall
Birmingham
Wales *Midland* Coventry
Radnor Worcester
Cardigan Warwick
Hereford
Northampton
Northampton
Carmarthen Brecknock
Gloucester
Pembroke
Oxford
Oxford Bucking ham
Swansea Monmouth
Glamorgan
Cardiff Bristol
Bath
Wiltshire
Somerset
Reading

Luftwaffe accidentally bombs the neutral Republic of Ireland on raids aimed at Belfast

Wexford

Norfolk
Norwich
Isle of Ely
West Suffolk
Huntingdon
Cambridge
Cambridge *Eastern*
Bedford Ipswich

Luton
Hertford
Middlesex
Essex
LONDON
Southend-Sea
Surrey Kent
Tunbridge Wells
South Eastern Dover
West Sussex East Sussex
Hampshire Brighton
Dunkirk
Calais

South Western
Devon
Dorset
Southampton
Portsmouth
Bournemouth
Boulogne-sur-Mer

Exeter

Cornwall
Plymouth

English Channel

France

N

0 50 km
0 50 miles

Cherbourg
LUFTFLOTTE 3
LUFTFLOTTE 2

Channel Islands

XXXX

THE BLITZ

Realizing that Britain would be susceptible to air attack in time of war, the British Government developed a complicated scheme to evacuate children from vulnerable cities to the countryside. Some evacuations even took children as far as distant Canada. The German night bombing of British cities, know as the 'Blitz', began in September 1940 and lasted in earnest until May 1941.

Most of the attacks centred on London. German aircraft raiding at night found London with great ease – in part by following the River Thames. Although Britain would suffer nearly 60,000 civilian dead – the majority from London – by the war's end, the carnage failed to cause the collapse of British morale. Seeking better results, by November 1940 the Germans began to strike less prepared cities, often in the British Midlands.

To locate the targets, the Germans employed X-Gerät radio beams. Emanating from different points in France, the radio beams would cross above the intended target, telling the bomb aimer to drop his load. This method was used to destroy much of Coventry in one massive November raid.

The British initially relied on searchlights and anti-aircraft guns for defence. However, some fighters were equipped with radar, enabling them to locate German night raiders. In the end the Blitz failed, and the Luftwaffe redeployed to the east to attack the Soviet Union.

symbol of British resolve. Attacks continued in the spring of 1941, often aimed at the industrial centres of the Midlands. Even so, Hitler's ambitions had changed, for he was readying for his climactic struggle with the Soviet Union. The bombing was intended to help Britain come to the realization that it could not win the war and should come to an accomodation, as Hitler had always wanted, but this end was not in sight. As a result, the Luftwaffe ended the Blitz in preparation for its role in 'Operation Barbarossa'.

Britain had survived, though at the cost of tens of thousands of civilian dead. In the epic struggle, the RAF had lost 1265 aircraft and the Luftwaffe some 1882 aircraft. It was the first time that a battle over the life of a nation had been decided solely in the air. The tiny band of brave pilots and crews of the RAF – many of them not British, but Czech or Polish exiles – had achieved victory, prompting Winston Churchill's now famous remark, 'Never in the field of human conflict was so much owed by so many to so few.'

Above: A German Luftwaffe ground crew works on the Daimler-Benz engine of a Me 109 fighter on the French Channel coast. *Reichsmarschall* **Hermann Göring had boasted to Hitler that the Luftwaffe would force Britain to surrender. But the courageous efforts of the British Royal Air Force – in which many Czech, Polish, French and even a few American pilots were also serving at the time – ensured that the danger of invasion was averted.**

The Air War in Europe

The strategic air campaign waged against Germany was the product of theories which were developed during the inter-war years. It was thought that a country could be bombed into submission through air power alone, but it would take the lives of many young Allied airmen – and helpless German citizens in cities such as Cologne and Dresden – to prove the theory false.

During World War I, aerial warfare and combat were in their infancy, but even so results of the first air war indicated that the military aircraft had the potential to be a war-winning weapon. While air power demonstrated its considerable worth in reconnaissance and ground-attack roles, many theorists paid the greatest heed to the role of the strategic bomber. During the Great War, German Zeppelins and Gotha bombers launched rather small bombing raids on British industrial and civilian targets. Results of the raids included near panic and a drop in industrial output far in excess of what the Germans expected.

In Italy in the wake of World War I, it was Giulio Douhet who first postulated as early as 1921 that bombers alone could win a war through the destruction of enemy industrial production and the population's will to fight. Douhet's theories found fertile ground in both Britain and the United States, for both nations sought a method to project their power into a continental war. In Britain, General Hugh Trenchard, the first commander of the Royal Air Force (RAF), was the prophet of air power, while General Billy Mitchell was to play a similar role in the United States.

The airpower theorists gained immeasurably from the experience of the Spanish Civil War. In aid of the Falangist Franco, Germany devoted the Condor Legion of aircraft to the conflict, which gained the most notoriety – or possibly infamy – for its raids on civilian targets, including the destruction of the Basque stronghold of Guernica. Casualties in the air raids were so high that they led some British theorists to believe that, upon the outbreak of war, London would suffer tens of thousands of deaths per day in a concentrated air attack. While such casualty figures were wildly overestimated, what is true is that Allied air theorists believed even more comprehensively in the war-winning power of the bomber.

Despite being particularly enamoured of the theory of strategic bombing, Bomber Command within Britain's RAF was nonetheless unprepared for the coming of World War II and had only a handful of medium bombers at its disposal in 1939 – too small and too few in number to have any effect on the outcome of the conflict. Even so, the RAF continued in its programmes to develop and produce heavy, four-engine bombers capable of attacks on the industrial and population centres of Germany. Eventually these aircraft, the Stirling, Lancaster and Halifax bombers, would form the backbone of a fleet of bombers designed to crush German resistance.

During 1939 and 1940, the initiative in the air war lay mainly with the Luftwaffe and included brief raids on Warsaw and Rotterdam – and the extended Battle of Britain and the Blitz. Locked in a life-or-death defensive struggle, the RAF did little to project its power over the skies of Germany in any organized fashion. In late 1939 a few, outdated Wellington bombers struck Germany's North Sea coast, with little result. Amid the Battle of Britain, the RAF carried out five weak raids on Berlin, during which only 29 of the 105 bombers involved even found their intended target. The proponents of strategic bombing, however, remained unfazed. With an adequate force of heavy bombers, bombing at night to avoid the worst of the German defensive measures, the RAF believed that it could still use strategic bombing to destroy both German will and the ability to resist.

Left: Allied bombs fall on a U-boat base. Unlike the British and later American air forces, the German Luftwaffe was very much tailored to fighting a tactical war against opponents on the battlefield, acting as 'flying artillery' in support of the panzers; it was less suited to the bombing of strategic targets such as factories and rail marshalling yards. Overall, though, the Luftwaffe had a significant advantage in the first years of World War II, with proven aircraft designs and experienced aircrews who had fought in the Spanish Civil War.

The Bombing of Europe 1939–41

- Bomber Command Headquarters
- Bomber Group Headquarters

Weight of bombs

- 25–1000 tonnes
- 1000–3000 tonnes
- 3000–4000 tonnes

NORWAY

SWEDEN

DENMARK

North
Sea

Copenhagen

Sylt

Flensburg

Kiel

Warnemünde
Rostock

Cuxhaven

Lubeck
Wismar

Bremerhaven

Hamburg

Stettin

Irish
Sea

York

Wilhelmshaven
Emden

Bremen

Berlin

UNITED
KINGDOM

Texel

NETH.

Oldenburg

Salzbergen

Osnabruck

Brunswick

Magdeburg

Grantham

Amsterdam
Schipol

Bielefeld

Huntingdon
Exning

Soesterberg

Munster

Merseburg

Abingdon

Rotterdam

Haamstede

Emmerich

Hamm
Soest

Paderborn

Kassel

High Wycombe
London

Flushing

Eindhoven

München–
gladbach

Moncheim
Cologne

See inset

GERMANY

Ostend

Koblenz

Prague

Dunkirk

Zeebrugge

Calais

Hazebrouck

Boulogne

Brussels

BELGIUM

Frankfurt

English Channel

Merville

Mannheim

Nuremberg

Cherbourg

Dieppe

Karlsruhe

le Havre

Stuttgart

Brest

Paris

Munich

Lorient

FRANCE

St Nazaire

La Pallice/
La Rochelle

Bern

SWITZERLAND

Bay of
Biscay

Royan

Geneva

Vichy
Occupied 11 Nov 1942

Ambares

Wesel

Milan

Venice

Bordeaux
Airfield

Bordeaux

Turin

Bottrapp

Lunen

Starkade

Gielen-Kirchen

Homberg
Huls

Wanne-Eickel

Dortmund

ITALY

Duisberg

Essen

Schwerte

Genoa

Krefeld

Ruhr

SPAIN

Munchen-
Gladbach

Dusseldorf

Reishaloz

THE BOMBING OF EUROPE 1939–41

The outbreak of war in Europe found the Royal Air Force (RAF) at only the beginning of a rearmament plan, and thus without enough heavy bombers to launch a strategic bombing campaign designed to force Germany from the war. Instead, under the command of Chief of the Air Staff Sir Charles Portal, it was decided that the RAF would launch a series of lesser raids against German industrial targets. Initially such attacks were undertaken by day in hopes of destroying facets of the German war industry through precision attacks. However, the raids – especially those on the port city of Lubeck and the industrial centres of the Ruhr – proved inaccurate and quite costly in terms of both men and machines.

The RAF also concentrated its efforts against German naval targets – specifically the submarine bases that served as ports for the deadly German U-boats taking part in the ongoing Battle of the Atlantic. The gigantic concrete U-boat pens at French ports on the Atlantic such as Lorient and St-Nazaire, though, proved nearly impossible to hit and almost impervious to damage.

Nevertheless, the proponents of strategic bombing argued that a shift to night-time area bombing attacks would provide war-winning results, given the requisite strength in heavy bombers to provide the saturation bombing of a target.

Above: A German anti-aircraft gun crew run towards its weapon on the French coast. The RAF pursued a policy of strategic bombing, although losses soon forced the British to conduct only night raids. By 1943, when the USAAF began its own bombing campaign in earnest, strategic targets in Germany were being attacked by both day and night, and German boys as young as 14 were operating the anti-aircraft guns.

THE BOMBING OF GERMANY 1941–42

In 1941, the RAF continued sporadic, night-time raids against German industrial targets. Results of the bombing, though, remained minimal and merely bothersome. Utilizing reconnaissance and Ultra intelligence in August 1941, Britain took stock of the strategic bombing offensive in the Butt Report. Churchill was disturbed to learn that in general RAF bombing missions missed their designated target by 8km (5 miles), with some bombers even straying up to 120km (75 miles) off course. Thus the RAF could not be relied upon to hit a target smaller than a city. Yet the Chief of the Air Staff, Sir Charles Portal, still remained convinced that strategic bombing was the key to victory. Portal contended that a fleet of 4000 heavy bombers could destroy Germany's cities, bringing the nation to its knees. Although somewhat taken aback that Germany's civilian population would now be seen as a legitimate target, Churchill approved the Area Bombing Directive. Thus an increasing number of RAF heavy bombers would be devoted to bombing German civilian targets, a move aimed at crushing enemy morale. To facilitate this new plan, Churchill appointed Arthur Harris as head of Bomber Command of the RAF. Harris, who would earn the nickname 'Bomber' Harris, was completely devoted to the idea that strategic bombing could crush Germany's will to resist.

Despite the fact the British bombed at night, German defensive advance had served to even the odds somewhat. A chain of radar stations enabled the Germans to detect many incoming attack forces, and increasingly Luftwaffe night fighters could rely on onboard short-range radar to find their elusive targets. Although losses began to mount, Harris hoped to overwhelm Luftwaffe defenses with sheer numbers. Needing victories to prove the validity of his scheme, Harris launched his first major area bombing raid on the German city of Lubeck in March 1942. Using a potent mixture of high-explosive and incendiary bombs, 242 RAF bombers laid waste

THOUSAND-BOMBER RAID

Hungry for a signal success, RAF Bomber Command's Arthur Harris developed 'Operation Millennium, the first thousand-bomber raid directed at the industrial city of Cologne. Realizing the possible propaganda effect of such a raid, Harris gathered a force of 1046 aircraft, including virtually every serviceable bomber in the country.

Using the new directional radio aid of Gee, the bombers formed up from some 98 different locations in Britain and flew out in three waves. The first wave of bombers struck the centre of Cologne with incendiary bombs, starting fires that would serve as the aiming point for subsequent waves. The raid lasted some 98 minutes, with 898 bombers actually reaching and bombing the target area.

In total, the RAF dropped 1478 tonnes (1455 tons) of bombs on Cologne, devastating the city and forcing the evacuation of 200,000 people. The cost of the raid to the RAF was 40 aircraft lost, a figure which represented only 3.8 per cent of the total deployed – the sheer size of the operation had overwhelmed the German defences in the area.

The raid gripped a British public in need of good news, even though the military results were less positive than expected. Harris nevertheless remained firm in his belief that strategic bombing represented the quickest road to victory.

to the centre of the port city. Although the raid was a potent propaganda victory for Harris, the industrial areas of Lubeck remained intact, and the morale of the citizenry did not crack. Harris, though, was certain that he was on the path towards victory – and he hoped that a single, monumental raid would prove his point.

A NEW LEVEL OF DESTRUCTIVENESS

Amassing all the forces at his disposal, Harris launched the first 'thousand-bomber' raid. After a series of feints designed to lessen German resistance, on the night of 30 May 1942, some 1046 bombers formed up from a total of 98 bases in Britain – a massive logistical undertaking – and struck the heart of the German city of Cologne. Again, the raid was a massive publicity success, devastating the heart of the city as it did for the loss of only 40 bombers. On a military level, however, the raid achieved little success – German industrial production did not fall, and civilian morale once again held firm. Three more raids of similar magnitude followed on other major industrial and population centres, with similar results. To many observers, the strategic bombing offensive seemed to be a failure, even though it continued to garner headlines. Harris, however, was still certain that more aerial destruction remained the key to victory, and finally he had a new weapon to hand to achieve this end – the might of the United States Army Air Force (USAAF).

Although distracted by events in the Pacific, the United States quickly sent elements of the US 8th Air Force to Britain in the wake of the Japanese attack on Pearl Harbor, arriving in force

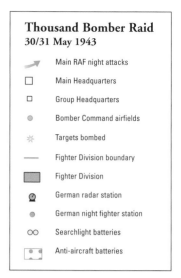

Thousand Bomber Raid
30/31 May 1943

↗ Main RAF night attacks
☐ Main Headquarters
☐ Group Headquarters
⦿ Bomber Command airfields
✳ Targets bombed
— Fighter Division boundary
▣ Fighter Division
⊕ German radar station
● German night fighter station
∞ Searchlight batteries
▦ Anti-aircraft batteries

Below: An Avro Lancaster, one of the mainstays of the RAF's bombing effort over Germany. Both Britain and the United States relied on four-engined bombers to reach targets throughout the Third Reich. The USAAF continued to use the B-17 Flying Fortress in Europe despite the B-29 Superfortress entering service, as the latter's greater range was needed in the Pacific to attack strategic targets in Japan.

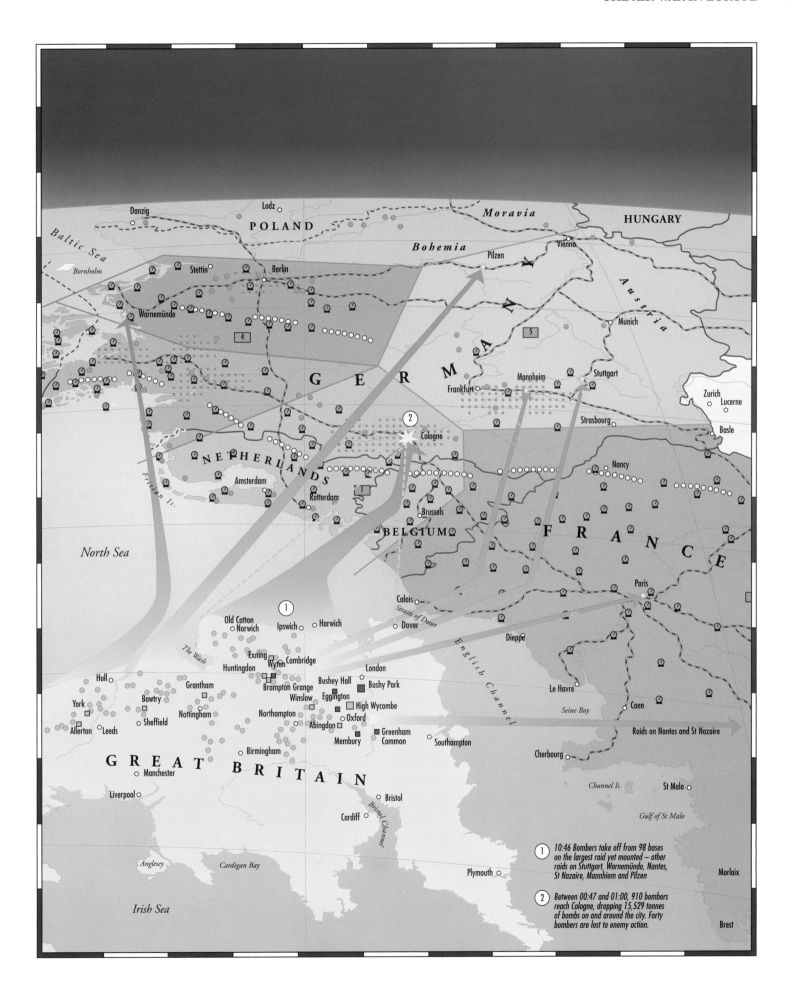

Danzig

Lodz

Baltic Sea

POLAND

Moravia

HUNGARY

Bornholm

Bohemia

Stettin

Berlin

Pilzen

Vienna

Warnemünde

G E R M A N Y

Austria

Munich

4

5

Mannheim

Stuttgart

Frankfurt

Zurich

Lucerne

Strasbourg

Basle

Cologne

2

NETHERLANDS

Nancy

Amsterdam

Rotterdam

1

Brussels

North Sea

BELGIUM

F R A N C E

Frisian Is.

Paris

Calais

Straits of Dover

Old Catton

Norwich

Ipswich

Harwich

Dover

Dieppe

1

The Wash

Exning

Cambridge

London

Le Havre

English Channel

Hull

Huntingdon

Wyton

Grantham

Bushey Hall

Bushy Park

Caen

York

Bawtry

Nottingham

Winslow

Eggington

Northampton

High Wycombe

Seine Bay

Brampton Grange

Leeds

Allerton

Sheffield

Abingdon

Oxford

Cherbourg

Membury

Greenham
Common

Southampton

Raids on Nantes and St Nazaire

Birmingham

G R E A T   B R I T A I N

Channel Is.

St Malo

Manchester

Liverpool

Bristol

Gulf of St Malo

Cardiff

Bristol Channel

Anglesey

Cardigan Bay

Plymouth

Morlaix

Irish Sea

Brest

1   10:46 Bombers take off from 98 bases
on the largest raid yet mounted – other
raids on Stuttgart, Warnemünde, Nantes,
St Nazaire, Mannheim and Pilzen

2   Between 00:47 and 01:00, 910 bombers
reach Cologne, dropping 15,529 tonnes
of bombs on and around the city. Forty
bombers are lost to enemy action.

by May 1942. The 8th Air Force relied on the strength of the B-24 Liberator and the B-17 Flying Fortress – mighty four-engined bombers bristling with defensive firepower. The British had chosen to bomb Germany at night, largely due to the fact that there were as yet no long-range fighters to protect the vulnerable bombers against German air attacks. The Americans, commanded by General H.H. 'Hap' Arnold, believed that their heavily armed bombers flying in tight formations could fend off German fighters, allowing for daylight bombing. In addition, the Americans possessed the new and superior Norden bombsight which they hoped would result in precision devastation of German industry. Initial US raids proved costly and rather inaccurate, but in January 1943, Britain and the United States agreed to the Combined Bomber Offensive. The RAF would bomb German cities by night, while the 8th Air Force would engage in destruction of industrial targets by day.

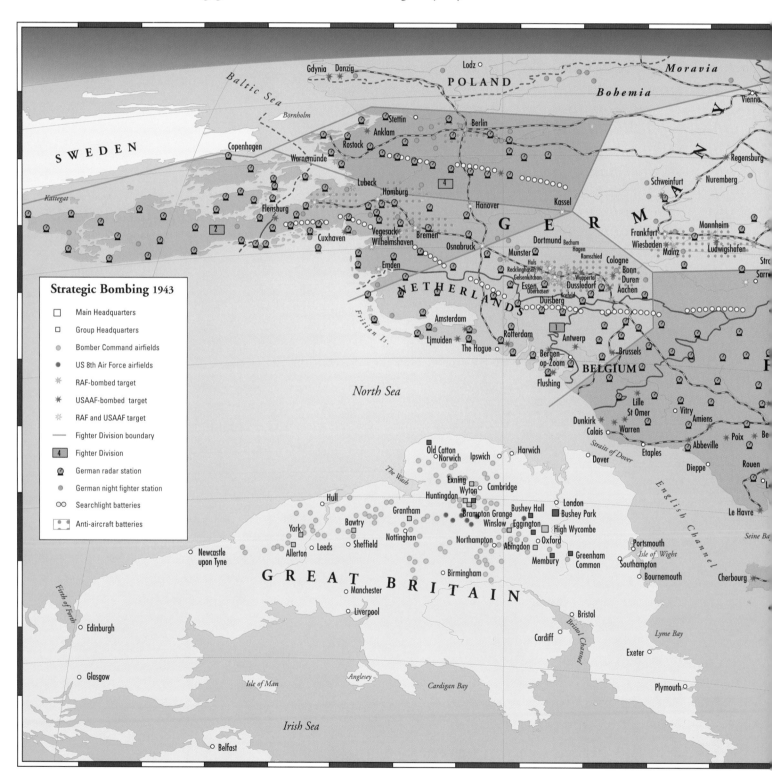

REAPING THE WHIRLWIND

The Allies demonstrated their awesome newfound power in a series of raids in late July and early August 1943 on the German port city of Hamburg. On the night of 24 July, some 800 RAF bombers destroyed much of central Hamburg. Next came two days of raids by the 8th Air Force. On the night of 26 July, the RAF returned, dropping incendiary bombs on the rubble below, starting innumerable fires. The conflagrations coalesced slowly into one mighty blaze over 3km (2 miles) in diameter, transforming into a giant firestorm. Winds around the firestorm whipped at some 320km/h (200mph) as its temperatures reached a high of 1500°F (800°C). In the end Hamburg was destroyed, and some 60,000 lives were lost – more than in the entire Battle of Britain. The Allies, though, could not keep up such a bombing pace. Large raids continued across Germany – notably over the industrial area of the Ruhr and Berlin – but none with the devastating impact of the Hamburg raid. Surprisingly, German industrial production actually went up in 1943, under the guidance of Albert Speer – who did his best to disperse German industry into the countryside, away from the vulnerable cities. In addition, losses among the bomber ranks continued to rise, as the Germans redoubled their efforts to build defensive fighter aircraft.

The 8th Air Force fared little better. Bombing German industrial targets mainly associated with aircraft production by day, the Americans did score significant successes. However, when the bombers strayed beyond the range of fighter escort, they often paid a prohibitive price. In August 1943 US aircraft struck at German industrial assets in the Regensburg area and at ball-bearing factories in Schweinfurt. Hampered by bad weather and new German fighter tactics, the Schweinfurt raid turned into a disaster. Nearly 40 bombers were destroyed, and a further 100 were damaged – and the ball-bearing factories received only little damage. During the same month, 117 US bombers took off from North Africa to bomb the Ploesti oil fields of Romania – 54

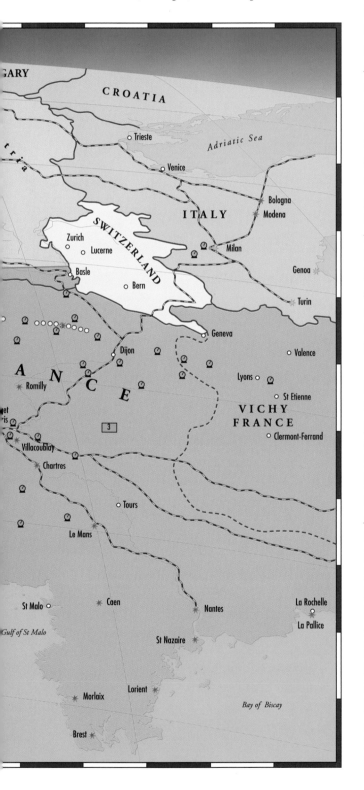

STRATEGIC BOMBING 1943

By 1943 Britain had built up its force of Halifax and Lancaster bombers, and the United States 8th Air Force – with its B-17 Flying Fortresses and B-24 Liberators – had joined the conflict. The Germans countered this bomber force with the construction of the Kammhuber Line of defences.

First, a belt of 'Wurzburg' radar installations detected the incoming Allied bombers. Next, a line of searchlights and anti-aircraft guns defended the approaches to the Third Reich – with a lesser belt defending Berlin. Finally, groups of fighter aircraft, often provided with onboard radar, would rise to meet the attackers, usually long after any defending fighters had been forced to return home.

During 1943 the RAF hammered Germany by night – again concentrating on the industrial area of the Ruhr and Berlin – while American formations attempted precision bombing of German industry by day. With the increase of German defensive capability in 1943, the Allies suffered heavy losses to their aircrews. They did, however, succeed in dropping some 203,200 tonnes (200,000 tons) of bombs on German cities. Even so, German industrial output continued to rise, and German civilian morale remained high.

DAMBUSTERS

During mid-1943, Bomber Command concentrated 43 raids on the main German industrial area of the Ruhr. The most daring of the raids was undertaken by the British 617 Squadron, known as the 'Dambusters'. The goal of the raid was to destroy the Moehne, Schelme, Eder and Sorpe dams, the source of most of the electricity in the region.

During arduous training in very difficult low-level bombing, the Dambusters practised releasing cylindrical bombs, which would skip along the water until they struck the dam, where they would then sink to the bottom and explode. Numbering only 19 aircraft, the squadron, led by Wing Commander Guy Gibson, had to face attack during much of their journey through German-held territory – losing three aircraft in the process. The majority of losses, though, came during the low and vulnerable approach over the Ruhr, when five aircraft were lost. The brave surviving Dambuster pilots succeeded in breaching both the Moehne and Eder dams. Even then the damage inflicted was not as great as had been expected, allowing the Germans to effect quick repairs.

Although lauded for their actions, the Dambusters had achieved little at a high price, leaving the future of bombing to more traditional attacks. Later in the war, however, 617 Squadron would achieve success by destroying the German battleship *Tirpitz*.

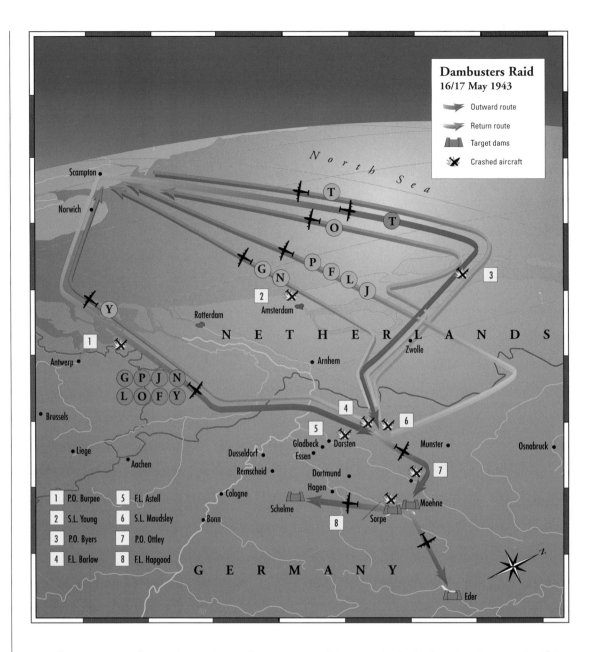

were lost to enemy fire and 522 airmen became casualties – again for little gain. As a result of the continuing losses, the United States called off further bombing missions beyond the range of fighter escort.

THE WAR COMES TO AN END

As 1944 and the Normandy invasion drew near, Allied air forces shifted the focus of their bombing campaign to northern France. With victory in Normandy secured and Germany facing invasion on two fronts, the strategic bombing campaign renewed in earnest in November 1944. The 8th Air Force, now under the command of General James Doolittle, along with the 15th Air Force based in Italy, began a series of raids on the German petroleum industry – and German petroleum production plummeted, further hindering the already sorely pressed Wehrmacht. The Germans had hoped that the new Me 262 jet fighter would tip the balance of the air war in their favour, but the jets were too few in number. In addition, the Allies now possessed the best all-round fighter of the war, the long range P-51 Mustang, to serve as escort to vulnerable bombers.

As the war neared its end, many questioned the need to visit further slaughter upon Germany's civilians. Even so, in February 1945, British and American bombers struck Dresden, causing another firestorm. More than 37,000 people died in the inferno – for a very limited military gain. It is quite possible that the Allies undertook the bombing of Dresden in part to impress the Soviets, who were only 80km (50 miles) away. In the wake of the controversial attack, the Allies ceased bombing of German civilian targets, and the strategic bombing campaign came to an end.

In the bombing campaign over Germany, some 400,000 civilians lost their lives, at the cost of 40,000 Allied aircraft lost and 160,000 airmen dead – US aircrews suffered one of the highest fatality rates of the war. The bombing campaign had failed to destroy either German industry or the German will to resist. Only in 1945 did strategic bombing achieve its best results. The bombing campaign did, however, divert valuable resources and millions of Germans from the front lines. In the end, strategic bombing did not live up to the hopes of its ardent supporters, but was a valuable tool in helping to achieve the Allied victory – even if at horrific cost.

SCHWEINFURT

On 17 August 1943, the 8th Air Force launched twin strikes on elements of the German aircraft industry in Regensburg and the ball-bearing factories of Schweinfurt. But bad weather and confusion led to disaster. Only 184 of the original 230 bombers struck Schweinfurt, dropping only 386 tonnes (380 tons) of bombs.

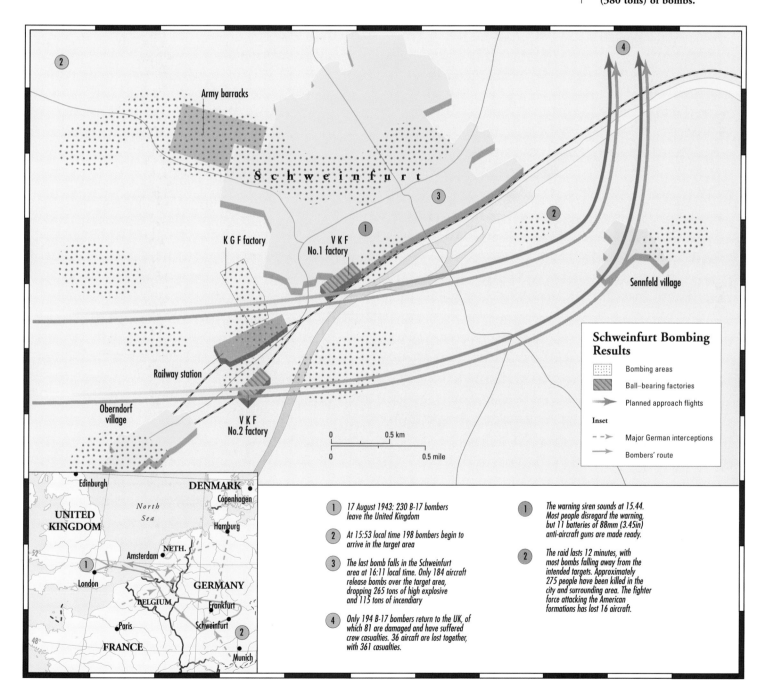

Schweinfurt Bombing Results

- :::::: Bombing areas
- ▨ Ball–bearing factories
- → Planned approach flights

Inset

- – – ▶ Major German interceptions
- → Bombers' route

① 17 August 1943: 230 B-17 bombers leave the United Kingdom

② At 15:53 local time 198 bombers begin to arrive in the target area

③ The last bomb falls in the Schweinfurt area at 16:11 local time. Only 184 aircraft release bombs over the target area, dropping 265 tons of high explosive and 115 tons of incendiary

④ Only 194 B-17 bombers return to the UK, of which 81 are damaged and have suffered crew casualties. 36 aircraft are lost together, with 361 casualties.

① The warning siren sounds at 15.44. Most people disregard the warning, but 11 batteries of 88mm (3.45in) anti-aircraft guns are made ready.

② The raid lasts 12 minutes, with most bombs falling away from the intended targets. Approximately 275 people have been killed in the city and surrounding area. The fighter force attacking the American formations has lost 16 aircraft.

The War in the Atlantic

Britain's continued fight against Hitler's Germany was wholly dependent on its supply
lines to the United States and to its colonies. If the U-boats of the German *Kriegsmarine* could sink
enough ships to starve Britain of raw materials and American armaments, it would be forced to sue
for peace. The Battle of the Atlantic would prove to be a bitter and drawn-out campaign.

Many in Britain expected that the main naval threat during World War I would come from the formidable German High
Seas Fleet, but for most of the war German capital ships remained in their home ports. The most deadly German naval
weapon was the U-boat. These stealthy, underwater craft invaded the Atlantic sea lanes and struck hard at the merchant shipping
that was Britain's very life blood. The situation became so bad in 1917 that Britain seemed to be only weeks from capitulation.
In the end, though, the institution of a system of convoys defeated the U-boat threat. The situation had been so close run,
however, that the Treaty of Versailles forbade Germany ever again to build submarines.

Hitler's rise to power led to the possibility of a second Battle of the Atlantic. The commander of the German Navy, Admiral
Erich Raeder, advocated a balance of surface ships and U-boats for the coming struggle. He was offset by the commander of the
German submarine service, Admiral Karl Dönitz, who contended that only massed numbers of U-boats could defeat Britain. The
early onset of World War II found Germany only at the beginning of an aggressive naval building programme. The German
surface fleet was very small, numbering three small 'pocket' battleships, two battlecruisers, eight cruisers and 21 destroyers. In
addition, Germany possessed 57 submarines, only 22 of which were capable of operations in the Atlantic. Although the Germans
hoped to harass the British with both surface raiders and submarines, they could not match the might of the British Home Fleet,
which boasted 15 battleships, 62 cruisers, 7 aircraft carriers, 178 destroyers and 56 submarines.

Even with this disparity, Dönitz argued that Germany, if it focused on building U-boats, could yet win the day. He contended
that a fleet of some 300 U-boats could strike the vulnerable Atlantic shipping lanes and sink 711,000 tonnes (700,000 tons) of
shipping per month, thus starving Britain into surrender. Dönitz had no doubt that Britain would once again rely on a convoy
system to defend merchant ships, but he had developed a new scheme to defeat convoys – so-called 'wolfpack' tactics. Once a
convoy was sighted, all of the German submarines in the area, using wireless communication, would join together in a pack and
attack the convoy when it was at its weakest: at night. The brash and confident Dönitz soon caught Hitler's attention.

Dönitz's beloved U-boats, though, still suffered from a myriad of drawbacks, for they were in essence submersibles, rather than
true submarines. Agile and fast on the surface, U-boats only submerged for defensive purposes. Underwater, they were slow and
cumbersome, and the time able to be spent submerged was quite limited. Thus U-boats operated and attacked in the main on
the surface. With little armament or armour, however, U-boats made very weak surface vessels, relying on their low silhouette and
stealth in attack. Any surface attack would inevitably drive a U-boat underwater, allowing even the slowest convoy to escape.

For the defence of merchant shipping during World War II, Britain once again relied on a convoy system, in which a group
of merchant ships steamed under the protection of a screen of warships. Escort ships carried sonar systems to detect submerged
U-boats. The ships carried depth charges as weaponry, which exploded when they reached a certain depth beneath the ocean's
surface. The escort ships' weapons systems, though, did have their weaknesses. Sonar faced forwards and was unable to detect a

**Left: A German sailor blows a whistle to signal the captain's arrival on board. The superiority of the British and later American surface navies meant
that Admiral Karl Dönitz pursued a strategy that focused largely on his U-boat fleet in the battle for the Atlantic. Nevertheless, the activities of such
ships as the *Graf Spee*, *Bismarck* and *Tirpitz* caused problems of their own for the Royal Navy. As the war progressed, however, the air superiority of
the Allies made leaving port a dangerous activity for any German vessel.**

BATTLE OF THE ATLANTIC I

Upon the outbreak of World War II, Germany's fledgling U-boat fleet operated out of bases such as Kiel in northern Germany. Admiral Karl Dönitz, the commander of the U-boat arm, had just 57 submarines, many of which were already outdated. To reach the Atlantic, the U-boats had to waste valuable time steaming through the North Sea, and then had to avoid the British blockades covering either the English Channel or the narrow gap between Norway and Scotland. It was a perilous journey, causing the loss of several valuable U-boats.

By the time the submarines reached the Atlantic, they only had enough fuel remaining to operate in the crowded Western Approaches to the British Isles. Making matters worse was the fact that most of these waters were within the range of British aircraft, leaving the U-boats susceptible to discovery and attack. As a result, German U-boats were only a nuisance, sinking some 222 Allied merchant ships, during the first phase of the Battle of the Atlantic. Dönitz tried hard to rectify the situation, constantly pressuring Hitler for more submarines to be built.

Despite Dönitz pressing his Führer for a production figure of 29 U-boats per month, however, Germany was able to average only two submarines a month during 1940.

submarine's depth, while the depth charges were dropped off of a ship's stern – only after a necessary loss of sonar contact.

THE WAR BEGINS

Upon the outbreak of war in September 1939, Dönitz attempted to launch a submarine campaign against the United Kingdom. With few U-boats at his disposal, and the routes to the Atlantic shipping lanes blocked by British warships, the submarines proved little more than a nuisance to Britain and its mighty fleet. The U-boats did achieve some notable successes, including the sinking of the British aircraft carrier *Courageous*. In a separate and stunning development, *U-47*, commanded by Gunther Prien, penetrated the British Home Fleet base at Scapa Flow and sank the battleship *Royal Oak* before escaping back to Germany. Between September 1939 and March 1940, German U-boats sank a total of only 900,000 tonnes (886,000 tons) of merchant shipping at the cost of 15 valuable submarines. Confined to the carefully patrolled waters around Britain, then, the few available German U-boats paid a prohibitive price to achieve disappointing results.

The naval war, though, had another side, for at the same time some 914,000 (900,000 tons) of Allied shipping was lost to German mines and surface raiders. Although some vessels of the German surface fleet, including the pocket battleship *Deutschland*, were recalled to Germany, others remained at sea to cause as much disruption to the sea lanes as possible. Off the coast of South America, the German pocket battleship *Graf Spee* initially found rather easy hunting, destroying nine merchant ships. The British Admiralty immediately sent a force to hunt down the German raider. On 13 December 1939, a British squadron numbering one heavy and two light cruisers discovered *Graf Spee* in the South Atlantic. Boasting heavier armament, the *Graf Spee* dealt harshly with her attackers, severely damaging the heavy cruiser *Exeter*; however, the German ship also received damage in the battle and put into the neutral port of Montevideo, Uruguay, for repairs. Captain Hans Langsdorff of the *Graf Spee* had made a critical error. While he languished in port, more British ships arrived to block his escape. Forced to leave Montevideo before repairs were complete, Langsdorff chose to scuttle *Graf Spee* rather than give the British the pleasure of her destruction. Afterwards Langsdorff committed suicide. Atlhough German surface raiders would pose an intermittent threat through much of World War II, their impact remained very limited.

It seemed that the British had the Battle of the Atlantic, such as it was, well in hand, but the German conquest of Norway and France in 1940 altered everything. U-boats and surface raiders could now operate out of the sheltered fjords of Norway and the

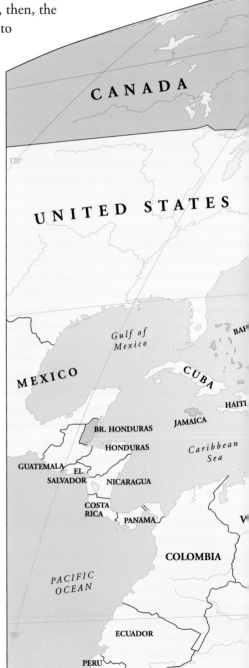

Atlantic ports of France, avoiding the British blockade. In addition, the sailing time of the U-boats was now much reduced, extending their action radius far out into the Atlantic sea lanes. Instead of doing battle in the crowded waters of the North Sea and the Western Approaches to Britain, the U-boats could now lose themselves in the vastness of the ocean, attacking their victims by surprise. The Battle of the Atlantic had suddenly become much more serious.

Operating out of newly captured French ports, the U-boats had much easier access to the vulnerable Atlantic shipping lanes by June of 1940. Although the British convoyed their merchant shipping, the convoy screen of warships had

Battle of the Atlantic I
September 1939–May 1940

- Border of Pan-American Neutrality Zone (1939)
- Extent of air escort cover
- Major convoy routes
- Allied merchant ships sunk by U-boats
- U-boats sunk
- Territory under Allied control
- Territory under Axis control
- Neutral territory

GREENLAND

Norwegian Sea

ICELAND

Arctic Circle

NORWAY

SWEDEN

LABRADOR

North Sea

DENMARK

NEWFOUNDLAND

IRELAND

UNITED KINGDOM

St. John's

NETH

BEL

GERMANY

Halifax

FRANCE

SWITZ

New York

ITALY

Azores

PORTUGAL

SPAIN

Gibraltar

Mediterranean Sea

Bermuda

Maderia

ALGERIA

TUNISIA

MOROCCO

Canary Is.

ATLANTIC OCEAN

WESTERN SAHARA

Africa

FRENCH WEST AFRICA

Cape Verde Is.

Dakar

GAMBIA

Pan–American Neutrality Zone

GUINEA-BISSAU

BRITISH GUIANA

SIERRA LEONE

DUTCH GUIANA

FRENCH GUIANA

Freetown

NIGERIA

LIBERIA

GOLD COAST

ZIL

St. Paul Rocks

BATTLE OF THE ATLANTIC II

Having conquered Norway and France, the Germans had broken the British blockade, allowing U-boats much easier access to the vital Atlantic shipping lanes. Although Britain relied on a system of convoys to protect merchant shipping, there was a shortage of both escort warships and air cover. Thus the few U-boats that Germany was able to place into the Atlantic scored remarkable successes in a period known by the Germans as the 'Happy Time'.

The submarine war moved into the Western Approaches where merchant shipping was abundant, and out of the dangerous waters of the North Sea. Additionally, as the capabilities and numbers of German submarines increased, the U-boats moved further out into the mid-Atlantic and the waters off of the African coast, far beyond British air cover. Losses to the U-boats were heavy, totalling 1.6 million tonnes from June through November 1940, but these losses remained sustainable as Britain devoted its resources to stemming any possible German invasion.

Convoy escorts were so few that there were only enough to escort merchant ships into the mid-Atlantic, where the escorts of a westbound convoy would then turn home, attaching themselves to an eastbound convoy – and leaving the westbound merchant ships to scatter without escort.

to remain very small, as the British held back ships to face the imminent threat of German invasion. Also, Britain could devote few aerial resources to the battle even as the Battle of Britain raged. Thus German U-boats possessed many advantages during 1940 and early 1941 – and U-boat commanders would refer to this period as the 'Happy Time'. Nonetheless, Germany still possessed too few U-boats truly to threaten Britain's existence. Attrition and slow production rates meant that Germany had no more U-boats in September 1940 than it had possessed at the outbreak of the conflict.

Thus 1940 was, in the main, a year of individual U-boat commanders striking unsuspecting convoys in single battle. It was during this year that the great U-boat aces, such as Otto Kretschmer, Wolfgang Luth and Gunther Prien, amassed their greatest successes. In general, U-boat commanders would lie in wait for a convoy on the surface in the Western Approaches, or further out into the Atlantic beyond the range of British air cover. Spotting a convoy, the U-boat would race ahead of the approaching ships, then submerge to periscope depth and attack as the convoy steamed past. Inevitably the few escort ships in the area would counterattack, forcing the U-boat to dive and suffer through a nerve-wracking barrage of depth charges. As yet, as the British had not honed their anti-submarine skills, most of the U-boats survived their ordeals, but the dramatic German U-boat successes of June 1940 still accounted for only 284,000 tonnes (280,000 tons) of merchant shipping, far below the stated goal of 711,000 tonnes (700,000 tons). As a result Dönitz ordered a change in tactics in September, having his submarines work together in wolfpacks for the first time. The results were dramatic, but worsening winter weather soon brought such operations to a halt. Dönitz was convinced, however, that, given a total of 300 U-boats, wolfpack tactics would destroy Britain.

Admiral Raeder added even more to the British list of concerns. The Germans converted nine merchant ships into disguised raiders in early 1941. These ships, including the famous *Atlantis*, plied the oceans of the world for the next three years picking off isolated merchants ships one at a time. By the end of the war, these raiders would sink some 130 ships totalling 864,000 tonnes (850,000 tons). Of even more concern to the British were the surviving German warships. In November 1940, the pocket battleship *Scheer* broke out into the Atlantic and sank 15 ships, while the *Scarnhorst* and *Gneisenau* entered the Atlantic in January to sink an additional 22 ships. The successes of these raids prompted Raeder to send the pride of the German Navy, the mighty battleship *Bismarck*, on its own voyage of destruction later in 1941.

END OF THE 'HAPPY TIME'

In 1941 several developments worked in Britain's favour in the Battle of the Atlantic. Taking command

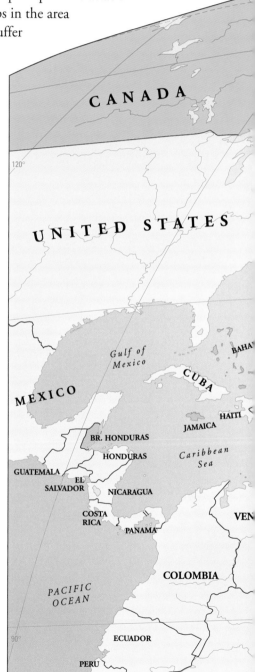

of the anti-submarine campaign was the energetic Admiral Percy Noble, Commander-in-Chief of the Western Approaches. Noble codified convoy tactics and lobbied the government for additional support and shipbuilding. Britain also benefited from the development of what was perhaps one of the most underappreciated weapons systems of World War II: the corvette. These small, ungainly warships were lightly armed and notoriously uncomfortable for their crews; however, in their favour, they were both cheap and easy to build, and were ideal as convoy escorts.

Britain also received aid from other sources in the war against the U-boat in 1941. The Royal Canadian Navy took over much of the task of convoy duty

Battle of the Atlantic II
June 1940–March 1941

——	Pan-American Neutrality Zone
——	Extent of air escort cover
– – –	Extent of surface escort cover
▭	Major convoy routes
•	Allied merchant ships sunk by U-boats
⚓	U-boats sunk
▨	Territory under Allied control
▨	Territory under Axis control
▨	Territory under Vichy government (unoccupied France)
▭	Neutral territory

GREENLAND

Norwegian Sea

From UK and Iceland July 1941   ICELAND   Surface escort Western Approaches

Surface escort from Newfoundland

From Newfoundland

Surface escort from Newfoundland

LABRADOR

NEWFOUNDLAND
• St. John's

NORWAY   SWEDEN

North Sea   DENMARK

IRELAND   UNITED KINGDOM

NETH
BEL
GERMANY

• Halifax

New York

FRANCE   SWITZ

VICHY FRANCE   ITALY

Bermuda

Londonderry Escort Zone

Azores

PORTUGAL   SPAIN

Maderia

• Gibraltar   *Mediterranean Sea*

ATLANTIC OCEAN

MOROCCO   ALGERIA   TUNISIA

Canary Is.

Pan–American Neutrality Zone

WESTERN SAHARA

A f r i c a
FRENCH WEST AFRICA

Cape Verde Is.

Dakar •
GAMBIA

GUINEA–BISSAU

BRITISH GUIANA
DUTCH GUIANA   FRENCH GUIANA

Freetown Escort Zone

• SIERRA LEONE
Freetown

NIGERIA

LIBERIA   GOLD COAST

ZIL

St. Paul Rocks

BATTLE OF THE ATLANTIC III

In 1941 the Germans still lacked the number of U-boats necessary to contest control of the Atlantic. On top of this, improvements in British convoy organization and the advent of a new type of escort, the corvette, which was quicker to produce meant that the convoys themselves were better protected. Increasing Canadian and American involvement in the submarine war also strengthened the British convoy system further.

By June 1941, convoys received protection for their entire journey across the Atlantic, and by September US forces had become involved in a 'secret' shooting war in the Atlantic against U-boats, engaging any U-boats they encountered despite their supposed neutrality.

As a result, the German U-boats had to seek their quarry further afield to avoid destruction. The most popular operational area for the U-boat commanders was the so-called 'mid-Atlantic gap'. Here, beyond the reach of Allied air cover, the U-boats were at their most effective. The German submariners also found good hunting again off the long west coast of Africa, preying on Britain-bound convoys from Sierra Leone.

in the western Atlantic, while the United States began to take a more active role in the Battle of the Atlantic as the year progressed. First the United States sent Britain a force of 50 badly needed destroyers in return for leases on British bases in the West Indies. The lend-lease programme also aided Britain in the construction of ships, and by September 1941 the United States had even taken responsibility for escorting convoys to the mid-Atlantic, in effect becoming involved in an undeclared war against the German U-boats.

Finally Britain gained an immeasurable edge in the Battle of the Atlantic in the field of cryptanalysis. British analysts at Bletchley Park, in an effort codenamed Ultra, achieved great success in decoding the German Enigma system of encryption, often aiding the Royal Navy in locating the elusive wolfpacks. In addition, British ships armed with High Frequency Direction Finding (HF/DF or 'Huff Duff') could also locate U-boats based on their radio transmissions. Thus, although the Germans still achieved intermittent successes, sinking some 1.5 million tonnes of shipping between April and December 1941, losses again remained sustainable even in the face of wolfpack tactics. Allied tactics had even resulted in some notable successes, including killing or capturing three of Germany's leading U-boat aces – Prien, Matz and Kretschmer – in an attack during March on a single convoy.

In May, the battleship *Bismarck*, commanded by Admiral Gunther Lutjens, broke out into the Atlantic to prey on Allied shipping. The British Admiralty quickly gathered its most powerful battleships to strike at the *Bismarck*. Off the south coast of Iceland on 24 May, the most powerful ship afloat, the *Hood*, accompanied by a new battleship *Prince of Wales*, made ready to do battle with *Bismarck*. The opponents opened fire upon each other at a range of more than 22km (14 miles). Almost immediately a German shell ripped through the outdated and weak armor of the *Hood*'s deck – detonating in a powder magazine. The resulting explosion ripped the *Hood* apart, killing all but three of *Hood*'s 1400-man crew. The *Prince of Wales*, also damaged, broke off the battle. The loss of the *Hood* stunned the British people, and the *Bismarck* seemed ready to run rampant in the Atlantic.

The *Bismarck*, though, had also received damage in the battle and had to make for the French coast at reduced speed, hoping to outdistance any British pursuit. On the evening of 26 May, a flight of outdated Swordfish biplanes from the aircraft carrier *Ark Royal* struck the *Bismarck*, jamming her rudder. Resisting all efforts at control, the German ship could only steam in wide circles as the might of the Royal Navy closed in for the kill. The next day the British battleships *Rodney* and *King George V* battered the *Bismarck* into a flaming hulk. Eventually the proud ship rolled over and sank beneath the waves, killing all but 110 of the 2000-man crew. The remainder of the Battle of the Atlantic would belong to the U-boats.

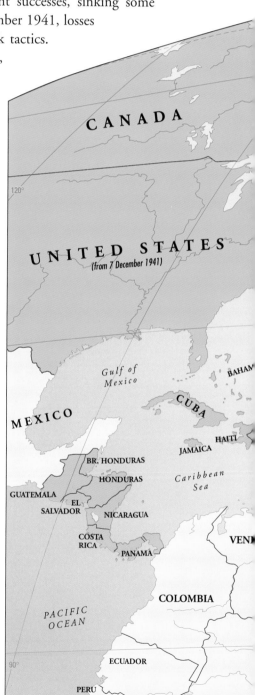

CRISIS POINT

The crisis of the Battle of the Atlantic came rather unexpectedly in 1942. British countermeasures and a scarcity of U-boats had conspired to keep the loss rate of merchant shipping to 183,000 tonnes (180,000 tons) per month, well below the stated requirement for German victory. The entrance of the United States into the conflict, however, suddenly gave the U-boats a decided and unforeseen advantage. Shipping in US waters had yet to be organized into convoys, and the United States had failed to impose blackouts on its coastal towns and cities.

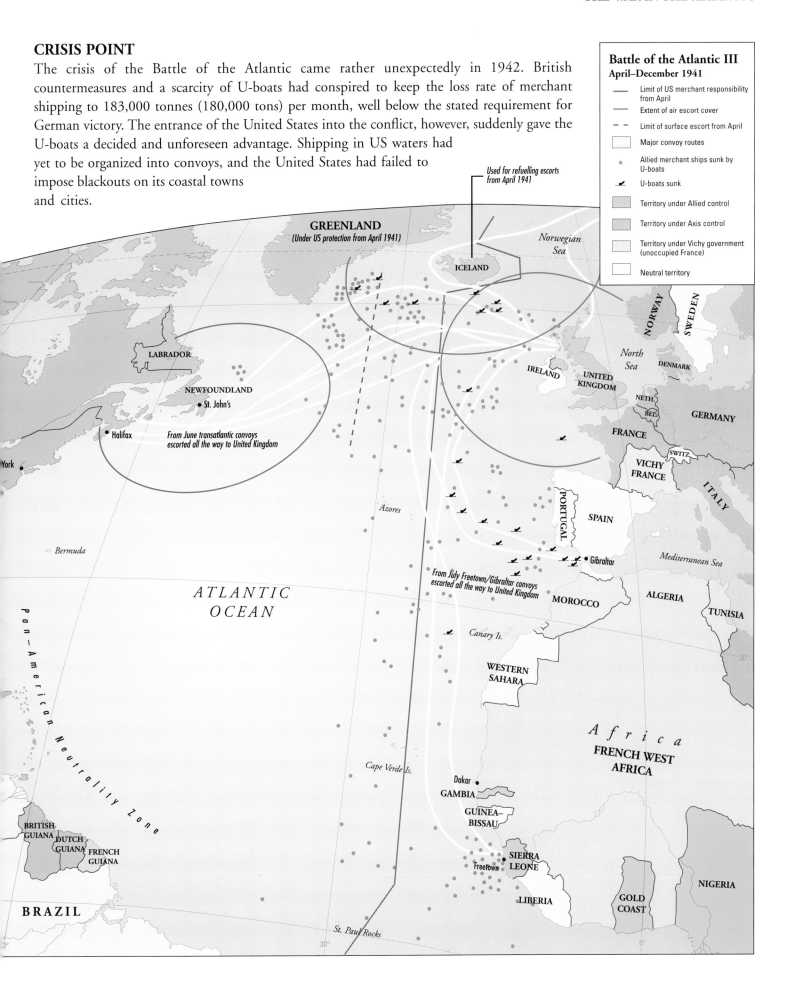

Battle of the Atlantic III
April–December 1941

— Limit of US merchant responsibility from April
— Extent of air escort cover
--- Limit of surface escort from April
☐ Major convoy routes
• Allied merchant ships sunk by U-boats
⚓ U-boats sunk
☐ Territory under Allied control
☐ Territory under Axis control
☐ Territory under Vichy government (unoccupied France)
☐ Neutral territory

Used for refuelling escorts from April 1941

GREENLAND
(Under US protection from April 1941)

Norwegian Sea

ICELAND

LABRADOR

NEWFOUNDLAND
• St. John's

Halifax

From June transatlantic convoys escorted all the way to United Kingdom

IRELAND

UNITED KINGDOM

North Sea

NORWAY SWEDEN

DENMARK

NETH.
BEL. GERMANY

FRANCE

SWITZ

VICHY FRANCE

ITALY

York

Azores

Bermuda

PORTUGAL SPAIN

Gibraltar

Mediterranean Sea

From July Freetown/Gibraltar convoys escorted all the way to United Kingdom

MOROCCO

ALGERIA

TUNISIA

ATLANTIC OCEAN

Canary Is.

WESTERN SAHARA

A f r i c a
FRENCH WEST AFRICA

Pan–American Neutrality Zone

Cape Verde Is.

Dakar •
GAMBIA

GUINEA–BISSAU

BRITISH GUIANA
DUTCH GUIANA
FRENCH GUIANA

SIERRA LEONE

Freetown •

LIBERIA

NIGERIA

GOLD COAST

BRAZIL

St. Paul Rocks

BATTLE OF THE ATLANTIC IV

The year 1942 brought on the crisis of the Battle of the Atlantic. Prompted by Dönitz, the U-boats left the Western Approaches of Britain and the mid-Atlantic, and made for the eastern coast of the United States in search of more vulnerable targets. Slow to adopt convoy measures, US ships steaming alone along the eastern seaboard proved easy prey for German submarines.

At first the United States chose to strike back by forming hunting groups of warships, a tactic long since abandoned by the Royal Navy as ineffective. Belatedly, in July, the United States instituted convoys along the east coast, but the U-boats only moved on to attack weaker prey in the Gulf of Mexico and off the coast of Venezuela, scoring notable successes against valuable oil tankers.

Even so, much of the traffic in this area was not bound for Britain to supply its war needs, serving to dilute the impact of the German successes. As the expanding US system of convoy came to include shipping even in these areas, the German U-boats – now numbering more than 300 and operating from the west coast of France – made ready once again to move back into the shipping lanes of the North Atlantic.

Realizing this, Dönitz sent as many U-boats as possible, still only a dozen, to prey upon the new targets provided by American oversight in what became known as the 'Second Happy Time'. The U-boats would linger offshore nearly invisible on the surface at night, and wait for single merchant ships, hopefully highly valuable tankers, to appear in their sights, silhouetted against the lights of coastal towns. The results were instant and dramatic. From February through May, U-boats destroyed over 508,000 tonnes (500,000 tons) of merchant shipping per month. Finally in June 1942 the U-boats exceeded the magic number of 711,000 (700,000 tons) of shipping per month – possibly enough to starve Britain into submission.

Although the danger to Britain was overestimated, due to the fact that many of the ships being sunk in US waters were not bound for Britain at all, the war in the Atlantic was nonetheless reaching a crisis point. The US Navy found itself stretched very thin, forced to fight a two-ocean war against Japan in the Pacific and against Germany in the Atlantic. At first most US naval resources went to the war against Japan, leaving the Battle of the Atlantic to be run on a shoestring budget. However, US President Franklin Roosevelt was a firm believer in the 'Europe First' strategy – identifying Germany as the most immediate threat. Acceptance of this strategy meant that American servicemen would soon be making their way to Europe in great numbers. Before that could take place, the U-boat threat had to be destroyed, lest the American army die at sea in a flurry of sunken troop transports.

By June, finally heeding British advice, the Americans instituted a convoy system on the US east coast. In response, the U-boats simply moved to more fertile hunting grounds – including the North Atlantic route to Russia, the Caribbean and the vulnerable coast of South America, even as the Allies scrambled to defend those areas adequately. At the same time, the Germans' submarine construction programme finally swung into high gear, and by August 1942 Dönitz could boast a fleet of 300 U-boats superior to those in service at the beginning of the conflict. Merchant shipping losses, which had fallen in the wake of the US institution of convoys, in November again rose to over 711,000 tonnes (700,000 tons) per month. Although the loss rate did not force Britain from the conflict, it posed an unacceptable risk to 'Operation Bolero', the gathering of US forces and material in Britain in preparation for D-Day.

FINAL MOVES

Admiral Dönitz hoped that the U-boat campaign of 1943 would achieve great success. No longer would his submarines work singly off the American coast as they had in the 'Second Happy Time'. Instead, his massive fleet of U-boats would re-enter the mid-Atlantic gap and finally put wolfpack tactics to use in

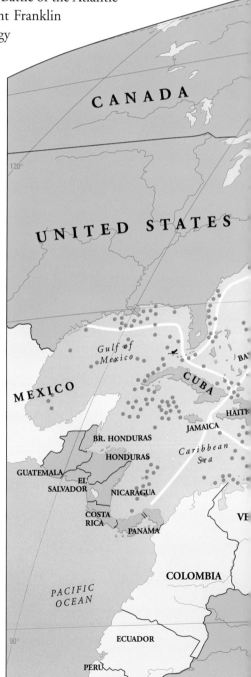

full force, hoping to score a decisive blow against Britain. In March 1943 all seemed well, as the wolfpacks destroyed more than 609,000 tonnes (600,000 tons) of merchant shipping – nearly all bound for Britain; however, the tide would soon turn against the U-boats amid an Allied counterattack.

Taking the offensive in support of 'Operation Bolero', the Allies found inspired leadership in the person of Admiral Max Horton, the new Commander-in-Chief of the Western Approaches. Aided by recent Ultra breakthroughs, Horton devised new and effective methods of both defence against and attack on German submarines.

Battle of the Atlantic IV
January 1942–February 1943

— Change ond operational control UK to US, August 1942
— Extent of air escort cover
--- UK escort stations to July 1942
▢ Major convoy routes
• Allied merchant ships sunk by U-boats
⚓ U-boats sunk
▨ Territory under Allied control
▨ Territory under Axis control
▢ Neutral territory

GREENLAND

Norwegian Sea

ICELAND
(Occupied by US from 11 July 1942)

Complete transatlantic surface escort implemented

LABRADOR

NEWFOUNDLAND

Home Station

IRELAND

UNITED KINGDOM

North Sea

NORWAY

SWEDEN

DENMARK

NETH.
BEL.
GERMANY

• St. John's

Halifax

FRANCE

SWITZ.

ITALY

York •

Bermuda

Azores

North Atlantic Station

PORTUGAL

SPAIN

Freetown/Gibraltar convoys escorted all the way to United Kingdom

• Gibraltar

Mediterranean Sea

ATLANTIC OCEAN

MOROCCO

ALGERIA

TUNISIA

Canary Is.

WESTERN SAHARA

A f r i c a
FRENCH WEST AFRICA

Cape Verde Is.

Dakar •

GAMBIA

GUINEA-BISSAU

West African Station

Freetown •

SIERRA LEONE

NIGERIA

GOLD COAST

LIBERIA

BRITISH GUIANA
DUTCH GUIANA
FRENCH GUIANA

BRAZIL

22 August 1942: Declares war on Germany South Atlantic seaboard air bases available for Allied convoy air cover

St. Paul Rocks

From Ascension I.

BATTLE OF THE ATLANTIC V

In 1943 the German U-boats returned to the North Atlantic hoping to cut off supplies to Britain and wreak havoc among the valuable troop transports taking part in 'Operation Bolero'. Operating in the mid-Atlantic, furthest from the threat of Allied air power, the U-boats scored initial successes early in the year – in March they sank over 609,000 tonnes (600,000 tons) of shipping.

However, the development of new tactics and technology on the part of the Allies spelled doom for the U-boats. Realizing the threat, the Allies had allocated more warships for service in the Atlantic. Some of the craft gave better protection to the convoys themselves. Others, operating in 'hunter–killer' groups and employing new forward-firing anti-submarine mortars, hunted down and destroyed the vulnerable U-boats.

Aircraft, armed with advanced radar and depth charges, located and attacked submarines with ease. As a result, by May 1943 Dönitz recalled his submarines from the Atlantic, for their losses had reached a prohibitive level. When Dönitz attempted to send his U-boats back into the Atlantic in September 1943, most never made it beyond the waters of the Bay of Biscay off the coast of France – hunted down and destroyed long before they could reach the Atlantic shipping lanes. The battle was effectively over.

The United States, under the command of Admiral Ernest King, began to devote more resources to the Battle of the Atlantic and to work more closely with the British. Convoys crossing the Atlantic enjoyed more protection than ever before. The number of Allied warships in the Atlantic was indeed so high as to allow for the creation of 'hunter-killer' groups. Convoy escorts by nature served a defensive role. The 'hunter–killer' groups were offensive in nature and could linger in an area to attack and destroy U-boats, rather than just driving them off and allowing them to survive.

The Allies also now employed new and improved anti-submarine weaponry. Along with more advanced sonar, many ships now carried 'Hedgehogs', which could launch a pattern of 24 projectiles over a ship's bow at a submarine without losing sonar contact. In addition, increased air power tipped the balance in the Battle of the Atlantic to the Allies' favour. Long-range aircraft could now range across the Atlantic and were armed with powerful new radar that could locate U-boats with ease – even at night. The aircraft also carried depth charges enabling them to attack U-boats single-handed. Thus, while convoys were better protected than ever, the U-boats could no longer hide from their more numerous and better equipped attackers. The tide of the Battle of the Atlantic had suddenly turned.

THE BATTLE IS LOST

In May 1943 the fate of Convoy ONS-5 demonstrated the new balance of the Battle of the Atlantic. Having located the convoy, several wolf packs gathered in an attempt to destroy it utterly. The convoy suffered attacks from more than 50 U-boats and lost nearly a third of its ships; however, the U-boats fared far worse. Located both by radar and by signals intelligence, the wolf packs faced relentless attacks by aircraft and hunter–killer groups. The carnage was unprecedented. In May alone, the Allies sank some 41 German U-boats – this was a rate of attrition far too high for the meager results gained against Convoy ONS-5. As a consequence, Dönitz ordered his precious U-boats out of the dangerous North Atlantic, and he would later write in his memoirs that in May 1943 he realized that Germany had lost the Battle of the Atlantic.

Dönitz still retained hope that new developments, including acoustic torpedoes and a new type of submarine dubbed the 'Walter' class, would eventually alter the balance in the Battle of the Atlantic once again. In September 1943, the U-boats returned to the North Atlantic, but achieved little – at the cost of 25 U-boats destroyed. In early 1944, Dönitz ordered a renewed effort, only to lose 37 submarines and sink only three merchant ships. Most submarines were not even able to break out of their port areas in the Bay of Biscay before being located and sunk by marauding aircraft. No new German technology could alter the fact that the Battle of the Atlantic had already been decided.

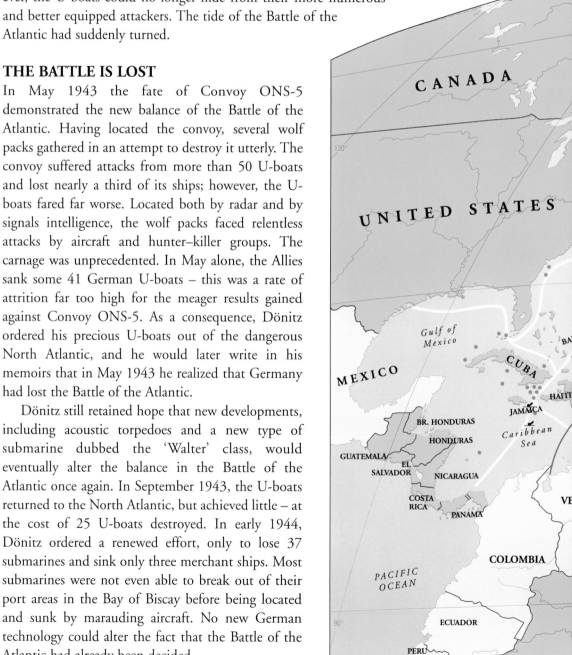

During the Battle of the Atlantic, U-boats sank 2848 Allied ships, accounting for some 14 million tonnes of shipping. Despite this, even at the height of the Atlantic war, Britain had never been brought near to surrender by the U-boats' activities. After some fits and starts, the Allies won a comprehensive victory over the Germans in the Atlantic. Of the 1170 submarines which were in German service in World War II, 784 were lost to Allied attacks. The fatality rate in the German U-boat arm ran at an astounding 75 per cent, higher even than that of the Japanese kamikaze. Remarkably, none of the troop transports carrying their cargo of millions of American soldiers to fight in Europe suffered any loss to U-boat attack.

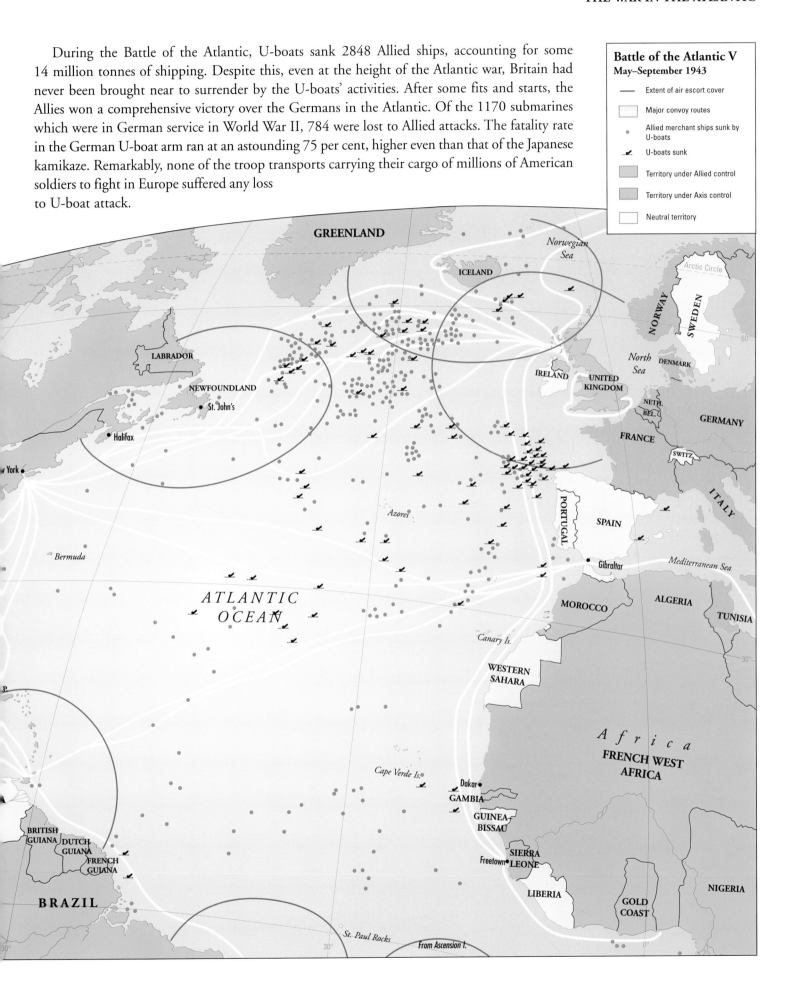

Battle of the Atlantic V
May–September 1943

— Extent of air escort cover

☐ Major convoy routes

• Allied merchant ships sunk by U-boats

⟋ U-boats sunk

▨ Territory under Allied control

▨ Territory under Axis control

☐ Neutral territory

North Africa and Italy

After the Fascist takeover of Italy Mussolini turned his ambitions to North Africa, where he saw the opportunity to create a new Roman Empire. Hitler's early success in Europe lead him to believe that Britain and France would soon be defeated and Mussolini felt he had to act quickly if Italy was to share the spoils of victory and prevent Germany siezing the Allies' colonial possessions in Africa.

After some debate, Italy chose to side with the Allies against the Central Powers in World War I, based in part on a promise, backed by Britain, of considerable territory along the eastern Adriatic coast at the conclusion of the conflict. At the treaty negotiations in Versailles, Italy pressed for its due – but instead only received a tiny amount of territory around the city of Trieste and the Trentino. Italy had suffered nearly 500,000 dead in the war – seemingly for nothing.

Mired in an economic slump after the war, the country faltered on the brink of revolution. A weak coalition government proved unable to deal with the deepening crisis, which led to a democratic breakdown as mobs of unemployed veterans took to the streets. Amid the chaos, the tiny Fascist Party of Benito Mussolini thrived. Achieving little in the way of electoral success, Mussolini's 'Black Shirts' instead battled in the streets against the forces of communism and socialism. In October 1922, the Black Shirts staged an audacious march on Rome. Taken aback, King Victor Emmanuel appointed the brash Mussolini premier – a move which facilitated the Fascist takeover of Italy.

Surprised by their success and forced to extemporize a coherent ideology, the Fascists advocated corporativism and ultra nationalism. When it came to foreign policy, the Fascist creed called for a rebirth of the old Roman Empire through conquest both in the Balkans and in North Africa. Realizing Italy's military and economic weakness, Mussolini placed his dreams of conquest on hold during a slow period of government-sponsored industrialization and rearmament.

The meteoric rise of Hitler, though, forced Italy's hand. Initially Mussolini was taken aback by Hitler's aggressive foreign policy; however, his continuing string of diplomatic successes against the western Allies soon won Mussolini's admiration and support. As Germany went from victory to victory, Italy also embarked on a period of aggression – seizing Ethiopia in 1936 and Albania in 1939. Even so, Mussolini remained much more controlled in his foreign policy than did Hitler. Again Mussolini realized his weaknesses, and consequently aimed for a series of small, colonial victories more akin to those of Britain and France in the previous century. The Italian leader warned Hitler that Italy would not be ready for any major conflict for several years.

The German attack on Poland and the later unleashing of the forces of blitzkrieg on France took Mussolini unawares. Echoing World War I, Italy remained out of the fray – contemplating its options. The rapid success of the German invasion of France, though, made Mussolini's decision fairly easy. It seemed that Hitler would quickly dominate Europe, leaving the rich colonial possessions of both France and Britain easy prey. As a result, Italy entered the war on 10 June 1940, eventually launching a singularly unsuccessful invasion of southern France. The lack of Italian success against a demoralized and nearly beaten foe should have served as a warning to Mussolini. Instead, the Italian dictator chose to overlook the obvious flaws in his military machine. Italian armour was poor, and the level of mechanization of its army was extremely low. In addition, the Italian economy was tiny and singularly unable to supply the needs of a nation at war. Even though his military was destined to be undergunned and poorly supplied, Mussolini remained firm in his belief that both Britain and France were on the brink of defeat and that Italy had to act

Left: The arrival of the *Afrika Korps* in North Africa was to change the course of the campaign. Under the direction of Erwin Rommel, who had achieved notable success with the 7th Panzer Division during the invasion of France, the Germans were able to halt the Allied advance and drive the British and Commonwealth troops back almost to the Nile itself. Although the desert war has – retrospectively – been seen as a sideshow, in fact it was the key Allied–Axis battleground from the fall of France until the invasion of the Balkans and the Soviet Union in 1941, and remained a drain on Nazi resources.

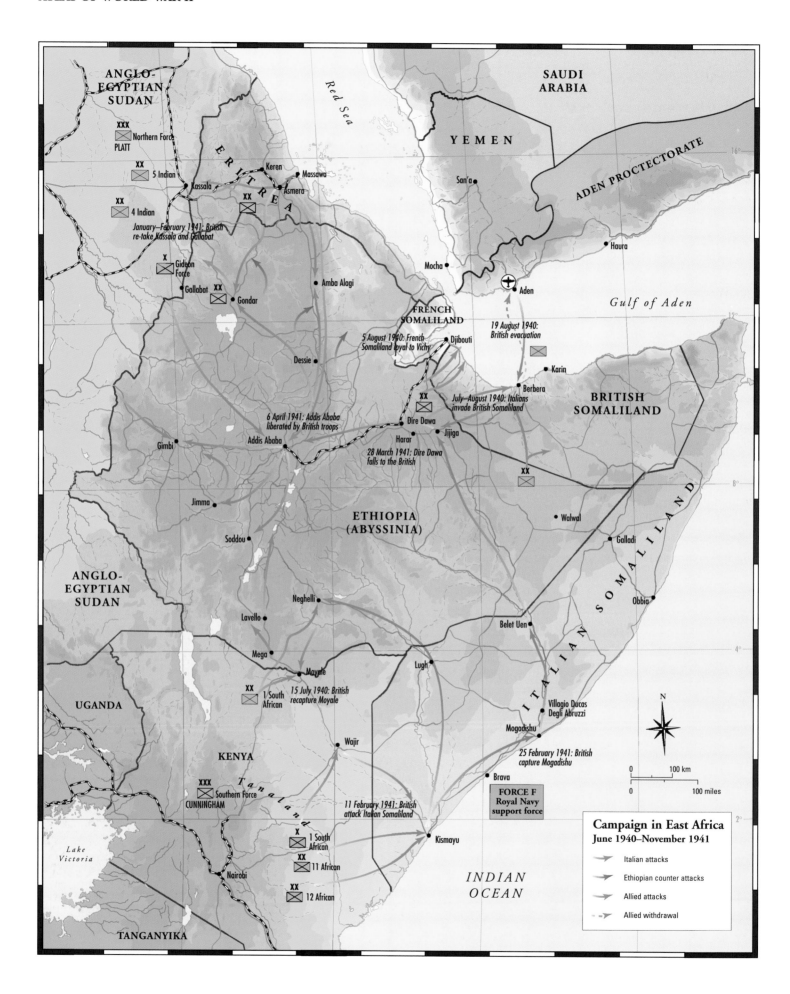

ANGLO-
EGYPTIAN
SUDAN

XXX
Northern Force
PLATT

XX
5 Indian

XX
4 Indian

January–February 1941: British re-take Kassala and Gallabat

X
Gideon
Force

Gallabat

XX
Gondar

Kassala

ERITREA

Keren

Massawa

Asmera

XX

Amba Alagi

Dessie

Gimbi

Addis Ababa

6 April 1941: Addis Ababa liberated by British troops

Jimma

Soddou

Neghelli

Lavello

Mega

Moyale

XX
1 South
African

15 July 1940: British recapture Moyale

ANGLO-
EGYPTIAN
SUDAN

UGANDA

KENYA

XXX
Southern Force
CUNNINGHAM

Tanaland

X
1 South
African

XX
11 African

XX
12 African

Nairobi

Lake
Victoria

TANGANYIKA

Red Sea

SAUDI
ARABIA

YEMEN

San'a

Mocha

Haura

ADEN PROCTECTORATE

Aden

19 August 1940: British evacuation

XX
Karin

Berbera

Gulf of Aden

BRITISH
SOMALILAND

Galladi

Obbia

ITALIAN SOMALILAND

FRENCH
SOMALILAND

5 August 1940: French Somaliland loyal to Vichy

Djibouti

July–August 1940: Italians invade British Somaliland

XX
Dire Dawa

Harar

Jijiga

28 March 1941: Dire Dawa falls to the British

ETHIOPIA
(ABYSSINIA)

Walwal

XX

Belet Uen

Lugh

Villagio Ducas
Degli Abruzzi

Mogadishu

25 February 1941: British capture Mogadishu

Brava

Wajir

11 February 1941: British attack Italian Somaliland

Kismayu

INDIAN
OCEAN

FORCE F
Royal Navy
support force

N

0 ——— 100 km
0 ——— 100 miles

Campaign in East Africa
June 1940–November 1941

→ Italian attacks
→ Ethiopian counter attacks
→ Allied attacks
- - → Allied withdrawal

THE ITALIANS IN EAST AFRICA

In July 1940, seeking to rebuild the Roman Empire, Mussolini's troops struck out of recently conquered Ethiopia at the vulnerable British Somaliland. Within days, the massive Italian force had driven the tiny British garrison from the area – leaving Italy in control of the Horn of Africa and threatening the valuable Red Sea trade routes.

Mussolini was aware that his army, though large, was weak in both armour and transport, and was made up largely of less-than-willing local conscripts. Consequently, the Italians did not attack the stronger British colonies in the area – Kenya and the Sudan – preferring instead to concentrate efforts further north against Egypt.

Fearing for the safety of their colonies and trade routes, the British gathered over 100,000 men – mainly South African, Indian and native African forces – to smash Italian power in East Africa. The Northern Force under General Platt struck first out of the Sudan, quickly conquering Eritrea. From Kenya the Southern Force, under General Cunningham, invaded Italian Somaliland.

Cunningham's troops drove to Mogadishu with blazing speed, then all the way to the Ethiopian capital of Addis Ababa in only four months. Mussolini had indeed been correct to question the ability of his East African forces, as their collapse presaged further Italian military difficulties in the ongoing war in Africa.

quickly to stop Germany stealing the spoils. The Italian army had only to brush away the feeble resistance of a few British soldiers in North Africa and the Roman Empire would be reborn.

THE FIRST MOVES

Mussolini and the Italians first looked towards the valuable British colonies in eastern Africa. Stationed in Ethiopia and Italian Somaliland, the Italians could call upon a massive force of some 200,000 soldiers – mainly local, colonial levies – under the command of the Duke of Aosta. On 3 August 1940, some 26 battalions invaded British Somaliland – a valuable colony guarding the entrance to the Red Sea – brushing aside the resistance of the tiny British garrison of 1500 men. Although Italian aggression in the area then came to a halt, British forces in the threatened colonies of Kenya and the Sudan made ready to counterattack.

Churchill was quite concerned that the Italian presence on the Red Sea would do great damage to critical British trade routes. As a result, Britain massed 75,000 troops in Kenya and 28,000 troops in the Sudan under the overall command of General Archibald Wavell. The first strike against the Italians fell in the north as two Indian divisions, under the command of General Platt, attacked into the Italian colony of Eritrea. An Italian force numbering more than 17,000 put up a fierce resistance to the invasion, holding out in the mountain fastness near Keren

Below: Fuelling a RAF Lockheed Hudson on an Egyptian airfield. Control of Egypt – and thus control of the Suez Canal – was vital for Britain's strategic interests. If the canal were lost, reinforcements and raw materials from Britain's empire and Commonwealth would take weeks longer to reach British ports, as they would have to be diverted around the Cape of Good Hope. The *Afrika Korps* therefore posed a serious strategic threat to Britain.

for 53 days, before being dislodged by an overwhelming British armoured attack. The collapse of Italian forces enabled the British to advance to the Eritrean capital of Asmera in early April, effectively ending resistance in the area.

In the south, British forces under the command of General Alan Cunningham invaded Italian Somaliland on 11 February 1941, brushing aside weak Italian forces and advancing to the critical port town of Mogadishu in just 14 days. Aided by effective and brutal Ethiopian partisans, Cunningham's forces swung north from Mogadishu, cut across Italian Somaliland and entered Ethiopia near Belet Uen. The poorly-equipped Italian forces put up little resistance to the British advance, and conscript Ethiopian forces deserted in droves. As a result, by 17 March, Cunningham was able to complete an amazing 640-km (400-mile) advance to Jijiga – effectively slicing Ethiopia in two. At the same time, a combined arms operation launched from the British protectorate of Aden had recaptured Berbera and driven the Italians from British Somaliland.

Cunningham then swung his force westwards and made for the Ethiopian capital of Addis Ababa. With their backs against the wall, the level of the Italians' resistance rose sharply, leading to a pitched battle near Dire Dawa, which, on 28 March, fell to the force of British arms, leading to the fall of Addis Ababa on 6 April 1941. British forces under Platt and Cunningham now

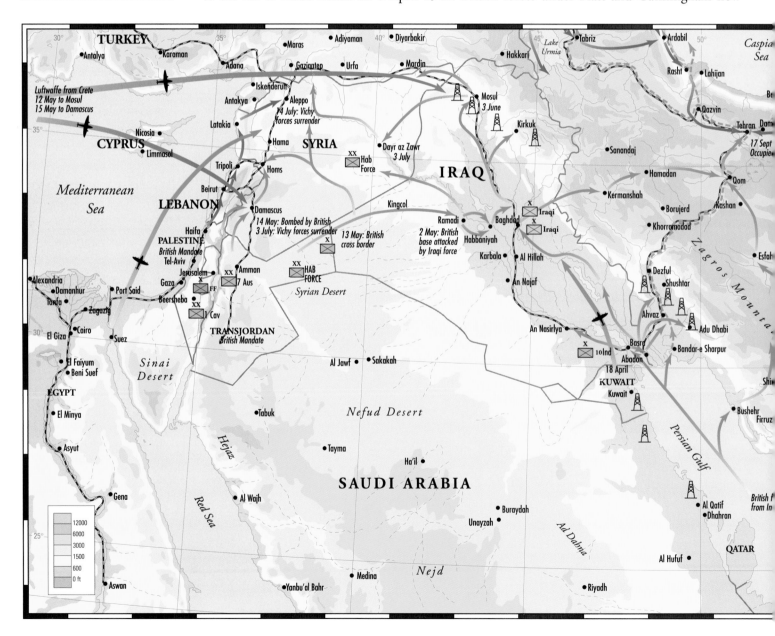

Iraq, Syria and Persia
April–September 1941

- Allied forces movements
- Free French forces movements
- Russian forces movements
- Allied bomber movements
- German bomber movements
- Allied supply routes
- Oilfield

converged on the 7000 remaining Italian soldiers under the command of the Duke of Aosta at Amba Alagi in Ethiopia. Aosta's surrender in May capped a mobile and dramatic campaign by the British in East Africa – at a time when the British population sorely needed positive wartime news.

CONFLICT IN THE MIDDLE EAST

In the Middle East, the fall of France had left Syria in the hands of the compliant Vichy government – posing a possible threat to valuable oil resources. The situation worsened in 1940 with the rise of anti-British feeling in neighbouring Iraq. Under a pro-British government for several years, Iraq was a major source of British oil and housed an important Royal Air Force (RAF) base at Habbaniya. However, on 3 April 1941, having received aid from German agents, Rashid Ali seized control of Iraq and appealed to Hitler for aid.

Quick to seize the proffered opportunity, the Germans dispatched military aid to Iraq aboard Luftwaffe aircraft, which had to land in Vichy-controlled Syria to refuel. Although the threat was in many ways minuscule, British forces reacted with great speed. On 17 April, hurriedly gathered Indian troops landed in southern Iraq to secure the oil fields of the region. Against very little resistance, the Indian brigade moved northwards, securing valuable oil pipelines as it advanced.

By May, the Indian force had reached Baghdad and Habbaniya – only to be attacked by Iraqi forces. After a short battle around the airfield, the Iraqis were defeated and Rashid Ali fled into exile. The pro-British government under Nuri-es-Said was reinstated; however, British troops remained in the area for the rest of the war to ensure the safety of the oil fields.

Churchill and the British nonetheless remained concerned regarding the fate of Syria. Hitler's attention having been diverted by the growing war in the Soviet Union, the Germans actually had no immediate plans to act in the Middle East and had long since withdrawn their aircraft from the area. Churchill, though, could not abide an open flank so near the critical oil fields. On 8 June 1941, therefore, British and Free French forces invaded Syria from Iraq and Palestine. The fighting was confused, as the British and Free French fought against rather stern resistance from the Vichy French forces in the area. The struggle, which pitted former French brothers-in-arms against each other, lasted for five weeks. Allied forces entered Damascus on 17 June and finally drove the Vichy French northwards to eventual surrender at Aleppo on 14 July 1941. As in Iraq, British forces would remain in both Syria and neighbouring Lebanon for the remainder of World War II.

Further to the east, Persia became important to the conflict with Hitler's invasion of the Soviet Union. As the war progressed, Persia served as a valuable supply route to the Soviet Union, which was beset by German blitzkrieg and in desperate need of all types of economic aid, especially oil from the Middle East. For its part, the Persian government seemed rather ambivalent towards the needs of the Allies and refused to expel German agents from its borders. Concerned once again over supply routes, in August 1941, both British and Soviet forces moved into Persia, meeting little resistance. On 17 September, Allied forces reached the Persian capital of Tehran and forced Shah Reza Pahlavi to abdicate in favour of his more tractable son. Britain and the Soviet Union left occupation forces behind in Persia, dividing the country into zones of influence. In January 1942, both nations agreed

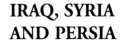

IRAQ, SYRIA AND PERSIA

During 1941, concern over critical oil supplies transformed the Middle East into a theatre of war. Churchill was worried that Syria, under the control of the pro-German Vichy regime, would form a springboard for German action against the oil fields of Iraq. British fears grew ever greater as German troops moved into Greece and across North Africa, seemingly aiming at conquest of the Middle East.

In April 1941, all of Churchill's fears became reality when Rashid Ali led a pro-German coup in Iraq – and requested German aid for his government. German aircraft flew to Damascus and Mosul in response. Reacting swiftly against the already foreseen difficulties, however, Britain dispatched an Indian brigade to secure the oil fields of southern Iraq and to drive on Baghdad. After brushing aside Iraqi resistance at Habbaniyah, the British forced Rashid Ali into exile and reinstated the pro-British government.

Still concerned that the Vichy French could pose a future threat, in June 1941 British and Free French forces invaded Syria from both Iraq and Palestine. After more than a month of unexpectedly strong resistance, the Allies prevailed over the Vichy French forces, accepting their surrender at Aleppo.

In September 1941, British and Russian forces occupied neighbouring Persia to protect the important oil supply route to the Soviet Union.

TANK ASSAULT

After Graziani's failed attack on Egypt with the Italian Tenth Army, the British counter-attacked. The Italian defensive line was a series of fortified camps near Sidi Barrani which were too far apart to be mutually supporting.

The British forces, under General O'Connor, possessed a critical edge in tanks, as the British Matilda was impervious to the weak Italian anti-tank guns. The British assault took nearly 40,000 prisoners, and the British captured 70,000 more in Bardia and Tobruk. O'Connor then sent a mobile force across the desert to Beda Fomm, ahead of the fleeing Italian troops, sealing their fate.

to exit Persia six months after the close of the conflict. As a result of Allied actions, Persia was to remain an important part of the Soviet supply line for the remainder of World War II.

ENTER THE *AFRIKA KORPS*

Mussolini held out the greatest hope for an attack on the British in Egypt, for victory there would sever the vital shipping route through the Suez Canal and leave the oil fields of the Middle East open to conquest. The odds seemed in Mussolini's favour, for the 250,000-man Italian Tenth Army, under the command of Marshal Rodolfo Graziani, faced a mere 36,000 British troops defending Egypt. When the Italian attack began on 13 September, the British defenders, under the overall command of Wavell and the field command of General Richard O'Connor, retreated beyond the town of Sidi Barrani, where Graziani halted his advance. The Italian commander was right to be cautious – the open desert was the realm of armoured, mobile warfare. Italian tanks were hopelessly outclassed by their British rivals, and were outnumbered more than two to one.

Hoping to resupply prior to another cautious advance, Graziani ordered the construction of a series of armed camps near Sidi Barrani. On 9 December 1940, however, O'Connor struck at a vulnerable gap between two of the Italian camps, circling behind them and surrounding them. The brilliant manoeuvre, dubbed Operation Compass, dislocated the entire Italian defensive system and succeeded in capturing nearly 40,000 prisoners. Shaken by the disaster, the Italian forces fled in retreat, losing first Bardia, then Tobruk – and an additional 70,000 prisoners. With the Italians in full retreat, O'Connor decided to take a great risk – the 6th Australian Division followed the Italian retreat down the coast road, while the 7th Armoured Division, known as the Desert Rats, struck out across the desert wastes, hoping to circle behind the Italians to cut off their retreat. On 7 February 1941, O'Connor's masterpiece was complete when the

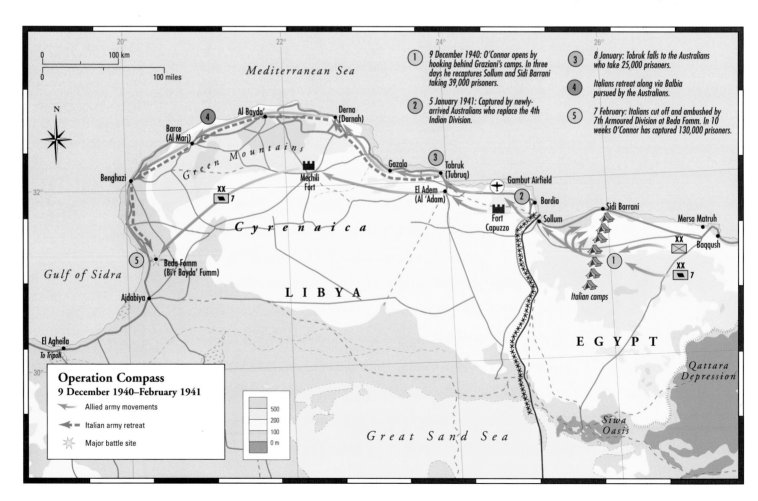

1. *9 December 1940: O'Connor opens by hooking behind Graziani's camps. In three days he recaptures Sollum and Sidi Barrani taking 39,000 prisoners.*

2. *5 January 1941: Captured by newly-arrived Australians who replace the 4th Indian Division.*

3. *8 January: Tobruk falls to the Australians who take 25,000 prisoners.*

4. *Italians retreat along via Balbia pursued by the Australians.*

5. *7 February: Italians cut off and ambushed by 7th Armoured Division at Beda Fomm. In 10 weeks O'Connor has captured 130,000 prisoners.*

Operation Compass
9 December 1940–February 1941

⬿ Allied army movements

◀ ▬ Italian army retreat

✳ Major battle site

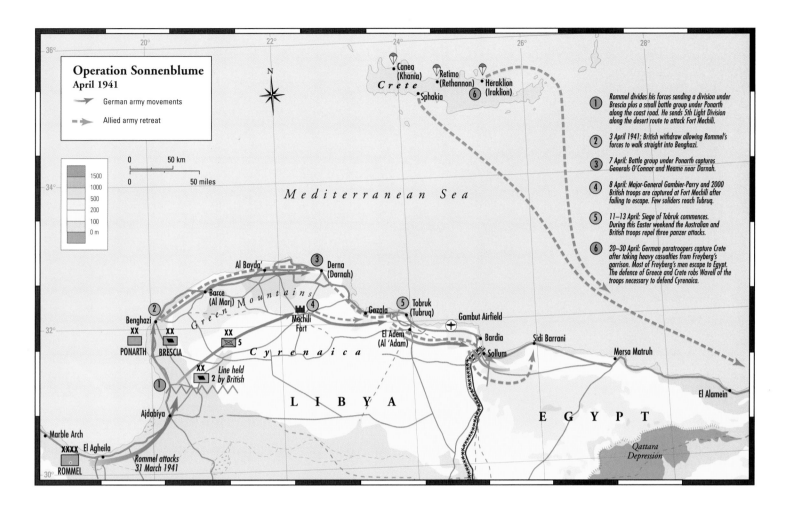

Operation Sonnenblume
April 1941

German army movements

Allied army retreat

1. Rommel divides his forces sending a division under Brescia plus a small battle group under Ponarth along the coast road. He sends 5th Light Division along the desert route to attack Fort Mechili.

2. 3 April 1941: British withdraw allowing Rommel's forces to walk straight into Benghazi.

3. 7 April: Battle group under Ponarth captures Generals O'Connor and Neame near Darnah.

4. 8 April: Major-General Gambier-Parry and 2000 British troops are captured at Fort Mechili after failing to escape. Few soliders reach Tubruq.

5. 11–13 April: Siege of Tobruk commences. During this Easter weekend the Australian and British troops repel three panzer attacks.

6. 20–30 April: German paratroopers capture Crete after taking heavy casualties from Freyberg's garrison. Most of Freyberg's men escape to Egypt. The defence of Greece and Crete robs Wavell of the troops necessary to defend Cyrenaica.

Desert Rats reached Beda Fomm in time to block the Italian withdrawal, trapping the remainder of the luckless Tenth Army. It was a great victory; the British had captured 130,000 men, 845 guns and 380 tanks, at the cost of fewer than 2000 casualties – all in a space of 10 weeks.

The situation, however, rapidly changed. Churchill removed forces from Wavell's command for the defence of Greece – leaving only a covering force to defend Cyrenaica. At the same time, Hitler came to the belated aid of his Axis partner, devoting the 5th Light Division and the 15th Panzer Division to the struggle in North Africa. Although chronically understrength and often poorly supplied, what became known as the *Afrika Korps* would gain great fame under the command of General Erwin Rommel – a master of armoured warfare. Initially Rommel, under titular Italian command, was mandated only to defend the line near El Agheila. Sensing British weakness, though, Rommel on 31 March chose to attack – even before the entire *Afrika Korps* had arrived on the continent. After a brief struggle, the British 2nd Armoured Division retreated from defensive positions at Mersa Brega, opening the way for Rommel's advance.

With the British in retreat, Rommel sent part of his force down the coast road towards Benghazi, while the 5th Light Division struck out across the desert towards Mechili. Despite the fact that Rommel's forces were scattered and running short on fuel, the British mustered no counterattack. Indeed, their retreat turned into a disaster when, on 7 April, German forces captured O'Connor himself and much of the British command structure in Darnah. Harried but still in good order, elements of the 9th Australian Division and the 2nd Armoured Division fell back on the port city of Tobruk and dug in – in an attempt to deny the critical forward port city to the Germans. Rommel's forces struck the defensive bastion of Tobruk on 12 April, but were repulsed. Unconcerned, the *Afrika Korps* rushed forwards into Egypt, intending to deal with the Tobruk garrison at its leisure.

AFRIKA KORPS

Sent to North Africa to save the Italians from disaster, Rommel's *Afrika Korps* arrived when British defences were weakened to send forces to Greece. Seizing his chance, Rommel disobeyed orders and attacked.

Catching the British by surprise, Rommel proved he was a master of desert warfare. He sent the 5th Light Division across the desert to try to cut off the British retreat. Although O'Connor was captured, the *Afrika Korps* – weakened and short on supplies – was unable to capture Tobruk. With a lengthy supply line and a vulnerable flank, Rommel halted on the Egyptian frontier to prepare for a new offensive.

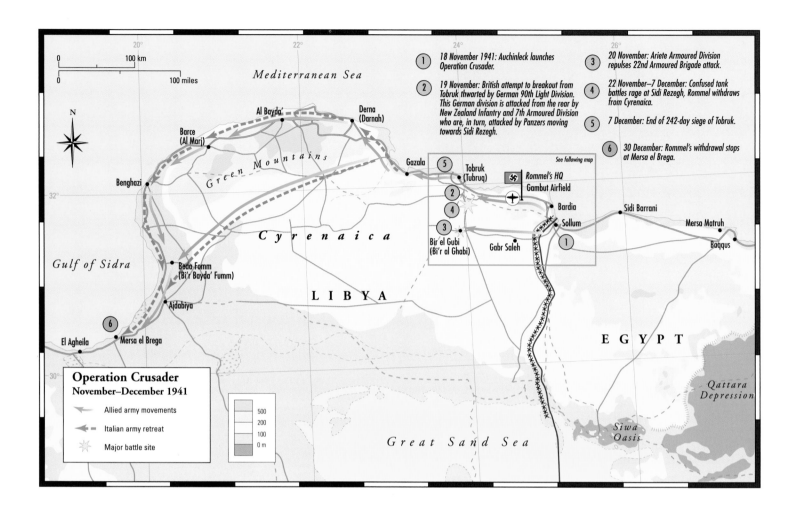

1. *18 November 1941: Auchinleck launches Operation Crusader.*

2. *19 November: British attempt to breakout from Tobruk thwarted by German 90th Light Division. This German division is attacked from the rear by New Zealand Infantry and 7th Armoured Division who are, in turn, attacked by Panzers moving towards Sidi Rezegh.*

3. *20 November: Ariete Armoured Division repulses 22nd Armoured Brigade attack.*

4. *22 November–7 December: Confused tank battles rage at Sidi Rezegh, Rommel withdraws from Cyrenaica.*

5. *7 December: End of 242-day siege of Tobruk.*

6. *30 December: Rommel's withdrawal stops at Mersa el Brega.*

Operation Crusader
November–December 1941

→ Allied army movements

◄- - Italian army retreat

✳ Major battle site

CRUSADER

On 18 November 1941, the Eighth Army under General Alan Cunningham launched Operation Crusader, designed to relieve Tobruk. While infantry pinned the Axis defenders to the north in place, British armour swung south. Catching the *Afrika Korps* by surprise, British forces captured Rommel's headquarters at Gambut Airfield and came within 19km (12 miles) of Tobruk.

There followed a series of confused battles near Bir el Gubi and Sidi Razegh. Realizing the danger to his supply lines, on 4 December Rommel retreated. After a short battle at Gazala, the Axis forces withdrew from Cyrenaica.

Although Rommel pushed light forces into Egypt, the *Afrika Korps* was now critically short on supplies, relying on a logistic support line that ran all the way back to Tripoli. Forced to revert to a defensive posture and wait for supplies and reinforcements, Rommel paid more attention to the siege of Tobruk, for the need of a forward port was now critical. However, the Tobruk garrison, relying on the power of artillery, held out against all odds – making Rommel's task very difficult. At the same time, much of the British force that had been sent to defend Greece returned to Egypt, having failed to stem the Axis tide in the Balkans.

BRITISH COUNTERATTACK

With Rommel in obvious logistical trouble, Wavell sought to strike the weakened *Afrika Korps* and relieve Tobruk. Resupplied with armour – achieving a four-to-one superiority over the *Afrika Korps* – Wavell planned to assault the centre of the Axis defensive line while the Desert Rats swung to the south to exploit the attack. On 15 June 1941, the British launched the ambitious Operation Battleaxe and almost immediately faced disaster. The Germans had perfected the art of using their deadly 88mm (3.45in) anti-aircraft guns in an anti-tank role. The British moved forwards, with their Matilda and Cruiser tanks in small units, and found themselves outranged and outgunned by German 88mm tank traps at the Halfaya Pass and Hafid Ridge. In a single day, the British lost half of their tanks to the deadly 88s. The next day Rommel, who was proving as skilful in the defensive as he was in the attack, countered with an armoured thrust that drove the British back to their original positions. In the stunning setback, the British had lost a total of 91 tanks and had only succeeded in destroying 12. Shocked by the reverse, Churchill replaced Wavell with General Claude Auchinleck in the Middle East, rushing supplies and reinforcements to the area. The augmented British force was rechristened the Eighth Army, which was placed

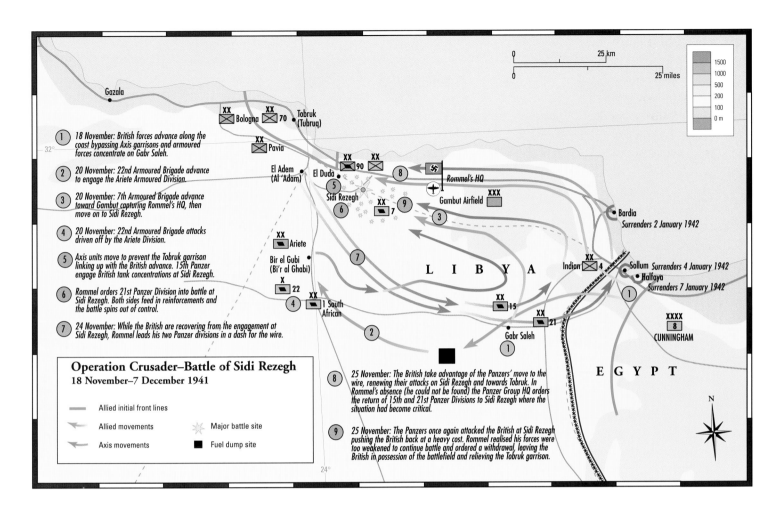

Operation Crusader–Battle of Sidi Rezegh
18 November–7 December 1941

1 18 November: British forces advance along the coast bypassing Axis garrisons and armoured forces concentrate on Gabr Saleh.

2 20 November: 22nd Armoured Brigade advance to engage the Ariete Armoured Division.

3 20 November: 7th Armoured Brigade advance toward Gambut capturing Rommel's HQ, then move on to Sidi Rezegh.

4 20 November: 22nd Armoured Brigade attacks driven off by the Ariete Division.

5 Axis units move to prevent the Tobruk garrison linking up with the British advance. 15th Panzer engage British tank concentrations at Sidi Rezegh.

6 Rommel orders 21st Panzer Division into battle at Sidi Rezegh. Both sides feed in reinforcements and the battle spins out of control.

7 24 November: While the British are recovering from the engagement at Sidi Rezegh, Rommel leads his two Panzer divisions in a dash for the wire.

Allied initial front lines

Allied movements — Major battle site

Axis movements — Fuel dump site

8 25 November: The British take advantage of the Panzers' move to the wire, renewing their attacks on Sidi Rezegh and towards Tobruk. In Rommel's absence (he could not be found) the Panzer Group HQ orders the return of 15th and 21st Panzer Divisions to Sidi Rezegh where the situation had become critical.

9 25 November: The Panzers once again attacked the British at Sidi Rezegh pushing the British back at a heavy cost. Rommel realised his forces were too weakened to continue battle and ordered a withdrawal, leaving the British in possession of the battlefield and relieving the Tobruk garrison.

SIDI REZEGH

Operation Crusader's most critical phase was the confused fighting at Sidi Rezegh, taken by the British 7th Armoured Brigade on 20 November 1941. The *Afrika Korps* gathered 150 tanks, along with infantry and 88s, to launch a counterattack, ousting the British and splitting their forces in two. Rommel's remaining armour – fewer than 100 tanks – drove east, hoping to cut off the British in Libya. Unfazed, Auchinleck ordered the attack to continue, resulting in a link-up with the Tobruk garrison. Rommel struck again at Sidi Rezegh, but failed to stem the British advance. Down to 60 tanks, on 4 December he admitted defeat and withdrew.

under the operational command of General Alan Cunningham.

Soon Cunningham could call upon 700 tanks and command of the air. Hitler, however, was distracted by the ongoing struggle in Russia, and sent few reinforcements to Rommel – leaving the *Afrika Korps* with only 320 tanks, half of which were inferior Italian models. With his newfound strength, Cunningham proposed to attack, using the infantry to pin the Axis defenders in place near the Halfaya Pass, while British armour swung south around Axis defences to strike towards Tobruk. The British plan, dubbed Operation Crusader, was sound, but their armoured tactics were poor, tending towards dispersing their tanks and giving Rommel a chance of victory.

Cunningham launched Operation Crusader on 18 November 1941 and initially met with great success, with the 7th Armoured Brigade capturing Rommel's headquarters and penetrating to Sidi Rezegh – only 19km (12 miles) from Tobruk. Further south, the 22nd Armoured Brigade penetrated as far as Bir el Gubi, threatening to flank the entire Axis position. The situation was dire, but again Rommel proved a master of defensive warfare. Employing 88s in anti-tank roles, the Germans were able to stem the advance of the 7th Armoured at Sidi Rezegh, while the Italian Ariete Division halted the 22nd Armoured at Bir el Gubi. The fighting was intense and confused, especially at Sidi Rezegh, leaving the British stunned and with only 14 per cent of their armoured force intact. While the British regrouped and brought up new armour from the rear, Rommel made a brash bid for victory on 24 November by sending his few remaining tanks on a dash to the east, towards the Halfaya Pass, in a bid to cut off and destroy the now-exposed British armour.

Shaken by the bold move, Cunningham was ready to withdraw, but Auchinleck, realizing that Rommel was in a very weak position, personally ordered the offensive to continue and replaced Cunningham in command with General Neil Ritchie. While Rommel moved east, British armour linked up with the Tobruk garrison on 27 November. Running low on fuel, harassed

FRESH ATTACK

General Rommel realized that the British had weakened their forces in North Africa and, on 21 January 1942, attacked at Mersa Brega outside Ajdabiya. After a confused struggle, the 1st Armoured Division withdrew with Rommel in pursuit.

Near Msus Rommel swung northward in an attempt to cross difficult, but undefended, terrain and reach Benghazi to cut off the British retreat. Though the Germans reached the coast on 28 January the British managed to smash their way through. At this point Rommel chose to pause and resupply and British forces used the lull to retreat to prepared defensive positions at Gazala.

from the air and with his vital supply lines nearly severed, Rommel struck back towards Sidi Rezegh and Tobruk, still hoping to snatch victory from the jaws of defeat. Again superior German all-arms coordination proved critical, as Rommel expelled the British from Sidi Rezegh in a seesaw struggle. Auchinleck, though, stood firm – realizing that Rommel was running out of time and supplies – and ordered a further offensive to the west to cut off the Axis escape route.

Reduced to a force of only 60 tanks, on 4 December Rommel chose to retreat to Gazala, pursued by the victorious Eighth Army. Although Rommel had hoped to remain on the defensive at Gazala, his weakened force could not hold against British flanking actions, and the retreat continued all the way to El Agheila, the place where Rommel had started his audacious offensive only eight months before.

ROMMEL RETURNS

It seemed that the tide of war had turned irrevocably against the *Afrika Korps*, but the outbreak of war in the Far East again forced Britain to strip forces from North Africa – tipping the balance back towards the Axis powers. Rommel quickly recognized his newfound advantage and seized the initiative. Having received promotion and the command of the newly designated *Panzerarmee Afrika*, on 21 January Rommel ordered the attack on British positions near Mersa Brega, initiating a British withdrawal after heavy losses. Rommel pursued the retreating British formations to Msus, then suddenly shifted his advance northwards towards the coast, hoping to cut off British forces at Benghazi, and reached the coast on 28 January, completing the encirclement. The developing situation had been so confused that Rommel nearly landed his observation aircraft in a British encampment. Although victorious, many of the Axis forces were widely dispersed, a factor which allowed, in a confused night engagement on 29 January, a daring

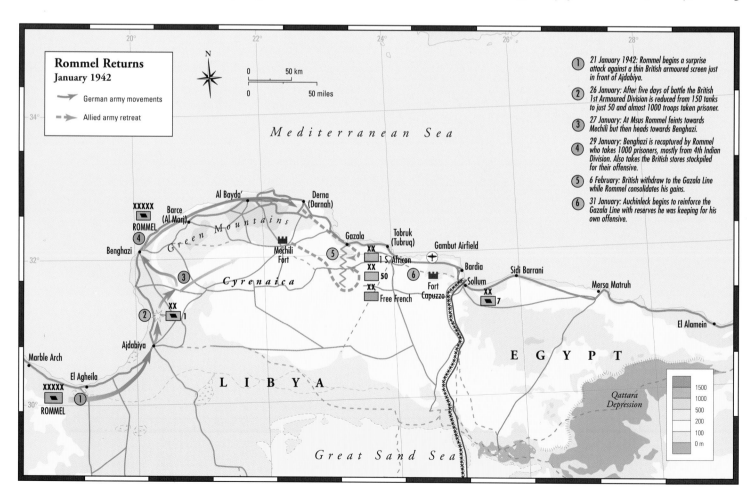

British escape from the trap. The Germans had captured valuable supplies at Benghazi, but their continuing logistical woes caused Rommel momentarily to halt his advance, while the British retreated to a defensive position at Gazala. At this point, many within the *Panzerarmee Afrika* urged Rommel to devote his energies to the destruction of the British Mediterranean bastion of Malta, in an attempt to rectify the continuing supply imbalance. Rommel, however, decided that the time was ripe instead to continue the advance – aimed at the seizure of the fabled British defensive bastion of Tobruk.

The situation for attack was quite risky, for the British occupied strong defensive positions at Gazala, and Axis supplies remained chronically low. Although the Germans had command of the air and an equality in infantry forces – they had only 560 tanks compared to the British strength of 849 tanks, the latter including many powerful US-built Grant tanks. Rommel's plan called for Axis mobile forces to sweep southwards around extensive British minefields and the Free French bastion at Bir Hacheim. German forces would then move northwards past Bir el Gubi to sever British supply lines and bring the British armour to battle.

On 26 May 1942, Axis forces moved forwards into battle, but were forced to halt near Bir el Gubi. Stymied, Rommel found himself at a distinct disadvantage – having to rely on long supply lines that were interdicted by the stubborn resistance of the Free French at Bir Hacheim. His forces were so near to running out of fuel that Rommel actually considered asking the British for surrender terms. However, the master of improvisation was to gamble yet again – this time on a frontal assault on the British 150th Brigade manning the original defensive line. On 2 June, and with little time to spare, the Axis infantry broke through the British defences, opening a new and direct line of supply to Rommel's armour. Even as the Axis battle plan teetered near disaster, the British launched poorly coordinated assaults on the German force stranded near Bir el Gubi in

TOBRUK FALLS

On 26 May 1942, Rommel pre-empted a possible British attack near Gazala with his own offensive. After a feint in the north, Axis mobile forces swung south around the deadly minefields and the Free French bastion at Bir Hacheim. However, the British held firm near Bir el Gubi, forcing Rommel to halt while striking at the British 150th Brigade in order to open a supply line. Barely achieving success in the face of disorganized British assaults, Rommel resumed the attack on 13 June. His victory was so stunning that the British, with only 70 tanks left, abandoned Tobruk, retreating to El Alamein in Egypt.

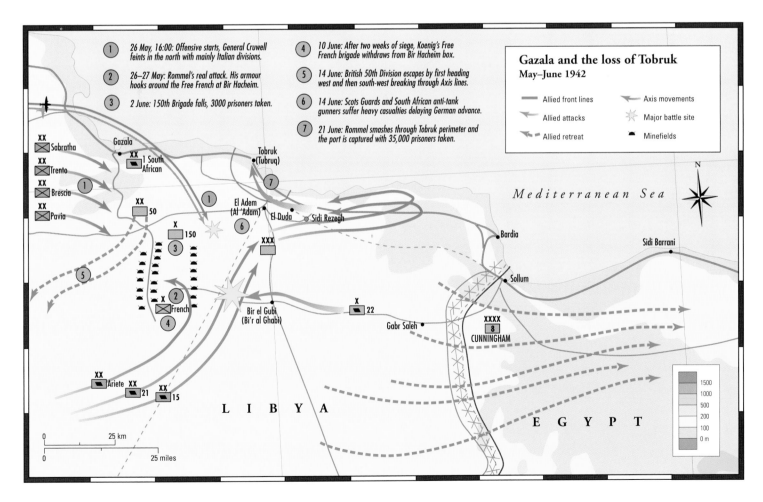

1 26 May, 16:00: Offensive starts, General Cruwell feints in the north with mainly Italian divisions.

2 26–27 May: Rommel's real attack. His armour hooks around the Free French at Bir Hacheim.

3 2 June: 150th Brigade falls, 3000 prisoners taken.

4 10 June: After two weeks of siege, Koenig's Free French brigade withdraws from Bir Hacheim box.

5 14 June: British 50th Division escapes by first heading west and then south-west breaking through Axis lines.

6 14 June: Scots Guards and South African anti-tank gunners suffer heavy casualties delaying German advance.

7 21 June: Rommel smashes through Tobruk perimeter and the port is captured with 35,000 prisoners taken.

Gazala and the loss of Tobruk
May–June 1942

Allied front lines
Allied attacks
Allied retreat
Axis movements
Major battle site
Minefields

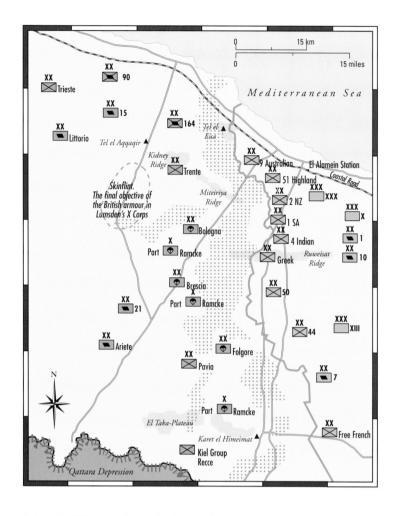

The Eve of Battle
23 October 1942

- Allied frontline
- Allied objective
- Axis minefields

an area dubbed 'The Cauldron'. Had the British been more persistent or better organized, they might have achieved victory. Instead tanks, with little support, threw themselves at the enemy lines and the German 88s. In one attack the British lost 50 out of 70 tanks, and the balance of battle began to shift back towards Rommel once more.

After the fall of Bir Hacheim on 10 June, Rommel – with a remaining force of 184 tanks – attacked British armour – with a remaining force of 247 tanks – and advanced towards Tobruk. Moving forwards with power and precision, Rommel crushed British resistance – destroying 138 tanks and driving the British back in disarray. Caught by surprise by the crushing nature of its defeat, the Eighth Army was not able to mount a stern defence of Tobruk, which finally fell on 21 June 1942. To the British, the fall of Tobruk signified disaster – causing Auchinleck to sack Ritchie as commander of Eighth Army. To the Germans, the fall of Tobruk was a godsend, having allowed them to seize tons of valuable supplies and a critical forward port. Rommel, promoted to Field Marshal and convinced that the British were beaten, asked for permission to invade Egypt and push on to Cairo and the Suez Canal. Although the *Afrika Korps* was near

Below: British Crusader tanks during the second battle of El Alamein. Armoured forces were the key to victory in the desert war, with its wide, open spaces. After the invasion of the Soviet Union, the Allied forces usually outnumbered the German tanks, and by 1942 American Grant tanks with 75mm (2.95in) guns capable of knocking out the German panzers became available to the British and Commonwealth forces in large numbers.

MONTY'S VICTORY

British forces had held firm in defence at El Alamein, with their flanks anchored on the Mediterranean Sea to the north and the impassable sands of the Qattara Depression to the south. Behind intricate minefields, the Eighth Army fought off two desperate German offensives in late June and August. Then the new British command team of General Alexander and General Montgomery presided over a rapid build-up of men and material, as Churchill finally made the war in North Africa his highest priority.

By late October 1942, the British advantage in the area was overwhelming, with 250,000 men, 1200 tanks and 750 aircraft against an Axis force of only 80,000 men, 489 tanks and 675 aircraft. On 23 October, Montgomery launched the first phase of his carefully planned offensive dubbed Operation Lightfoot. The XIII Corps under General Horrocks launched a diversionary attack near the Qattara Depression. Further north, the X Corps under General Lumsden pressed through the German minefields towards Kidney Ridge.

The surprise move, executed with a grim tenacity, forced Rommel's hand. Gathering all of his mobile forces Rommel was forced to counterattack, launching his few remaining tanks against overwhelming British firepower. The balance in North Africa had now shifted irrevocably to the Allies.

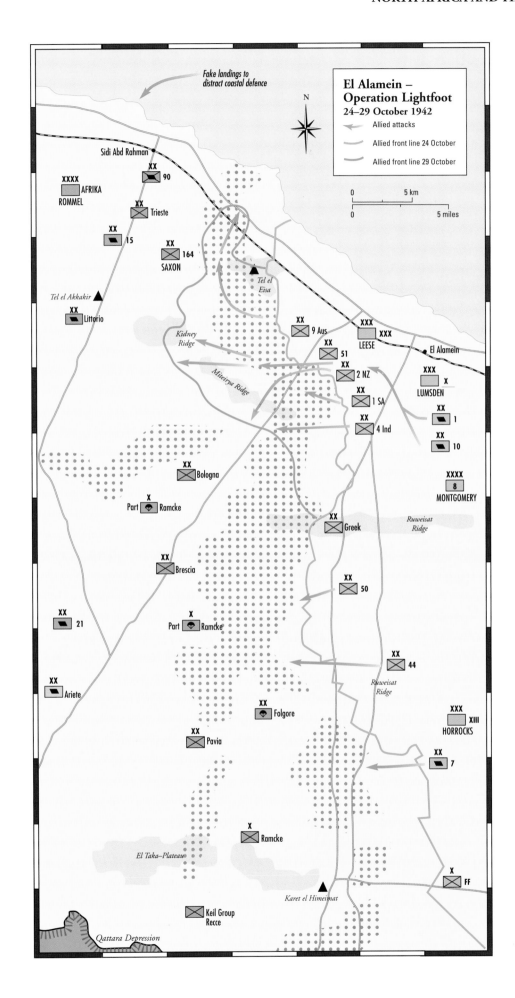

El Alamein –
Operation Lightfoot
24–29 October 1942

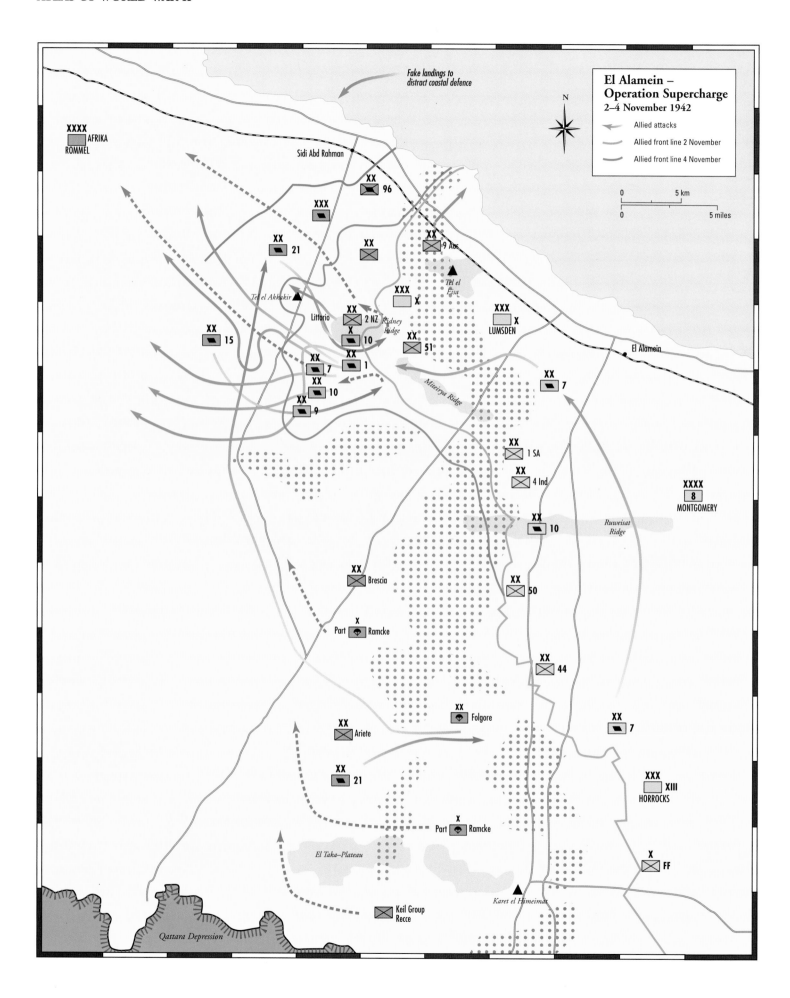

Fake landings to
distract coastal defence

El Alamein –
Operation Supercharge
2–4 November 1942

Allied attacks

Allied front line 2 November

Allied front line 4 November

N

0   5 km

0   5 miles

XXXX
AFRIKA
ROMMEL

Sidi Abd Rahman

XX
96

XXX

XX
21

XX

XX
9 Arc

Tel el Eisa

Tel el Akkakir

XXX
X

XXX
X
LUMSDEN

XX
2 NZ   Ridney
Ridge

Littorio

XX
15

X
10

XX
51

XX
7
1

XX
10

XX
9

Miteirya Ridge

El Alamein

XX
7

XX
1 SA

XX
4 Ind

XXXX
8
MONTGOMERY

XX
10   Ruweisat
Ridge

XX
Brescia

X
Part   Ramcke

XX
50

XX
44

XX
Folgore

XX
Ariete

XX
21

XX
7

XXX
XIII
HORROCKS

X
Part   Ramcke

El Taka–Plateau

X
FF

Karet el Himeimat

XX
Keil Group
Recce

Qattara Depression

BREAKOUT

Having broken into the German defensive system near Kidney Ridge, General Montgomery did not plan to use manoeuvre to surround the German defenders. Instead he chose to use his superiority in numbers and firepower to draw Rommel into a futile attack, forcing a battle of attrition. Rommel, rightly fearing a British breakthrough, obliged.

The German 15th and 21st Panzer Divisions attacked British defences near Kidney Ridge on 27 August, but were repulsed having lost more than half of their armoured force. Although British armoured losses had been high, they were sustainable, whereas German losses were not.

With an overwhelming edge in armour, Montgomery chose to launch a breakout attempt dubbed Operation Supercharge. Heralded by a massive artillery barrage, British and Dominion infantry opened a gap in the German lines exploited by British armour. Although defensive fire from German 88mm (3.45in) anti-tank guns exacted a fearsome toll – the 9th Armoured Brigade losing 70 of its 94 tanks – Montgomery relentlessly pressed forward.

With his forces nearing total collapse, Rommel – after convincing a reluctant Hitler – finally chose to retreat. Sacrificing the majority of the forces of his Italian allies, Rommel eventually made good his escape with only a single, cobbled-together brigade and 36 tanks left at his disposal.

exhaustion, Hitler agreed, and Rommel pursued the retreating British, who prepared to make a stand at a new defensive bastion outside El Alamein in Egypt.

TOWARDS DECISIVE BATTLE

In hot pursuit, Rommel's forces arrived at El Alamein on 30 June and endeavoured to keep their victorious momentum intact by attacking the very next day. British forces, however, had chosen a wonderful defensive bottleneck at which to make their stand. Guarded by the sea to the north and the impassable sands of the Qattara Depression to the south, the British system at El Alamein possessed no vulnerable flank – denying Rommel his favoured indirect approach towards victory. Instead, Axis forces struck the British defences head on, and failed to break through while suffering heavy losses. Down to a force of only 26 operational tanks, Rommel shifted to the defensive while awaiting the arrival of new supplies and reinforcements. Although Auchinleck had achieved a sort of victory by holding Rommel at bay, Churchill nonetheless had him replaced in command by General Harold Alexander, while placing operational control of the Eighth Army in the hands of General Bernard Montgomery.

In the face of near disaster, the British again began to lavish supplies on their forces in Egypt. It quickly became apparent to Rommel that the *Afrika Korps*, at the end of a long and vulnerable

Below: An *Afrika Korps* machine-gun team secure in a rocky position. The desert war was characterized by the use of strongpoints occupied by well dug-in infantry protected by reams of barbed wire and minefields coupled with fast-moving battles fought by 'fleets' of opposing tanks. At night, the tanks would combine in guarded camps to safeguard them from being picked off one by one by raiders.

WAR OF SUPPLY

The war in North Africa was in many ways a war of supplies, as both British and Axis supply ships had to ply the dangerous waters of the Mediterranean to keep the armies in North Africa alive. The balance of power in the Mediterranean initially favoured the Italians, but the British Mediterranean Fleet, based at Alexandria in Egypt, quickly redressed the balance by executing a daring air strike on Taranto and through a stirring victory at Cape Matapan.

However, German entry into the conflict and resulting Axis victories on land in Greece and North Africa again tipped the balance against the British. Unlike the war in the Atlantic, all of the Mediterranean was subject to air attack. Axis victories had seized all of the major air bases of the central Mediterranean – leaving British supply lines in dire danger.

The British retained only the tiny island of Malta, just 110km (70 miles) south of Sicily, as a vital air and sea link in the area. Submarines and aircraft based at Malta could strike at virtually any Axis supply route, often taking a heavy toll on valuable shipping. As a result Malta became the target of incessant bombing and lived with the constant threat of invasion. The garrison there would remain intact, however, playing a pivotal role in the Mediterranean conflict. In recognition of its role, the island was awarded the George Cross, the highest civilian honour, by King George VI.

supply line and virtually ignored in favour of the continuing struggle in the Soviet Union, could only lose the struggle to resupply – and thus he chose to attack once again. On 30 August, the Axis forces moved forwards between the Alam Nayil Ridge and the Qattara Depression – but were outnumbered more than two-to-one in tanks. While the British could now rely on advanced US Grant and Sherman tanks, half of Rommel's force was made up of nearly useless Italian tanks. At first, Rommel's attack bogged down in a minefield, then ran afoul of the British 22nd Armoured Brigade at the Alam Halfa Ridge. Nearly cut off, and constantly pounded from the air, Axis forces had to retreat quickly to avoid disaster.

By October, the Eighth Army numbered 250,000 men, 1200 tanks and 750 aircraft, while Axis forces numbered only 80,000 men, 489 tanks (280 of which were obsolete Italian models) and 675 aircraft. Montgomery, a much more able armoured commander than his predecessors, planned to use his overwhelming material edge in a set-piece battle dubbed Operation Lightfoot. Opening the offensive on 23 October, the 7th Armoured Division launched a diversionary attack against the German lines near the Qattara Depression. Next the main British force, led by the 1st and 10th Armoured Divisions and aided by overwhelming artillery support, struck the Axis lines further north near Miteirya Ridge. Although the British paid a heavy price, losing nearly 300 tanks, their penetration threatened the entire German defensive position. Rommel threw virtually all of his mobile forces into the fray to stem the British advance. The move played into Montgomery's hands, as he had hoped to draw the German armour into vulnerable attacks against his all-arms formations – a tactic used by Rommel so often in the past.

BREAKTHROUGH

Forced to improvise, on 27 August, Rommel launched his strongest counterattack of the entire battle, throwing the 21st and 15th Panzer Divisions against the mass of British armour, infantry and artillery in the area around Kidney Ridge. The attack, involving 148 tanks, quickly broke upon a wall of concentrated defensive firepower and constant air attacks. With only 77 tanks remaining, Rommel called a halt to the attack and had to work hard to prevent a British breakthrough.

Although he had not gained the expected amount of ground, Montgomery was quite pleased. Having reduced Axis power through attrition, he now planned a breakthrough offensive dubbed 'Operation Supercharge'. While Rommel pondered a withdrawal to defensive positions outside Fuka, the British struck. On 2 November, the British infantry and artillery attacked first, opening a gap exploited by British armour. Rommel quickly moved his remaining mobile units and armour to the area south of Kidney Ridge, and his 88s exacted a fearsome toll on the attackers. The British 9th Armoured Brigade lost 70 of its 94 tanks; however, still the British came forward. The Germans, too, paid a prohibitive price in battle, losing all but 24 of their precious 88mm (3.45in) anti-tank weapons.

Realizing that his counterstroke had failed, Rommel now made ready to retreat, but received orders from Hitler to stand fast. Losing a day before he could dissuade Hitler from his misguided notion, Rommel and his *Panzerarmee Afrika* narrowly avoided total destruction at the hands of the advancing British. Most of the Axis infantry and mechanized forces were brought to battle by the advancing British and destroyed, while the elite forces of the German *Afrika Korps* gathered what transport and supplies they could to make good their escape. With

a force of only 36 tanks and a motley assortment of survivors from various units that together equalled only one brigade, the Germans quit Egypt and fled for their lives from Montgomery's powerful, confident and victorious Eighth Army.

MEDITERRANEAN NAVAL OPERATIONS

The back-and-forth struggle for North Africa often hinged upon the availability of supplies carried by merchant ships plying the dangerous waters of the Mediterranean Sea. British supply lines to the area were already long and dangerous, running southwards across the Atlantic and through the Straits of Gibraltar. It was the entrance of Italy into the conflict, however, that made the situation dire, for the Italian Navy possessed six battleships, 18 cruisers, 60 destroyers and more than 100 submarines. Outnumbered and outgunned, the British Mediterranean Fleet, under the command of Admiral Andrew Cunningham – along with Force H based at Gibraltar – had to protect the vital supply lines to Africa, as well as support the isolated British base at Malta. Of vital importance, the tiny island of Malta sat astride Axis supply lines to North Africa and represented the only British forward air base in the central Mediterranean. Sporting a tiny naval force and air contingent, the British garrison at Malta periodically took a heavy toll on Axis supply shipments, but faced constant bombing and the threat of invasion. Indeed, tiny Malta became one of the focal points of the conflict in North Africa.

Although at a numerical disadvantage, the British retained a significant technological edge on their Italian foes. The Mediterranean Fleet had superior intelligence due to Ultra intercepts, the use of radar afforded the British a night-fighting capability the Italians lacked and the British were

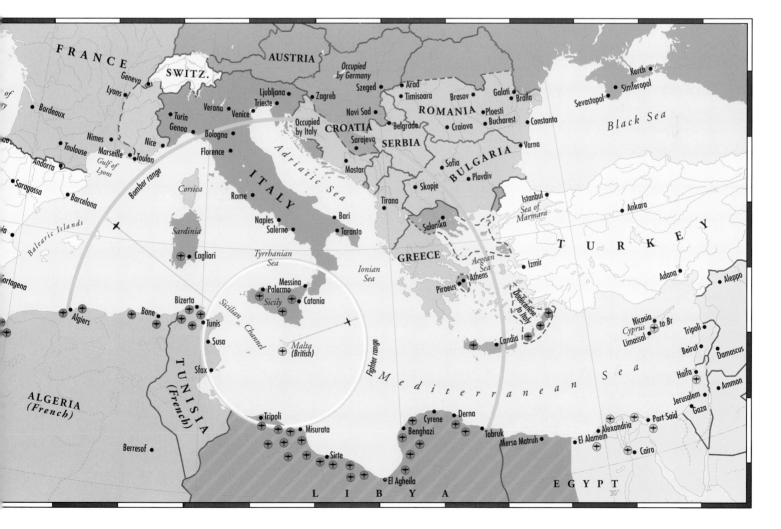

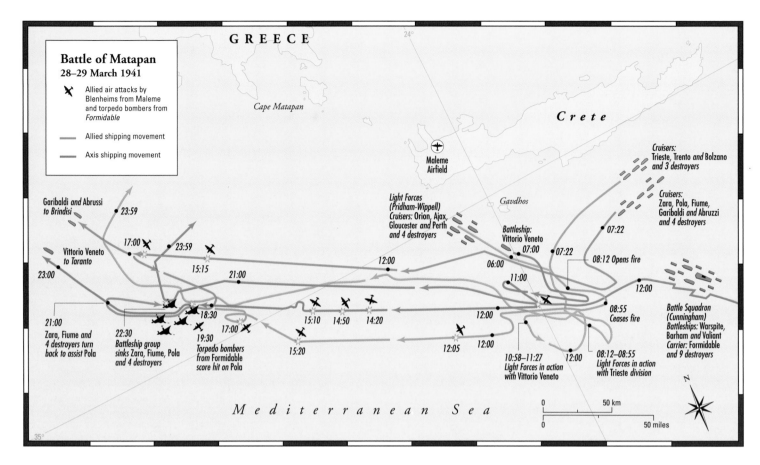

CAPE MATAPAN

On 27 March 1941, the British Mediterranean Fleet under Admiral Cunningham sank three Italian cruisers and two destroyers, and damaged the battleship *Vittorio Veneto* at the cost of only one aircraft lost.

TARANTO

On 11 November 1940, the British Mediterranean Fleet attacked the Italian naval base at Taranto. The aircraft carrier *Illustrious* launched a flight of 21 Swordfish torpedo bombers. Arriving in two waves at night, 10 aircraft dropped flares, while the remaining 11 dropped their torpedoes. The British attack successfully sank one battleship, while badly damaging two others and two cruisers.

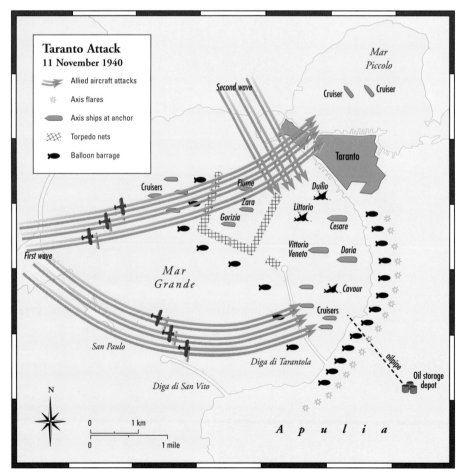

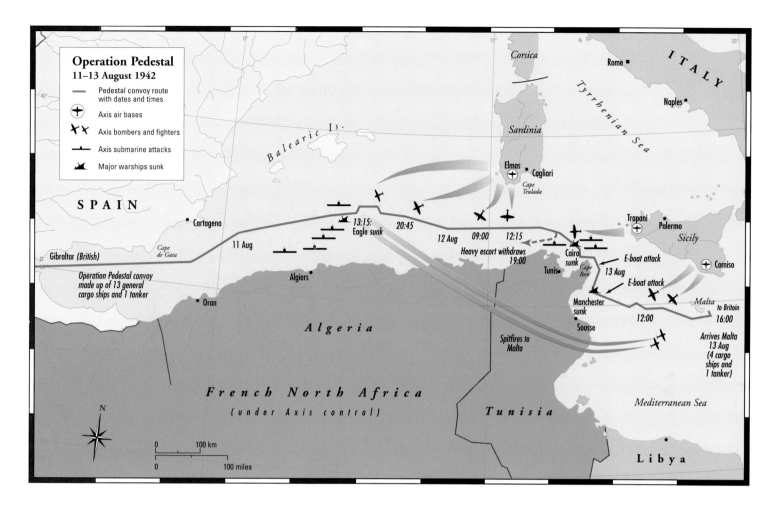

Operation Pedestal
11–13 August 1942

- Pedestal convoy route with dates and times
- Axis air bases
- Axis bombers and fighters
- Axis submarine attacks
- Major warships sunk

PEDESTAL

On 10 August 1942, a large convoy numbering 14 merchant ships, 3 aircraft carriers, 2 battleships, 4 cruisers and 14 destroyers left Gibraltar to resupply Malta, which was short of supplies. The convoy, dubbed Operation Pedestal, faced constant attack by Axis aircraft and submarines.

At 1.15 the next afternoon the aircraft carrier *Eagle* was sunk. Attacks were so severe that some of the heavier British ships were forced away, while three cruisers and a destroyer were lost. Finally, at noon on 13 August, the remnants of the convoy reached Malta. Only five ships arrived safely, but one of these was a precious oil tanker.

able to call upon the services of the aircraft carriers *Illustrious* and *Formidable*. Ever an aggressive commander, Cunningham looked past his numerical inferiority to seize the initiative. Afraid that the remnants of the French fleet would fall into German hands, in July 1940 Cunningham destroyed its remaining forces at Mers el Kebir and Oran. Next, in November 1940, the Mediterranean Fleet launched a daring, pre-emptive strike on the main Italian fleet base at Taranto. The British aircraft carrier *Illustrious* stole to within striking distance of the supposedly safe fleet base and launched a flight of 21 outdated Swordfish biplanes. Flying at night, the daring pilots launched 11 torpedoes at the moored Italian fleet, sinking one battleship and crippling two others, including the powerful *Littorio*, along with two cruisers. The successful attack helped to redress the balance of power in the Mediterranean and forced the remnants of the Italian Navy to move to distant bases on Italy's west coast – and left the Italians reticent to test British power.

Ebbing Italian fortunes in North Africa, along with British intervention in Greece, forced the Italian Navy from its lethargy. Initially reluctant to attack British shipping in and around Greece, the entry of the Germans into the conflict there helped to force the Italians into action. On 27 March, a considerable Italian naval force formed off the coast of Sicily – including one battleship, the *Vittorio Veneto*, eight cruisers and nine destroyers – hoping to destroy British shipping north of Crete. However, due to an intelligence break, the British were aware of Italian intentions and put to sea from Alexandria the very same day with a force of three battleships and an aircraft carrier, along with an assortment of cruisers and destroyers. The next morning, in an action known as the Battle of Cape Matapan, a flight of torpedo bombers caught the Italian force unawares, damaging the *Vittorio Veneto* and disabling the heavy cruiser *Pola*. While part of Iachino's fleet limped homeward with the *Vittorio Veneto*, some remained behind with the stricken *Pola*. In a night battle, British surface ships struck the remaining Italian forces, sinking

TORCH

On 8 November 1942, a joint Anglo-American force, under the command of General Dwight Eisenhower, launched Operation Torch. Over 600 ships, some sailing directly from the United States, carried over 70,000 men to strike at Casablanca, Oran and Algiers in the North African colonies of Vichy France. Although many had resisted at first, by 11 November, the Vichy commander, Admiral Darlan, convinced most of his forces to join with the Allies. The British and American forces were consequently able to drive quickly on Tunisia, forcing the newly reinforced Axis troops there into a shrinking pocket.

TUNISIA

After El Alamein, *Panzerarmee Afrika* was too weak to offer any real resistance to the victorious Eighth Army and could only form delaying positions at natural defensive lines. The situation was so bad that Rommel had to abandon 10,000 tons of vital supplies on 13 November, as his forces fled Tobruk. Rushing down the coast road, Axis forces narrowly avoided capture at Mersa Brega, falling back on a line of defences near Burerat and later near the vital port of Tripoli. At each juncture, Montgomery attempted flank manoeuvres to the south – leading to further Axis retreat. Finally, on 1 February, Rommel's exhausted men reached the safety of the Mareth Line in Tunisia.

three heavy cruisers and two destroyers. The victory was critical, leaving the Italian fleet in a defensive posture and unable to disrupt the coming British evacuation from Greece and Crete.

DECISION

The delicate balance of the war in the Mediterranean was altered by Germany's entrance into the war in North Africa. German aircraft based in Sicily and North Africa placed immediate pressure on British supply routes – and announced their presence by badly damaging the *Illustrious*. Lacking in air power, the British Mediterranean Fleet was spread thin in an effort to make certain that valuable shipping made it to Malta and North Africa. Thus the war settled into a convoy struggle, with both sides attempting to protect their supplies, while interdicting those of the enemy.

In 1942, German activity in the

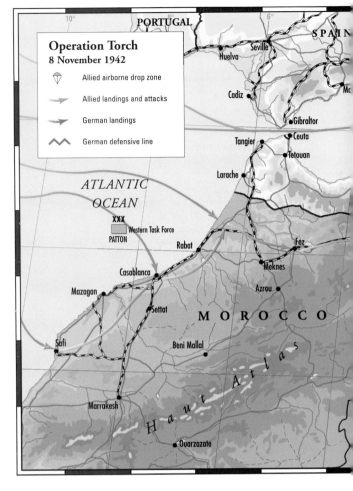

Mediterranean reached its zenith, leaving Malta and the British war effort in North Africa in peril. With the Luftwaffe in control of the skies, British convoys in the area took a heavy pounding, and the garrison on Malta ran critically low on all types of supplies. In an effort to stave off disaster, on 10 August 1942, the British launched a convoy of 14 merchant ships bound from Gibraltar to Malta – guarded by a powerful escort of three aircraft carriers, two battleships, four cruisers and 14 destroyers. Axis aircraft and submarines pressed relentless attacks on the convoy – sinking nine merchant ships, the aircraft carrier *Eagle*, three cruisers and a destroyer. Despite the heavy cost, enough merchant ships made it through, including the lone oil tanker, to avert the crisis in Malta.

In the end, the conclusion of the fighting in the Mediterranean was decided by the ebb and flow of battle in North Africa. With Germany sidetracked by war in Russia, in late 1942 the British – relying on supply routes outside the Mediterranean – were able to crush Rommel's force at El Alamein. The German retreat to Tunisia in the east, coupled with the Allied landings in West Africa, meant that critical advance air bases were seized and the balance in the air war in the Mediterranean was turned against the Luftwaffe. With newfound command of the air, the Allies severed Axis supply lines to Tunisia, helping to force their ultimate surrender. With the Luftwaffe defeated, the few remaining Italian surface ships and submarines were unable to oppose eventual Allied landings in Sicily – the war in the Mediterranean had come to a conclusion.

AXIS RETREAT AND ALLIED INVASION

Tattered, beaten and running short of supplies, Rommel's *Panzerarmee Afrika* headed west, with Montgomery's Eighth Army in hot pursuit. With a force of only 4000 men, 24 88mm (3.45in) guns, 40 artillery pieces and 11 serviceable tanks, Rommel rightly feared utter destruction. At

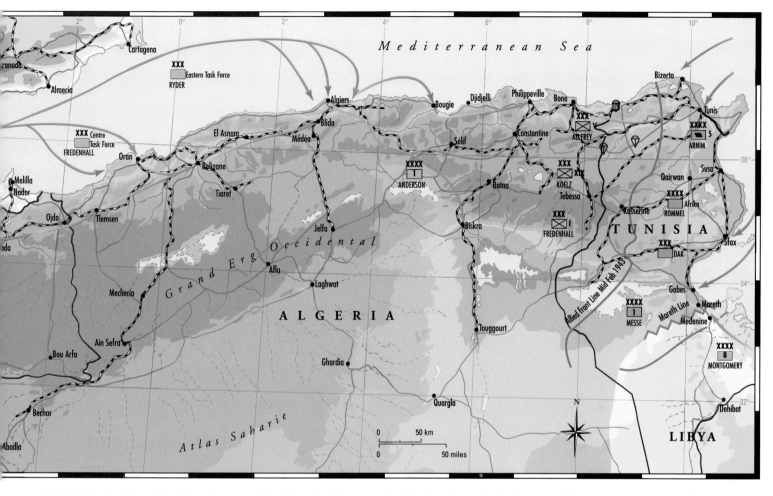

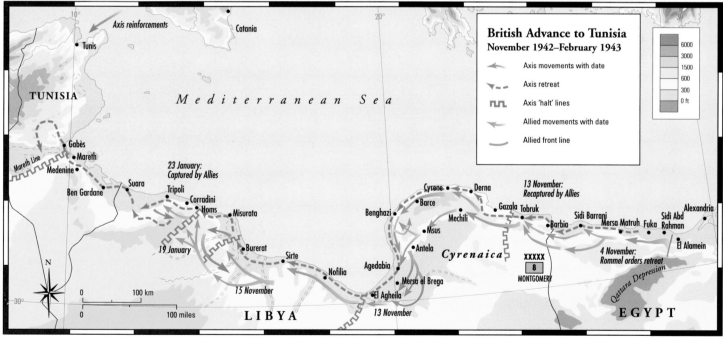

times Rommel would call halts at defensible points to allow his exhausted soldiers a break; however, at the first sign of a British flanking movement, the *Panzerarmee Afrika* would again escape, leaving a delaying force to cover its retreat. Montgomery advanced cautiously, missing a chance to flank Rommel at Mersa Brega. Under constant pressure, Rommel evacuated successive lines of defence in Libya, exiting the vital port of Tripoli on 23 January. On 1 February, he reached the safety of the Mareth Line in

Tunisia. At the end of a long supply line, Montgomery halted outside Tripoli to resupply. The German decision to retreat into Tunisia was largely forced by a new development in West Africa. Pressured to open a second front by the Soviets, but not yet ready to invade Europe, the Allies chose Operation Torch, the invasion of North Africa. Passing over several more senior generals, the Allies settled on General Dwight Eisenhower as overall commander. Hoping to catch Rommel in a vice, some Allied strategists advocated a landing as far east as Bone, near Tunisia. In the end, the plan was rejected as too risky, and the main Allied landings were made at Casablanca, Oran and Algiers in the North African colonies of Vichy France.

With over 100,000 men in the area, the Vichy French, if they chose to resist, were capable of significantly delaying the Allied plan. Following clandestine talks with the Vichy French on 8 November, a massive fleet of over 600 ships arrived off the various

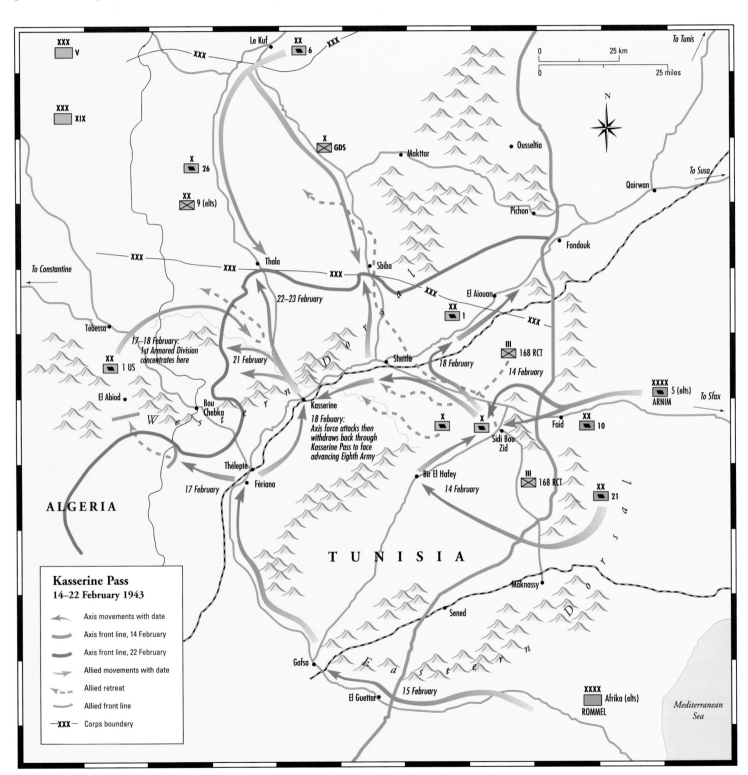

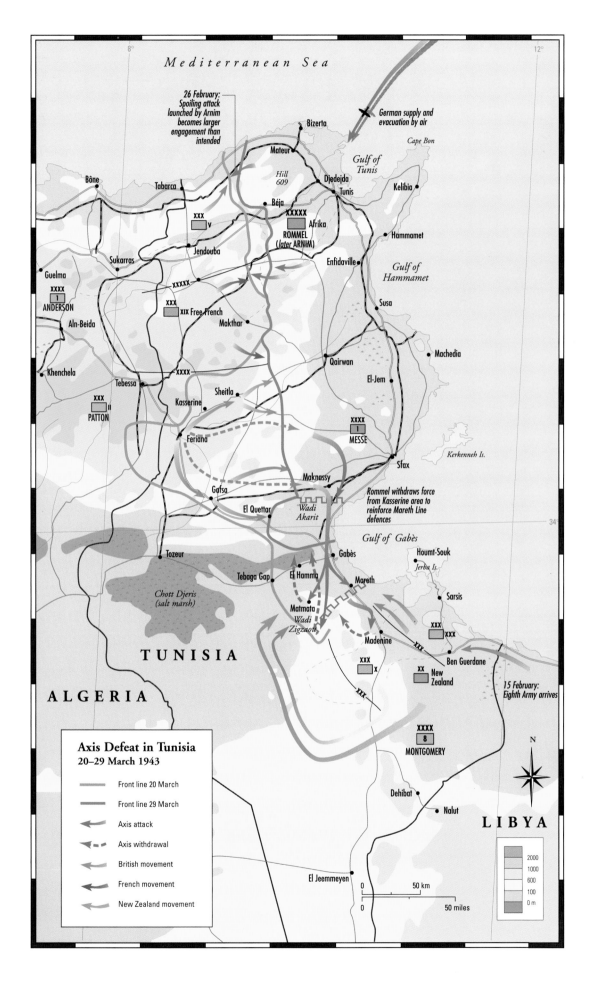

Mediterranean Sea

26 February: Spoiling attack launched by Arnim becomes larger engagement than intended

German supply and evacuation by air

Bizerta

Cape Bon

Mateur

Gulf of Tunis

Bône

Tabarca

Hill 609

Djedejda

Tunis

Kelibia

Béja

XXX V

XXXXX Afrika

ROMMEL (later ARNIM)

Hammamet

Jendouba

Sukarras

Enfidaville

Guelma

Gulf of Hammamet

XXXX 1 ANDERSON

XXXXX

Aln-Beida

XXX XIX Free French

Makthar

Susa

Khenchela

Machedia

Qairwan

XXXX

El-Jem

Tebessa

Sheitla

XXX II PATTON

Kasserine

XXXX 1 MESSE

Feriana

Kerkenneh Is.

Sfax

Maknassy

Gafsa

Rommel withdraws force from Kasserine area to reinforce Mareth Line defences

El Quettar

Wadi Akarit

Gulf of Gabès

Tozeur

Gabès

Houmt-Souk

Jerba Is.

Tebaga Gap

El Hamma

Mareth

Sarsis

Chott Djeris (salt marsh)

Matmata Wadi Zigzaou

XXX XXX

Madenine

TUNISIA

XXX x

XX New Zealand

Ben Guerdane

XXX

15 February: Eighth Army arrives

ALGERIA

XXXX 8 MONTGOMERY

N

Dehibat

Nalut

LIBYA

Axis Defeat in Tunisia
20–29 March 1943

⎯	Front line 20 March
⎯	Front line 29 March
←	Axis attack
⇠	Axis withdrawal
←	British movement
←	French movement
←	New Zealand movement

El Jeemmeyen

0   50 km

0   50 miles

2000
1000
600
100
0 m

KASSERINE

Rommel saw the opportunity for a riposte against the Americans in Tunisia, and proposed that his forces join with Arnim's Fifth Army in a drive on the major US supply base at Tebessa in Algeria. Arnim, though, gave only half-hearted support to the plan, attacking and taking Sidi Bou Zid on 14 February. Rommel then wanted to thrust towards the Kasserine Pass, but Arnim diverted considerable forces northwards towards Sbiba.

Frustrated, Rommel advanced on Kasserine nonetheless, and on 19 February won a stunning victory there over outmatched American forces. The attack was too weak and fell short of its goal, however, with Rommel forced to send troops back to the Mareth Line to face the advancing Montgomery.

After Kasserine, command of all Axis troops in Tunisia finally fell to Rommel. It was, however, too late, for the Allied forces' superiority in men and material became too great. The Germans undertook two spoiling attacks, one in the north under Arnim and the other a direct assault on Montgomery's defences at Medenine near the Mareth Line.

The Allies launched a two-pronged offensive to trap Axis forces on the Mareth Line, with the US II Corps advancing from Feriana towards the coast while Montgomery attempted to flank the line itself. The result was the German defenders retreating to Wadi Akarit, but they were defeated there as well and finally fell back on Enfidaville.

landing points. Vichy resistance was spotty, but heavy fighting broke out near Oran. On 11 November, the Vichy commander, Admiral Darlan, reached an agreement with Eisenhower and his forces joined the Allies. The special treatment afforded Darlan outraged the Free French leader Charles de Gaulle, but allowed Allied forces to race forward into Tunisia.

When Rommel arrived at the Mareth Line, the Axis command situation was muddled. Under nominal overall Italian command, Rommel led *Panzerarmee Afrika*, while most of the new reinforcements in Tunisia were in the Fifth Panzer Army commanded by General Jurgen von Arnim. While Montgomery loitered outside Tripoli, Rommel and Arnim saw the chance to strike the raw American forces in western Tunisia. Rommel proposed a thrust at the US supply base at Tebessa in Algeria, while Arnim wanted an assault much further north, in Tunisia, aimed at Beja. In the end, both attacks took place, leaving the attackers severely outnumbered by the Allied defenders.

On 14 February 1943, elements of Arnim's 21st Panzer Divison opened the fighting by crushing inexperienced troops of the US II Corps at Sidi Bou Zid, allowing the 21st Panzer to reach Sbeitla in only three days. Further south, Rommel had removed forces from the Mareth Line defences and moved north, advancing through Feriana and towards the bottleneck of Kasserine. Certain that a major victory beckoned, Rommel chafed at Arnim's desire for the 21st Panzer to continue northwards away from vulnerable Tebessa. Frustrated, Rommel flung the *Afrika Korps* and the 10th Panzer Division at the American defenders of the Kasserine Pass, which fell after a two-day struggle. Belatedly the Axis leadership realized that Arnim's failure to support Rommel had been critical, and placed Rommel in command of all Axis forces in Tunisia. The 10th Panzer moved towards Thala while Rommel rode with the *Afrika Korps* towards Tebessa.

Shaken, but not demoralized, the British and Americans rushed reinforcements to the scene and rained air attacks upon the advancing Germans. The Allied forces were too strong for Rommel's advance to continue, and Montgomery had arrived at the Mareth Line, held by a weak covering force. Thus the tactical masterpiece of Kasserine had failed to tip the balance. For the Americans, especially, the experience had been a rude awakening to the tactical prowess of the German military and the strength of its armoured units. In an effort to shake up his command structure, Eisenhower placed the US II Corps in the hands of a brash new commander: General George Patton.

By this time, Rommel had come to the conclusion that the Axis defense of Tunisia was doomed to failure. However, the Allied blockade meant that there was no way to withdraw the Axis forces from Africa – they would have to fight on. Eschewing an opportunity to withdraw to the most defensible line around Tunis, Rommel chose instead to launch further spoiling attacks upon Allied forces. On 26 February, Arnim struck Allied lines north of Beja, but suffered heavy losses for no gain, before having to retreat. On 6 March, Rommel followed with a frontal assault against Montgomery at Medenine, which was also repulsed.

THE FALL OF TUNISIA

With both his spirit and health failing, on 9 March 1943, Rommel departed North Africa for recuperation in Germany, leaving the faltering Axis army in the hands of Arnim. On 17 March 1943, the US II Corps under Patton attacked eastwards from Feriana, threatening the German defenders of the Mareth Line. Three days later, Montgomery added a costly frontal assault on

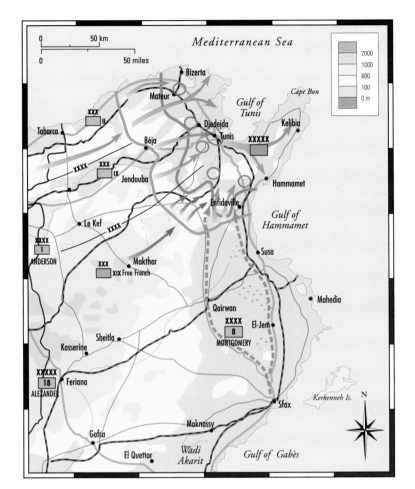

Capture of Tunis
April–May 1943

- Front line mid-April
- Front line 3 May
- Axis withdrawal
- British movement
- French movement
- Concentration of Axis surrenders 7–13 May

THE END IN AFRICA

The Axis defenders of Tunis were a great many in number, but the success of the Allied blockade caused major shortages in supplies of all types. Without air support and outnumbered six to one on the ground and 15 to one when it came to armour, the German and Italian effort in North Africa was nearing its end.

Montgomery opened the attack with a diversionary assault on the powerful German defenses near Enfidaville, followed by an attack by the British First Army and Free French forces in the centre of the German defensive system. Further north, the US II Corps struck towards Bizerta.

By May 1943, the German front lines had been constricted and Axis forces had run out of supplies. On 6 May, British forces launched Operation Vulcan with a punishing air and artillery barrage that wiped out the last of the German armour in the area.

Finally, in a hopeless situation, the remnants of the once-mighty *Afrika Korps* disintegrated, leaving the route to Tunis and Bizerta open, and both cities fell without a struggle. Across the northern Tunisian peninsula, Allied forces mopped up the last pockets of German resistance.

In a disaster that was equal to that of the Battle of Stalingrad in the Soviet Union (only a few months earlier), some 150,000 Axis forces fell into the hands of the Allies.

the German line – designed to pin the defenders in place. Further south, elements of the Eighth Army advanced around the flank of the Mareth Line, and on 27 February reached El Hamma. The move, though, had been too slow, and the majority of the German defenders had escaped north to a new line of defences at Wadi Akarit. Facing attack from the Americans in the west and the British in the south, on 6 April the German defensive line crumbled – resulting in a 240km (150-mile) retreat northwards to defences outside Enfidaville.

The Allies slowly drew up a massive force around the beleaguered Axis defenders of Tunis. In total, the Allies now enjoyed a 6:1 advantage in men, a 15:1 advantage in armour and nearly uncontested command of the skies over the battlefield. The attack on Tunis began with a diversionary assault by the Eighth Army near Enfidaville. The main attacks, though, came further north. The British First Army assaulted the centre of the German defences, while the US II Corps, now under the command of General Omar Bradley, attacked in the north. Lavish artillery support and continuous pressure resulted in II Corps nearing the critical city of Bizerta, around 120 km (75 miles) from Tunis, while General Arnim expended the remainder of his precious resources thwarting the simultaneous British advances. General Alexander, commanding the British First Army, then suspended the assault on Enfidaville, adding two additional armoured units to the First Army assault in the centre.

Below: Locals look on as British Valentine tanks enter Tunis. The surrender of the Axis forces in North Africa – so recently reinforced by Hitler – was a significant morale boost for the Allies. The world waited to see where the Allies would choose to land on the continent of Europe. President Roosevelt and his advisers were keen to land in France, while Churchill wanted to liberate Greece and the Balkans.

The First Army launched its climactic final assault, dubbed Operation Vulcan, on 6 May 1943, in the Medjerda Valley. Massive air and artillery attacks preceded the British advance, destroying the remaining German armour. German resistance consequently collapsed. British columns motored into Tunis unopposed, while the Americans took Bizerta without a fight. The war in North Africa had come to an end, as 150,000 Axis soldiers surrendered in a disaster some referred to as 'Tunisgrad'. The defeat was a massive blow to the morale of the Axis forces. Germany was now clearly on the defensive. The master tactician Rommel had succeeded admirably in battle with a paucity of forces; he had constantly bombarded the German High Command with requests for more men. Hitler had ignored his call for support when victory had beckoned, but ironically sent lavish reinforcements to the area in time to surrender after defeat was assured.

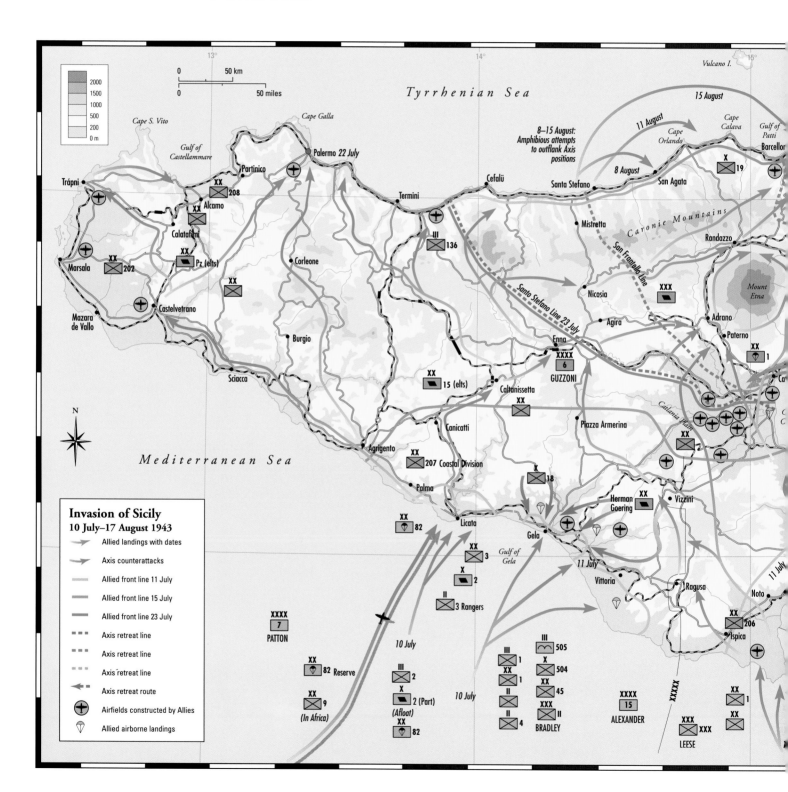

Invasion of Sicily
10 July–17 August 1943

- Allied landings with dates
- Axis counterattacks
- Allied front line 11 July
- Allied front line 15 July
- Allied front line 23 July
- Axis retreat line
- Axis retreat line
- Axis retreat line
- Axis retreat route
- Airfields constructed by Allies
- Allied airborne landings

THE INVASION OF SICILY

The Allies chose next to launch Operation Husky: the invasion of Sicily. With Eisenhower in overall command, British General Alexander served as the field commander of the operation. His plan called for Montgomery's Eighth Army to land near Siracusa and drive north on Messina. Patton and his Seventh Army would land on the southern coast of Sicily and serve as a flank guard for Montgomery's advance. Mussolini had hoped to defend Sicily with only Italian troops, but by the time of the invasion two German Panzer Divisions were also on hand – under the command of Field Marshal Albert Kesselring.

On 10 July 1943 the Allies struck, catching the Axis defenders by surprise, with many Italian divisions collapsing in the face of the assault. Aware of the problem, Kesselring withdrew most of his forces to the area around Mount Etna in an attempt to hold open the escape route to Messina and eventually Italy itself. Thus the way lay open for the Allied advance. Montgomery paused to regroup before being held up around Mount Etna by Kesselring's crack troops. Further west, Patton's Seventh Army crashed through weak Italian resistance and, on 22 July, captured Palermo on Sicily's northern coast.

Now both Allied armies drove on Messina, with the battle turning into something of a race to capture the port city. Patton's drive, though, quickly slowed as he now faced German defenders. Leaving delaying forces behind, on 11 August, the Germans began their withdrawal across the narrow Straits of Messina. Although the Allies attempted a number of amphibious landings to cut off the retreating Germans – and the fact that, in the face of crumbling resistance, on 17 August Patton won the race to Messina – Kesselring's forces made good their escape.

THE INVASION OF ITALY

The fall of Sicily had wide-ranging repercussions. On 24 July, King Victor Emmanuel III dismissed Mussolini, placing him under arrest and naming Marshal Pietro Badoglio as the new head of the Italian government. Badoglio quickly began to seek a separate peace with the Allies. Expecting treachery, the Germans rushed additional forces to Italy to face an imminent Allied invasion. In addition, German special forces rescued Mussolini from his mountaintop prison. Hitler installed Mussolini as the puppet ruler of a new Fascist state in Northern Italy. All the while, Badoglio walked a tightrope – hoping to complete a secret deal to join the Allies, while avoiding Hitler's wrath. Controversially, the Allies relented in their call for unconditional surrender, and Italy exited the Axis and joined the Allies on 3 September 1943.

On the same day, Montgomery's Eighth Army crossed the Straits of Messina and landed on the toe of the Italian boot with no resistance. Six days later, additional elements of Montgomery's force landed at Taranto, again unopposed. The main Allied force, though, landed at Salerno, south of Naples, and faced a stern test. Here the Anglo-American Fifth Army under General Mark Clark landed on a beach surrounded by mountains which offered the Germans strong defensive positions. The German 29th Division launched a strong counterattack. Nearly driven back into the sea, Clark's force held at a last-ditch defensive line with rear echelon troops. Finally, after six days of bitter fighting, Clark's Fifth

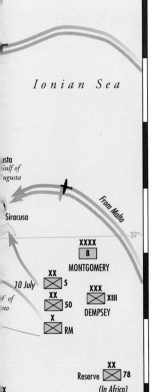

OPERATION HUSKY

On 10 July 1943, the Allies launched Operation Husky, the invasion of Sicily, with Patton's Seventh Army landing in the area of Licata in southern Sicily and Montgomery's Eighth Army landing near Siracusa.

With the Italian forces crumbling, the Axis commander in the area, Kesselring, realized that the defence of Sicily was hopeless. Montgomery, driving northwards on Messina, forced Kesselring to concentrate his crack German divisions in the rugged terrain of Mount Etna in an effort to preserve his only escape route. In the south, Patton, who was only supposed to provide Montgomery with flank protection, faced weak Italian resistance.

As a result, Patton thundered northwards and, on 22 July, captured Palermo. Chafing at Montgomery's slow advance, Patton now swung to the west and towards Messina. Patton, though, soon fell afoul of successive German lines of defence, which slowed the breakneck speed of his advance.

With the noose tightening, Kesselring received belated permission to evacuate Axis forces from Sicily and, only narrowly avoiding several Allied attempts to turn his flank, on 16 August made good his escape – a single day before Patton won his personal race with Montgomery and captured the town of Messina.

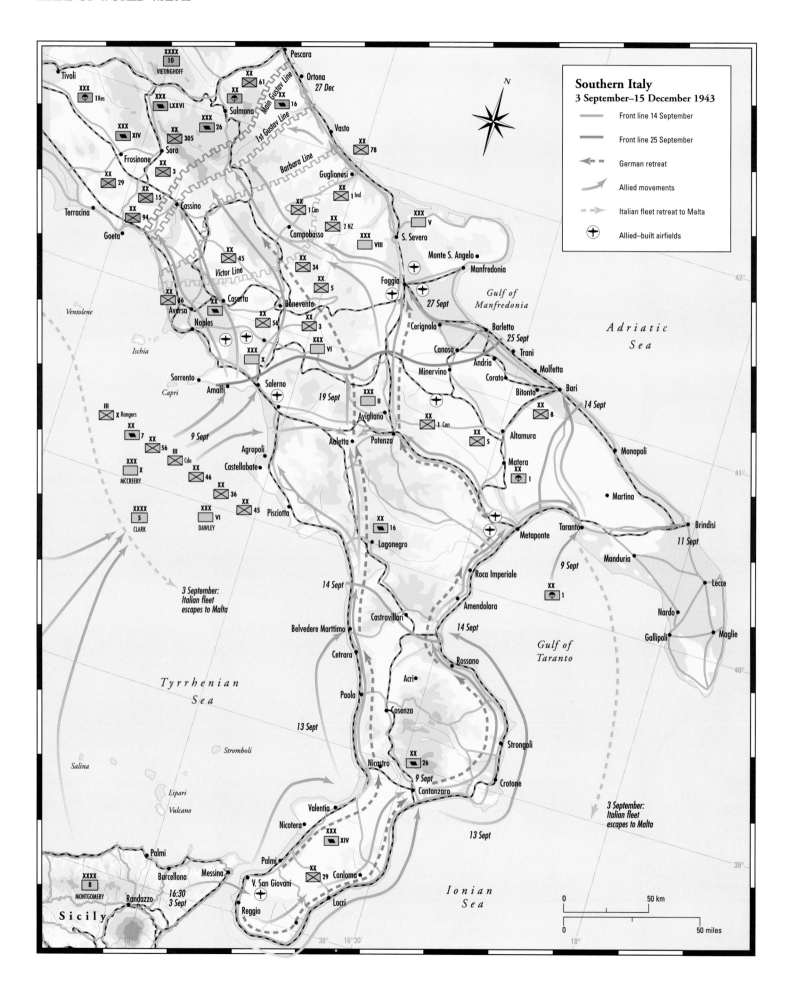

Southern Italy
3 September–15 December 1943

Front line 14 September	
Front line 25 September	
German retreat	
Allied movements	
Italian fleet retreat to Malta	
Allied–built airfields	

ITALY INVADED

On 3 September 1943, Montgomery's Eighth Army crossed the Straits of Messina, meeting little resistance from the Axis forces. Six days later, additional elements of the Eighth Army landed at Taranto – with similar results.

On 9 September, units of General Mark Clark's Fifth Army undertook Operation Avalanche, the landings on the Italian peninsula at Salerno. Many in the US command structure had advocated landings north of the critical city of Naples, but were overruled due to the fact that Salerno was within reach of Allied air cover based in Sicily.

A ring of hills surrounding Salerno, however, were to provide cover for the German 29th *Panzergrenadier* Division, which struck hard at the Fifth Army, almost causing the failure of the entire operation. Only after six days of bitter struggle, and the arrival of reinforcements from the American 82nd Airborne Division, did the tide begin to turn towards the Allies.

Finally forced from their defences, the German Tenth Army withdrew northwards to a series of holding positions in the rugged river valleys of the Apennine Mountains.

In a struggle reminiscent of World War I, Allied forces slogged northwards against mounting German resistance until they reached the Gustav Line – a prepared position so powerful that the Germans planned to hold the Allied armies there indefinitely.

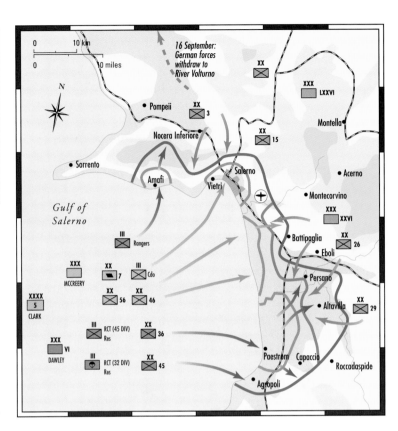

Landings at Salerno
9–16 September 1943

- German front line 14 Sept.
- Allied front line 11 Sept.
- Allied front line 9 Sept.
- German movements
- British movements
- U.S. movement

Army linked up with Montgomery advancing from the south.

Slowly the German forces gave ground, fighting a desperate rearguard action among the rocky defiles of the Apennine Mountains. The German Tenth Army, led by Heinrich Vietinghoff, used a series of delaying positions and fought with great skill, slowing the Allied advance to a crawl. At the same time, the Germans were busy preparing the Gustav Line, anchored on the chokepoint at Monte Cassino. Allied forces slowly encountered these formidable defences, and the attack ground to an exhausted halt, with the Fifth Army alone having suffered 90,000 casualties to the fighting and the poor weather.

Below: US troops of the 38th Infantry Division, 3rd Infantry Regiment come ashore from their landing craft on a beach near Salerno. These troops are reinforcements – the original Allied landings at Salerno met with stiff resistance from the German 29th *Panzergrenadier* Division.

ANZIO

In January 1944, Allied forces struck across the Liri Valley towards Monte Cassino – the hub of the German defensive network known as the Gustav Line – in an attempt to draw attention away from the impending landings at Anzio.

The landings, which took place on 22 January, surprised the German defenders. With the agreement of General Mark Clark, however, the landing forces did not seize their advantage, but instead chose to strengthen defences. Having missed their chance to score a major victory, Allied forces had to concentrate instead on direct assaults against the mighty Gustav Line.

CASSINO

The German position on the Gustav Line overlooked any attempt by the Allies to advance across the low-lying Liri Valley. Monte Cassino, topped by an historic medieval abbey, formed the linchpin of the defensive network. In January, partly to divert attention from Anzio, Clark's forces attacked across the Liri – but came to grief on the strong German defences. Convinced that the Germans were using the abbey as an observation post, in February a raid by 200 bombers destroyed the historic structure, but a follow-up ground attack failed.

Finally, in mid-May 1944, the Allies gathered 20 divisions for a major assault, managing to evict the German defenders from their defensive bastion.

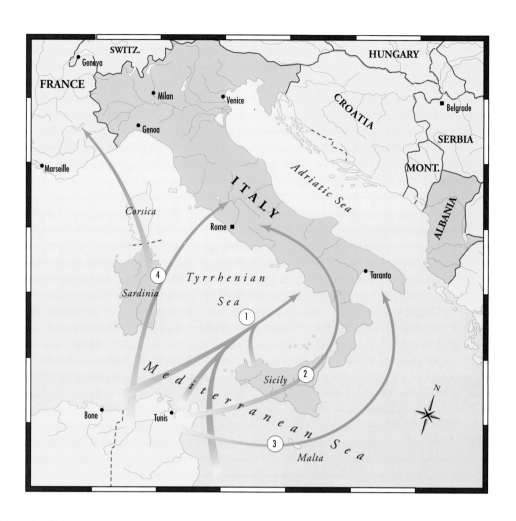

THE GUSTAV LINE

At the end of 1943, a major command shift took place in the Allied forces in Italy. In preparation for the invasion of Normandy, Eisenhower and Montgomery left the theatre, leaving Alexander in command of Allied forces in Italy, while General Oliver Leese took command of the Eighth Army. The German defences along the Gustav Line were daunting, including gun pits, concrete bunkers, barbed wire and minefields, manned by 15 German divisions as part of the Tenth Army. Against the nearly impregnable defences, Alexander chose a two-pronged offensive, involving an attack by Mark Clark's Fifth Army across the Liri Valley against Monte Cassino, the linchpin of the German defensive system.

Although Clark did not achieve a breakthrough, he did succeed in pinning the German defenders in place. On 22 January 1944, the second phase of the Allied offensive, a landing at Anzio behind the Gustav Line, caught the Germans by surprise. In Operation Shingle, the US VI Corps of the Fifth Army, under the command of General John Lucas, landed at Anzio against very light opposition. The plan called for the VI Corps to move out to the Alban Hills, some 30km (20 miles) inland, to flank the defenders of the Gustav Line, causing their withdrawal. Convinced, though, that the crafty Kesselring would react quickly, Clark allowed Lucas to halt to build up defensive strength before moving inland. The considerable pause gave the Germans the opportunity to react. Gathering nine divisions, against only three divisions located at Anzio, the Germans halted the cautious Anzio advance, laying siege to the unfortunate Allied soldiers holding the beachhead. The chance for a quick overthrow of the Gustav Line had been lost.

Operational Plans
1942–43

1. Operation Avalanche (US Fifth Army)
2. Operation Baytown (British Eighth Army)
3. Operation Slapstick (British Eighth Army)
4. Other projected moves

With the failure of the Allied advance at Anzio, Alexander had once again to rely on more direct methods. Further attempts to cross the Liri and Rapido rivers towards Cassino met with costly failure. In February, believing that the Germans were using the historic monastery at Monte Cassino as a vantage point, he ordered 200 bombers to destroy the building. However, the Germans – who had not been in the monastery – now occupied and fortified its ruins, making their defensive position stronger than ever before, and they repulsed an Indian assault on their position. By 20th February the attack had failed. In March, Alexander attempted to use air power to his advantage, as some 500 bombers laid waste to Cassino itself. Allied forces hoped to advance into the ruined town before the Germans could react, but were repulsed, with heavy losses.

With repeated failures at the Gustav Line, and the impending invasion of Normandy, Supreme Allied Command began to question the wisdom of the bloody fighting in Italy. However, Alexander argued his case, receiving permission for one last offensive dubbed 'Operation Diadem'. First Allied bombers pounded German supply lines in Operation Strangle. Next, 20 Allied divisions, with lavish fire support, attacked seven determined but overmatched German divisions. The successful assault was a true Allied affair. Free French forces, under the command of General Alphonse Juin, struck through the most rugged terrain of the entire German defensive system, west of the Liri River. The Germans considered the terrain impassable and did little in its defence; however, the French persevered and achieved the first penetration of the Gustav Line. With their positions compromised, the Germans began to retreat, although they continued to fight a bitter rearguard action. A British unit captured the town of Cassino, while Polish forces, on 18 May, finally reached the summit of the tortuous mountain to seize the abbey itself – or rather what remained of it after the heavy fighting.

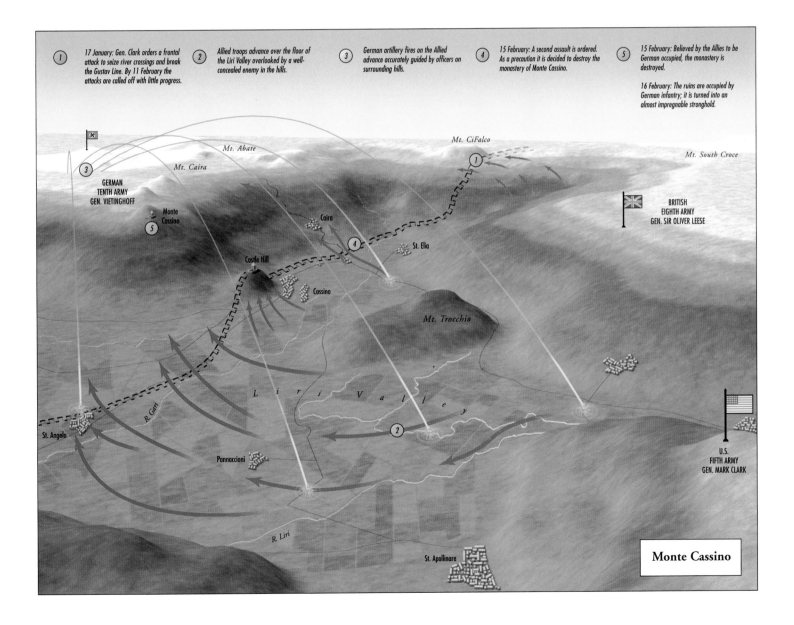

1   17 January: Gen. Clark orders a frontal attack to seize river crossings and break the Gustav Line. By 11 February the attacks are called off with little progress.

2   Allied troops advance over the floor of the Liri Valley overlooked by a well-concealed enemy in the hills.

3   German artillery fires on the Allied advance accurately guided by officers on surrounding hills.

4   15 February: A second assault is ordered. As a precaution it is decided to destroy the monastery of Monte Cassino.

5   15 February: Believed by the Allies to be German occupied, the monastery is destroyed.

16 February: The ruins are occupied by German infantry; it is turned into an almost impregnable stronghold.

Monte Cassino

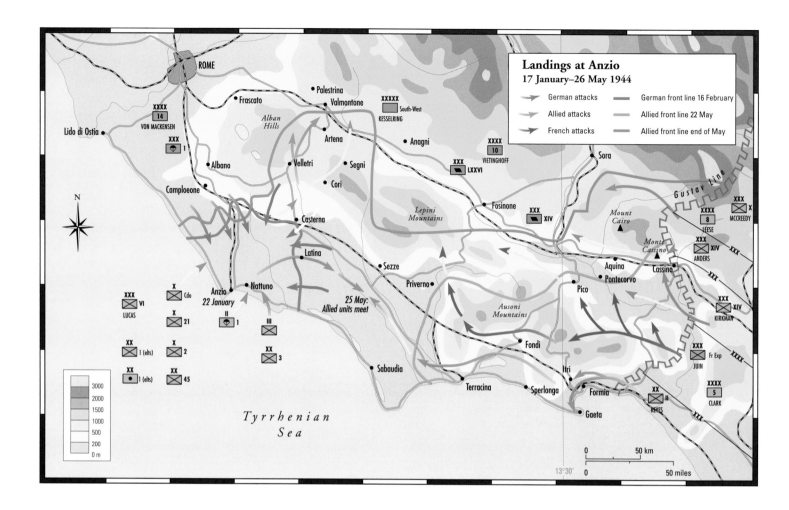

RETREAT AND THE LIBERATION OF ROME

The Allies had achieved another hard-fought victory, but again one marred by failure. Having heavily reinforced the Anzio beachhead, Alexander now ordered Clark to drive inland towards Valmontone. Seizing the critical road junction would cut off the German retreat from the Gustav Line and destroy the remnants of the Tenth Army as they struggled northwards. Clark, though, had different ideas – he wanted his American troops to have the honour of liberating the city of Rome just 53km (33 miles) to the north. Accordingly, Clark dispatched the majority of his forces northwards, while only a small contingent advanced on Valmontone. The weakness of Clark's foray to the east allowed the Germans to escape. Kesselring ordered Rome declared as an open city to prevent its destruction and, on 4 June, Clark's forces rolled in, capturing the Italian capital, but at the cost of a critical missed opportunity.

Once again Vietinghoff's Tenth Army retreated northwards, fighting skilful delaying actions in the rugged terrain. Held at arm's length by German rearguards, the Allied forces, delayed, too, by capturing important Italian cities including Leghorn and Florence, were unable to close with and destroy the harried German defenders. First halting at the Viterbo Line just north of Rome, then at the Albert Line near Perugia, the Germans again forced the Allies into difficult battles on favourable terrain. All the while, German reinforcements were streaming in from the Eastern Front as work progressed on the next major German blocking position, the Gothic Line. The Germans had succeeded in retreating 240km (150 miles) to the northern Apennine Mountains.

ALEXANDER'S SIDESHOW

With the Normandy invasion, the campaign in Italy became something of a sideshow. Alexander lost more and more of his forces to the ongoing struggle in the west. The development frustrated

MOVE NORTH

After the fall of the Gustav Line, Clark could have cut off the Germans by advancing east from Anzio. Instead he chose to move north on Rome. Declared an open city by Kesselring, on 4 June, the Italian capital fell without a struggle. It was a great propaganda victory, but it still allowed Vietinghoff's Tenth Army to escape.

The Germans held delaying positions against the Allies at the Vierbo Line and the Albert Line. During the epic 240km (150-mile) retreat, German reinforcements were arriving from the Eastern Front, and the next major defensive position north of Florence, dubbed the Gothic Line, was prepared.

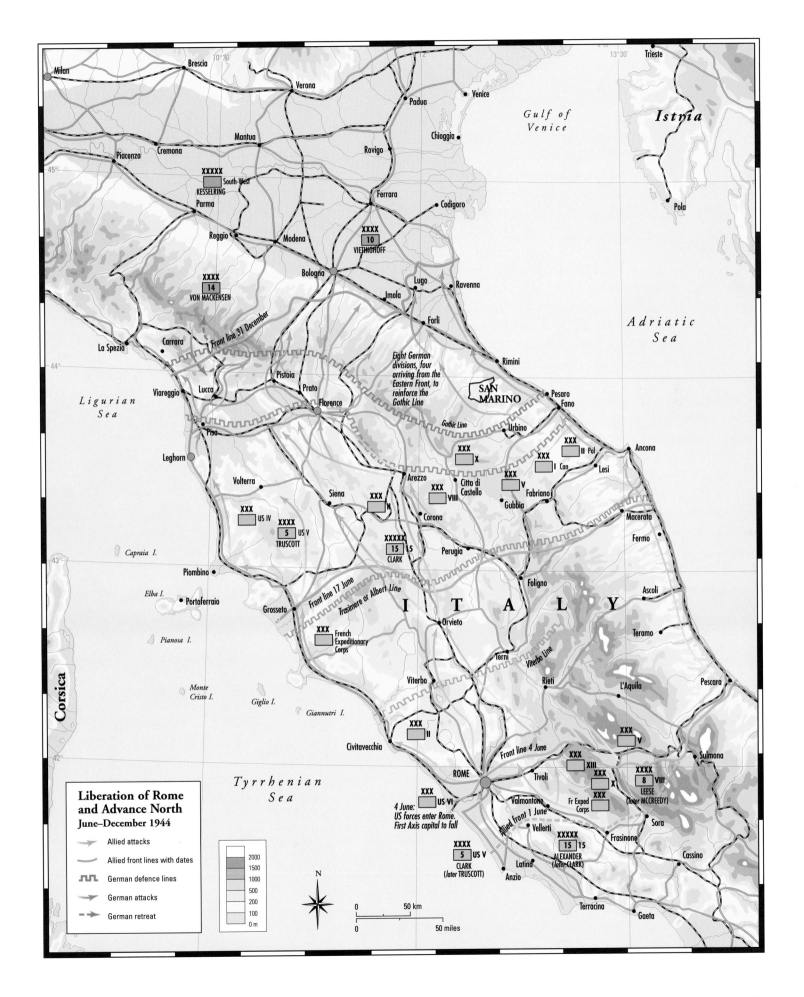

Milan
Brescia
Verona
Padua
Venice
Chioggia
Gulf of Venice
Istria
Trieste
Pola
Mantua
Cremona
Piacenza
Reggio
Parma
XXXXX South-West KESSELRING
Modena
Ferrara
Codigoro
XXXX 10 VIETINGHOFF
Bologna
Lugo
Ravenna
XXXX 14 VON MACKENSEN
Imola
Forli
Adriatic Sea
Front line 31 December
La Spezia
Carrara
Pistoia
Prato
Rimini
Eight German divisions, four arriving from the Eastern Front, to reinforce the Gothic Line
SAN MARINO
Pesaro
Fano
Ligurian Sea
Viareggio
Lucca
Pisa
Florence
Gothic Line
Urbino
XXX II Pol
Ancona
Leghorn
Volterra
Siena
Arezzo
XXX X
XXX I Can
Lesi
XXX V
Citta di Castello
Fabriano
XXX VIII
Corona
Gubbia
Macerata
XXX US IV
XXX IX
XXXX 5 US V TRUSCOTT
Fermo
Capraia I.
XXXXX 15 15 CLARK
Perugia
Foligno
Ascoli
Piombino
Elba I.
Portoferraio
Grosseto
Front line 17 June
Trasimere or Albert Line
ITALY
Orvieto
Teramo
Monte Cristo I.
Pianosa I.
Terni
Viterbo Line
Rieti
L'Aquila
Pescara
Giglio I.
Giannutri I.
XXX French Expeditionary Corps
Viterbo
Tyrrhenian Sea
XXX II
Civitavecchia
Front line 4 June
ROME
Tivoli
XXX V
Sulmona
XXX XIII
XXX X
XXXX 8 VIII LEESE (later MCCREEDY)
Corsica
4 June: US forces enter Rome. First Axis capital to fall
XXX US VI
Valmontone
Fr Exped Corps
Sora
Allied front 1 June
Velletri
XXXXX 15 15 ALEXANDER (later CLARK)
Frasinone
XXXX 5 US V CLARK (later TRUSCOTT)
Latina
Anzio
Cassino
Terracina
Gaeta

Liberation of Rome and Advance North
June–December 1944

→ Allied attacks
— Allied front lines with dates
⊓⊔ German defence lines
→ German attacks
⇢ German retreat

2000
1500
1000
500
200
100
0 m

N

0   50 km
0   50 miles

Alexander, who hoped to break the Gothic Line and conquer the remainder of Italy in 1944. He even held out hope that his forces could advance through the Alps as far as Vienna. Although his hopes were likely misguided, even with reduced forces – now representing more than 25 Allied nations – Alexander was able to orchestrate a breakthrough of the Gothic Line north of Florence. Despite being surprised by the speed of the Allied action and advance, the Tenth Army fought doggedly in the rugged terrain, limiting the Allied breakthrough. Finally, the combination of strong German defences, exhaustion, and the onset of winter weather served to halt the Allied advance.

VICTORY

In 1945, Allied forces in Italy possessed an overwhelming numerical and material advantage. On 9 April 1945, after a three-month lull, the British Eighth Army – now commanded by General Richard McReery – struck German defences outside Bologna on the Reno and Senio rivers. In addition, British forces launched an amphibious operation across Lake Comacchio, catching the Germans by surprise and threatening the flank of their defences. In the space of only 10 days, the Eighth Army had broken through the last major German defences and into the open lands beyond. Further west, Clark's Fifth Army rushed northwards towards Parma.

With the situation desperate, Vietinghoff requested to withdraw his beleaguered forces to the natural defensive line of the Po River. Hitler, however, refused. Realizing the critical nature of the situation, though, Vietinghoff disobeyed Hitler's orders – but it was too late. Aware of German intentions, Allied armour hurtled towards the Po, reaching the river in advance of the retreating Germans and finally cutting them off. The victory was complete and the German defence of Italy crumbled. Realizing the war in Italy was over, Vietinghoff sought terms from the Allies and, on 2 May 1945, agreed to unconditional surrender.

As the situation fell apart, Mussolini – the once mighty dictator who had of late only served as Hitler's puppet in a fictitious Fascist state – fled for exile in Switzerland. Tired of war and disgusted by German domination of their country, Italian partisans haunted the rugged approaches to the Alps. On 28 April, a group of partisans captured Mussolini and his mistress, Clara Petacci, and shot them to death.

The war was over, but the question remained: was the fighting in Italy worth the effort and sacrifice? Obviously Churchill had been mistaken in the notion that Italy represented the 'soft underbelly' of Axis Europe. There had been no breakout from Italy, and the war there was to have only a marginal effect on overall German strategy. Some historians claim that the Allied effort in Italy did serve to divert valuable German resources from the Western Front. However, at what cost? The invasion of Sicily – or perhaps a move into southern Italy only – would have diverted considerable German forces at a far lesser cost to the Allies. The move northwards by the Allies had enabled a lesser German force to make splendid use of the close and rugged country. In the end, Allied resources in Italy would have been better utilized elsewhere.

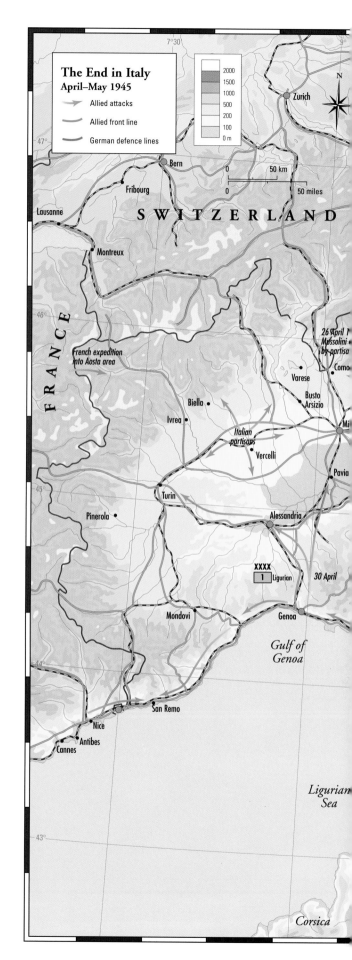

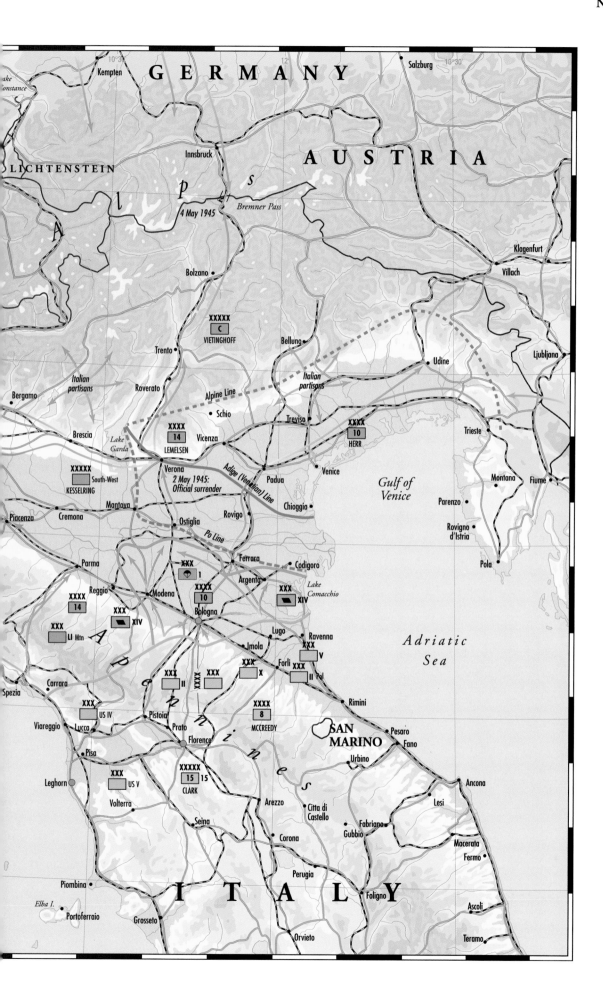

ALLIED VICTORY

Although the Germans had intended to hold for the winter at the Gothic Line, the speed of the Allied advance in September forced a breach in the powerful defensive position. Surprised but still an effective fighting force, the German defenders fell back in the rugged terrain and held south of Bologna at the onset of winter.

The Allies struck again on 9 April 1945. In the east, the Eighth Army, which had chased the Germans ever since El Alamein, broke through near Bologna, while the Americans shattered the German defences further west. Outnumbered and running short on supplies, Vietinghoff sought permission to withdraw his forces behind the natural defensive line of the Po River. Divorced from reality, though, Hitler refused – forcing Vietinghoff to take matters into his own hands.

It was, however, too late for further military action. The German Tenth Army had been destroyed and Vietinghoff could only ask for terms of surrender. On 2 May 1945, the Germans surrendered unconditionally outside Verona – and the war in Italy came to an end.

Some American forces drove northwards to link with their colleagues advancing south through Austria, joining up at the Brenner Pass in the last few days of the war itself.

The Eastern Front

The crushing of the Soviet Union and Communism had long been one of Hitler's ambitions. Although briefly distracted by events in the Balkans, on 22 June 1941 he unleashed a vast and powerful army to conquer more land for Germany. Unfortunately for Nazi Germany, the Russians were not crushed, and a mere four years later Soviet forces would occupy the Reich's capital.

The war in Eastern Europe will forever be associated with the bitter battles and horrendous casualty rates sustained in the fighting between Germany and the Soviet Union that followed Hitler's attack on Russia in June 1941. The first fighting in this theatre, however, took place just over six months prior to Operation Barbarossa, with the Italian invasion of Greece, which marked the commencement of the war in the Balkans.

The peace settlements after the Great War had given Transylvania to Romania, despite the fact that there were some two million members of the Magyar race (the Sicules) living in the region. The government in Budapest was well aware that the Sicules wished to remain Hungarian and, in the summer of 1940, made efforts to persuade the Romanians to return the province to them. Diplomacy proved unworkable, and it seemed as though the two nations would go to war. This was not to Hitler's liking, as he did not wish to see access to vital oil supplies in Romania being threatened by a conflict. The Axis powers offered to mediate, and appeared to have reached a compromise: Romania retained western Transylvania, while the areas occupied by the Sicules returned to Hungarian control. Regrettably for the Romanians, this meant that three million of them now found themselves under Hungarian rule. Resentment in Romania led to the Prime Minister, General Ion Antonescu, orchestrating the abdication of King Carol II and his replacement by his son, Prince Michael. Antonescu then requested military aid from Germany, and Hitler was only too happy to send troops, who began arriving in October 1940.

In itself, this was not enough to start a war. The first phase of the fighting in the Balkans began as a result of Mussolini's hubris – irritated that Hitler had not told him about the occupation of Romania, he decided to demonstrate his importance by invading Greece. Not for the first time, his generals were horrified; when he found out about the plan, so was Hitler. He travelled to Italy to try to talk Mussolini out of the invasion, but when he arrived on 28 October he was met by a jubilant *Duce*, who told him that his troops had crossed the Greek frontier that morning. Sadly for Mussolini, his troops fared badly – a Greek counterattack pushed into Albania, and by the end of the year there was little sign that there would be an early Italian victory; worse still for the Axis powers, British forces landed in Crete and Lemnos, and the Royal Air Force (RAF) was sent to the Peloponnese to provide air support.

This was to prove an irritating distraction for Hitler, who had no desire to see the opening of a Balkan front while he was in the midst of planning for the conquest of the Soviet Union. Although Hitler and Stalin's non-aggression pact had held, there was no disguising the fact that it was, as Churchill remarked, 'an unnatural act' between two bitterly opposed ideologies. Even while Britain appeared to be on the brink of defeat, Hitler's thoughts were focused well away from the United Kingdom – on 31 July 1940, he had told his generals that he intended to wipe out Russia. Equally, there can be little doubt that Stalin knew that he would, at some point, have to fight against Nazi Germany. This unreal atmosphere persisted until June 1941, when Hitler's great plan was enacted. At the time, Hitler was at the height of his power; when he said that Russia would be utterly defeated by the autumn, his success up to that time meant that there was little reason to disbelieve him.

Left: Soldiers of the Wehrmacht during the first snowfalls of winter 1941. Hitler and his general staff had expected the Soviet campaign to be completed before winter set in; however, the late start to the invasion brought about by the diversion in the Balkans in April 1941 meant that the German armies were unable to reach Moscow in time. As a consequence, many German soldiers, ill equipped for the harsh conditions, suffered frostbite from the extreme cold of the Russian winter. A special drive to collect winter clothing had to be launched in Germany to provide for the exposed troops.

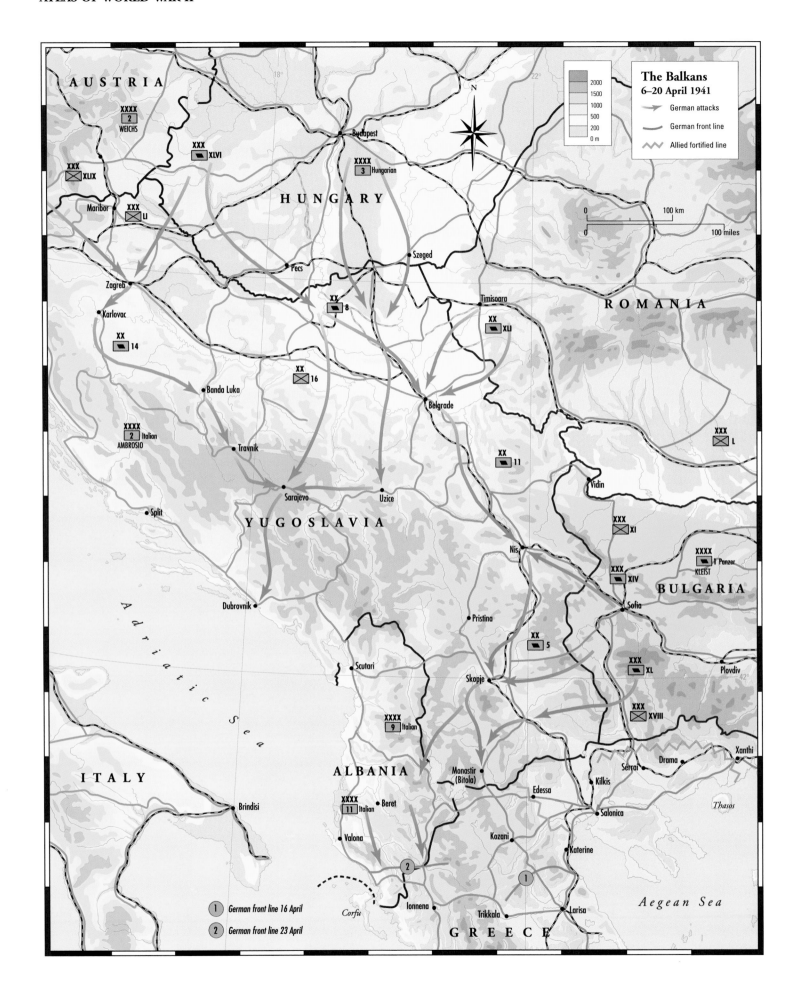

The Balkans
6–20 April 1941

German attacks
German front line
Allied fortified line

2000
1500
1000
500
200
0 m

N

0   100 km

0   100 miles

AUSTRIA

XXXX
2
WEICHS

XXX
XLVI

XXX
XLIX

Maribor

XXX
LI

Budapest

XXXX
3   Hungarian

HUNGARY

Szeged

Pecs

ROMANIA

Timisoara

XXX
XLI

Zagreb

Karlovac

XX
14

XX
8

XX
16

Belgrade

XXX
L

Banda Luka

XXXX
2   Italian
AMBROSIO

Travnik

Sarajevo

Uzice

XX
11

Vidin

Split

YUGOSLAVIA

XXX
XI

Nis

XXX
XIV

XXXX
T Panzer
KLEIST

BULGARIA

Dubrovnik

A d r i a t i c   S e a

Pristina

XX
5

XXX
XL

Plovdiv

Scutari

Skopje

Sofia

XXX
XVIII

ITALY

XXXX
9   Italian

ALBANIA

Monastir
(Bitola)

Edessa

Xanthi

Drama

Serrai

Kilkis

Brindisi

XXXX
11   Italian

Beret

Valona

Kozani

Salonica

Thasos

Katerine

2

1

Corfu

Ionnena

Trikkala

Larisa

A e g e a n   S e a

GREECE

1   German front line 16 April

2   German front line 23 April

YUGOSLAVIA AND GREECE

Troops for the invasion of Yugoslavia formed up in Romania, Bulgaria and Germany. A large force rolled over the border early on the morning of 6 April 1941. Simultaneously, the Luftwaffe launched a massive air assault on Belgrade, in which some 17,000 civilians were killed.

Within a week, German forces had covered more than 300 miles (480km), reaching the city of Belgrade on 13 April. Sarajevo fell two days later, and the Yugoslavs surrendered on 17 April, although much of the Yugoslav army continued to fight a bitter guerrilla war against the occupiers.

The attack on Greece was to coincide with that on Yugoslavia. At 05:15 on 6 April 1941, German forces crossed into Greece. The Greeks held out vigorously; however, although the German advance was slowed, it could not be stopped. By 11 April, the Germans had come into contact with the Anglo–Greek force under Field Marshal Sir Henry Maitland Wilson.

The British had only 100 tanks against 500 or more German panzers, and they were forced back. The British troops were evacuated to Crete, and Greece surrendered on 21 April.

An airborne attack against Crete was launched on 25 April. German paratroops suffered horrendous casualties, but the Germans quickly gained a foothold. On 27 April, British evacuation of the island began.

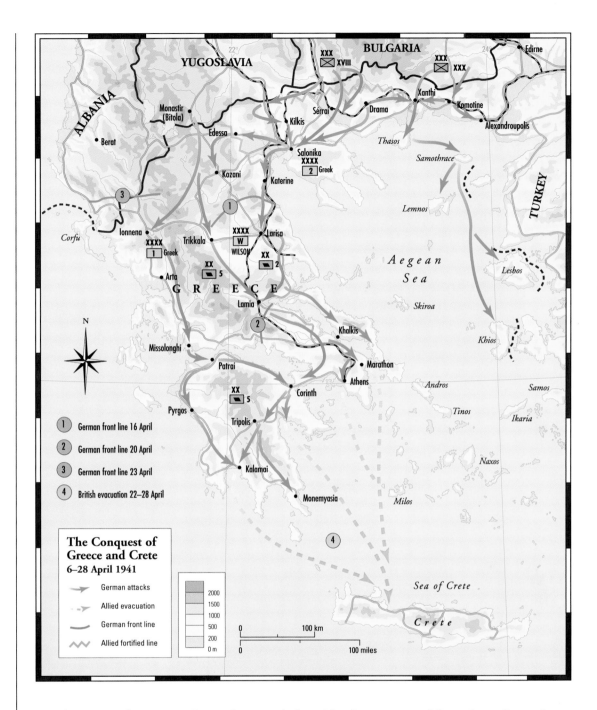

The war on the Eastern Front, then, might be said to have stemmed from the unfettered egos of two dictators. A mixture of overconfidence, delusion and vanity set them upon the path that led to the destruction of their regimes.

THE BALKANS

The lack of Italian success in the Balkans convinced Hitler of the need to assist his ally or otherwise risk the Axis being embarrassed by Mussolini's failure. Hitler ordered his generals to plan for an invasion of Greece for March 1941. The plan was complicated by the fact that Yugoslavia lay in the path of the invasion; however, the government in Belgrade was painfully aware of the fact that three of its neighbours claimed parts of its territory and, further, that antagonizing the Germans might prompt them to assist in the dismemberment of the country. The Regent, Prince Paul, joined the Tripartite Pact, in effect allying with Germany, but this act provoked an anti-German coup just two days later.

The new anti-German government was well aware of the threat it faced, and it made determined efforts to seek support from Moscow as a potential protector against Nazi aggression. Negotiations produced a treaty of friendship between the Soviet Union and Yugoslavia, signed on 5 April, but this was almost worthless. It did not guarantee military assistance in the event of an attack on the country, and, more pertinently, almost before the ink had dried on the document, German forces had launched their attack.

On 6 April 1941, the German assault on Yugoslavia opened with bombing raids against Belgrade, while German armour pushed across the border. The defenders were unable to resist the weight of the German attack and were quickly driven back. On 17 April, the position was hopeless, and the Yugoslav army surrendered.

Below: A German StuG III self-propelled assault gun in the shadow of Athen's Acropolis. Although the intervention in the Balkans on Mussolini's behalf was an inconvenience for Hitler's plans for the Soviet Union, it did once more prove the supposed invincibility of the German war machine and the blitzkrieg. The high cost of capturing Crete, however, convinced Hitler that paratroops had no place in modern warfare, and he forbade their future use.

BARBAROSSA

The German plan for Operation Barbarossa involved three Army Groups (North, South and Centre), with the bulk of the forces concentrated in Army Groups North and Centre.

Army Group Centre, which contained around half the German armour, was to shatter Soviet forces in Belorussia before turning to assist Army Group North in the drive on Leningrad. Army Group South, meanwhile, was to deal with Soviet forces in the Ukraine, attacking from Romania in a drive to the River Dnieper. Once destruction of the Soviet Army had been completed, phase two of the operation would see an attack on Moscow.

The invasion began with air attacks against key Soviet targets such as supply dumps and airfields, and initially all went well; however, Soviet resistance continued. As their armies advanced, Hitler's generals began to press him to allow them to focus upon taking Moscow, exploiting their armoured strength to do so. They failed to persuade Hitler, who insisted that his armoured forces should move to support Army Groups North and South, even though the terrain in the north was not suitable for armoured operations.

By early September 1941, Germany's Army Group North had reached Lake Lagoda, isolating Leningrad; Army Group South, meanwhile, had succeeded in taking Kiev. Only now did Hitler finally authorize the attack on Moscow.

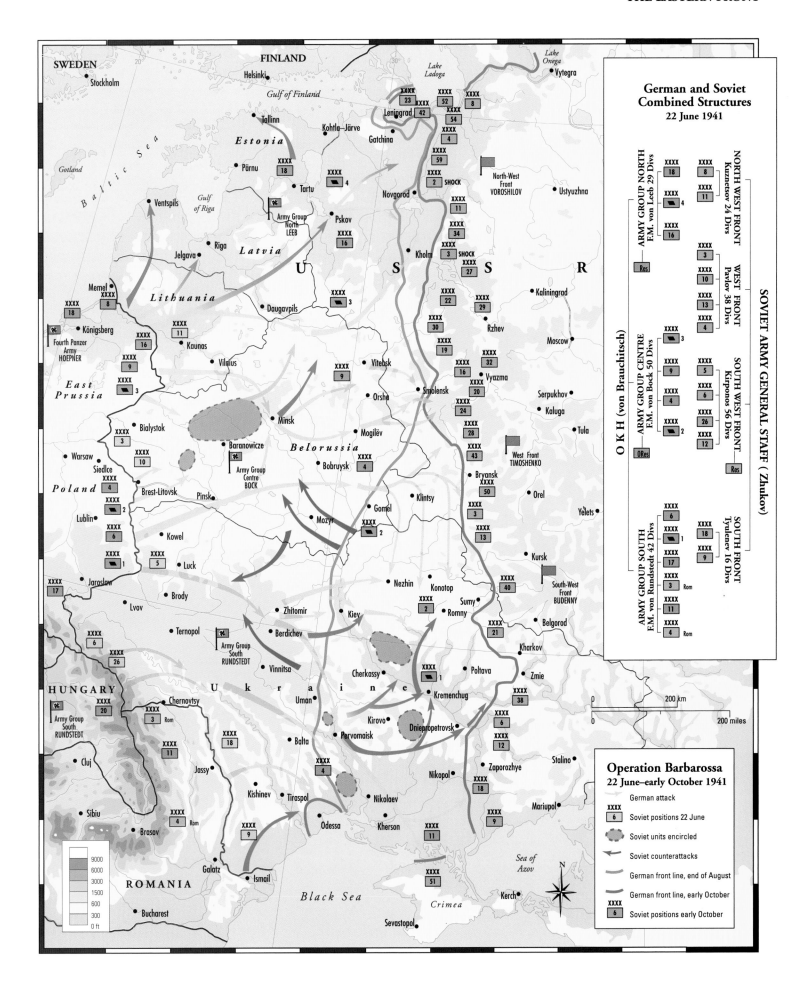

German and Soviet Combined Structures 22 June 1941

Operation Barbarossa 22 June–early October 1941

- German attack
- Soviet positions 22 June
- Soviet units encircled
- Soviet counterattacks
- German front line, end of August
- German front line, early October
- Soviet positions early October

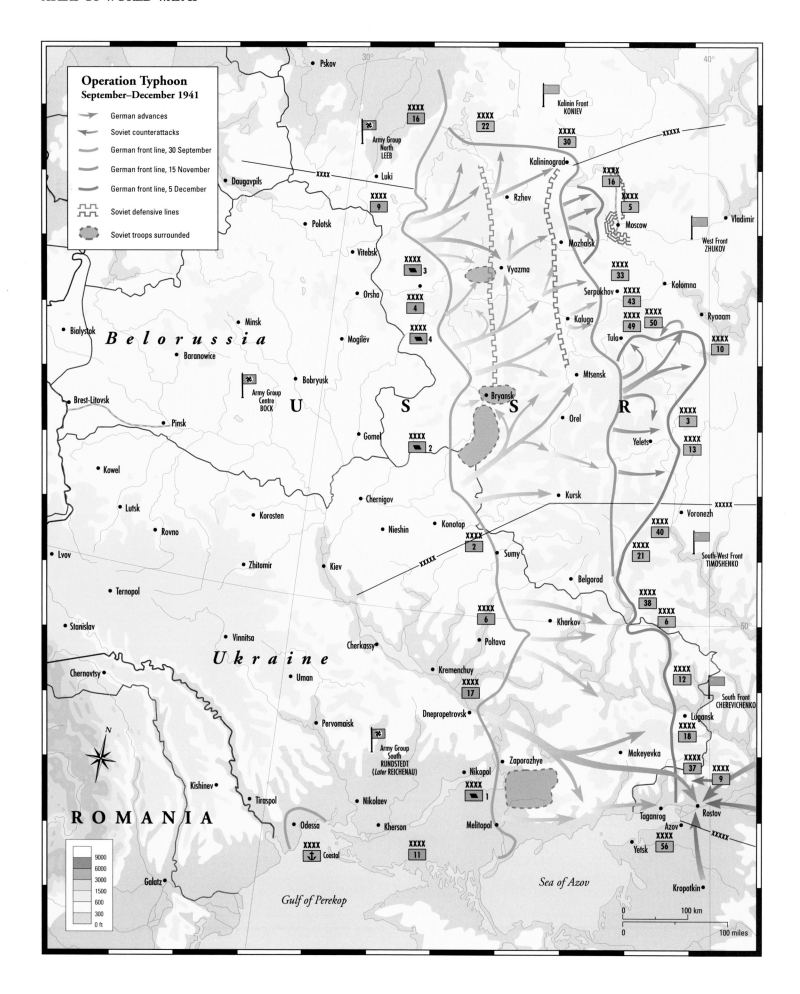

Operation Typhoon
September–December 1941

→ German advances
← Soviet counterattacks
～ German front line, 30 September
～ German front line, 15 November
～ German front line, 5 December
Soviet defensive lines
Soviet troops surrounded

Pskov

30°

40°

Kalinin Front
KONIEV

XXXX
16

XXXX
22

XXXX
30

XXXXX

Army Group
North
LEEB

Luki

Kalininograd

XXXX
16

XXXX
5

XXXX
9

Daugavpils

XXXX

Rzhev

Moscow

Vladimir

West Front
ZHUKOV

Polotsk

Mozhalsk

Vitebsk

Vyazma

XXXX
33

XXXX
3

Serpukhov

XXXX
43

Kolomna

Minsk

Orsha

XXXX
4

Kaluga

XXXX
49

XXXX
50

Ryaaam

Belorussia

Mogilëv

XXXX
4

Tula

XXXX
10

Bialystok

Baranowice

Mtsensk

Army Group
Centre
BOCK

Bobryusk

U   S   S   R

Bryansk

Orel

XXXX
3

Brest-Litovsk

Gomel

XXXX
2

Yelets

XXXX
13

Pinsk

Kowel

Chernigov

Kursk

XXXXX

Lutsk

Korosten

Nieshin

Konotop

Voronezh

Rovno

XXXX
40

Lvov

Kiev

XXXX
2

Sumy

XXXX
21

South-West Front
TIMOSHENKO

Zhitomir

Belgorod

XXXXX

Ternopol

Stanislav

Kharkov

XXXX
38

XXXX
6

Vinnitsa

Ukraine

Cherkassy

XXXX
6

Poltava

Chernovtsy

Uman

Kremenchuy

XXXX
12

XXXX
17

South Front
CHEREVICHENKO

Pervomaisk

Dnepropetrovsk

Lugansk

XXXX
18

Army Group
South
RUNDSTEDT
(Later REICHENAU)

Zaporozhye

Makeyevka

XXXX
37

Kishinev

Nikopol

XXXX
9

ROMANIA

Tiraspol

XXXX
1

Nikolaev

Melitopol

Taganrog

Rostov

Odessa

Kherson

Azov

XXXXX

XXXX
⚓ Coastal

XXXX
11

XXXX
56

Yetsk

Galatz

Sea of Azov

Kropotkin

9000
6000
3000
1500
600
300
0 ft

0   100 km

0   100 miles

Gulf of Perekop

N

OPERATION TYPHOON

While the failure to hold Smolensk was a blow to the Russians, the rigorous defence of the city had delayed the German advance on Moscow. This bought time for the Russians to evacuate industry and key workers from the area, sending them far to the east, safely away from the war zone.

After refusing to make Moscow his priority at the outset, Hitler issued orders on 2 October 1941 that the Soviet capital should be taken. The intensity of fighting increased as the Germans approached the capital, for both sides had come to realize the importance of the factor of time for their plans.

For the Germans, it was imperative that they seize Moscow before the winter set in, while the Russians needed to ensure that the government could be evacuated before the Germans were able to capture the capital, while bringing in new troops from Siberia.

Two German assaults against Moscow failed, and the early onset of winter meant that the practicality of continuing the attack all but disappeared. Hitler gave instructions for a temporary suspension of operations on 8 December. This marked the end of Barbarossa.

While the Germans had succeeded in inflicting massive damage upon the Russians, they had not captured their main objectives; nor were the Soviets on the brink of defeat. It was quite clear that a rapid German victory was no longer possible.

Above: Endless lines of Russian prisoners seen from a German Storch observation aircraft. So many prisoners were taken by the Germans during Operation Barbarossa that they struggled to cope with them, and some prisoners were allowed to escape and form the partisan bands which would subsequently prove a significant thorn in Germany's side. Many prisoners were used as slave labour for German industrial projects.

While the Yugoslavs were under attack, the first German units entered Greece. Greek and British forces fought hard, but could not hold the enemy back. On 19 April, the decision to evacuate the British Expeditionary Force was taken and, two days later, the Greek army surrendered. The Germans then moved on to Crete to deny the RAF a base from which it could attack the Romanian airfields. An airborne invasion of the island began on 25 April and, after two days of heavy fighting, the British began to evacuate. With the removal of the threat from the Balkans, the scene was now set for the German attack on Russia.

OPERATION BARBAROSSA

Hitler's desire to attack the Soviet Union was finally realized on 22 June 1941. The invasion was an enormous affair. Two armies each some three million strong faced one another, with a potential area of operations of vast scale. Despite this, the Germans did have some advantages. The first was the age-old benefit of surprise: when the attack occurred, it was some time before Stalin could believe that the non-aggression pact had been brought to a clear end, making it difficult for the Russian forces to react as quickly as they might have wished. Furthermore, Stalin's brutal purging of the Red Army in the years prior to Operation Barbarossa meant that it had lost most of its best leaders; as a result, many senior commanders were less than adept, and the performance of their troops brought this fact into stark relief. Finally, the German troops had much more experience than their opponents.

This was not enough, however, to guarantee success. The German High Command (*Oberkommando der Wehrmacht*; OKW) was well aware that the Russians could, if given the chance, simply melt away into the vast Russian interior, and wait for the depredations of the winter to come to their assistance. To overcome this, it was clear that a rapid advance would be required to guarantee victory. There was a considerable difference of opinion between Hitler and his High Command as to how success could be best achieved. While the OKW saw a rapid thrust upon Moscow as the obvious solution, Hitler preferred to destroy Soviet forces in the Baltic and to achieve the symbolic victory of taking Leningrad, the birthplace of the Bolshevik revolution. Despite protests, Hitler would not be moved, and the main effort of the invasion was to be directed against Leningrad; only after success was achieved here would the Führer permit the focus of the attack to be turned upon Moscow.

When Operation Barbarossa began, it appeared that Hitler's confidence was well founded. The Soviet forces suffered enormous losses, and the advance was rapid. However, despite their swift advance in the early days, by mid-July the Germans were facing difficulties in supplying their forward troops, while there were many pockets of Soviet forces as yet undefeated all along the line of advance. As well as increased supply problems, the Germans faced worrying casualty levels – by the end of August 1941, 10 per cent of the Field Army had been killed, wounded or gone missing, while the slow rate of replacement meant that the army was now 200,000 men below strength. By September, it was clear that the Soviets had learned from the utter catastrophe that had befallen them in June and July, and it was clear that defeating them would be a more difficult task than Hitler had first appreciated.

OPERATION TYPHOON

On 6 September 1941, Hitler issued Directive No. 35, making Moscow the next objective. The bulk of the panzer forces would concentrate under Army Group Centre, but it would take the remainder of the month for them to regroup. The concept underpinning Operation Typhoon was familiar. Armour would penetrate deep into enemy lines, encircling Soviet forces, which would then be destroyed by the infantry armies. While this sounded simple enough, conditions in Russia were problematic. The autumn rains meant that the Russian road system (such as it was) became impassable; this in turn meant that rapid movement of armour was all but impossible, while even the horse-drawn transport upon which the German army was dependent was severely inconvenienced. Although there would be a brief opportunity to move between the end of the rains and the onset of winter, this offered little to the Germans: their planning was based upon the assumption that the Russians would have just 60 divisions left at that point in the campaign, when they in fact had 212 (even though fewer than 100 could be considered fully operational).

As well as the benefits afforded the Soviets by the weather, Stalin's conviction that Japan was far more likely to attack the Americans than the Soviet Union meant that he felt confident enough to move some of his experienced divisions from the Far East. Also, Marshal Georgy Zhukov, previously removed from his post by Stalin and effectively exiled to the east, was given command of the battle for Moscow.

In the first days of Typhoon, the Germans enjoyed considerable success. However, Russian resistance remained determined, marked by counterattacks. Early in November, the OKW was forced to admit that it would be unable to take Moscow or to defeat the Soviet Union before 1942. To make matters worse, the Russians had carefully husbanded nine reserve divisions and launched a counteroffensive in early December. The sensible response to this was for the German forces to withdraw; Hitler, however, would not permit this, and sacked all three Army Group commanders, as well as removing a number of others.

Having lost momentum in their attack, the Germans made a new effort to reinvigorate Operation Typhoon on 4 December 1941, unaware that the Russians were putting the finishing touches to their plans for a counterattack.

The next day, Soviet forces moved forwards on the Kalinin front, while, on the West and Southwest fronts, last-minute preparations were made for attacks on 6 December. The Kalinin attack achieved almost total surprise. Despite the movement of large numbers of troops and all the preparations associated with a large offensive, German intelligence totally failed to spot any of the warning signs. The Germans were completely wrong-footed, and chaos reigned for some

COUNTERBLOW

The Soviet counterattack in early 1942 made use of infiltration tactics, rather than massed attacks against German strongpoints. Cossacks and Soviet ski units ignored the near-impassable road network, instead moving across country to outflank the Germans, who were compelled to pull back or risk being overrun.

The Germans were not helped by the appallingly cold weather conditions, as the Luftwaffe's aircraft were unable to fly, and German soldiers could not call on their usual air support. To their consternation, Soviet Frontal Aviation managed to assemble a force of some 350 aircraft – all of which had been carefully cared for in hangars, rather than left outside – and these carried out a number of attacks against German airfields, destroying as many as 1400 aircraft according to some estimates. The Red Army also enjoyed the benefits of air support for perhaps the first time in the war, and this assisted in its advance.

This was not the end to German woes, as the panzer arm began to encounter notable numbers of the T-34 tank for the first time. The T-34 was a far different beast to any enemy armour encountered to date by the Germans, for it was a match for their best tanks. Although the T-34s were not yet available in large numbers, the warning signs were clear: the German armoured superiority seen in the blitzkrieg since 1939 was under serious threat.

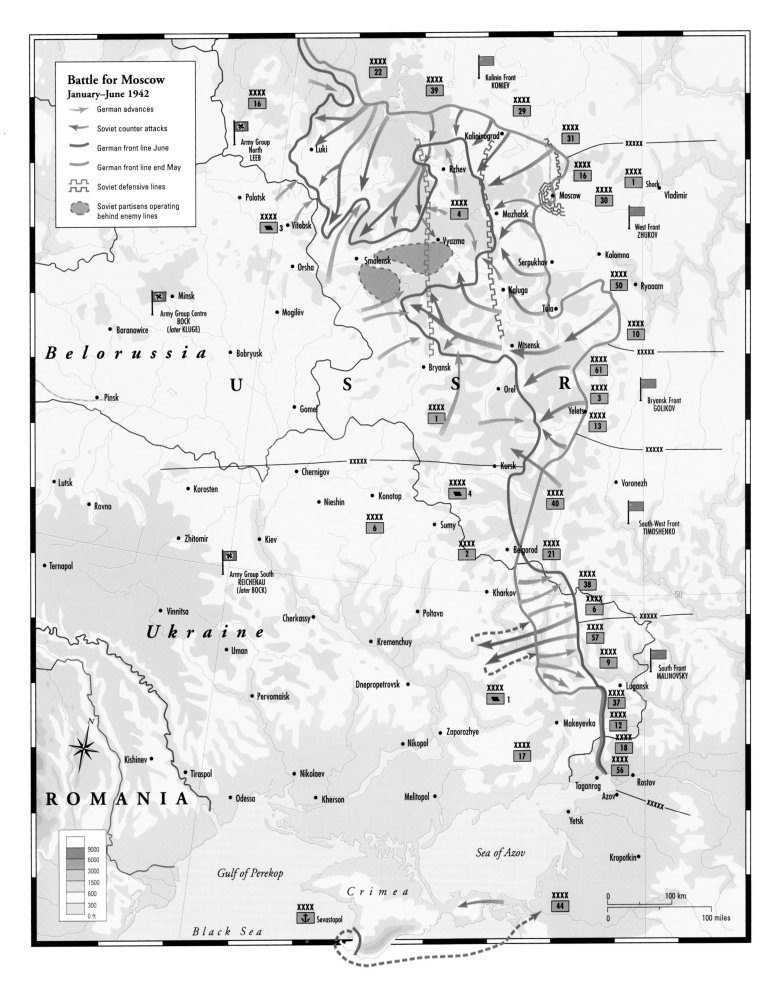

Battle for Moscow
January–June 1942

→ German advances

← Soviet counter attacks

〰 German front line June

〰 German front line end May

⌐⌐ Soviet defensive lines

▨ Soviet partisans operating behind enemy lines

XXXX
22

XXXX
16

XXXX
39

Kalinin Front
KONIEV

XXXX
29

Army Group North
LEEB

Luki

Kalininograd

XXXX
31

XXXXX

Polotsk

Rzhev

XXXX
16

XXXX
1 Shock

Vladimir

XXXX
30

XXXX
3 Vitebsk

Orsha

Smolensk

Vyazma

XXXX
4

Mozhalsk

Moscow

Serpukhov

Kolomna

West Front
ZHUKOV

Minsk

Army Group Centre
BOCK
(later KLUGE)

Mogilëv

Kaluga

Tula

XXXX
50 Ryaaam

Baranowice

Bobryusk

Belorussia

U

S

S

Bryansk

Mtsensk

XXXX
10

XXXXX

Pinsk

Gomel

Orel

R

Yelets

XXXX
61

XXXX
3

Bryansk Front
GOLIKOV

XXXX
1

XXXX
13

XXXXX

Lutsk

Chernigov

XXXXX

Kursk

Voronezh

Korosten

XXXX
4

XXXX
40

Rovno

Nieshin

Konotop

South-West Front
TIMOSHENKO

XXXX
6

Zhitomir

Kiev

Sumy

XXXX
2

Belgorod

XXXX
21

Ternapol

Army Group South
REICHENAU
(later BOCK)

Ukraine

Vinnitsa

Cherkassy

Poltava

Kharkov

XXXX
38

XXXX
6

XXXXX

Uman

Kremenchuy

XXXX
57

XXXX
9

South Front
MALINOVSKY

Pervomaisk

Dnepropetrovsk

XXXX
1

Lugansk

XXXX
37

Makeyevka

XXXX
12

Kishinev

Zaporozhye

XXXX
18

Nikopol

XXXX
56

R O M A N I A

Tiraspol

Nikolaev

Melitopol

XXXX
17

Taganrog

Rostov

Odessa

Kherson

Azov

Yetsk

XXXXX

Kropotkin

9000
6000
3000
1500
600
300
0 ft

Gulf of Perekop

Sea of Azov

Crimea

Sevastopol

XXXX
44

0   100 km

0   100 miles

Black Sea

107

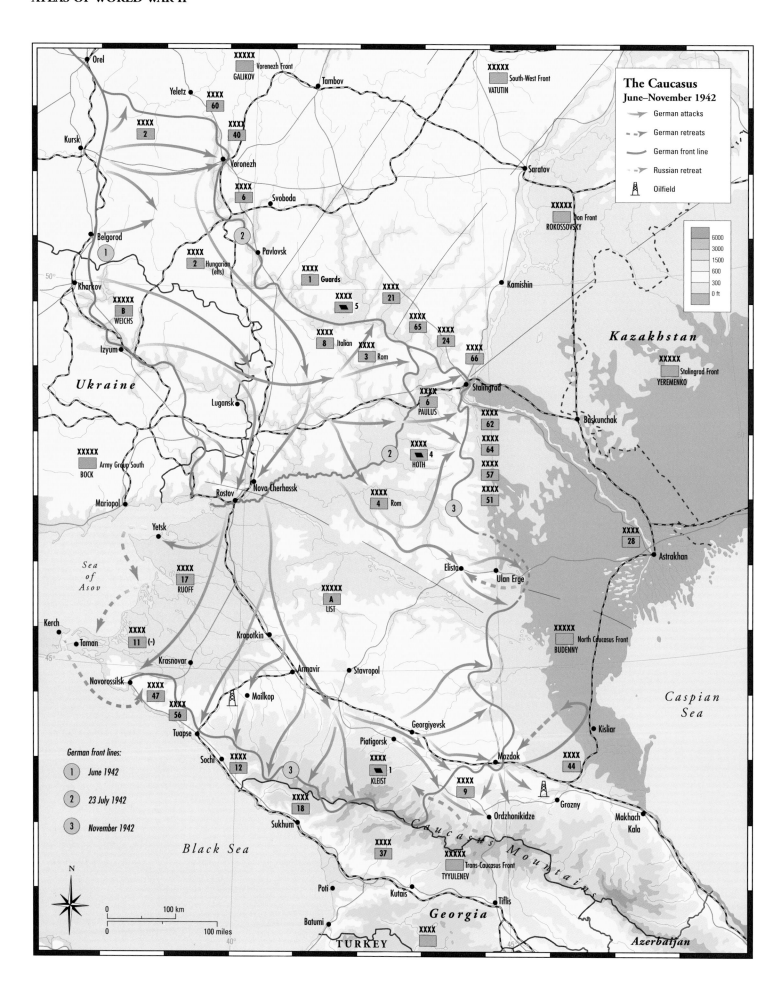

The Caucasus
June–November 1942

German attacks
German retreats
German front line
Russian retreat
Oilfield

6000
3000
1500
600
300
0 ft

Orel

XXXXX
Vorenezh Front
GALIKOV

XXXXX
South-West Front
VATUTIN

Yeletz

XXXX
60

Tambov

Saratov

XXXX
2

Kursk

XXXX
40

XXXX
6

Svoboda

Voronezh

XXXXX
Don Front
ROKOSSOVSKY

Belgorod

1

2

Pavlovsk

Kazakhstan

XXXX
2
Hungarian
(elts)

XXXX
1   Guards

Kamishin

Kharkov

XXXXX
B
WEICHS

XXXX
2

XXXX
5

XXXX
21

Izyum

XXXX
8   Italian

XXXX
65

XXXX
24

XXXX
3   Rom

XXXX
66

XXXXX
Stalingrad Front
YEREMENKO

Ukraine

Lugansk

Stalingrad

Baskunchak

XXXX
6
PAULUS

XXXX
62

XXXXX
Army Group South
BOCK

2

XXXX
4
HOTH

XXXX
64

XXXX
57

Mariopol

Rostov

Nova Cherhassk

XXXX
4   Rom

3

XXXX
51

XXXX
28

Yetsk

Astrakhan

Sea
of
Asov

XXXX
17
RUOFF

Elista

Ulan Erge

XXXXX
A
LIST

Kerch

XXXX
11 (–)

Taman

Krasnovar

Kropotkin

XXXXX
North Caucasus Front
BUDENNY

Caspian
Sea

Novorossilsk

XXXX
47

Armavir

Stavropol

XXXX
56

Tuapse

Georgiyevsk

Mailkop

Kisliar

German front lines:

1   June 1942

Sochi

XXXX
12

3

Piatigorsk

XXXX
1
KLEIST

Mozdok

XXXX
44

2   23 July 1942

XXXX
18

XXXX
9

Grozny

Makhach
Kala

3   November 1942

Sukhum

Ordzhonikidze

N

XXXX
37

XXXXX
Trans-Caucasus Front
TYYULENEV

Caucasus Mountains

Black Sea

Georgia

Poti

Kutais

Tiflis

0   100 km

0   100 miles

Batumi

TURKEY

XXXX

Azerbaijan

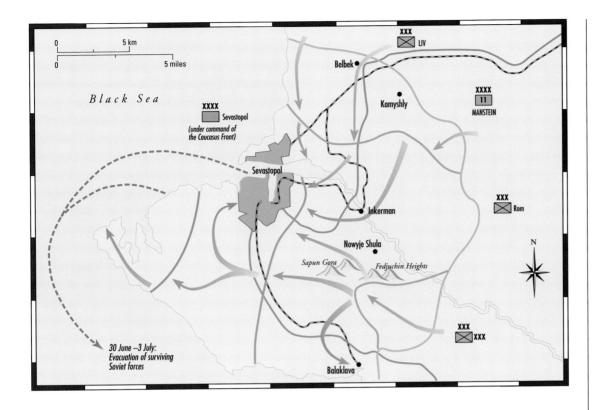

THE SOUTH

The first German assault on Sevastopol – on 30 October 1941 – failed, and the attack was not renewed until 17 December. German efforts were complicated by a Russian amphibious landing on the east of the Crimea, which was only finally repelled in February 1942. Eventually, the Germans systematically began to dislodge the port's defenders. A hasty evacuation enabled some of the Russian survivors to escape.

While the siege at Sevastopol was reaching its conclusion, a German offensive in the Caucasus was scheduled for 18 May 1942. This plan was unhinged when a Soviet attack to retake Kharkov was launched six days before the German start date. Despite being caught off guard, the Germans improvised an effective response, before turning to the offensive.

Although three whole Soviet Armies were destroyed, the German attempt to seize Voronezh failed, prompting Hitler to sack General Bock and divide his command into Army Groups A and B. Hitler then ordered the capture of the Black Sea ports and the Caucasus oilfields, failing to appreciate that the Soviets had withdrawn to stronger defensive positions.

Hitler's goals were not to be realized, even though his forces did manage to gain substantial amounts of ground and to threaten the Black Sea coastal cities. In some ways, this was the high point of German fortunes, as things soon took a dramatic turn for the worse.

time. General Zhukov used the First Shock Army and the Tenth and Twentieth Armies to assault around Moscow, and the German salients to the north and south of the city collapsed under the weight of the attack. Despite this, though, there was no general German retreat.

The attacks on the West and Southwest fronts did not have the same benefit of surprise as that on the Kalinin front, but this did not make an appreciable difference. German units were caught off guard, and for the first time on the Eastern Front as a whole, the initiative had passed to the Soviets. Stalin hoped that the counteroffensive would yield decisive results, but this was almost certainly too optimistic an assessment of what could be achieved by his troops at this point in the war. Thus, while Russian counterattacks continued, the Red Army could not exploit the impetus gained. The Germans settled into strongly constructed defensive positions known as 'hedgehogs', and the pace of the Soviet advance began to slow.

By spring 1942, both sides were at a standstill. Although Stalin's hoped-for decisive blow against the Germans had not materialized, there were a number of implications. Despite advice from his generals, Hitler ordered that there should be no general retirement in the face of the enemy onslaught. Although there is little doubt that Hitler's refusal to take professional military advice cost him dear later in the war, this case was rather different. While German units were forced to fall back or risk annihilation, the lack of a general retreat was in fact beneficial. It is quite possible that if one had been ordered, a repetition of the chaotic retreat by Napoleon's forces in 1812 could have followed. As it was, the Germans remained in a reasonably favourable position as a result. This served only to convince Hitler that he could afford to ignore the advice of his generals, setting him on a disastrous path where he would totally ignore military realities to achieve a grandiose objective beyond the means of the forces at his disposal.

The failure to take Moscow did not dishearten Hitler sufficiently to dent his confidence in his planning. Instead, he turned his attention to the Caucasus and Southern Russia, seeing potentially enormous gains to be made from success here. There were a number of key considerations that led to Hitler's decision. The majority of Soviet oil supplies came from the region, and, if the region could be captured, the Red Army would rapidly face a serious crisis for want of oil. In addition, Hitler would also benefit, for the captured oil facilities could be employed for provisioning his own troops: no longer would he face the dire possibility of running out of fuel and the near inevitable consequences. While these considerations perhaps ignored the possibility of the Russians destroying the facilities to deny them to the Nazis for some considerable time, they were enough to persuade Hitler to lay plans for 1942's operations.

The plans that emerged for the first phase of the operations called for the River Volga to be cut above Stalingrad, preventing oil supplies from reaching the Russians. This would be followed by an attack against the Caucasian oilfields, with an advance over the Caucasian Mountains to achieve this end.

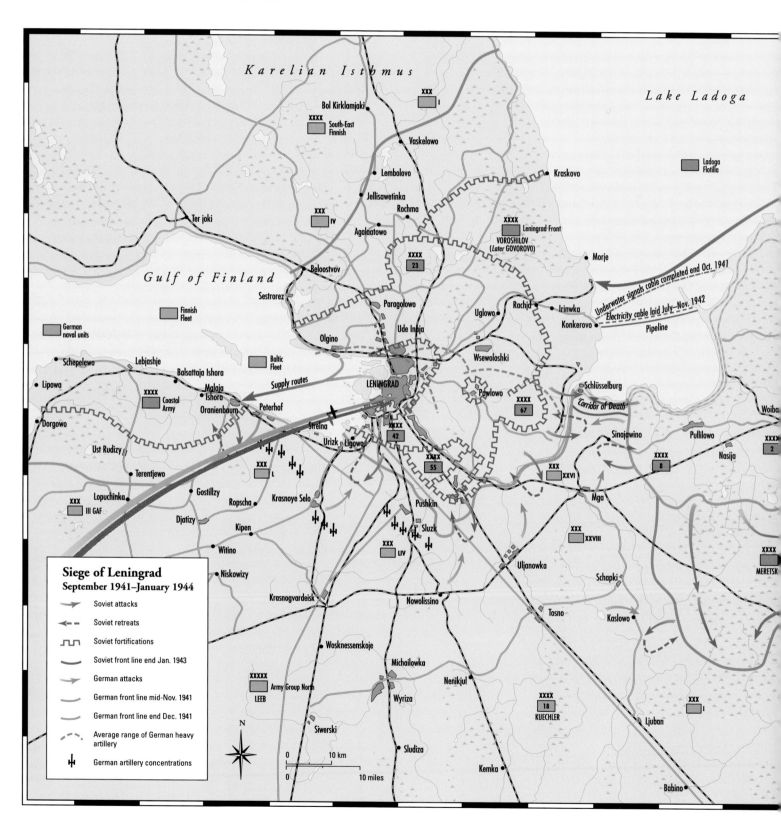

Siege of Leningrad
September 1941–January 1944

- ➤ Soviet attacks
- ◀- - Soviet retreats
- ⊓⊔⊓ Soviet fortifications
- ── Soviet front line end Jan. 1943
- ➤ German attacks
- ── German front line mid-Nov. 1941
- ── German front line end Dec. 1941
- ⌐ ⌐ Average range of German heavy artillery
- ✠ German artillery concentrations

N

0   10 km

0   10 miles

While these plans were being made, the siege of Sevastopol was drawing to a bloody finale. Even before Operation Typhoon had ended, German forces had successfully captured the Crimean peninsula, apart from the city, which had been taken under siege. An initial attack had been beaten off, and it was not until mid-December that the effort to take Sevastopol was renewed. Fighting dragged on, until by early June the Germans were ready for their final thrust. Beginning on 6/7 July 1942, the assault took 27 days. The garrison of 106,000 Soviet soldiers, sailors and marines fought desperately, until it became clear that they could not hold the Germans any longer. Stalin ordered an evacuation, commencing on 30 June. Those left in the garrison covered the withdrawal, often fighting to the death. Finally, on 4 July, the Germans were able to claim victory, and the port fell into their hands.

The main offensive ran into difficulties when the Russians staged an attack of their own, but continued to make good progress, reaching the Don in July 1942. Army Group A's advance was swift, but ended amid great irony – shortly after occupying the Maykop oilfield, the Germans ran out of fuel and could not attain their main objective. The focus of their attention now turned to Stalingrad.

LENINGRAD

As the birthplace of the Russian Revolution, Leningrad held a special place in both German and Soviet considerations, because its possession was particularly symbolic. This fact certainly influenced Hitler's decision-making, as he made the capture of the city one of the key objectives in Operation Barbarossa, despite the opposition of his generals, who considered the attack to be a distraction from the business of taking Moscow. By the time Hitler allowed the effort to be switched towards the Soviet capital, it was too late – and Leningrad remained defiant.

Initially, the German advance towards Leningrad made reasonable progress, but this was slower than had been anticipated. The Russian forces in the path of Army Group North put up far stiffer resistance than had been anticipated, and this had the effect both of reducing the combat power of the advancing Germans and enabling the city authorities to make some preparations for the defence, even though aspects of these were to prove inadequate. The first German artillery shells landed in the city on 1 September 1941, and a week later, land communications between Leningrad and the rest of the Soviet Union were cut off. The encirclement of the city was completed by 15 September and a siege began.

The city came under bombardment both from artillery and air attack; however, the demands of Barbarossa and the shift of focus towards Moscow meant that the German forces facing Leningrad were not strong enough to launch an immediate attack. The Russians, meanwhile, made preparations to keep the city supplied, using roads up to the shores of Lake Lagoda, then ferrying provisions in by barge. These supply efforts were not enough to keep Leningrad's citizens adequately supplied; within a matter of weeks, the failure to build up food stocks prior to the arrival of the Germans was brought home to the population. Rations were reduced as foodstuffs ran out, and the citizens faced a daily battle to survive as temperatures fell to among the lowest in half a century. As the

Summer supply route from 'lifeline' road

Novaya Ladoga

'Lifeline' road completed 6 December 1941

Kisselaja

Wolkow

XXXX 54

Tscherenzovo

Pcheva

Oskui

XXXX 4

LENINGRAD

German forces had cut off the city of Leningrad by mid-September. The city was saved by the fact that Lake Lagoda at least allowed some supplies to be brought in, especially when the water froze to sufficient thickness to permit road convoys to drive across. The Germans bombed the lake in an effort to break the ice.

The fall of Tikhvin on 9 November prompted desperate Soviet efforts to keep the city resupplied. A roadway was hastily carved through the forests to keep a route open to the shores of the lake. Thousands of labourers died in the effort to complete the road; with a grim irony, Russian troops retook Tikhvin three days after it was completed. Despite this success, Operation Sinyavino (August–October 1941) failed to relieve Leningrad, as did Operation Lyuban (January–April 1942).

Another attempt to lift the blockade (also Operation Sinyavino) was made in August 1942, but this failed. Finally, the Sixty-Seventh Army and 2nd Shock Army succeeded in punching a narrow corridor through to the city on 18 January 1943. Within a week, a new road and a railway line had been constructed, taking much-needed supplies into the city. Although the Germans continued to besiege the city, they could not cut the corridor: by the end of 1943, it was clear that the huge sacrifices made by the citizens of Leningrad had not been in vain.

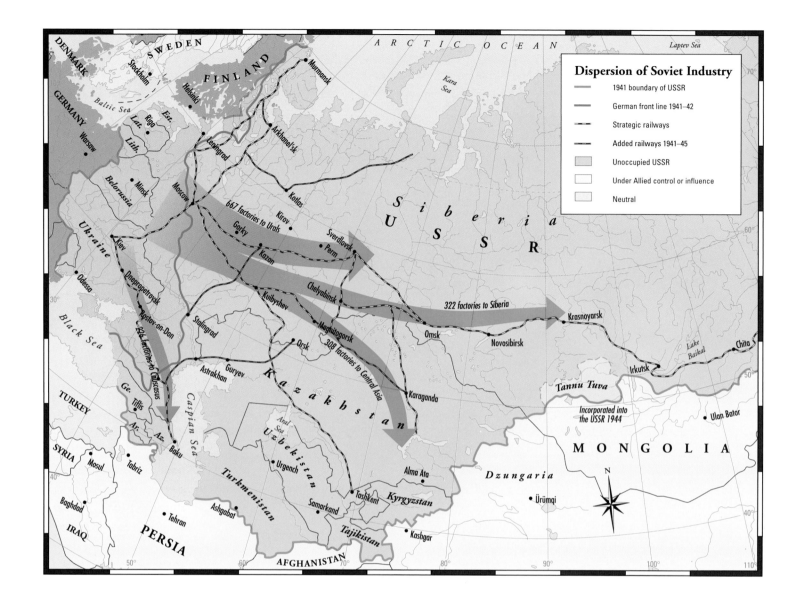

situation worsened, the Leningrad Scientific Institute developed artificial flour from shell packaging, and a variety of substances such as sawdust were added to the 'bread' that resulted. Only a tenth of the daily calorific requirements was provided by the food available, and people subsequently died in their thousands. The situation was made even worse on 9 November, when the Germans took Tikhvin, from where the supply convoys to Lake Lagoda originated. The town was recaptured a month later, and by this time the lake had frozen sufficiently to allow lorries to drive straight across; even so, the amount of supplies brought in was still inadequate.

Efforts to lift the blockade in 1941 and 1942 failed, but a fresh attempt in January 1943 brought success. A narrow corridor between Lake Lagoda and German positions was established, through which supply convoys could travel, albeit at considerable danger from enemy artillery. The Germans remained blockading Leningrad for the rest of 1943, and it was not until 1944 that Russian efforts to lift the siege entirely bore fruit.

THE DISPERSAL OF SOVIET INDUSTRY

One of Stalin's major achievements as Soviet leader was to drive forward the mass industrialization of his country, although this success was forever tarnished by the vast human cost that was paid to achieve this.

Communist leaders were well aware that one of the primary causes of Russia's failure in World War I had been a lack of industry to provide the war material necessary to fight a modern conflict. Other European nations had been fearful of the sheer size of the Russian army throughout the nineteenth century, but once World War I was under way, it became clear that Russian troops were poorly equipped. The Allied intervention in Russia in 1918–19 and the clear threat presented to the survival of the

SOVIET INDUSTRY

The sheer scale of Soviet war industry is difficult to imagine. Almost as soon as war started in June 1941, the State Defence Committee ordered the rapid dispersal of industries based in the west of the Soviet Union, evacuating them to the Urals, Siberia and Central Asia. Within six months, 1532 factories had been dismantled and shipped east to their new location. By mid-1942, only about 300 of these plants had not restarted production.

These developments meant that Soviet industry produced 238,000,000 tons of munitions in 1942, in comparison with 63,000,000 tons in 1940 – and this despite the disruption created when the factories were moved. Between 1943 and 1945, the Soviet Union produced more than 80,000 aircraft, 73,000 armoured vehicles and 324,000 artillery pieces. Factories such as that at Cheliabinisk were colossal – the plant had no fewer than 64 assembly lines.

There were some deficiencies in this mammoth effort – over two-thirds of motor transport in Soviet service in 1945 came from the Western Allies. Britain and America also supplied a considerable number of aircraft and other items. However, even this contribution was dwarfed by indigenous production: 14,795 aircraft reached the Soviet Union from the United States during the war, a figure representing about four months' Soviet aircraft production.

Above: Greatcoated German infantry move gingerly forwards in support of a tank. The lack of metalled roads caused the Germans immense problems in the Soviet Union, as vehicles broke down frequently and required more maintenance than usual. Supplies were difficult to bring up to the front line, especially as the Wehrmacht advanced deep into the country. Rain and summer heat produced vast quantities of mud and dust, respectively.

Bolshevik regime convinced Soviet leaders that they needed to create vast industrial capacity to ensure that any future army placed in the field would be suitably equipped.

The programme of industrialization was immense and carefully thought out. Huge industrial complexes were established deep in the Soviet interior. The much-heralded city of Magnitogorsk served as a spectacular demonstration of the scale of industrialization that took place. In 1928, it had a mere 25 inhabitants; four years later, after the habitation had been chosen as the location for a new industrial city, there were no fewer than 250,000 people living there.

Much of the Soviet Union's basic heavy industry was set up far to the east of the Urals, in Siberia or Central Asia, which had the advantage of placing it well beyond the range of German air attack once the war started.

Light industry was a different matter, however, and a great deal of this sector was well within reach of an invading army. As soon as the war began in 1941, the Soviet State Defence Committee oversaw a mass exodus of factories and workers, evacuating whole businesses from the western borderlands and deep into the heart of the Soviet Union. Although there was naturally considerable disruption to these industries as they moved, once re-established, they began to produce vast quantities of war material. The labour force was sustained by the conscription of women, children and the elderly to replace the men of fighting age – as early as the autumn of 1941, only a few months after the German invasion, 70 per cent of the industrial workforce in the Moscow area was female.

Once industries had been successfully relocated, production increased dramatically. Although the Russians had access to just one-third of the steel and coal supplies available to Germany in 1942, their factories produced twice as much war material again. One of the key advantages enjoyed by Russian industry was the fact that many factories had dual production capabilities: the majority of the output would comprise materials needed for agriculture or other aspects of industrial production, with the rest made up of war material such as tanks or rifles. When war broke out, the factories simply reversed the proportion of each product – a tractor factory, for instance, might have produced both tractors and tanks in peacetime, with a ration of 80:20 in favour of the tractors. Once war broke out, the ration would be reversed and 80 per cent of production would be in the form of armoured vehicles instead.

STALINGRAD AND KHARKOV

As with Leningrad, Stalingrad had particular symbolic significance in the fighting on the Eastern Front. Hitler felt that its capture would be a particular blow to the Soviet regime, while it would have immense propaganda benefits for the Nazis. Stalingrad was not the primary aim of Hitler's 1942 campaign plans, given the focus on destroying the Russian forces on the River Don and the subsequent advance on the Caucasian oilfields. As part of these plans, Stalingrad was to be neutralized

The Battle for Stalingrad
September 1942–February 1943

- Russian attacks
- German counter-attacks
- German retreats
- German front line
- Limit of Russian artillery
- Russian air support

STALINGRAD

The fighting in and around Stalingrad from September 1942 through to February 1943 was some of the most ferocious of the war. The German attacks petered out by mid-October. In November, Soviet forces surrounded the city and slowly tightened their grip. Relief attempts and air resupply failed to prevent the Germans' defeat.

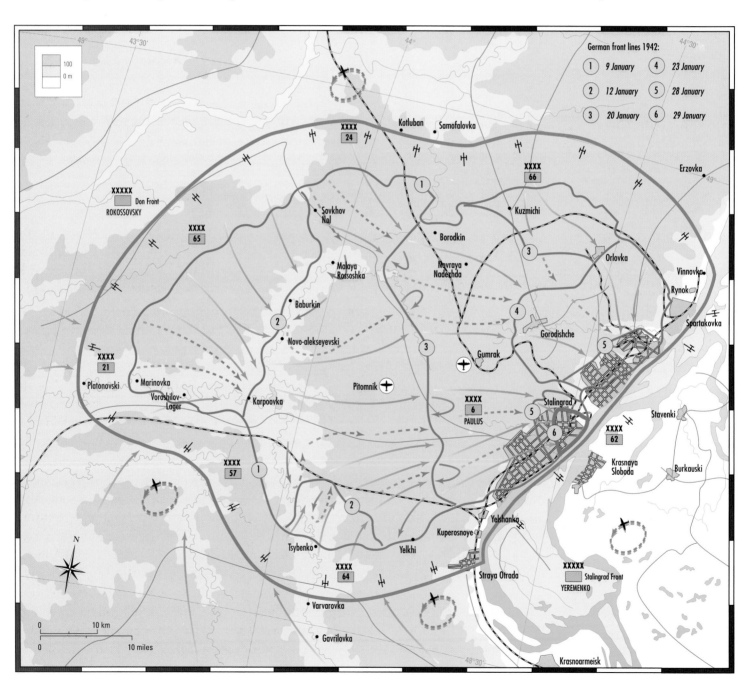

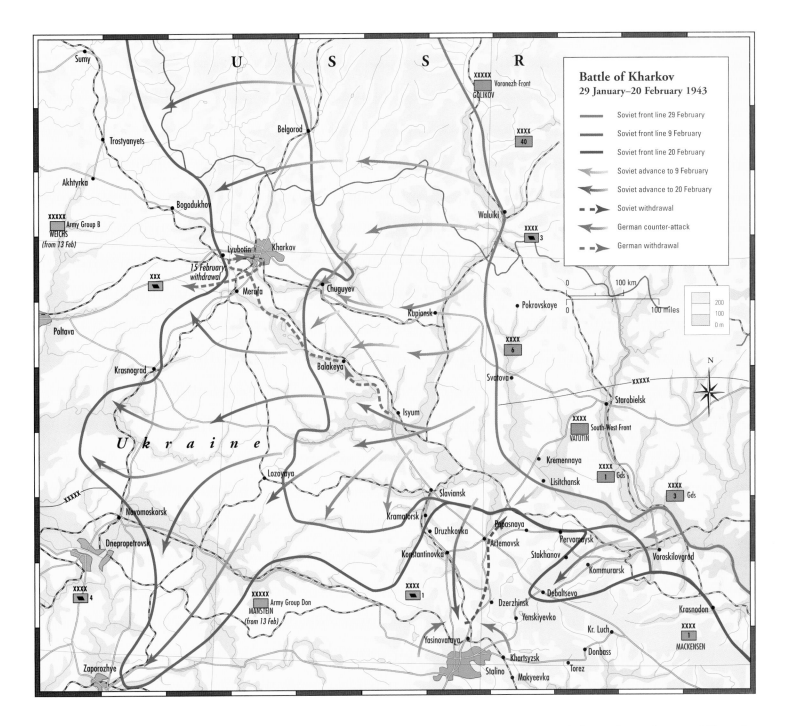

Battle of Kharkov
29 January–20 February 1943

———	Soviet front line 29 February
———	Soviet front line 9 February
———	Soviet front line 20 February
◄—	Soviet advance to 9 February
◄—	Soviet advance to 20 February
◄- - -	Soviet withdrawal
◄—	German counter-attack
►- - -	German withdrawal

KHARKOV

Eager to exploit their success, the Russians launched further attacks, aiming for Kharkov. They enjoyed early success, retaking the city, but as fresh German troops arrived their momentum began to fade. Poor weather and a lack of resupply forced the Southwest Front onto the defensive north of Kursk.

or captured, thus denying its industrial output and transport links to the Red Army. When the Red Army staged its counteroffensive at Voronezh in mid-July, Hitler seems to have taken the opportunity to change the emphasis of his campaign: Stalingrad was to be assaulted, with the oilfields remaining a priority as well. This represented a diversion of effort, which was potentially dangerous; although this was pointed out to the Führer, he overruled objections and the Sixth Army, under General Friederich von Paulus, was assigned the task of taking the city. Paulus did not have enough troops to encircle Russian positions, however, and was instead forced to conduct a frontal assault into urban terrain.

Stalingrad was defended by Lieutenant General Vasily Chuikov's Sixty-Second Army. Chuikov took command just three days before the assault began, but sought to exploit the urban conditions to make it extremely difficult for the Germans to coordinate their air force, infantry and armour. The battle started on 14 September 1942, beginning weeks of ferocious fighting.

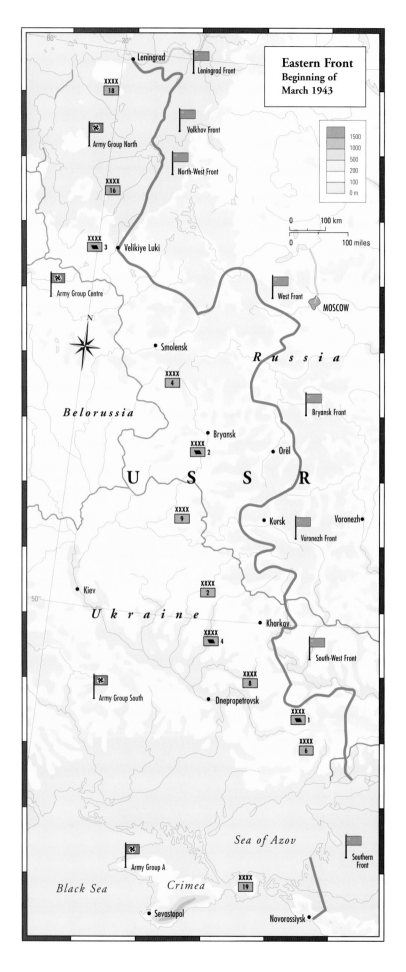

Although the Germans made some progress, they did not manage to dislodge the tenacious defenders.

While the battle raged, the Soviet High Command prepared a counteroffensive. Operation Uranus deployed more than 1.05 million Russian troops, seeking to encircle Stalingrad from north and south. The offensive was launched from the northern sector on 19 November, followed the next day by that from the south. On 23 November, the two Soviet forces linked up, cutting off the Germans. Hitler refused permission to surrender; however, once German efforts to relieve the city failed, it was clear that the position was hopeless. Paulus surrendered on 31 January 1943, and, two days later, the German forces in the northern pocket in the city capitulated as well.

The Russians were anxious to exploit their success and began a series of operations coinciding with the surrender at Stalingrad. The Voronezh front attacked sequentially from the south on 29 January 1943 and punched a huge gap in German lines. Circumstances overtook Hitler's instructions that Kharkov be held at all costs: Russian units entered the city on 15 February, and over the next 24 hours bitter street fighting took place. German forces fought their way out of the city, and, by the end of the 16th, the Russians controlled Kharkov once more. They continued with their offensive, and it was clear that if something were not done swiftly, Army Group Don, under Field Marshal Erich von Manstein, might be cut off and destroyed.

THE EASTERN FRONT, MARCH 1943

The Russian success at Stalingrad marked a turning point in the war in the East, although it was to be some time before the impact of the victory was to be fully exploited. After the Russian advance to Kharkov, the Germans were left aware of the calibre of their opponents. Although the Russians had lost millions of men, and considerable territory, they were not only still capable of offensive action, but also beginning to inflict serious damage upon the Germans. Stalingrad had been a disaster, and the loss of Kharkov left Army Group Don at risk of obliteration. Army Group A had narrowly avoided destruction and had been forced to leave the Caucasus, apart from the Taman peninsula and the Novorissiisk coastal area opposite the Soviet Southern Front.

While the Germans were facing up to the serious problems confronting them, the Russians were implementing some of the hard-won lessons of the past 18 months into practice. The most important changes occurred at the high-command level. Stalin had come to appreciate that his military judgement was not as good as that of his generals, so began to allow them to exercise their own initiative. While his

GERMAN VICTORY

By early March 1943, the Eastern Front had taken on a new aspect. Although the Germans still held large tracts of Soviet territory, they had taken a fearful battering, suffering massive losses during the winter, culminating in the disaster at Stalingrad. In contrast, although the Russians, too, had suffered serious losses, they were still putting new, well-equipped divisions into the field, and the whole Red Army was fighting better than it had before as a result of reforms in command and the learning and heeding of lessons from past battles.

The increased effectiveness of the Soviet forces had been demonstrated at Stalingrad and the subsequent offensives that had seen the recapture of Kharkov. Army Group Don was under serious threat from the Russian forces around the city, and Field Marshal Manstein's solution was a daring German counterattack. He assembled an army of 24 reconstituted divisions and launched an assault on 20 February 1943, forcing the Russians back over the River Donets.

Kharkov fell to the Germans once more, and this brought the winter campaigns of 1942–43 to a conclusion, both sides being exhausted. However, although Manstein's counterattack rescued the German position in southern Russia, it could not disguise the fact that three entire German armies had been destroyed in the fighting, together with three other Axis armies.

final approval was still required for major operations, Soviet High Command ceased to be simply a staff for implementing Stalin's plans. The appointment of General Georgy Zhukov as Stalin's deputy and Colonel General Aleksander Vasilevsky as Chief of Staff was swiftly followed by a reorganisation of the Red Army's command structure. Political interference at the tactical and operational levels was removed and full command vested solely in military officers rather than political commissars. Thus, by early 1943, while the Red Army was not quite the 'finished article' it was moving towards its ultimate position as an effective and irresistible force in the East.

KHARKOV RETAKEN

There were still some obstacles facing the Russians, not least in the form of skilled German commanders. Perhaps the most clear-cut example of this came from Manstein, as he sought to rescue Army Group Don's perilous position. Manstein appreciated that the Soviet efforts during

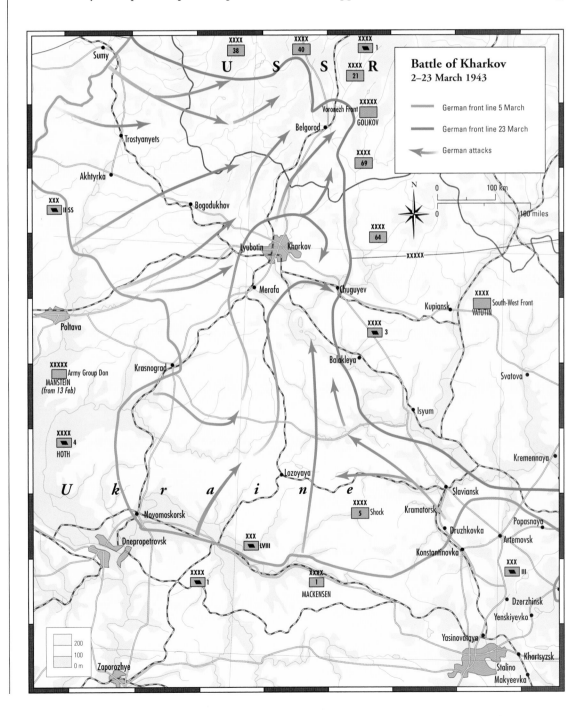

January and February 1943 had overextended their supply lines and reduced the density of their line and, seeking to strengthen his army group's position, decided that he would launch a counterattack. This was a potentially risky course of action, but Manstein felt that the deficiencies in the Red Army forces as a result of recent operations would be sufficient to ensure success. On 20 February, he launched the first phase of the counterattack, which fell upon the Russian Sixth Army. Over the next few days, the advance continued, with the Russians apparently unable to respond in a timely fashion to the threat. Kharkov was recaptured on 14 March; however, the Russians reinforced and were able to stabilize the front before a significant breakthrough could be made. The battle exhausted both sides, and the onset of the spring thaw brought campaigning to a halt as both sides sought to regroup.

EASTERN FRONT

The end of Manstein's counteroffensive left a significant salient in the Russian lines, centred on the town of Kursk. Hitler decided that this offered an opportunity to destroy the two Soviet fronts (Central and Voronezh) which held the area. Hitler was convinced that success would inevitably follow if his forces were equipped with enough of the new Tiger and Panther tanks and more of the self-propelled guns that were coming off the production lines. The validity of this idea was perhaps rather dubious, but a more serious problem came from the fact that German factories were simply unable to meet demand for the new weapons. This prompted Hitler to postpone his planned offensive until enough were available – giving the Soviets time to recover from the winter's fighting and increase their strength. Furthermore, Soviet intelligence-gathering capabilities were improving, and the delays in launching an operation

Below: A Soviet anti-tank gun supports the advance of the Red Army. By 1943, the Russian forces were not the pushover they once were, and the Germans no longer possessed air superiority, which had allowed them to batter any defensive position into submission. Although the Red Army could not yet hold the initiative, the resources of the Soviet Union and the support of the Western Allies would ensure that it could only improve as a fighting force.

NEW GERMAN OFFENSIVE

The large salient that had developed beyond Kursk was an obvious point for a German offensive, as it was vulnerable to the sort of pincer movement that had characterized early successes in Operation Barbarossa.

Good intelligence meant that, by early April 1943, Zhukov was convinced that the next German attack would be in the Kursk area, allowing him to make preparations. Troops were brought in from other fronts to defend the salient, while plans were made to follow this up with a huge counteroffensive along the entire southern part of the front.

By early July, the Germans had concentrated nearly 3000 tanks and assault guns around the salient. While this force was being built up, the Soviets prepared seven incredibly strong defence lines between April and July, while reserves were positioned opposite the largest German concentrations to deny them a decisive advantage. The Russians also set up a further line well behind the salient.

Nearly 1,000,000 men and 3300 tanks faced the Germans, with another 380,000 men and 600 tanks in reserve – and this was only in the tactical defences. The operational line behind the salient had 500,000 men and another 1500 tanks. Hitler's decisive offensive was about to begin with his troops heavily outnumbered by well-protected opponents in strong defensive positions and with massive reserves.

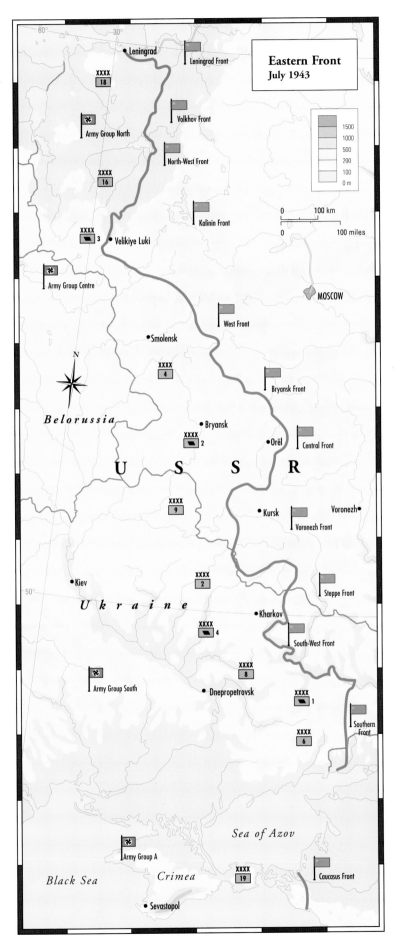

Eastern Front
July 1943

provided the Russians with an excellent opportunity to discover the details of the plan.

On the German side, Hitler's generals were far from impressed with the idea that they should launch another offensive when it was put to them in early May 1943. They questioned whether or not the resources for such a venture would actually be available and disagreed with Hitler's postponements in order to wait for new equipment: they pointed to the fact that delay would allow the Russians more time to increase their strength, with possibly disastrous consequences for the offensive. Not for the first time, Hitler refused to listen to his military commanders and continued with the plan. General Heinz Guderian, the inspector general of Panzer forces, was utterly opposed to the idea of any offensive in Russia. He noted that the German position in North Africa was untenable and would soon collapse, while the likelihood of an Anglo-American-led invasion of Europe increased daily. Rather than squander armour in another battle in the East, Guderian argued that the new tanks should be kept for facing the invasion forces. He felt strongly that German troops in the Soviet Union should adopt a defensive posture, and not gamble on offensive action at all.

Hitler ignored this advice as well. Finally, he set the date for the offensive at 5 July 1943, a day which would mark the start of the largest armoured battle in history.

KURSK

Hitler's bold plan to conduct a decisive offensive against the Russians in the Kursk salient was beset by delays as he waited for sufficient Tiger and Panther tanks to become available for his armoured forces. Finally, the 5 July start date for Operation Citadel (the code name for the Kursk operation) had arrived.

Army Group South had conducted several preparatory operations on 4 July to secure the starting positions for Citadel, the attack proper beginning at 05:30 the next morning. Three Panzer and five infantry divisions from Army Group North led the assault, and managed to gain around 10km (six miles); however, this progress was simply down to the fact that the Russians had pulled back to their second defensive belt. After taking a little more ground on the second day, the Germans came to a standstill, having taken heavy losses. Army Group South initially encountered problems caused by bad weather, which made crossing streams and rivers extremely difficult. Nonetheless, the first line of Russian defences was breached, and, by nightfall on 5 July, the Germans had managed to advance around 11km (seven miles). By 11 July, 2nd SS Panzer Corps had reached

KURSK

To destroy the Kursk Salient, the Germans launched near-simultaneous attacks from north and south. In the North, General Walter Model's Ninth Army met heavy resistance and made only six miles in the first day. To the south the furthest advance being of 19 km (12 mile). The southern flank managed to maintain its advance until it reached the Prokhorovka. The massive tank battle that took place there from 11 July proved decisive.

Although the Germans destroyed over 400 Soviet tanks, these losses could be borne with relative ease; the German loss of over 100 armoured vehicles was far more serious. The failure of German units to break through meant this was the first occasion upon which a German offensive had failed to penetrate the Russian defences to any depth.

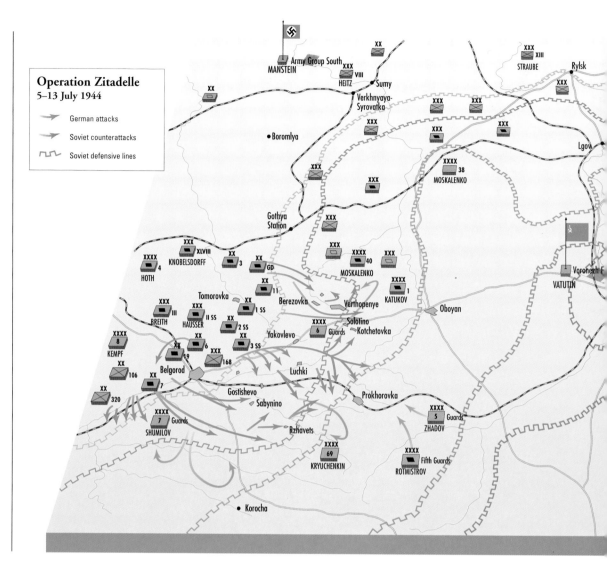

Operation Zitadelle
5–13 July 1944

→ German attacks

→ Soviet counterattacks

⌐⌐⌐ Soviet defensive lines

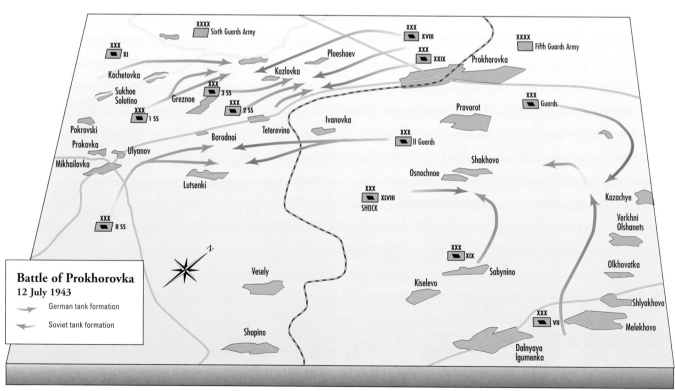

Battle of Prokhorovka
12 July 1943

→ German tank formation

→ Soviet tank formation

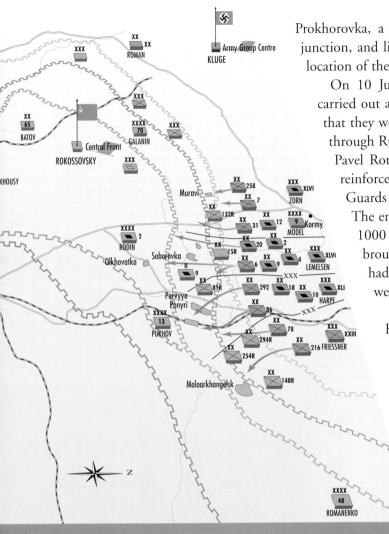

Prokhorovka, a small village most notable up until this point for its railway junction, and little else. All that was to change, as it would swiftly become the location of the largest tank battle in history.

On 10 July, General Vatutin, commander of the Voronezh Front, had carried out an assessment of German intentions, and reached the conclusion that they would seek to attack through Prokhorovka, in an attempt to break through Russian defences. Vatutin promptly redeployed Lieutenant General Pavel Rotmistrov's Fifth Guards Tank Army to the area so that it could reinforce the positions there. Once it had reached its position, the Fifth Guards Tank Army was ordered by Vatutin to launch a counterattack. The end result was an enormous battle on 12 July, in which more than 1000 tanks participated. After 36 hours' fighting, the Germans were brought to a halt. Although they had destroyed more tanks than they had lost, they had lost the initiative. Any plans to renew the offensive were ended by events elsewhere.

On 10 July, an Anglo-American invasion force landed in Sicily. Hitler correctly concluded that an invasion of Italy would soon follow, with potentially unfortunate results. The morale of the Italian High Command had declined significantly in recent months, and Hitler suspected that an Allied invasion of the mainland would lead to an Italian capitulation. As a result, the Führer decided that he must reinforce his units in the west, at the expense of Operation Citadel. Hitler called off the attack, and gave orders for the transfer of a number of units to the western front; in some cases, such as that of II SS Panzer Corps, the transfer was hampered by the fact that they were in contact with Soviet forces at the time and had to extricate themselves from the battle before they could obey their instructions.

As a result of Hitler's instructions, the only option available for the German forces enmeshed around Kursk was to carry out a fighting withdrawal towards the positions from which they had started on 5 July – the worst fears of Hitler's generals in the region had been realized.

ADVANCE TO THE DNIEPER

As the northern element of the German attack at Kursk ground to a halt against ferocious Russian resistance, the Soviet Western Front (General Sokolovsky) launched Operation Kutuzov, an attack against Second Panzer Army. The German forces were understandably distracted by their own offensive, and Kutuzov came as a great surprise. The German defences were quickly overrun, with Russian units threatening to cut the lines of communication of Model's Ninth Army before being checked. Kutuzov was swiftly followed by an offensive towards Orël by General Popov's Bryansk Front. Orël was the key road and rail junction in the region, and the prospect of losing it was of key concern to the Germans. Orël fell after a week, and the Russians continued to push forwards; by the middle of August, the German positions on the northern shoulder became untenable, and had to be abandoned. The Germans fell back to prepared defensive positions some 120 km (75 miles) away to the west.

While operations against the northern shoulder were taking place, the Russians did not ignore the enemy positions to the south. The Steppe Front (General Knoen) and General Vatutin's Voronezh Front launched their own offensive (Operation Polkovodets Rumyantsev), aiming to destroy the German southern shoulder of the salient before moving on the recapture Belograd and Kharkov.

When Rumyantsev began on 3 August, the Germans were again taken by surprise. They had correctly assessed that both the Steppe and Voronezh Fronts had taken heavy losses during the fighting at Kursk. They had, however, completely underestimated the Russians' ability to bring replacements into the line, and had made few preparations to meet an enemy assault.

Rumyantsev enjoyed considerable early success: Belograd had fallen by the end of the second day, allowing an advance to be

Above: Finnish stormtroopers wait for the order to attack. The conflict between the Finns and the Russians had begun in the Winter War of 1939–40. The Finns saw the German invasion as an opportunity to regain lost territory; however, the change in Germany's fortunes led Finland to make peace in 1944.

made towards Bogodukhov and Kharkov. A German counterattack was to prove fruitless, and Kharkov changed hands for the fourth – and final – time on 21 August 1943. As Operation Rumyantsev moved onwards, General Rokossovsky's Central Front launched an offensive of its own from Kursk, acting as a link between the offensives to the north and south; at the same time the Southwestern and Southern Fronts began attacks of their own against Army Group South.

By mid-September 1943, the offensive had driven Army Group South back across the Dnieper. A bridgehead across the river was secured by a Soviet advance party on 23 September, with the main force reaching the river along a frontage stretching from Gomel to Zaporozhye. The offensive continued, and, by 25 October, the Soviet advance had cut off German forces in the Crimea. Another German counterattack battered some of the Soviet advanced forces around the key German supply hub at Krivoi Rog, but this was not enough to prevent the Russians advancing on Kiev. The offensive here began on 3 November, and the city was back in Soviet hands within 48 hours.

As Christmas approached, the Germans were left holding just a few small sections of the western bank of the Dnieper, hoping to hold on until the Soviet offensive had exhausted itself. Initial signs that the Russians had lost momentum were misleading, though: they had no intention of slackening off their pace for the remainder of 1943 now that they held the initiative.

LIBERATING THE UKRAINE AND CRIMEA

Contrary to German expectations that the 1943 offensives would end in December as a result of fatigue among Soviet forces, the Russians had in fact made plans to begin the reconquest of Western Ukraine prior to the end of the year. Early on 24 December 1943, 1st Ukrainian Front launched a massive preparatory bombardment against Army Group South's positions to the west of Kiev. Once this had been completed, assault divisions were thrown into battle and made short work of the opposition. At the end of the day, Russian units had advanced up to 32km (20 miles), with the Germans in disarray. Their position was saved, however, when rain began to fall on Christmas Day. The deluge turned the countryside into mud, making it extremely difficult for the Soviet armour to maintain its initial pace. Nonetheless, the attack continued. German forces were pushed back, and the rail link between Army Group Centre and Army Group South was cut on 5 January 1944. As a result of the offensive, a hole 240km (150 miles) wide and 80km (50 miles) deep was punched into the German front before it began to slow down.

The loss of momentum was temporary, however, as the 2nd Ukrainian Front launched an offensive of its own, reaching the outskirts of Kirovgrad. After two weeks' preparation, both the 1st and 2nd Ukrainian Fronts attacked, trapping 50,000 Germans in the Korsun-Shevchenkovsky salient.

Hitler initially refused to allow any effort to break out, ordering a counteroffensive. This was initially successful; however, unseasonably warm weather turned the ground into a quagmire, and German armour was literally bogged down. Orders permitting a retreat from the Korsun-Shevchenkovsky pocket were given, but after an orderly beginning, this collapsed into a rout

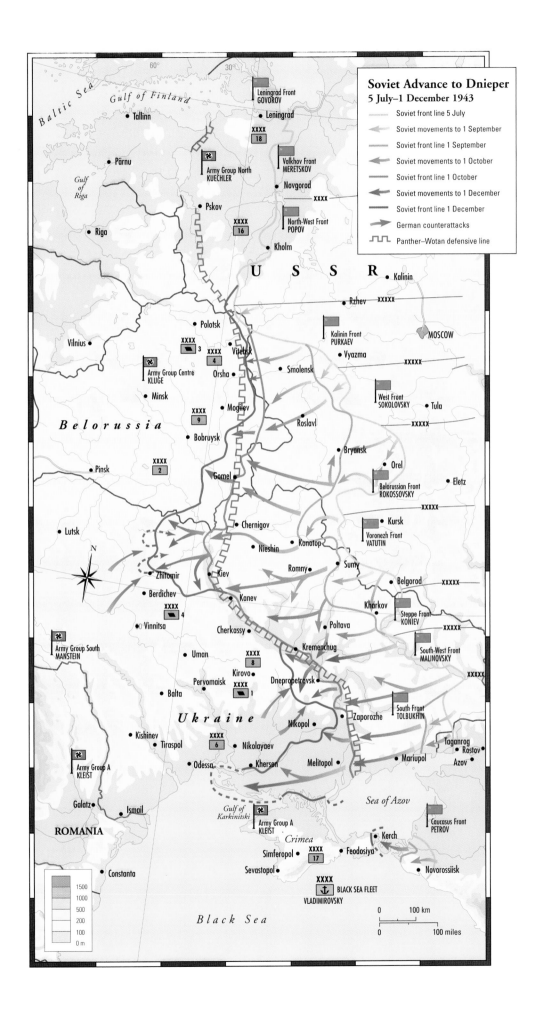

The map legend reads:

Soviet Advance to Dnieper
5 July–1 December 1943

- Soviet front line 5 July
- Soviet movements to 1 September
- Soviet front line 1 September
- Soviet movements to 1 October
- Soviet front line 1 October
- Soviet movements to 1 December
- Soviet front line 1 December
- German counterattacks
- Panther–Wotan defensive line

SOVIET ADVANCE

The events following Kursk came as a massive blow to German forces on the Eastern Front. Their losses could just be sustained; however, without any respite to the Russian onslaught, it was clear that they would be in serious danger of reaching a point where they simply could not bring troops into the line swiftly enough to counter the Soviet attacks.

This was amply illustrated by Operation Rumyantsev. The two Soviet fronts involved had suffered enormous losses in the fighting at Kursk, and it seemed inconceivable that they would be able to do anything other than regroup in preparation for further operations. At the very least, German commanders thought that these two forces would remain inactive until the end of August 1943. In fact, the fronts were reinforced rapidly, so that, when fighting resumed in early August, the Germans found themselves outnumbered by nearly 3:1, facing nearly 700,000 Russians.

Skilful use of combined arms armies and with tank armies meant that the Russians were able to batter their way through German lines relatively swiftly. The German commanders were skilled professionals, but the conditions they faced were all but impossible. Some counterattacks succeeded in slowing the Russian advance to the River Dnieper, but did not come near to halting it. Soviet troops now lined the river banks, waiting to make their next move.

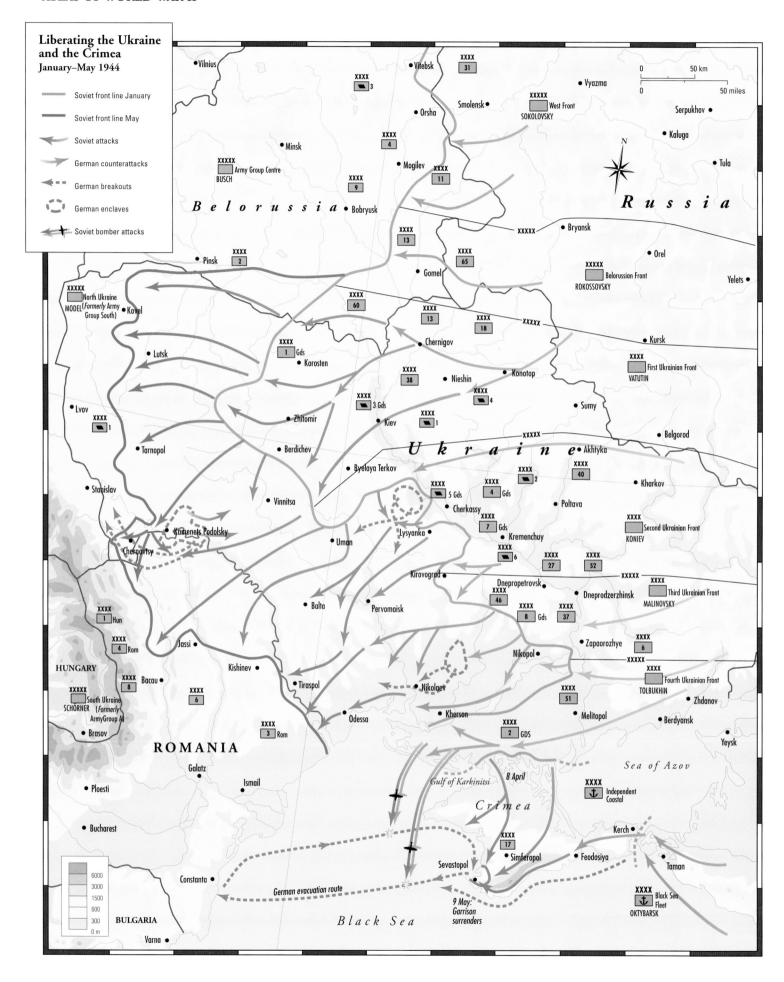

Liberating the Ukraine and the Crimea
January–May 1944

Soviet front line January
Soviet front line May
Soviet attacks
German counterattacks
German breakouts
German enclaves
Soviet bomber attacks

Vilnius
Vitebsk
XXXX 31
Vyazma
XXXX 3
Smolensk
Serpukhov
Orsha
XXXXX West Front
SOKOLOVSKY
Kaluga
Minsk
XXXX 4
Mogilev
Tula
XXXXX Army Group Centre
BUSCH
XXXX 11
R u s s i a
XXXX 9
B e l o r u s s i a
Bobruysk
Bryansk
XXXX 13
XXXXX
Pinsk
XXXX 2
XXXX 65
Orel
XXXXX North Ukraine
MODEL (*Formerly Army Group South*)
Kovel
Gomel
XXXXX Belorussian Front
ROKOSSOVSKY
Yelets
XXXX 60
Lutsk
XXXX 13
XXXX 18
Kursk
Chernigov
XXXX 1 Gds
Korosten
Konotop
XXXX First Ukrainian Front
VATUTIN
Lvov
XXXX 38
Nieshin
XXXX 4
Sumy
XXXX 1
XXXX 3 Gds
XXXX 1
Belgorod
Kiev
Zhitomir
U k r a i n e
Akhtyka
Tarnopol
Berdichev
XXXX 40
XXXX 2
Kharkov
Byelaya Terkov
Stanislav
XXXX 5 Gds
XXXX 4 Gds
Vinnitsa
Cherkassy
Poltava
XXXX 7 Gds
XXXX Second Ukrainian Front
KONIEV
Kamenets Podolsky
Uman
Lysyanka
Kremenchuy
XXXX 6
Chernovtsy
XXXX 27
XXXX 52
Kirovograd
Dnepropetrovsk
XXXXX
XXXX 46
Dneprodzerzhinsk
XXXX Third Ukrainian Front
MALINOVSKY
XXXX 1 Hun
Balta
Pervomaisk
XXXX 8 Gds
XXXX 37
XXXX 4 Rom
Jassi
Zapaorozhye
XXXX 6
HUNGARY
Nikopol
XXXXX
Kishinev
XXXX Fourth Ukrainian Front
TOLBUKHIN
XXXX 8
Bacau
Tiraspol
XXXX 51
Zhdanov
XXXXX South Ukraine
SCHÖRNER (*Formerly Army Group A*)
XXXX 6
Nikolaev
Kherson
Melitopol
Berdyansk
Brasov
XXXX 2 GDS
Odessa
Yeysk
R O M A N I A
XXXX 3 Rom
Sea of Azov
Galatz
8 April
XXXX Independent Coastal
Ismail
Gulf of Karkinitsi
Ploesti
C r i m e a
Kerch
Bucharest
XXXX 17
Feodosiya
Taman
Sevastopol
Simferopol
Constanta
XXXX Black Sea Fleet
OKTYBARSK
German evacuation route
9 May: Garrison surrenders
BULGARIA
B l a c k   S e a
Varna

50 km
50 miles
N

6000
3000
1500
600
300
0 m

THE UKRAINE

As the post-Kursk offensive slowed on Vatutin's 1st Ukrainian Front, a new one was begun by Koniev's 2nd Ukrainian Front. By 7 January 1944, Koniev's troops had broken through Army Group A and were on the outskirts of Kirovgrad. Both the 1st and 2nd Ukrainian Fronts paused to regroup, and, at dawn on 24 January 1944, an artillery barrage marked the opening of the assault.

Vatutin's troops attacked from the southeast, shattering the first line of enemy defences. 6th Guards Tank Army was sent through the breach to advance on Zvenigorodka at all possible speed. The town fell late that evening, trapping the German forces in the Korsun-Shevchenkovsky pocket.

Hitler's orders to hold the pocket were simply impossible to fulfil, and he allowed a breakout attempt. Although this succeeded, the disaster of losing so many men in the torrents of the Gniloi Tikitsch river demonstrated just how much of a rout the Ukrainian campaign had become.

The Crimea was to prove little different. Tolbukhin's offensive lasted just over a month. By 16 April 1944, German forces had been driven back to Sevastopol. The city came under assault on 6 May, and an evacuation was begun. The Russians took Sevastopol on 10 May. Before the offensive, the German Seventeenth Army had been some 150,000 strong: fewer than 40,000 men made it out of Crimea.

as command and control broke down. Thousands of Germans were killed trying to cross the Gniloi Tikitsch river, which was in full spate as a result of the thaw caused by the warm weather. Despite this, some 30,000 German troops escaped out of the 50,000 trapped, but they were in no condition to be returned to the front line in the near future. Stalin's initial anger at the escape of so many Germans was alleviated when he noted the parallels with Alexander Nevsky's destruction of the Teutonic Knights in 1242. The propaganda opportunity was exploited to the full, and Koniev was promoted to Marshal of the Soviet Union.

Soviet momentum did not slacken, and, on 4 March, Koniev and Vatutin launched a new assault that threw the Germans back across the Dniestr, capturing Chernovtsy, the last rail link connecting German forces in Poland and the southern Soviet Union. This was followed by an offensive by Malinkovsky's 3rd Ukrainian Front and Tolbukhin's 4th Ukrainian Front. Malinkovsky captured Odessa, while Tolbukhin's attack in the Crimea began on 8 April. After a month's fighting, the remains of the German Seventeenth Army were evacuated from the peninsula by sea, and the Crimea was liberated.

LENINGRAD AND THE KARELIAN FRONT

In January 1944, the Germans were distracted by the disasters befalling them in the south of the Soviet Union, and Army Group North's attention was focused on the increased likelihood of a Russian offensive in Belorussia. This meant that they missed the preparations for an offensive designed to clear German forces from the approaches to Leningrad. General Govorov's Leningrad Front and General Meretsov's Volkhov Front combined for the offensive in the Novgorod-Luga sector, beginning on 14 January. After an hour-long bombardment, a massed infantry assault was put in against the German first line. This was rapidly carried, and over the next few days the flanks of the German Eighteenth Army were destroyed.

Below: A Soviet shell lands near a German tank crossing a snowy landscape. In 1943, the Germans introduced two new tanks, the Tiger and the Panther, to counter the excellent Russian T-34 tank. Although the Tiger and Panther were more than equal to the T-34, the Germans were not able to produce them in sufficient quantities to make an impact against the huge numbers available to the Red Army.

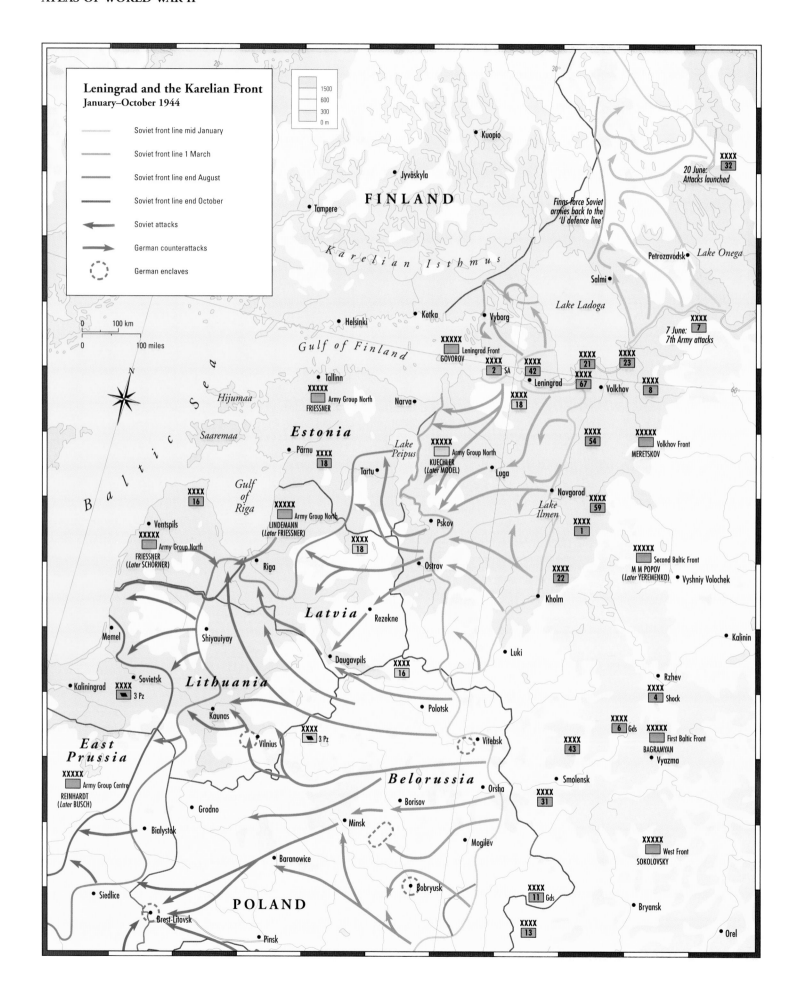

Leningrad and the Karelian Front
January–October 1944

Soviet front line mid January

Soviet front line 1 March

Soviet front line end August

Soviet front line end October

Soviet attacks

German counterattacks

German enclaves

1500
600
300
0 m

0   100 km
0   100 miles

N

FINLAND

• Kuopio

• Jyväskyla

• Tampere

Karelian Isthmus

20 June:
Attacks launched

XXXX
32

Finns force Soviet armies back to the 'U defence line'

• Petrozavodsk

Lake Onega

• Salmi

Lake Ladoga

• Helsinki

• Kotka

• Vyborg

XXXX
7
7 June:
7th Army attacks

Gulf of Finland

XXXXX
Leningrad Front
GOVOROV

XXXX
2 SA

XXXX
42

XXXX
21

XXXX
23

• Tallinn

XXXXX
Army Group North
FRIESSNER

Narva •

XXXX
67

XXXX
18

• Leningrad

• Volkhov

XXXX
8

Hijumaa

Baltic Sea

Estonia

Saaremaa

• Pärnu

XXXX
18

Lake Peipus

• Tartu

XXXXX
Army Group North
KUECHLER
(*Later* MODEL)

• Luga

XXXX
54

XXXXX
Volkhov Front
MERETSKOV

Gulf of Riga

XXXX
16

XXXXX
Army Group North
LINDEMANN
(*Later* FRIESSNER)

• Ventspils

XXXXX
Army Group North
FRIESSNER
(*Later* SCHORNER)

• Riga

XXXX
18

• Pskov

• Ostrov

XXXX
22

• Novgorod

XXXX
59

Lake Ilmen

XXXX
1

XXXXX
Second Baltic Front
M M POPOV
(*Later* YEREMENKO)

• Kholm

• Vyshniy Volochek

• Memel

Latvia

• Shiyauiyay

• Rezekne

• Daugavpils

XXXX
16

• Luki

• Kalinin

• Kaliningrad

XXXX
3 Pz

• Sovietsk

Lithuania

• Kaunas

XXXX
3 Pz

• Polotsk

• Vitebsk

XXXX
4 Shock

• Rzhev

XXXX
6 Gds

XXXXX
First Baltic Front
BAGRAMYAN

*East
Prussia*

XXXXX
Army Group Centre
REINHARDT
(*Later* BUSCH)

• Vilnius

Belorussia

• Grodno

• Minsk

• Borisov

• Orsha

• Mogilev

XXXX
43

• Vyazma

• Smolensk

XXXX
31

XXXXX
West Front
SOKOLOVSKY

• Bialystok

• Baranowice

• Bobryusk

XXXX
11 Gds

• Bryansk

• Siedlice

POLAND

• Brest-Litovsk

• Pinsk

XXXX
13

• Orel

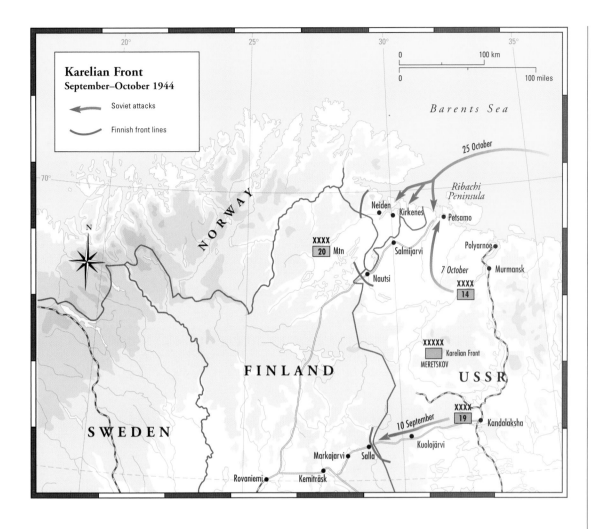

THE NORTH

By early 1944, the siege of Leningrad had been under way for 15 months, and lifting it had long been a goal for the Soviet leadership. Although a corridor had been opened into the city in 1943, this was well within range of German artillery fire. As a result, in conjunction with the offensives that liberated the Ukraine and the Crimea, a new effort was made to drive the Germans back on the Leningrad front.

The offensive, beginning on 14 January 1944, did not match those taking place in the south in terms of speed and success, as a result of commanders unfamiliar with the tactical methods now employed with such effect by other Soviet generals. This meant that the pursuit of the Germans was slow and poorly coordinated, and the Germans avoided the planned encirclement.

Nonetheless, by 30 January, the siege of Leningrad was lifted, although the last German units were not ejected from Leningrad region until summer.

Operations in the Karelian Isthmus were intended to bring the conflict with Finland to an end; outnumbered by Soviet forces that were far more adept than those that had participated in the Winter War, it was no surprise that the Finns had to fall back as the Russians retook territory that had been theirs until 1941. An armistice soon followed, while the Russians focused upon driving the Germans out of the Soviet Union completely.

Despite this success, there were a number of shortcomings in the Russian attack. A number of the formation commanders involved in the offensive had spent much, if not all, of the war in the Leningrad area and thus been denied the opportunity to participate in (and learn from) the offensives elsewhere in the Soviet Union. As a result, the initial phase of the operation was marked by some tactical shortcomings, not least the use of unsupported infantry and lack of coordination between the different arms. Govorov became particularly frustrated with these failings as his forces appeared unable to pursue the retreating Germans at the sort of pace he had intended.

Even though the Russians were not as effective in this sector as elsewhere, the Germans sustained heavy losses in the face of Russian attacks. Although the troops remained in good order, they were pushed backwards as town after town fell to the Russians; once again, the slowness of the Soviet pursuit meant that they were able to avoid disaster. However, despite this disappointment, the Russians had achieved their aim. By 30 January, German forces had been driven back between 80 and 100km (50 and 60 miles), while they had also been cleared from the railway line linking Moscow and Leningrad. While it was not until August that all German units were driven from the Leningrad region, the battle was won by the end of January; the siege was over.

All that remained was to remove Finnish forces from the territory that they had occupied since 1941. General Meretskov's Volkhov Front was disbanded in February 1944 as operations around Leningrad evolved, and he was given command of the Karelian Front. On 10 June, Meretskov launched the Svir-Petrozavodsk offensive, while the Leningrad front attacked the Karelian Isthmus near Vyborg. Operations lasted until 9 August, when the Finns were driven back to the line of the 1939 Finnish-Soviet border. Aware that there was nothing more that they could do, the Finns sought peace, an armistice being signed on 4 September 1944.

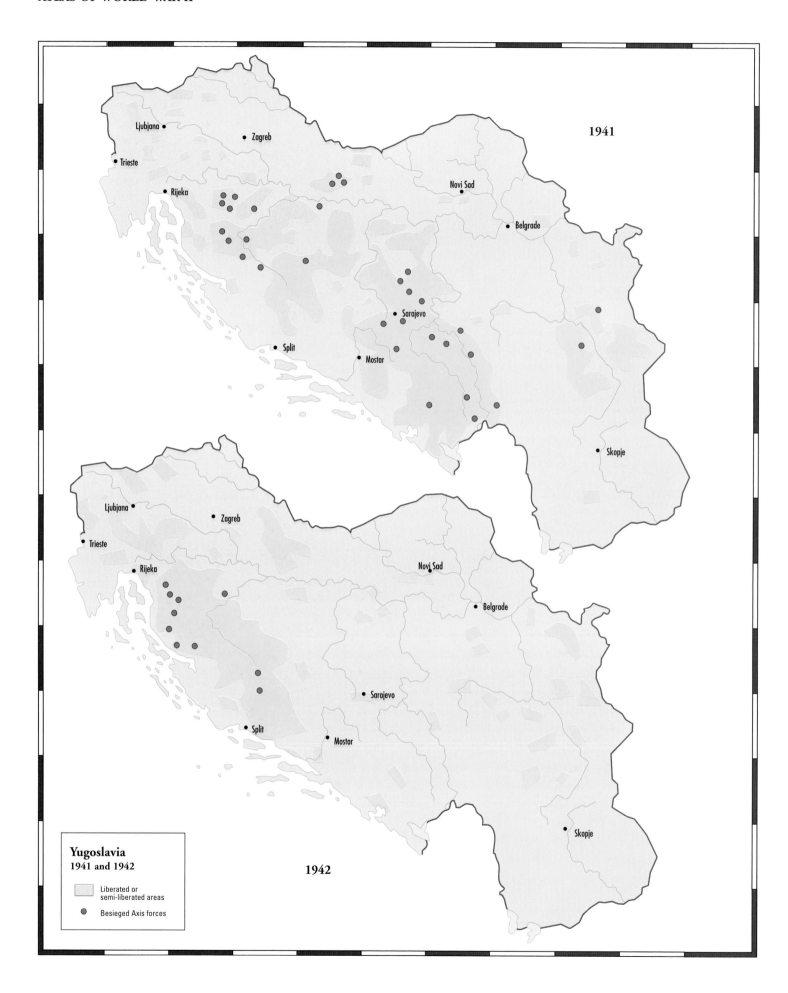

1941

Ljubljana
Zagreb
Trieste
Rijeka
Novi Sad
Belgrade
Sarajevo
Split
Mostar
Skopje

Ljubljana
Zagreb
Trieste
Rijeka
Novi Sad
Belgrade
Sarajevo
Split
Mostar
Skopje

1942

Yugoslavia
1941 and 1942

Liberated or
semi-liberated areas

Besieged Axis forces

YUGOSLAVIA

Once the Germans had taken the surrender of the Yugoslav army on 17 April 1941, any expectations that the country would settle down and accept its occupation were rapidly dashed. A leading communist activist, Josip Broz – known to his associates as 'Comrade Tito' – began organizing resistance. On 4 July 1941, Tito published a widely circulated proclamation calling upon the inhabitants of Yugoslavia to rise against the occupiers. Within three days, the call had been heeded in Serbia; within three weeks, every region of Yugoslavia was in revolt.

By September 1941, two-thirds of Serbia was under partisan control. This prompted the Germans to embark on full-scale offensive operations throughout the whole of Yugoslavia. The first German offensive began in mid-1941, and, although the partisans were forced to retreat, they were not destroyed by the time the offensive ended in early 1942. The German response to this was to launch another attack almost immediately, and this time the partisans were driven back. The second offensive merged into a third (between April and June 1942), in which the Germans sought to bring Tito's forces out into the open so that they could be defeated; however, this failed. Hitler's determination to smash the partisans led to a fourth offensive in early 1943. The partisans sustained heavy losses, but mauled Italian forces in the process. A fifth German offensive followed immediately, with similar results – the partisans were forced to retreat, but were not destroyed. Shortly after the end of the offensive, the partisans were able to exploit

PARTISANS

Partisan activity in Yugoslavia caused immense difficulties for the Germans. Under the leadership of Josip Broz ('Tito'), the partisan movement proved effective, not least since many of its members had military experience. Within a few months, the partisan movement had 70,000 members. As the Germans were unable to control all of Yugoslavia, the partisans were able to run large parts of the country themselves, with some German garrisons living in a state of siege.

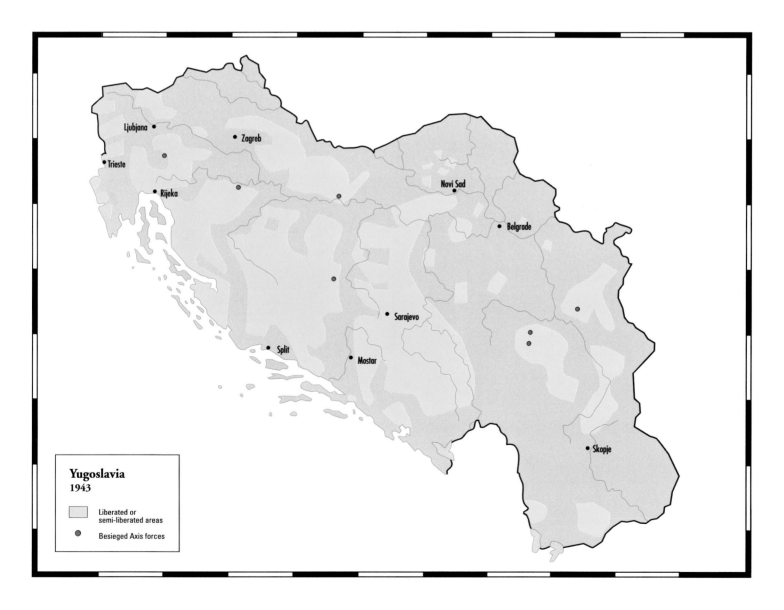

Yugoslavia
1943

Liberated or
semi-liberated areas

Besieged Axis forces

Italy's capitulation and take control of Dalmatia, Croatia and Slovenia, gaining some recruits from the Italian army in the process.

By the end of 1943, there were some 300,000 partisans at large, controlling more than 60 per cent of Yugoslavia. Two more German offensives were launched in 1944 with the hope of finally defeating the partisans and releasing sorely needed men for the Eastern Front. Although the seventh offensive was marked by an airborne attack against Tito's headquarters, he managed to escape. This was to be the last German offensive action in Yugoslavia. The war was turning against them, and it would not be long before the partisans began the final push to liberate their country.

Operation Bagration

Even before the end of the Soviets' successful spring 1944 offensive, the Soviet High Command had carried out extensive analysis of its options for future offensive action against the Third Reich. It rejected an operation in the Balkans for the sensible reason that this would be in danger of overextending Soviet supply lines over what was difficult terrain. Other options were debated, until it was finally agreed that an attack should be mounted in June against German forces in Belorussia, with the initial aim of recapturing the city of Minsk. This offensive, which was code-named Operation Bagration after a famed Russian commander of the nineteenth century who had fought Napoleon, would consist of a main thrust against Army Group Centre's

Below: A machine-gun post watches for any Soviet activity. Although the Wehrmacht had lost the initiative on the Eastern Front after the battle of Kursk, it still remained a dangerous opponent which was more than capable of mounting a successful counterattack. Any such successes, however, were only on a local level – the tide of the war was now clearly running in the Allies' favour.

BAGRATION

Operation Bagration began shortly after the Allied invasion of Normandy on 6 June 1944, with the deliberate aim of stretching the Germans to breaking point. On 23 June, four Soviet fronts attacked in the central sector of the front.

The aim of the offensive was simple: to encircle the German army groups in the Minsk–Vitebsk–Rogachev triangle. The Soviets enjoyed air superiority and a considerable advantage in manpower. They encircled German LIII Corps, then the Fourth Army. In each case, Hitler refused permission to withdraw, or gave his approval only when it was too late.

The Germans faced a series of disasters as a result. First, IX Corps was destroyed at Vitebsk. Then, on 29 June, 70,000 men of Ninth Army were trapped in the Bobruysk pocket before the Russians stormed the city.

Following a Soviet breakthrough at Orsha, Fourth Army was left in an untenable position. Although General Tippelskirch disobeyed orders and withdrew, by 30 June his forces were largely trapped to the east of the River Berezina, where they were killed or captured en masse. By the end of August, Soviet forces were in the Baltic states, Poland and on the Romanian border.

Operation Bagration marked the heaviest German defeat of World War II. Nearly half a million men had been lost in only a few months; it would not be long before the Red Army entered Germany itself.

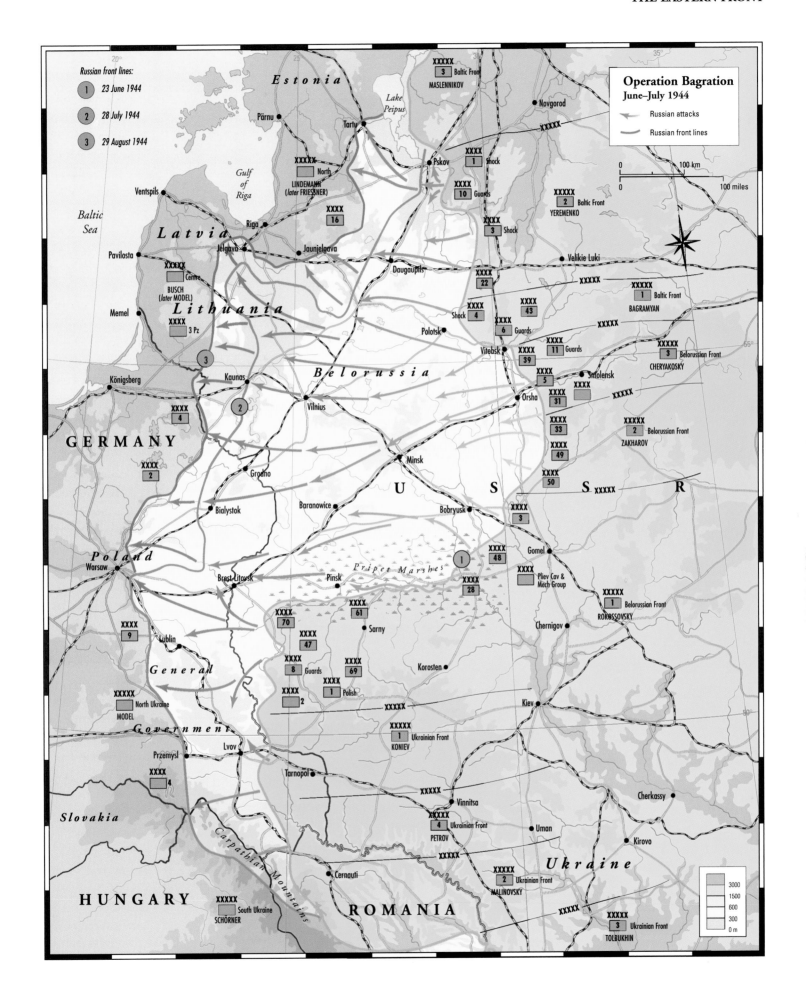

Russian front lines:

1 23 June 1944

2 28 July 1944

3 29 August 1944

Operation Bagration
June–July 1944

Russian attacks

Russian front lines

0   100 km
0   100 miles

Estonia

Baltic Sea

Latvia

Lithuania

GERMANY

Poland

Warsaw

General

Government

Slovakia

HUNGARY

Pärnu

Tartu

Lake Peipus

Novgorod

Pskov

Velikie Luki

Ventspils

Gulf of Riga

Riga

Jaunjelgava

Daugaupils

Pavilosta

Jelgava

Memel

Königsberg

Kaunas

Vilnius

Groдno

Bialystok

Baranowice

Minsk

Bobryusk

Gomel

Chernigov

Kiev

Cherkassy

Uman

Kirovo

Vinnitsa

Tarnopol

Lvov

Przemysl

Cernauti

ROMANIA

Ukraine

Belorussia

U S S R

Polotsk

Vitebsk

Orsha

Smolensk

Pripet Marshes

Pinsk

Sarny

Korosten

Lublin

Brest-Litovsk

Carpathian Mountains

XXXX 3 Baltic Front
MASLENNIKOV

XXXXX North
LINDEMANN
(later FRIESSNER)

XXXX 16

XXXX 1 Shock

XXXX 10 Guards

XXXX 3 Shock

XXXXX 2 Baltic Front
YEREMENKO

XXXX 22

XXXX 4 Shock

XXXX 6 Guards

XXXX 43

XXXXX 1 Baltic Front
BAGRAMYAN

XXXX 11 Guards

XXXXX 3 Belorussian Front
CHERYAKOSKY

XXXX 39

XXXX 5

XXXX 31

XXXX 33

XXXX 49

XXXX 50

XXXXX 2 Belorussian Front
ZAKHAROV

XXXX 3

XXXX 48

XXXXX 1 Belorussian Front
ROKOSSOVSKY

XXXX Pliev Cav &
Mech Group

XXXX 28

XXXX 61

XXXX 70

XXXX 47

XXXX 8 Guards

XXXX 69

XXXX 1 Polish

XXXX 2

XXXXX North Ukraine
MODEL

XXXX 9

XXXXX 1 Ukrainian Front
KONIEV

XXXX 4

XXXXX 4 Ukrainian Front
PETROV

XXXXX 2 Ukrainian Front
MALINOVSKY

XXXXX South Ukraine
SCHÖRNER

XXXXX 3 Ukrainian Front
TOLBUKHIN

XXXXX Centre
BUSCH
(later MODEL)

XXXX 3 Pz

XXXX 4

XXXX 2

3000
1500
600
300
0 m

131

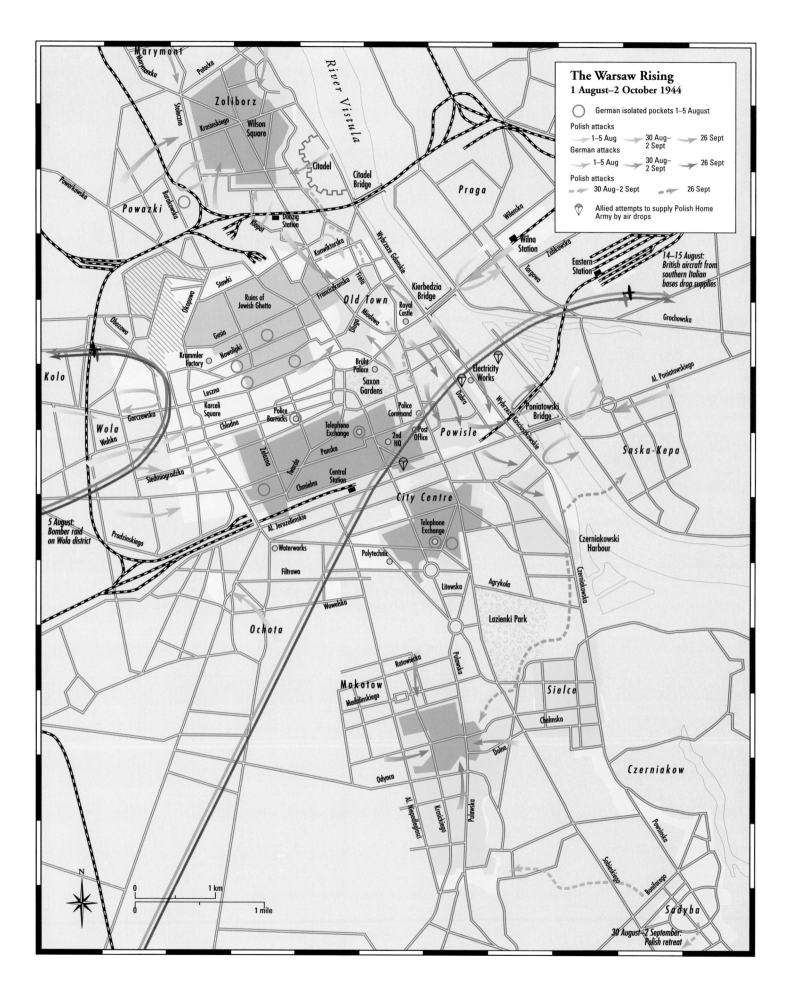

The Warsaw Rising
1 August–2 October 1944

German isolated pockets 1–5 August

Polish attacks
1–5 Aug | 30 Aug–2 Sept | 26 Sept

German attacks
1–5 Aug | 30 Aug–2 Sept | 26 Sept

Polish attacks
30 Aug–2 Sept | 26 Sept

Allied attempts to supply Polish Home Army by air drops

Marymont
Marmoncka
Potocka
Stołeczna
Zoliborz
Krasińskiego
Wilson Square
Powarkowska
Burakowska
Powazki
Citadel
Citadel Bridge

River Vistula

Praga
Wileńska
Wilna Station
Żabkowska
Targowa
Eastern Station

14–15 August: British aircraft from southern Italian bases drop supplies

Danzig Station
Klapol
Konwiktorska
Stawki
Ruins of Jewish Ghetto
Franciszkańska
Freta
Old Town
Wybrzeże Gdańskie
Kierbedzia Bridge
Grochowska
Okopowa
Gesia
Długa
Miodowa
Royal Castle
Okbowa
Kolo
Krammler Factory
Nowolipki
Brüht Palace
Saxon Gardens
Electricity Works
Dobra
Al. Poniatowskiego
Leszno
Police Command
Wola
Wolska
Gorczewska
Karceli Square
Chłodna
Police Barracks
Telephone Exchange
2nd HQ
Post Office
Powiśle
Poniatowski Bridge
Saska-Kepa
Siedmiogrodzka
Zelazna
Twarda
Panska
Chmielna
Central Station
Wybrzeże Kościuszkowskie
5 August: Bomber raid on Wola district
Pradzinskiego
City Centre
Telephone Exchange
Czerniakowski Harbour
Al. Jerozolimskie
Waterworks
Polytechnic
Czerniakowska
Filtrowa
Litewska
Agrykola
Lazienki Park
Ochota
Wawelska
Puławska
Sielce
Ratowiecka
Chelmska
Makotow
Madalinskiego
Dolna
Odynca
Al. Niepodleglosci
Krasickiego
Puławska
Czerniakow
Powsinska
Sobieskiego
Bonifatego
30 August–2 September: Polish retreat
Sadyba

N
0   1 km
0   1 mile

THE RISING

The Polish Home Army's efforts to liberate Warsaw were ultimately thwarted by the lack of support provided from nearby Soviet forces. Stalin's determination to ensure that the exiled government was not in any position to return to power meant that he was more than content to leave the Poles to their fate.

The Home Army was at a disadvantage from the outset. It had relatively limited arms and equipment, while the Germans, despite having sustained grievous losses against the Russians, were equipped with sufficient tanks, artillery and heavy weapons to be able to suppress the revolt unless outside assistance arrived.

In the initial stages of the rising, the Germans were cleared from parts of Warsaw; however, the Home Army was unable to seize the bridges over the River Vistula, preventing them from linking with the Russians. Once the Germans responded in full, bitter street fighting raged across Warsaw as the Poles were pushed back.

Obeying orders from Heinrich Himmler, German troops executed large numbers of civilians, and began razing the city of Warsaw to the ground. When fighting ended on 2 October, at least 75 per cent of the city's buildings had been destroyed (some estimates say over 90 per cent), while estimates of casualties range from between 150,000 and 200,000 Poles killed, along with some 17,000 Germans.

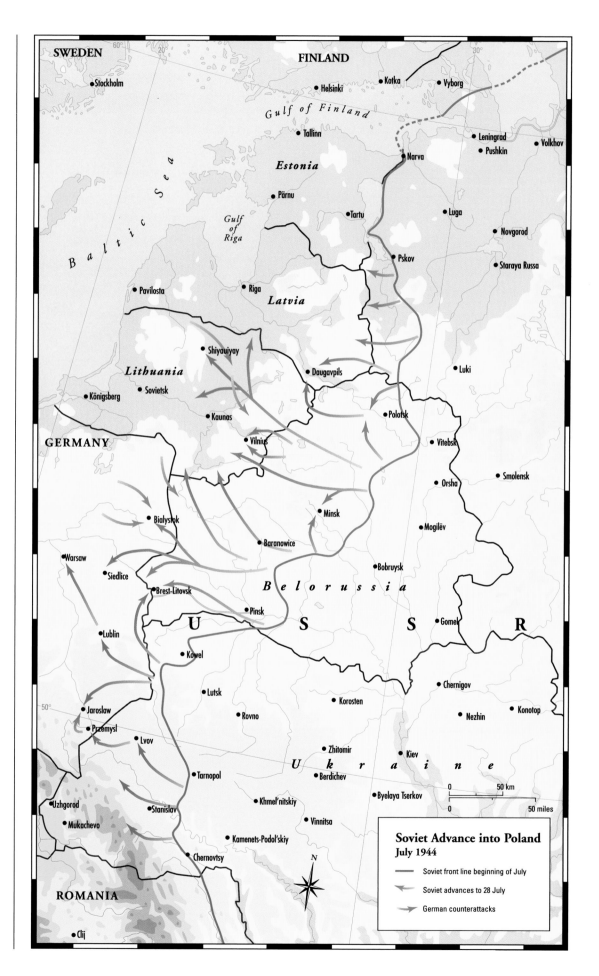

Soviet Advance into Poland
July 1944

Soviet front line beginning of July

Soviet advances to 28 July

German counterattacks

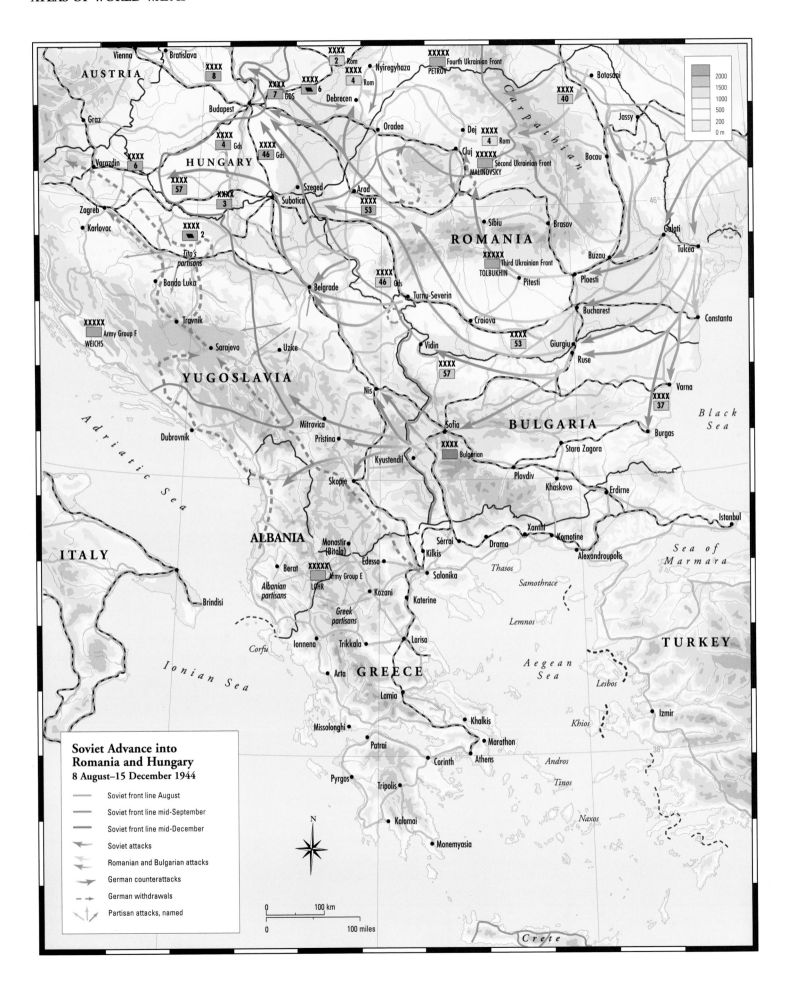

AUSTRIA

Vienna
Bratislava

XXXX
8

Graz

XXXX
2 Rom

Nyiregyhaza

XXXXX
PETROV Fourth Ukrainian Front

Botosani

XXXX
7 Gds

XXXX
6

Budapest

XXXX
4 Rom

Debrecen

Oradea

Dej

XXXX
4 Rom

XXXX
40

Jassy

XXXX
4 Gds

Cluj

Second Ukrainian Front
MALINOVSKY

Bocau

XXXX
6

Varazdin

HUNGARY

XXXX
46 Gds

Sibiu

Brasov

46°

XXXX
57

Szeged

Arad

XXXX
3

Subotica

XXXX
53

ROMANIA

Zagreb

Karlovac

XXXX
2

Tito's
partisans

XXXXX
TOLBUKHIN Third Ukrainian Front

Buzau

Galati

Tulcea

Banda Luka

Belgrade

XXXX
46 Gds

Turnu-Severin

Craiova

Vidin

Ploesti

Pitesti

Bucharest

Constanta

XXXXX
WEICHS Army Group F

Travnik

Sarajevo

Uzice

YUGOSLAVIA

Nis

XXXX
53

XXXX
57

Giurgiu

Ruse

Varna

Dubrovnik

Mitrovica

Pristina

Sofia

BULGARIA

XXXX
37

Black
Sea

Burgas

A d r i a t i c   S e a

Kyustendil

Skopje

XXXX
Bulgarian

Stara Zagora

Plovdiv

Khaskovo

Erdirne

ITALY

ALBANIA

Monastir
(Bitala)

Berat

XXXXX
LOHR Army Group E

Edessa

Kilkis

Kozani

Xanthi

Drama

Komotine

Alexandroupolis

Istanbul

Sérrai

Salonika

Thasos

Samothrace

Sea of
Marmara

TURKEY

Brindisi

Albanian
partisans

Greek
partisans

Corfu

Ionnena

Trikkala

Larisa

Lemnos

Aegean
Sea

Lesbos

Izmir

Arta

GREECE

Ionian Sea

Lamia

Khalkis

Missolonghi

Patrai

Corinth

Marathon

Athens

Khios

Andros

Naxos

Tinos

38°

Pyrgos

Tripolis

Kalamai

Monemvasia

N

**Soviet Advance into
Romania and Hungary**
8 August–15 December 1944

Soviet front line August

Soviet front line mid-September

Soviet front line mid-December

Soviet attacks

Romanian and Bulgarian attacks

German counterattacks

German withdrawals

Partisan attacks, named

0   100 km

0   100 miles

Crete

2000
1500
1000
500
200
0 m

BALKAN LIBERATION

The Russian advance into Romania was helped immensely by a distinct lack of fervour on the part of Romanian forces fighting for the Axis. The offensive by 2nd and 3rd Ukrainian Fronts began on 20 August. Although the 3rd ran into two German divisions around Bendery, the Romanian forces elsewhere on the front put up only limited resistance, and soon faded away as the Russians drove through them and on towards their objectives.

The German–Romanian front collapsed, and German Sixth Army, in a bulge to the south east of Iassy, was compelled to pull back swiftly to avoid total disaster. This gave King Carol II the opportunity to dismiss Antonescu, the pro-Nazi Romanian Prime Minister.

The king immediately sent emissaries to negotiate for an armistice with the Allies. In light of this, a mixed German battle group headed for Bucharest, but soon discovered that, although the Romanians had been most reluctant to fight the Russians, they had no such qualms when it came to resisting the German forces.

The battle group's failure to take the capital prompted the German commander General Friessner to order the killing of King Carol II in an air strike: the attempt failed, but many Romanian civilians were killed in the process, and the attack effectively united the country in approving the decision to declare war on Germany.

Above: A Red Army anti-tank rifle team waits for targets to present themselves, as a T-34 with tank-riding infantry rolls past during a battle in Hungary. By 1944, the Red Army had become a highly effective fighting force with skilled generals, commanders and non-commissioned officers. Adapting the blitzkrieg strategy to their own purposes, the Soviet forces continually struck at their ever-weakening German opponents.

forces around Minsk, to be followed by subsequent advances into Poland and Romania as the German defences crumbled.

On 23 June, a massive two-hour bombardment across the entire depth of the German positions marked the start of the main part of the offensive. Within 24 hours, German forces in Vitebsk had been cut off and destroyed by 1st Baltic and 3rd Belorussian Fronts. The 1st Belorussian Front encircled Bobruisk on 27 June, trapping most of the German Ninth Army. Mogliev was also on the verge of being encircled (this time by 2nd Belorussian Front), with the German 4th Army being trapped there. It was clear that Army Group Centre would be destroyed without rapid withdrawals, but Hitler only granted permission for this with reluctance. As the Russian advance continued almost inexorably, Hitler sacked Field Marshal Busch, the Army Group's commander.

Army Group North endured an equally torrid time as the Soviets advanced; by 3 July, German troops around Minsk had been trapped, and the city fell to the Soviets the next day. Some 43,000 Germans were killed in fierce fighting over the next seven days.

Having taken Minsk, the Russians pushed on into Lithuania, heading for Vilnius. They reached here on 8 July, and encircled the city, although about half the garrison was able to escape before it fell five days later. The 2nd Belorussian Front pushed on to within 80km (50 miles) of East Prussia, while 1st Belorussian punched its way into Poland and crossed the Vistula. Finally, after 68 days, Bagration ended on 29 August. Soviet forces had advanced between 545 and 600km (340 and 375 miles) along a 1120km (700-mile) frontage. Bagration inflicted massive and near irreparable damage on Army Group Centre, and battered the other German formations that stood against the advance. The offensive placed the Soviets in an ideal position to advance on toward Germany itself.

THE WARSAW RISING

The German occupation of Poland had been marked by considerable brutality towards the inhabitants of Warsaw, most notably those of the Jewish ghetto, and the Warsaw rising of 1944

had its roots firmly in these events. In 1942, some 300,000 Jews had been transported to the concentration camp at Treblinka; when reports of what was going on there filtered back to the Ghetto, a resistance organization was formed to fight back.

An attempt to remove more Jews from the Ghetto in January 1943 was met by gunfire from the inhabitants. After sporadic fighting, the German troops withdrew. This encouraged a larger display of resistance on 19 April 1943, when German units again entered the Ghetto with the intention of deporting inhabitants to concentration camps. More than 700 resistance fighters took on the Germans, holding out for nearly a month. The Germans crushed the rising, shooting 7000 captives and sending around another 50,000 to the camps.

DRIVE ON BUDAPEST

The situation in the Balkans deteriorated rapidly for the Germans in the aftermath of the Red Army's drive towards Romania. Hitler had always been concerned about his partners in the Balkans, and his suspicions were confirmed when the Red Army neared their territory. Both the Romanians and the Bulgarians were swift to change sides.

The possibility of German forces being isolated in Greece, Crete and Albania prompted the Germans to withdraw. The focus of the fighting switched to the Greek civil war between the communists and the royalists. The royalists enjoyed British support, but communist hopes of aid from Stalin were not realized; Stalin was quite content for Greece to be in the British sphere of influence, and the Greek communists were left to fend for themselves.

By early September, Russian forces had entered eastern Hungary, and, between 6 and 28 October 1944, the 2nd Ukrainian Front undertook operations to destroy Germany's Army Group South and Army Group F, to permit the 4th Ukrainian Front to advance upon Budapest.

Meanwhile, German forces in Yugoslavia were facing defeat as the Red Army linked up with Tito's partisans. Although Belgrade fell on 15 October, German forces continued fighting until May 1945; the last elements were only dealt with a week after Hitler's death.

These initial acts of resistance encouraged the inhabitants of Warsaw, and it was decided that they would launch a large-scale insurgency coincident with the approach of an Allied army. On 1 August 1944, with the Red Army to the east of the city, some 40,000 to 50,000 men and women began an uprising. The fighters intended to hold out for between two and six days, giving enough time for the Russians to arrive and liberate the city.

This assessment was not unreasonable. Marshal Rokossovsky's initial plan was for his troops to be in Warsaw on 2 August, but circumstances militated against the Polish Home Army's plans. First, Rokossovsky's 1st Belorussian Front required time to regroup and establish its supply lines, having suffered 28 per cent casualties in its advance to Poland. Furthermore, a vigorous counterattack by four German divisions pushed the Russians back. A further complication came in the form of Stalin. The Home Army was loyal to the exiled government in London, while Stalin wished to pass power in Poland to a communist 'Polish National Committee'. Once the Home Army declared that it represented the legitimate government of Poland, Stalin refused to support the uprising and turned down plans by Rokossovsky to take Warsaw.

THE GERMAN REACTION

The Germans responded vigorously to the uprising, forcing the Home Army into ever smaller areas of Warsaw, and six weeks into the rising, surrender terms were sought from the Germans. Negotiations broke down, as the 1st Belorussian Front began moving again on 10 September. As

Liberation of Greece
October–November 1944

→ British Army arrive 12 October

◄-- German withdrawal complete by 4 November

⬭ ELAS Partisan Group

⬭ EOA Partisan Group

⬭ ES Partisan Group

⬭ SNOF Partisan Group

⬭ PAO Partisan Group

⬭ EDES Partisan Group

⬭ EKKA Partisan Group

they advanced towards Warsaw, however, the Germans made sure that they pushed the Home Army away from the west bank of the Vistula, to prevent linkage with the Soviets. Anglo-American attempts to supply the Poles by air were thwarted by Stalin's refusal to permit aircraft to land in Russian-held territory. Even though he later changed his mind, it was too late. The Home Army was forced to surrender on 2 October.

ROMANIA AND POLAND

By early August 1944, Soviet offensives in the north and centre of the front were enjoying considerable success, and the Soviet High Command turned to planning for an attack into Romania. It was decided that the 2nd Ukrainian Front would attack German and Romanian defences to the north west of Iasi, then drive into the rear of the German Sixth Army. The 3rd Ukrainian Front would attack at Bendery, break through the enemy lines and join with the 2nd Ukrainian Front. Further forces would exploit the breakthrough and head for Bucharest and the oilfields at Ploetsi.

The offensive began on 20 August and, although the attack at Bendery was held up, Romanian forces collapsed in the northern sector. The Russian advance continued, and it was clear that, with the exception of the resistance in the north, the Romanian front had caved in. King Carol II took the opportunity to sack his government, and sought an armistice with the Russians. The German response was an assassination attempt against the king on 24 August, an act which only served to turn the Romanians against their erstwhile allies – Romania declared war on Germany the next day. By the end of the month, the precious oilfields were occupied, and the Red Army was able to enter Bucharest. German forces were compelled to withdraw.

Advance to Königsberg
October 1944 – April 1945

Soviet front line end October
Soviet front line April
Soviet attacks
German withdrawals
German enclave

1500
600
300
0 m

0   100 km
0   100 miles

FINLAND
Karelian Isthmus

Jyväskyla
Tampere
Helsinki
Kotka

Gulf of Finland

XXXXX Leningrad Front GOVOROV

Tallinn
Narva

Estonia
Pärnu
Tartu
Lake Peipus
Pskov

XXXXX Army Group North SCHÖRNER *(to Jan)*

Gulf of Riga

Ventspils
XXXXX Army Group North *(later Courland)*
Riga

XXXXX Second Baltic Front M M POPOV *(later YEREMENKO)*
Ostrov

Latvia
Rezekne

Baltic Sea

Memel
Shiyauiyay
XXXXX First Baltic Front BAGRAMYAN
Daugavpils

Königsberg
Tilsit
XXXX 3 PZ

Lithuania
Kaunas
XXXXX Third Belorussian Front CHERNYAKOVSKY *(to Feb)*
Vilnia
Polotsk

Belorussia

XXXXX Army Group Centre

East Prussia

THE BALKANS

The Russians took little time to exploit their success in Romania, and were greatly aided by the situation in Bulgaria. Although the Bulgarians were members of the Axis, at the same time they were not at war with the Soviet Union. The government in Sofia was all-too-keen to reassert neutrality, and ordered that the German forces withdrawing from Romania should hand over their weapons, promptly interning the unarmed soldiers.

The government then sought armistice terms with the United States and Britain, but could not avoid a declaration of war being made by the Soviet Union on 5 September 1944. The Soviet 3rd Ukrainian Front simply continued its march west and invaded, but the Bulgarians followed a pattern similar to that of the Romanians: a new government emerged, and it promptly proceeded to declare war on Germany

KÖNIGSBERG

As the Russians advanced through the Baltic States, German forces became compressed into the area around the Gulf of Riga, before being driven into Courland, where they remained. The Soviet effort switched in January 1945 towards East Prussia and Königsberg.

Despite the fact that the Soviet commander General Chernakovsky died on 18 January, his replacement, General Vasilevsky, regrouped 3rd Belorussian Front and renewed the assault against the Germans in early March. He targeted the German Fourth Army's positions at Heiligenbeil, before moving on to Königsberg itself. Fierce fighting took place in the area between 13 and 28 March 1945, at the end of which the Fourth Army had all but ceased to exist. Even before the last shots were fired at Heiligenbeil, Vaslievsky redeployed his forces for the attack on Königsberg.

The German commander in the city, General Otto Lasch, did his best to establish defensive lines, using the old nineteenth-century defences as the basis of his positions. The outer line was based upon twelve massive forts built between 1874 and 1882, while the inner line relied upon interior forts of similar vintage. Although well built, they were little match for Soviet artillery. The Germans were pushed back inexorably, and Königsberg simply could not be held. Lasch surrendered on 10 April 1945.

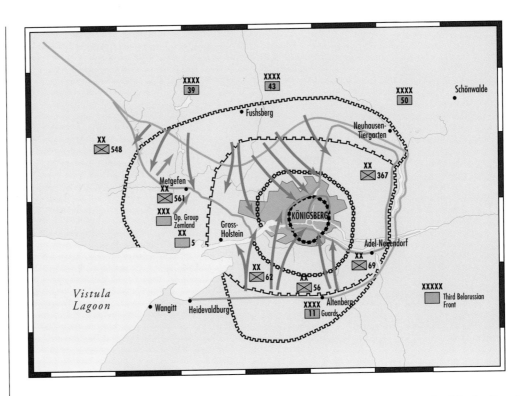

Battle for Königsberg

— German front line 5 April
— German front line 8 April
— German front line 9 April
→ German counterattack
← Soviet attacks

German defensive lines
⌐⌐⌐⌐ Outer defences
⌐⌐⌐ First position
-o-o-o- Second position
▪▪▪▪ Third position

on 9 September. The Bulgarian army joined with the Russians, and marched on towards Yugoslavia.

Those elements of Russian forces in Romania swept around the southeastern part of the Carpathian mountains, while the 3rd Ukrainian Front moved along the line of the Danube towards Yugoslavia. The 3rd Ukrainian Front briefly paused to resupply, then crossed into Yugoslavia on 25 September. The Russians joined with the partisans and marched on the Yugoslav capital, Belgrade, reaching there on 15 October 1944.

The situation in Greece was equally as bad for the Germans, who began a withdrawal with the situation in Yugoslavia adding urgency to their retreat. For nearly three years, they had been confronted by a resistance movement which consisted of communist and pro-royalist elements. The resistance movement was complicated by the fact that there were a number of different groups, all of whom mistrusted one another. While there may have been mistrust between the pro-communist and pro-royalist groups, there was outright enmity between the two generic factions, whose hostility to one another was only surpassed by their hatred of the Germans.

On 12 October 1944, British troops landed in Greece, with the intention of assisting the exiled government to return to power. They found themselves present at the start of a bitter civil war: Greece was liberated by 4 November 1944, but fighting would continue for some years.

By early 1945, the German position had become perilous. Bridgeheads in the north at Memel and Courland were in danger of being cut off. Soviet troops were in control of most of the Baltic states' territory, with the next phase of their advance being designed to clear the Germans from East Prussia.

On 13 January 1945, the 3rd Belorussian Front attacked towards Königsberg. The offensive did not go smoothly, as the Germans put up stiff resistance, leaving the attack in danger of stalling. Marshal Chernyakovsky redeployed his forces and broke through the German lines on 20 January, with his forces heading for Königsberg. Within a week, Russian forces had nearly surrounded the city. Their tanks nearly made it into Königsberg, but were stopped in the nick of

Above: Hungarian troops prepare a defensive position before the arrival of the Red Army. Hungary had been one of Hitler's more willing allies, and the Soviet forces had to fight hard until the fall of the capital, Budapest. Other Axis countries proved less difficult for the Russian forces; Romania and Bulgaria quickly switched allegiances when the opportunity arose.

THE SIEGE OF BUDAPEST

The offensive against the Hungarian capital began with an attack through the Dukla Pass on 6 October 1944. German counterattacks caused some delay to the Russian advance, but, although they demonstrated that the Germans were far from beaten, they were not enough to prevent the Russians encircling the twin cities of Buda and Pest on 24 December 1944.

The Russians dealt with Pest first, but the layout of the city – large, easily fortified factories and streets that were difficult for tanks to operate in – meant that the task of an attacking force was extremely difficult. The Russians advanced one building at a time, finally reaching the city's racecourse on 12 January 1945. This had been used to fly supplies in to the Germans, and its loss meant that the defenders could not hold out for long; they surrendered on 18 January. Buda was equally difficult to take, and another slow advance was required, street by street, until 12 February when an attempt to break out by 16,000 of the garrison was annihilated. The few remaining in Buda surrendered the next day.

The Soviet advance then turned towards Austria. Within a month of the offensive opening (on 16 March 1945), Russian troops were on the outskirts of Vienna. Fighting was fierce between 5 and 9 April, but the Soviets had gained the upper hand by 10 April; the city fell three days later.

time by six German assault guns that drove the Soviet armour back. The Russians completed the encirclement of the city on 29/30 January, and laid siege.

The siege of Königsberg was lifted on 19 February when the German 5th Panzer and 1st Infantry Divisions broke through Russian lines, joining with elements of XXVIII Corps attacking out of Samland. This created a narrow corridor from the city to Pillau, allowing evacuation of civilians. A lull in the fighting followed, not least because Chernyakovsky had been killed the day before. His replacement, General Vasilevsky, arrived with instructions to incorporate the 1st Baltic Front into his new command. Taking over command and making the necessary arrangements to coordinate his forces took Vasilevsky a little time; however, he was soon ready to go on the attack again.

The German forces, commanded by General Lasch, had used the lull in the fighting profitably, to enhance their defences along the fortifications already in the city. This was not enough to hold the Soviets off, however, and Lasch made clear that he thought that an evacuation should begin. He was permitted to begin a limited evacuation, but, before this was completed, the Russians attacked on 2 April.

The Eleventh Guards Army led the Soviet assault, and by 6 April they had broken through the German lines. Two days later, the Guards Army linked up with the Soviet Forty-Third Army, cutting the last link between Königsberg and the rest of East Prussia. Lasch knew that the position was untenable and, on 10 April, anxious to avoid unnecessary casualties, surrendered.

BUDAPEST AND VIENNA

After their successes against German forces in Romania, the Red Army advanced into Hungary. The decision of the Romanian and Bulgarian governments to join with the Soviets presented Hitler's remaining ally, Hungary, with serious problems. Hitler tried to encourage the leader, Admiral Horthy, that he should remain in the fight, promising to give Hungary parts of Romania

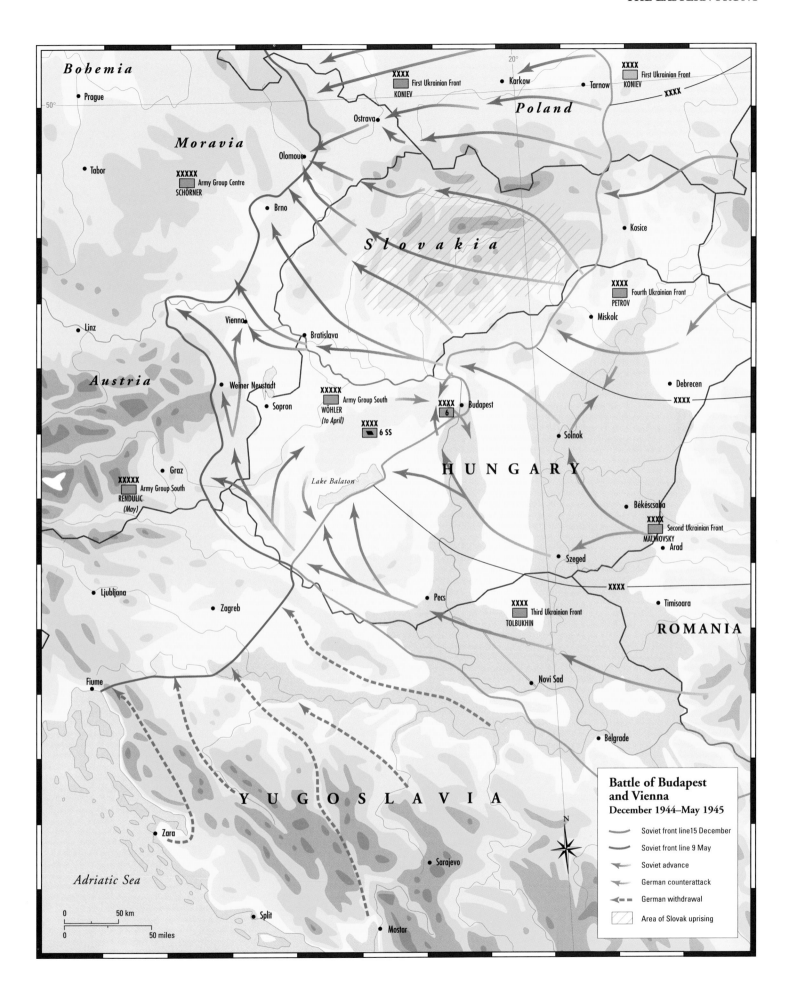

Bohemia

• Prague

Moravia

• Tabor

XXXXX ◻ Army Group Centre
SCHÖRNER

Ostrava •

Olomouc •

• Brno

S l o v a k i a

XXXX ◻ First Ukrainian Front
KONIEV

• Karkow

• Tarnow

Poland

XXXX ◻ First Ukrainian Front
KONIEV

XXXX

• Kosice

XXXX ◻ Fourth Ukrainian Front
PETROV

• Miskolc

• Linz

Austria

Vienna •

Bratislava •

• Weiner Neustadt

• Sopron

XXXXX ◻ Army Group South
WÖHLER
(to April)

XXXX ◼ 6 SS

XXXX ◻ 6 • Budapest

• Debrecen

XXXX

• Solnok

H U N G A R Y

• Graz

XXXXX ◻ Army Group South
RENDULIC
(May)

Lake Balaton

• Békéscsaba

XXXX ◻ Second Ukrainian Front
MALINOVSKY

• Arad

• Ljubljana

• Zagreb

• Pecs

• Szeged

XXXX

• Timisoara

R O M A N I A

XXXX ◻ Third Ukrainian Front
TOLBUKHIN

• Fiume

• Novi Sad

• Belgrade

Y U G O S L A V I A

• Zara

• Sarajevo

Adriatic Sea

0   50 km

0   50 miles

• Split

• Mostar

**Battle of Budapest
and Vienna**
December 1944–May 1945

———— Soviet front line 15 December

———— Soviet front line 9 May

⟵ Soviet advance

⟵ German counterattack

⟵ ⟵ German withdrawal

▨ Area of Slovak uprising

N

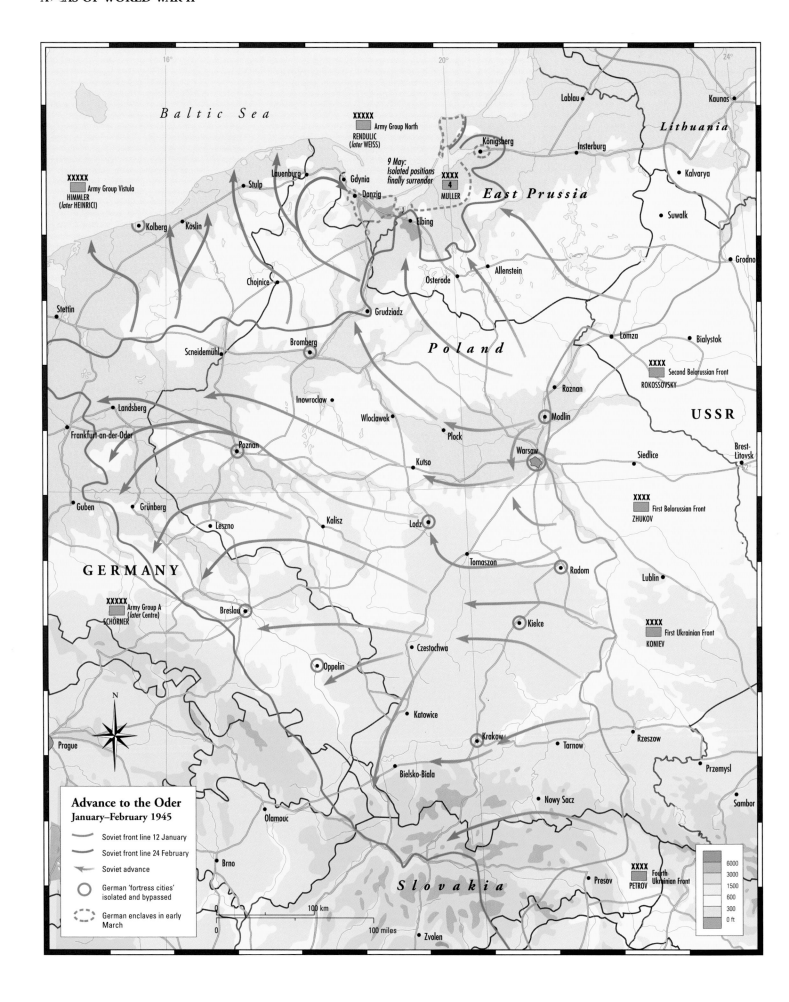

Baltic Sea

Lablau

Kaunas

Lithuania

XXXXX
Army Group North
RENDULIC
(*later* WEISS)

Königsberg

Insterburg

Kalvarya

9 May:
Isolated positions
finally surrender

XXXX
4
MULLER

East Prussia

Suwalk

Lauenburg

Gdynia

XXXXX
Army Group Vistula
HIMMLER
(*later* HEINRICI)

Danzig

Stulp

Grodno

Kolberg

Koslin

Elbing

Osterode

Allenstein

Chojnice

Grudziadz

Poland

Lomza

Bialystok

Stettin

Scneidemühl

Bromberg

Inowroclaw

XXXX
Second Belorussian Front
ROKOSSOVSKY

Roznan

U S S R

Landsberg

Wloclawek

Modlin

Frankfurt-an-der-Oder

Poznan

Plock

Warsaw

Siedlice

Brest-
Litovsk

Guben

Grünberg

Leszno

Kalisz

Kutso

Lodz

XXXX
First Belorussian Front
ZHUKOV

G E R M A N Y

Tomaszon

Radom

Lublin

XXXXX
Army Group A
(*later* Centre)
SCHÖRNER

Breslau

Kielce

XXXX
First Ukrainian Front
KONIEV

Oppelin

Czestochwa

Katowice

Krakow

Tarnow

Rzeszow

Prague

Bielsko-Biala

Przemysl

Nowy Sacz

Sambor

Advance to the Oder
January–February 1945

⎯⎯⎯ Soviet front line 12 January

⎯⎯⎯ Soviet front line 24 February

⟵ Soviet advance

◯ German 'fortress cities' isolated and bypassed

⬭ German enclaves in early March

Olamouc

Brno

Slovakia

Presov

100 km

100 miles

Zvolen

	6000
	3000
	1500
	600
	300
	0 ft

that it claimed as its territory. While this was popular with the Hungarian population in general, Horthy was not convinced, wondering exactly how Hitler proposed to overturn the disasters that were now enveloping his forces. Horthy opened secret negotiations with the Russians, but this was not enough to prevent the Soviets from launching an offensive on 6 October 1944. Within three days, Soviet forces were less than 112km (70 miles) away from Budapest, causing panic in the Hungarian capital.

Horthy's lack of resolution in dealing with the Russians persuaded Hitler that a change in leadership was required in Budapest, and a team of SS commandos, led by Otto Skorzeny, kidnapped Horthy's son in an attempt stiffen the Hungarian leader's resolve. Horthy stepped down instead, and the pro-Nazi Ferenc Szálasi was installed in his place on 16 October. The situation had improved by this point, as, six days before the leadership change, two German panzer divisions had managed to cut off three of the attacking Soviet corps. The Russians took four days to extricate themselves from their predicament, gravely delaying them. Another spectacular German success came when the town of Nyíregyháza was recaptured on 20 October, badly mauling another three Soviet corps in the process.

These successes may have demonstrated that the Germans were not beaten yet, but did not mark anything like a turning point. The Russian advance resumed, and, by the end of the month, Russian tanks were within 80km (50 miles) of Budapest.

General Malinkovski asked for five days to prepare his 2nd Ukrainian Front for the attack against Budapest, but was ordered by Stalin to attack immediately. The assault moved slowly, being joined by the 3rd Ukrainian Front as it went. Although Budapest was surrounded by Christmas, it took several more weeks of bitter street fighting before first Pest, then Buda were seized, with Buda falling on 13 February 1945.

Earlier operations around Lake Balaton gave the Russians the ideal opportunity to exploit their success and push into Austria; this would allow the capture of Vienna and put the Soviets in a position to destroy the remaining German forces in Hungary. The attack towards Vienna began on 16 March, and a methodical advance took the Soviets forward. By 5 April, they were within eight kilometres (five miles) of Vienna, and fighting for the Austrian capital began. After only eight days of fighting, Vienna fell to the Russians.

ADVANCE TO THE ODER

By late 1944, Hitler's attention had turned from the Eastern Front to the daring but over-optimistic Ardennes offensive. Despite protestations from his generals, he resolutely refused to accept that the Ardennes operation left Germany vulnerable to another Soviet attack in the East. He argued that the Soviets were not in a position to begin another offensive, as they had been fighting constantly for four months.

In fact, the Ardennes offensive worked in favour of the Russians, just as the German generals feared. Committing troops in Western Europe meant that they were not available to act as a reserve against a Russian attack. To deal with the Hungarian crisis, Hitler had been forced to denude the Vistula of forces. This simply assisted the Russians, who had in fact begun plans for their 1945 offensives in October 1944.

Some 2,200,000 Russian troops were assembled opposite the Vistula and were in position by early January. To assist with the fighting in the west, Stalin brought the start date of the offensive forward eight days to 12 January 1945. The offensive began at 04:30 in a blizzard, with a massive bombardment against German positions. After 30 minutes, the bombardment eased, and troops were sent forwards. They penetrated the German lines to a depth of up to three kilometres (two miles) in places before they were halted.

At 10:00, another huge bombardment, lasting for an hour and three-quarters, was laid down upon the German lines. The Fourth Panzer Army's headquarters was obliterated in the process,

TO THE ODER

The Soviet Vistula–Oder operation was remarkable in size and scope of achievement. Hitler's decision to go on the offensive in the west meant that troops that could have been employed against the Russians were otherwise engaged, and there was little chance of getting them back to the Eastern Front in time to meet any renewed Russian attack. Hitler's misplaced confidence that four months of near-constant fighting would prevent the Russians from attacking for some time meant that he did not maintain adequate reserves in the East. Some 400,000 German troops were left facing 2,200,000 Russians.

The Vistula–Oder operation began on 12 January 1945 and made rapid progress. The German forces crumbled in the face of a massive artillery bombardment, and they were forced to withdraw from Warsaw as their position collapsed. Hitler's response was to sack a number of generals and increase his grip on the army – reducing yet further its ability to show any initiative in the defence. Kraków and Silesia fell swiftly, and by the end of the month, Zukhov's Front was on the banks of the Oder.

Stalin ordered the end of the offensive on 2 February to allow time to prepare for an attack against Berlin itself, bringing to an end a hugely successful operation, which had gained over 480km (300 miles) in two weeks and destroyed Army Group Centre in the process.

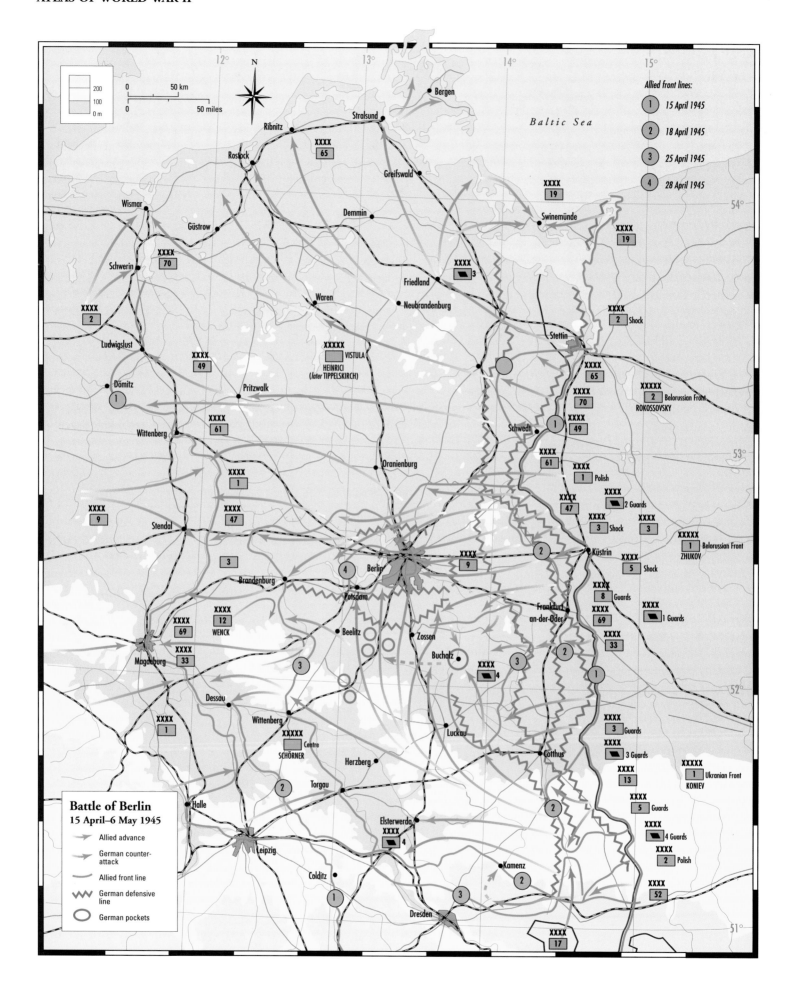

Baltic Sea

Bergen

Stralsund

Ribnitz

Rostock

XXXX
65

Greifswald

XXXX
19

Swinemünde

Wismar

Güstrow

Demmin

Schwerin

XXXX
70

Waren

Friedland

XXXX
3

Neubrandenburg

XXXX
2

Ludwigslust

Dömitz

XXXX
49

XXXXX
VISTULA
HEINRICI
(later TIPPELSKIRCH)

Pritzwalk

Stettin

Swinemünde

XXXX
19

XXXX
2 Shock

1

XXXX
65

XXXX
70

XXXX
2 Belorussian Front
ROKOSSOVSKY

Wittenberg

XXXX
61

Oranienburg

Schwedt

1

XXXX
49

XXXX
9

XXXX
1

XXXX
47

Stendal

XXXX
61

1 Polish

XXXX
47

XXXX
2 Guards

XXXX
3 Shock

XXXX
3

XXXXX
1 Belorussian Front
ZHUKOV

3

Brandenburg

Berlin

4

XXXX
9

2

Küstrin

XXXX
5 Shock

Potsdam

XXXX
12
WENCK

XXXX
69

Beelitz

Zossen

Frankfurt
an-der-Oder

XXXX
8 Guards

XXXX
69

XXXX
1 Guards

Magdeburg

XXXX
33

3

Buchalz

XXXX
4

3

2

XXXX
33

1

Dessau

Wittenberg

XXXXX
Centre
SCHÖRNER

Luckau

XXXX
3 Guards

XXXX
3 Guards

XXXX
1
XXXX
1 Ukranian Front
KONIEV

XXXX
13

Herzberg

Cottbus

2

Torgau

Halle

XXXX
5 Guards

Elsterwerda

XXXX
4

2

XXXX
4 Guards

Leipzig

Colditz

Kamenz

XXXX
2 Polish

1

3

2

XXXX
52

Dresden

XXXX
17

Battle of Berlin
15 April–6 May 1945

→ Allied advance

→ German counter-attack

— Allied front line

〜 German defensive line

◯ German pockets

Allied front lines:

1 15 April 1945

2 18 April 1945

3 25 April 1945

4 28 April 1945

GERMANY OVERRUN

Although Berlin was the main objective of the Soviet operation, consideration had to be given to defeating all of Germany. This meant that either the Western powers would have to push up to meet the Soviets near Berlin, or, conversely, that the Russians would have to drive beyond Berlin to meet with their allies. Stalin far preferred the latter option, and it was a point of view shared by the Americans, who were in no hurry to reach Berlin themselves (despite grave warnings from Britain's Winston Churchill of the consequences).

On the Western Front, the Allies drove forwards, heading towards the River Elbe, while the Russians carried out several manoeuvres. Rokossovsky's 2nd Belorussian Front attacked to the northwest, sweeping to the coast, tying down German forces that might have sought to aid the defence of Berlin in the process. Other elements of Rokossovksy's force pushed west to meet the Western Allies.

To the south, part of Koniev's 1st Ukranian Front swung to the north to threaten the southern suburbs of Berlin, while the remainder headed towards the Elbe. Elements of Zhukov's 1st Belorussian Front bypassed Berlin and pushed into the area around Brandenburg. Caught between the two sides, the Germans stood little chance. The first meeting of American and Russian troops occurred at Torgau on the Elbe. It was not long before only small pockets of enemy resistance remained.

and the formation lost all ability to fight, collapsing into confusion as the Russian tanks and infantry attacked. Some of them remained in their trenches, unable to move, with their will shattered by the massive bombardment. Others simply turned and ran in the face of the enemy attack.

The Soviet assault rapidly broke through German lines, and by the end of the day, had reached a depth of 22km (14 miles) along a 40km (25-mile) front. The next day, Russian tanks charged across the icy countryside, cutting the lines of communication between Warsaw and Kraków. The Germans were forced to withdraw from Warsaw, leaving Kraków and Silesia as the next targets for the Russians. Koniev's 1st Ukrainian Front was given the task of taking Kraków and Silesia, and was then to head for Bresalu. Kraków fell easily, when the Germans withdrew to avoid being encircled.

Silesia was more difficult, as it was heavily industrialized and offered good defensive opportunities. To avoid a repetition of Stalingrad, Koniev turned his forces through 90° and drove along the right bank of the Oder. Again, the Germans withdrew rather than risk encirclement.

Zhukov trapped 60,000 Germans in Poznan, then drove forwards to the Oder, which his forward elements reached on the last day of January. The Fifth Shock Army crossed the river as the last act of the offensive, which was halted on Stalin's orders on 2 February 1945. There were two practical reasons for this. First, a thaw had set in, making it impossible to cross rivers until the water in them had gone down. With his belief in divine providence, Hitler viewed the thaw as a sign that his fortunes would soon change – an incredible piece of optimism. Secondly, Stalin appreciated that his troops would need to have time to prepare for the assault against the final prize: Berlin itself.

BERLIN THE TARGET

By March 1945, it was quite clear that Berlin would soon be a battleground. Hitler issued orders for the defence of the Nazi capital, but these were long on rhetoric and lacking in detail. To make matters worse, Hitler's overwhelming confidence meant that effort to turn Berlin into a fortress had not been fully implemented: indeed, solid defensive positions were notable by their absence in many parts of the city.

Despite these difficulties, by the second week in April, a plan for defending Berlin had been drawn up, but the reality of the German situation was clear. Units were extremely short of ammunition, particularly for artillery, and movement was hampered by a shortage of fuel. Supplies were not transported because there were no vehicles to move them, tanks were unable to shift positions and the Luftwaffe was all but gone, grounded by lack of fuel for its remaining aircraft. Finally, although the Berlin garrison was a million-strong, many of the soldiers defending the city were boys under military age or men who had been too old or unfit to serve with the army before. Many lacked anything other than rudimentary training, although all were determined to defend against the Russians, particularly given the stories of the treatment meted out to German civilians by Soviet troops in areas already under their control.

Hitler himself had moved to the fortified bunker underneath the Chancellery building, making overoptimistic plans to throw the Russians back. His spirits rose on 12 April when news arrived that President Roosevelt had died. Hitler saw this as a positive omen and thought that he might, after all, negotiate a settlement now that one of the leading proponents of unconditional surrender was dead. Over the next two days, Hitler began to think that success could still be achieved when news came that German troops had inflicted a serious reverse upon American bridgeheads over the River Elbe.

This was all illusory: the death of their president and a tactical setback were not going to dissuade the Americans from prosecuting the war to a finish. Hitler's optimism also completely ignored the fact that the Soviet armies were very near to beginning their attack. The Soviets had

BERLIN

The main Soviet effort against Berlin was to be carried out by Zhukov's 1st Belorussian Front with the aim of taking the Seelow Heights. The massive bombardment that fell on the German lines on 16 April failed to kill many defenders, who had temporarily withdrawn.

Over the course of the next day, a massive attritional battle developed. Zhukov's plan was abandoned, and he used his reserve of six armoured formations – intended to exploit a breakthrough – to try to force a gap, which also failed. Zhukov was well aware that his rival Koniev was having far more success to the south of the city, and the threat from Stalin that he would give Koniev the prize of Berlin led Zhukov to threaten his commanders that they would be sent to fight as private soldiers if they did not succeed.

In the end, the weight of the Soviet forces told against the Germans. Gaps started to appear in the German lines on 18 April and, the next day, a breakthrough was made. The 1st Belorussian and 1st Ukrainian Fronts now pushed on into Berlin, aiming to encircle the enemy defenders. Their advance continued over the next few days, until the Germans were left with a small escape corridor by 27 April. This corridor was broken into the next day, and resistance was all but over. The upper floors of the Reichstag were taken on 30 April; however, fighting in the cellars continued until 2 May.

Above: A famous doctored propaganda photograph of Soviet fighter-bombers shown over the Reichstag in Berlin, with a T-34 tank in the foreground. Fighting continued in the basement of the building for two days after the Hammer and Sickle was flown from its rooftop. Elsewhere – in Yugoslavia and Czechoslovakia, for example – die-hard Nazi supporters were to fight on for another week before finally capitulating.

implemented a massive build-up since February, carrying out the largest and most complex redeployment of forces in history so that they were in the most favourable position to assault the enemy capital. More than 2,500,000 men, 6000 tanks and armoured fighting vehicles, 45,000 guns and rocket launchers, along with supplies ranging from food to artillery shells, were moved into place by mid-April 1945.

To make matters more difficult for the defenders, British and American forces were pushing ever deeper into western Germany, demonstrating the danger of fighting a war on two fronts. Stalin was concerned that the Americans might try to steal some of his glory by taking Berlin themselves, despite assurances that they had no intention of doing this. Stalin did not have long to wait – on 16 April, the attack against Berlin itself began.

THE END OF THE REICH

The plan of attack against Berlin was brutally simple in conception: Soviet forces would launch a number of attacks along a wide front, with the intention of encircling German forces and then destroying them. Zhukov's 1st Belorussian Front, which was closest to the capital, would attack from its positions near Küstrin on the west bank of the River Oder, heading direct for Berlin. Koniev would use his 1st Ukrainian Front to cross the Neisse and attack the southwest approaches to the enemy capital, while Rokossovsky would attack in the area around Stettin to ensure that the remnants of Third Panzer Army could not be used to reinforce the beleaguered German defenders in Berlin.

This plan caused Koniev considerable irritation. His rivalry with Zhukov had become intense, and he was extremely jealous that he would not have the opportunity to take Berlin, even if it seemed obvious that the task should fall to Stalin's nominated deputy commander. This apparently trivial case of ego was to be of some importance in the battle that followed, and it was exploited to good effect by Stalin as he urged his subordinates on.

At 03:00 on 16 April 1945, Zhukov's forces launched their attack, aiming to take the Seelow Heights. An enormous bombardment landed more than 1,000,000 shells on German positions and was accompanied by a heavy bombing raid. In the Vistula–Oder operation, such massive firepower had subdued the enemy to the point of near passivity, but this was not the case now. Zhukov's forces did not break through that day, while Koniev enjoyed some success. After a second day of fighting in which Koniev made more gains, Stalin (prompted by a suggestion from Koniev) threatened that he might allow Koniev to seize Berlin if Zhukov could not capture the Seelow Heights. This threat energized Zhukov, who through a mixture of blandishments and threats urged his subordinate commanders to greater efforts. Although little progress was made on 18 April, the pressure on the German lines began to tell, and Zhukov's forces broke through the next day.

On 21 April, Zhukov's Third and Fifth Shock Armies entered the suburbs of Berlin, then advanced towards the centre. Koniev's troops reached the Tetlow canal by the end of 22 April, pushing towards Zhukov's forces. On 24 April, 1st Ukrainian and 1st Belorussian Fronts met on the River Havel, encircling Berlin. A methodical, street-by-street battle then began, with the Germans being pushed ever further back. Their last line of resistance was fractured on 28 April. Two days later, Hitler killed himself in his bunker, and the Reichstag itself was taken. The Berlin garrison surrendered on 2 May, and mopping up continued for a few more days. On 8 May 1945, Germany surrendered unconditionally: the war in Europe was finally over.

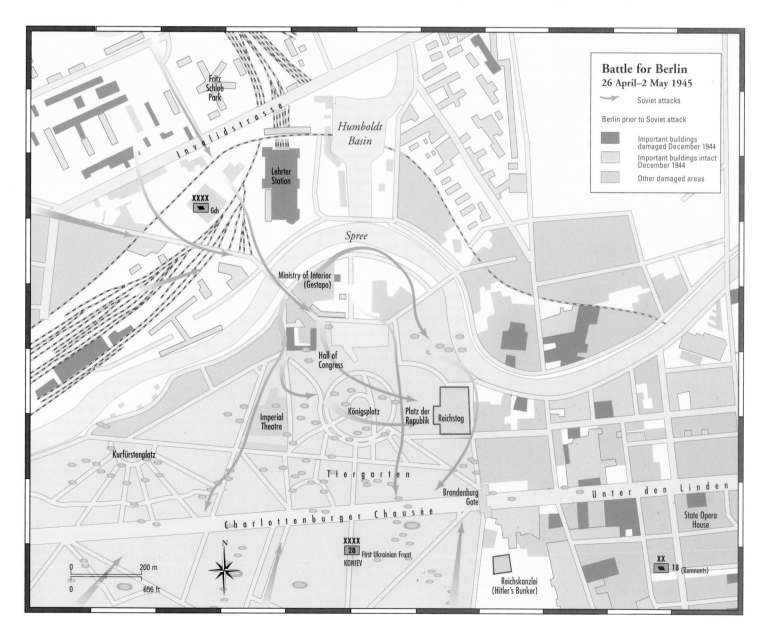

The Western Front

On 6 June 1944, American, British and Canadian forces landed on the beaches of Normandy, opening the second front in northwest Europe. After a few months of hard fighting, the road to Berlin lay open, but Allied logistics and a stiffening of German resistance prevented the war's end in 1944. The cold winter prolonged the war, and it was to be May 1945 before hostilities finally ceased.

The Western Front of World War II was a far more complex construction than that between 1914 and 1918. While the Western Front in World War I was clearly defined in that troops from the opposing sides faced one another in France and Belgium from the first day of the conflict to the last, and was regarded by the participants as the decisive theatre in the war, the pattern in World War II was very different, with no major fighting on land in northwest Europe for more than three years.

The first phase of the war in the west had been marked by very little activity; the so-called 'Phoney War'. British and French troops had spent their time training. All this changed in February 1940, when Hitler ordered the start of planning for an invasion of Norway to secure German access to iron ore. In April 1940, the Germans invaded Denmark and Norway. While Denmark capitulated almost immediately, the French and British sent troops to assist the Norwegians. Although the Allies enjoyed some success, by early May the majority of the Allied troops had been forced to withdraw.

Anglo-French priorities were dramatically altered by the German invasion of the Low Countries on 10 May 1940. The Netherlands, a nation that had not fought a war since 1830, had been invaded and forced to surrender in just four days, following a massive terror-bombing raid against Rotterdam by the Luftwaffe. The Belgian army fought with considerable vigour and courage against the invading Germans, but were hampered by the fact that, although France and Britain wished to send help, they were prevented from moving into Belgium by that country's desire to remain neutral. While British and French troops did reach the River Dyle and begin to aid the defence, the Germans were able to outflank them from the Netherlands, forcing the Allies to fall back. Belgium surrendered on 28 May, and the British and French fell back towards the Channel coast. The majority of British troops reached Dunkirk, and, in an error of judgement, Hitler stopped the pursuit by his panzers just long enough to allow the British to withdraw. Dunkirk proved a remarkable success (even if it represented a crushing defeat for the Allies), in that more than 335,000 British and French troops were evacuated.

BRITAIN ISOLATED

At this point, with the surrender of France, the front line on the Western Front might be said to have shifted to England's south coast. Unlike previous conflicts, the front shifted from the land to the air. The success of the Royal Air Force (RAF) in the Battle of Britain ensured that the Germans would not be able to invade – at least not in 1940. With the invasion of the Soviet Union in June 1941, the campaign in the west remained very much one conducted in the air, with RAF Bomber Command carrying out raids against Germany. These raids had to serve as the 'second front' for the purposes of carrying the fight to the enemy, as it was quite clear that British forces would not be able to return to Europe for some time. The entry of the United States into the war meant that an invasion of the continent would be possible; however, even this would take time. There were a few excursions onto French soil, with the commando raids on targets such as St Nazaire and Bruneval, which helped to boost civilian morale, and notably the

Left: An American tank column in the south of France. The Americans were keen to transfer troops and equipment from the Italian theatre – which had become of secondary importance in their view – to the main effort against Germany. The landings in southern France in August 1944 were known as 'Operation Dragoon', and Winston Churchill, the British Prime Minister, liked to say that he had been 'dragooned' into agreeing to go ahead with the plan when he would have preferred a landing in either Greece or the Balkans.

Canadian disaster at Dieppe, where important lessons were learned for the Normandy landings which undoubtedly helped save lives in the long run. But these raids were never intended to lead to permanent bridgeheads on the continent, and the front remained effectively in the English Channel. All that changed once the invasion of France took place in June 1944 – the more traditional concept of a 'front' returned, with Anglo-American forces (and their allies) driving the Germans back until their final defeat in 1945.

GLOBAL STRATEGY

World War II cannot be considered to have been a truly global conflict until the middle of 1941. Although the United States was not a combatant at the time that the Germans invaded Russia, nonetheless its role in the Battle of the Atlantic meant that it could hardly claim to be absolutely neutral. The lend-lease deal with the United Kingdom, coupled with the actions of the US Navy's

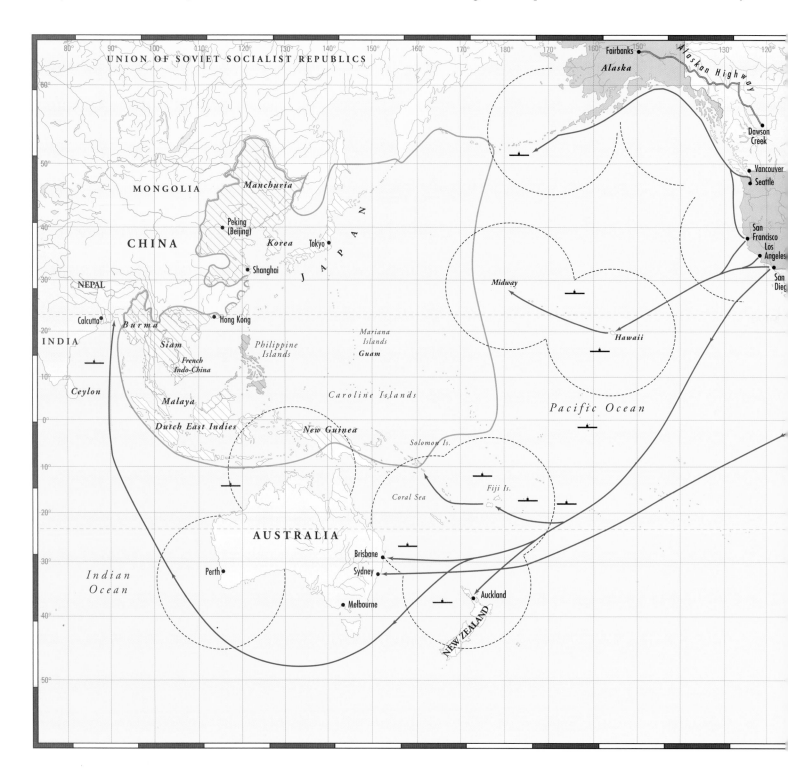

GLOBAL VIEW

The geographical extent of World
War II was enormous. Almost
every part of the globe played
some role in strategy, with the
sea routes between the United
States and Britain being of
particular importance. While the

Allies had agreed that Germany
should be their first priority, the
war in the Pacific could hardly
be said to have been ignored in
American planning.

The United States was the hub
of global strategy because its
phenomenal industrial strength
meant that it was able to drive

the war in both the Pacific and
western Europe. Although Soviet
industry was in many respects
even more prolific in terms of
military output, even the Red
Army was dependent upon
American factories for its trucks
and jeeps. As the Russians
inflicted increasingly heavy

reverses on the Germans, the
Anglo-American invasion of
Europe became the prime focus
for strategy; once the greater
threat of Hitler's Germany was
defeated, the Japanese would face
the full might of the US war
machine, culminating in their
utter defeat in August 1945.

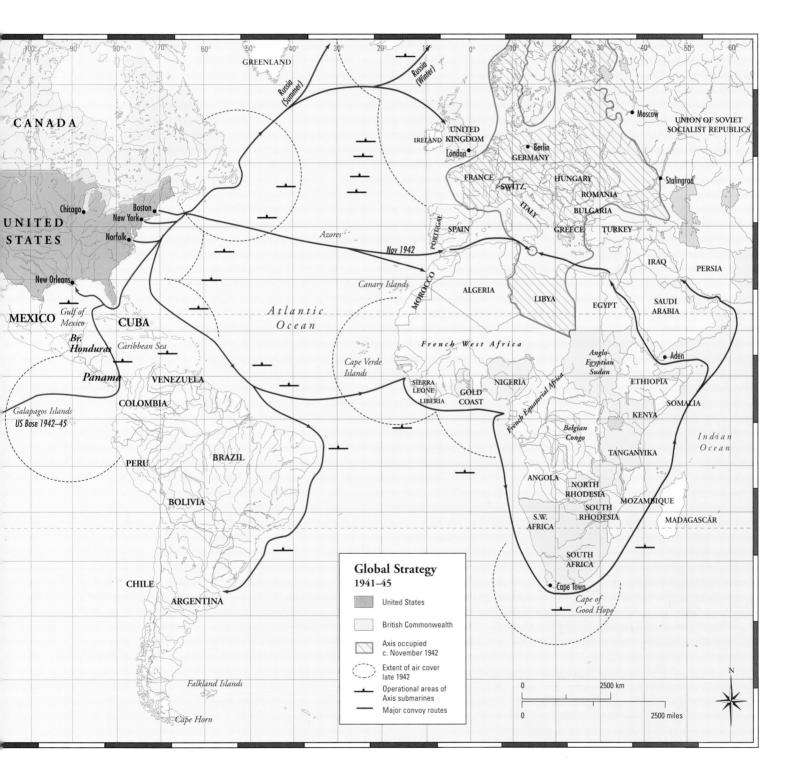

neutrality patrols, which covered everything from broadcasting the whereabouts of U-boats (enabling ships travelling to Britain to sail around the threat) to depth-charging them, meant that Hitler considered the United States to be at war with Germany in all but name. When the Japanese attacked Pearl Harbor, Hitler neatly solved the potential dilemma for US President Franklin Roosevelt of whether or not America should declare war upon Germany by stating that his country was at war with the United States.

Agreement between the British and Americans that the defeat of Germany would take priority meant that the Battle of the Atlantic intensified as a build-up of American troops and equipment in Britain took place, while the war in North Africa and the Mediterranean was prosecuted with some success: German forces in Tunisia surrendered in 1943, and Italy was invaded the same year. Pressure from the Soviet leader Stalin for a second front meant that an invasion of Europe had to be planned for as soon as was possible, and it was agreed in May 1943 that this operation would take place in 1944. As the invasion of Europe was planned, American operations in the Pacific began the long process of 'island hopping' towards Japan.

THE COSSAC PLAN

The Anglo–American conference in Casablanca in January 1943 set the priorities for future operations, including agreement that the unconditional surrender of Germany was the Allied goal. To achieve this, it was clear that an invasion of western Europe would be needed. The Americans had planned for this almost since their entry into the war, and initial schemes for an invasion as early as 1942 had caused considerable alarm to the British. The disastrous raid on

A map used by the D-Day planners to show the shipping lanes for the armada that carried and escorted the Allied armies across the Channel to the Normandy beaches. Each lane had to be swept in secret for German mines, with warships stationed either side of the convoys to prevent any German attacks on them by submarine or fast attack craft. Artificial harbours were also towed across with the convoys to protect them from any Channel storms.

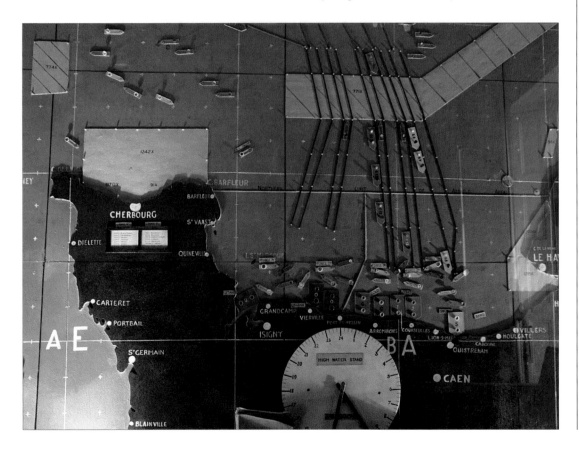

OVERLORD

The build-up for Overlord turned much of southern England into a giant military training camp: 1,500,000 American troops were to be based in Britain by May 1944, along with 50,000 tanks. Around 1,750,000 British troops and several hundred thousand from the British Empire and the Dominions, along with men from countries under occupation, would form the invading armies.

Another 1,000,000 men were still in the United States, and would be transported directly to France once the invasion had succeeded in capturing a suitable French port.

The plan for the invasion included an airborne assault to secure the flanks of the landing area. Three divisions were to land on the beaches on the first day, with additional forces to follow quickly afterwards. Once the beachhead was established, Caen was to be secured; while British forces fixed the German forces, US units would break out into France.

After Eisenhower was appointed Supreme Allied Commander, COSSAC was amalgamated into the Supreme Headquarters Allied Expeditionary Force (SHAEF). Field Marshal Montgomery was given the task of commanding the invasion forces, and made several refinements to the plan. Instead of three divisions, Montgomery increased the invasion force to five divisions, with three British/Canadian and two American beaches.

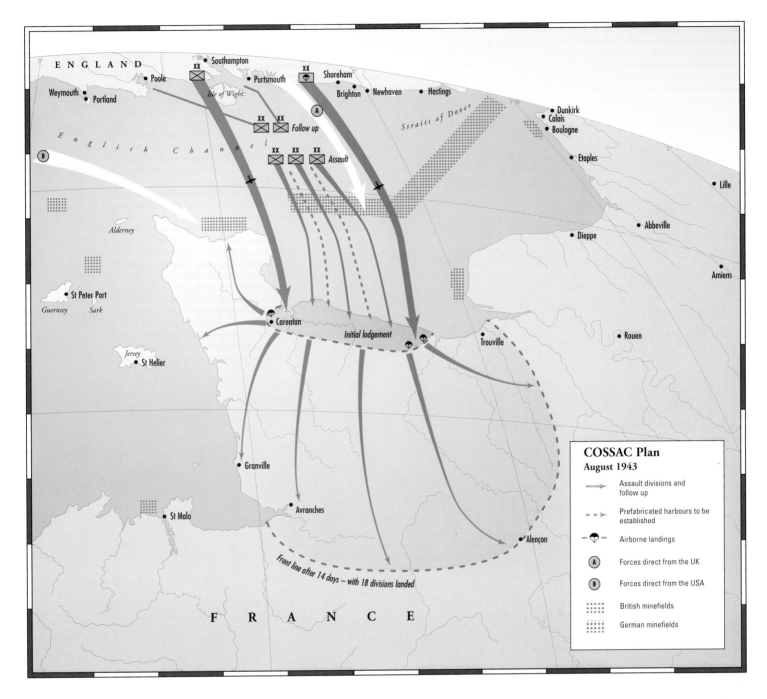

ENGLAND

Southampton
Poole
Weymouth • Portland
Isle of Wight
Portsmouth
Shoreham
Brighton • Newhaven • Hastings
Straits of Dover
Dunkirk
Calais
Boulogne
Etaples
Lille
English Channel
Follow up
Assault
Alderney
Abbeville
Dieppe
Amiens
St Peter Port
Guernsey   Sark
Carentan
Initial lodgement
Trouville
Rouen
Jersey
St Helier
Granville
Avranches
St Malo
Alençon
Front line after 14 days – with 18 divisions landed

F R A N C E

COSSAC Plan
August 1943

Assault divisions and follow up

Prefabricated harbours to be established

Airborne landings

Ⓐ Forces direct from the UK

Ⓑ Forces direct from the USA

British minefields

German minefields

Dieppe in August 1942 convinced the Americans that some delay in opening the second front was required, but their plan – Operation Round Up – remained extant as the basis for the landings when they did come.

To put the detail necessary to make Round Up a practical operation in place, the British Prime Minister Winston Churchill and President Roosevelt agreed to the establishment of a combined planning staff. General Sir Frederick Morgan was appointed Chief of Staff to the Supreme Allied Commander (COSSAC), and given the task of planning the invasion, even though the supreme commander for the operation had yet to be appointed. Once Morgan's staff had been appointed, the first task was to choose the location for the invasion. It was agreed that the landing area would need clear, open beaches, and the choice was narrowed to the Pas de Calais, Brittany or Normandy.

While the Pas de Calais offered the shortest distance across the Channel (and the shortest distance from France into Germany), there were a number of factors that counted against this location. The first was that the area was so obviously a good choice for a landing that the Germans were making considerable efforts to fortify it. Also, the exits from the beaches around the Pas de Calais were restricted, which would make it difficult to move armour and heavy equipment forward: it soon became clear that landings would have to be made on the Belgian coast or at the Seine estuary ports to allow such material to be landed. Finally, the Kentish

TWO FRONTS

When D-Day took place on 6 June 1944, Hitler still controlled large parts of Europe. His one hope of avoiding utter defeat was to secure a separate peace with the Western Allies, to enable him to hold off the advancing Red Army. While Hitler may have held hopes for such a result, the likelihood of the Allies abandoning their aim of forcing an unconditional surrender was in fact extremely remote.

Once a foothold had been established in Normandy, the liberation of western Europe could begin in earnest. The weight of Allied pressure in the west, in Italy and on the Eastern Front meant that the Germans were denied the time and space in which to operate effectively. Hitler's increasingly frail grasp upon the reality of his situation meant that his troops were sacrificed needlessly as they attempted to carry out orders to defend untenable positions, and led to such flights of fancy as the Ardennes Offensive, which was never going to achieve the goals set for it. It is debatable whether the loss of Antwerp would have forced the Allies to seek peace.

As a result, by September 1944, the Germans had been removed from the Soviet Union, France, Belgium and most of Italy. Although the war would go on for another eight months, the result could no longer be in doubt. Increasing pressure from all sides meant that it was a question of when, rather than if, Germany would be invaded, defeated and occupied.

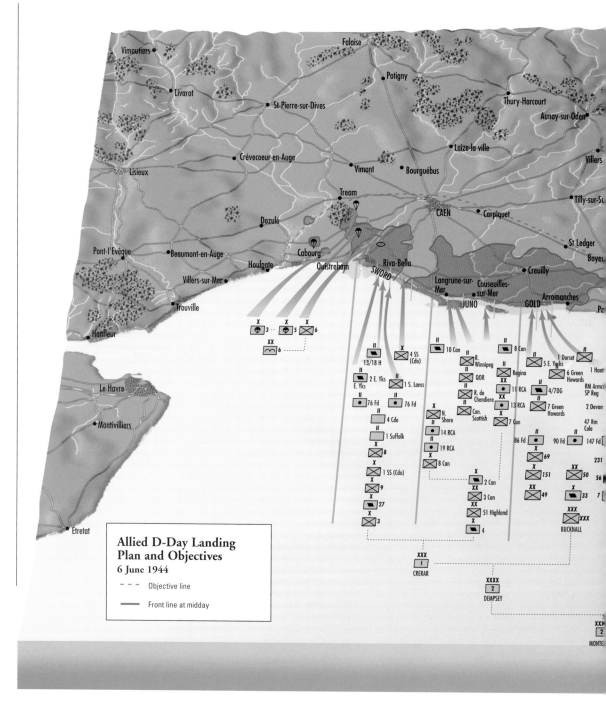

Allied D-Day Landing Plan and Objectives
6 June 1944

- - - Objective line

—— Front line at midday

ports were simply not big enough to accommodate the whole landing fleet, which would demand that some vessels sail from Portsmouth and Southampton – a journey of more than 160km (100 miles) within range of German shore batteries.

The Pas de Calais having been rejected, attention was turned to Brittany. Although the Brittany option had some support in COSSAC, the naval staffs were opposed, as the area was subject to violent and unpredictable storms that could seriously interfere with the landings. In addition to these concerns, the facts that the distance between Brittany and Germany would present massive challenges to Allied logistics and that the provision of air cover from the United Kingdom would be extremely difficult conspired to ensure that COSSAC recommended Normandy as the location for the invasion; this was confirmed in June 1943, by which time Round Up had been renamed Overlord. In response to demands from Stalin, the date for the invasion was set for May 1944.

NORMANDY

After a cancellation because of bad weather in the Channel on 5 June, Operation Overlord began on 6 June 1944. The airborne assaults suffered from some problems. Although landings by glider were successful, the paratroops landed in a variety of locations, and it took a great deal of time for them to form up into their units. The seaborne elements disembarked on the five landing beaches of *Sword, Juno* and *Gold* (British and Canadian formations) and *Omaha* and *Utah* (American). The invasion forces made it ashore without serious difficulty at four of the beaches, but Omaha beach was a different matter. Armoured support for the landing had been launched too far from the beach, and the majority of the tanks were swamped. Stiff resistance meant that there were times during 6 June when it appeared that Omaha would have to be abandoned. By nightfall, the crisis had passed, and Omaha, along with the other beaches, was secure, although casualties there of around 3000 were the heaviest of the day.

Once ashore, the Allies concentrated upon making their position absolutely secure. By 10 June, the five landing areas had been consolidated into a single lodgement, and the Americans were pushing inland towards Cherbourg. British attempts to take Caen

BREAKOUT

By July 1944, the planning for the Allied breakout from Normandy was marked by considerable doubt and controversy, as the Germans seemed capable of thwarting the Allies' every attempted move. Progress had been slow, with the ground favouring the defenders, and the British and Canadian forces had run into considerable opposition as they attempted to take Caen.

Nevertheless, while there was no denying that the delay in defeating the Germans opposite the British sector represented a setback, it did serve the intended purpose of preventing the Germans reinforcing the American sector.

Operation Cobra, the American attempt to breakout, was to begin in unfavourable circumstances, and, by the evening of 25 July, Eisenhower feared that the offensive would fail. However, General 'Lightning Joe' Collins' VII Corps punched through the German lines and continued to charge forwards in the face of relatively light opposition. After 50 days of fighting, the Americans had achieved the longed-for breakout. On 30 July, they entered Brittany.

General George S. Patton's newly arrived Third Army then pushed through the gap created at Avranches and began a rapid exploitation of the battlefield. Patton's formations tore through the German rear areas, and, by 6 August 1944, the breakout from Normandy had at last been made.

ran into heavy resistance, and three separate attempts to take the city failed. However, these efforts drew German forces on to the British and fixed them in place, giving the Americans the opportunity to build up their forces and to break out once ready.

BREAKOUT PLAN

On 18 June 1944, Field Marshal Montgomery issued a directive calling for the capture of Caen by the British and Cherbourg by the Americans within five days. Bad weather was to delay these operations, and the Americans were not able to secure Cherbourg until 27 June. The British attempt to take Caen was thwarted by fierce German resistance, but at least had the benefit of drawing two more German armoured divisions into the defence of the city, making them unable to redeploy swiftly so as to meet any threats elsewhere.

By the end of June, over 875,000 men had been landed in Normandy, but concerns persisted among some commanders about the speed at which the operation was progressing. By early July, the invasion forces were no more than 24km (15 miles) inland at any point, which meant that they had taken just one-fifth of the ground that had been anticipated in the original plan. Fears of a stalemate were growing, and by the second week in July it seemed as though Montgomery was the only commander with any sense of optimism left. On 10 July, he issued instructions for the breakout from Normandy. General Omar Bradley's First US Army would attack towards Avranches, after which the lead element of US Third Army (VIII Corps) would strike into Brittany. To assist, General Sir Miles Dempsey's British Second Army would attack through the open countryside to the east of Caen.

Dempsey was to begin his attack, Operation Goodwood, on 18 July, with Bradley's offensive, Operation Cobra, starting the next day. Until St-Lô was captured, however, it was impossible for Bradley to start his attack, and this was only achieved on the morning of 19 July, putting Cobra back until 24 July.

On the afternoon of 19 July, just as it appeared that success had been achieved, the armoured element of Goodwood ran into extremely heavy resistance, and was brought to a halt short of Bourgébus Ridge. Heavy rain on 20 July brought the attack to a complete standstill. It appeared that Goodwood had failed utterly. In fact, Montgomery's aim of drawing in German armour had worked. Thirteen German divisions now faced the British, while nine were opposite the Americans. Only two of these divisions were armoured.

Cobra did not begin well: American bombers sent in to action to destroy enemy positions managed to drop some of their bombs short and onto US troops. However, the bombing destroyed more than 60 per cent of the Panzer *Lehr* Division, and, by the end of the first day, American forces had advanced some 3600m (4000 yards). The advance continued until, on 27 July, the US 2nd Armored Division fought its way through into open country: the breakthrough had finally been achieved.

Once the breakthrough had been made, it became clear that the Germans were in danger of being encircled. On 3 August, Hitler ordered

Breakout Plan
22 July–6 August

Front line at 24:00 hrs

that an armoured assault against General George S. Patton's forces should be launched around the town of Mortain. Hitler's plan seemed simple enough – four armoured divisions would attack across the base of the Cotentin Peninsula to Avranches, splitting Patton's forces in two. This action would immediately force a halt to the advance.

The difficulty with this plan was that it totally failed to take account of Allied air power. German generals were horrified at Hitler's plan because they knew only too well what air attack could do to their forces; indeed, the commander of the 116th Panzer Division was sacked when he refused to allow his troops to take part in the attack.

Although the attack, beginning on 6 August, secured Mortain itself, it could not secure the high ground to the east of the town, and, as soon as dawn broke on 7 August, British and American fighter bombers began incessant attacks on the German formations. The Mortain attack was defeated, and the Allies now had an opportunity to encircle and then destroy the Germans in Normandy. This could be achieved in one of two ways: either by bottling the forces up in the Argentan-Falaise area, or by carrying out a larger

Falaise Pocket
6–19 August 1944

— Front line 6 August
— Front line 16 August
— Front line 19 August

FALAISE

The failure of a counterattack at Mortain gave the Allies an opportunity to encircle the Germans in Normandy by bottling the forces up in the Argentan-Falaise area. As US forces headed to Argentan, the Canadian First Army attacked in the direction of Falaise. The first attempts to reach Falaise failed, but a second offensive was launched, and, on 15 August 1944, the Canadians finally entered Falaise.

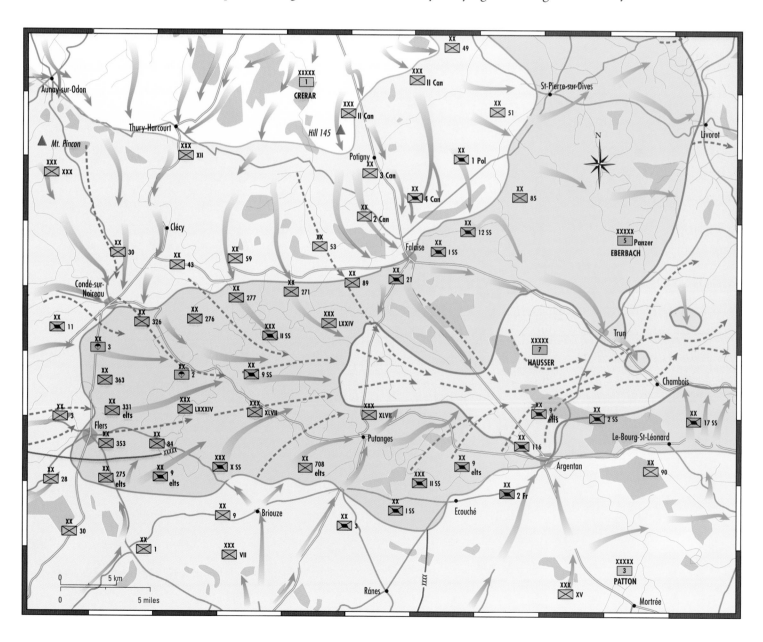

PARIS

The Germans carried out a reasonably ordered withdrawal from the Falaise pocket while the jaws remained open; some 40,000 men escaped. Once the pocket was closed, French forces moved on to retake Paris, which was now in revolt. Hitler's instructions that the city should be razed to the ground were ignored, and General Leclerc's troops liberated a city that was substantially intact, even after several days' fighting.

envelopment along the line of the River Seine. The former option was the one followed, as the defeat at Mortain forced the Germans back into the opening of a pocket which was already forming as US forces headed to Argentan, while Canadian First Army attacked in the direction of Falaise. Hitler initially refused to allow his troops to withdraw, but Field Marshal von Kluge ignored these instructions and began to pull forces back. This would prove to be too late for many Germans because the jaws of the trap were closing quickly.

The first attempts to reach Falaise as part of Operation Totalise had failed, but the need to reach the town prompted the launch of Operation Tractable, an immediate follow-on. The advance was slow; however, on 15 August, the Canadians finally entered Falaise, a week after they had started. The Germans carried out a reasonably ordered withdrawal from the pocket while the jaws remained open, and some 40,000 men were able to escape. Once the pocket was closed on 20 August, French forces moved on to retake Paris.

FALAISE AND THE LIBERATION OF PARIS

The day before the Falaise pocket closed, an uprising began in Paris, the inhabitants encouraged by the sounds of battle in the near distance. Eisenhower was not at all eager to advance on Paris,

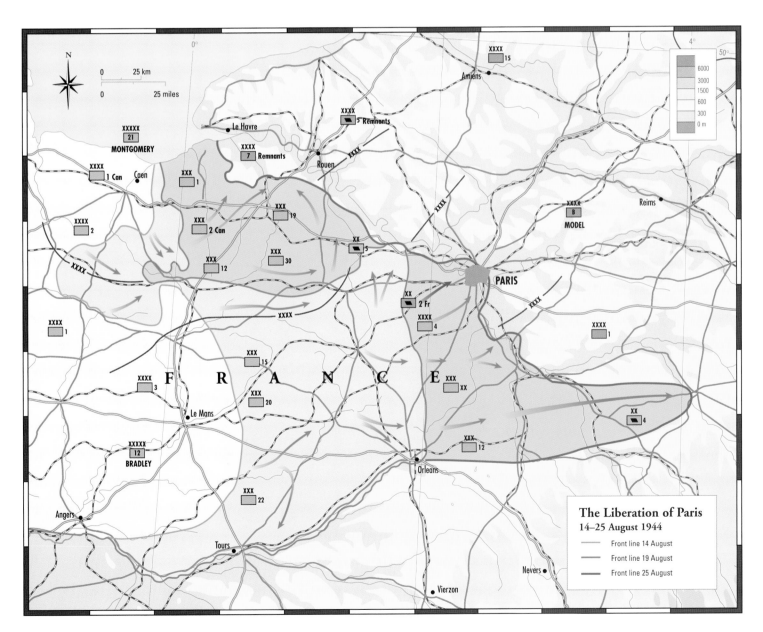

The Liberation of Paris
14–25 August 1944

Front line 14 August
Front line 19 August
Front line 25 August

Invasion of
Southern France
August 1944

— Allied front line 28 Aug.
← Allied attacks
→ German counterattacks
⌒ German strongholds
←-- German withdrawal

DRAGOON

Operation Anvil-Dragoon was driven more by the political necessity of ensuring that a recognized authority was restored in the south of France (preventing communist elements of the Resistance from establishing an administration) than military requirements. The invasion itself was a Franco-American effort, with limited British involvement. Some 94,000 soldiers embarked from Naples to form the initial seaborne wave of the invasion, and they were able to land with remarkably little resistance. The Germans put up barely any fight and were soon ordered to retreat northwards in order to defend Germany itself.

as it was militarily unimportant; however, pressure from General de Gaulle and the danger of a Communist takeover of the city by the Resistance meant that he was forced to change his mind. Stalin had been strongly criticised for allowing the Warsaw rebellion to be crushed by the Germans only a few weeks before, and Eisenhower was not keen to earn a similar reputation for ruthlessness. Forces were diverted towards the capital, headed by General Philippe Leclerc's French-manned 2nd Armoured Division, which had already attempted a reconnaissance in force towards the city. Slightly behind Leclerc was the US 4th Division.

The first French troops made their way into Paris on the evening of 24 August 1944, with the rest of 2nd Armoured Division following the next morning. Paris fell the same day, and was entered in triumph by de Gaulle 24 hours later. Hitler's instructions that the city should be razed to the ground were ignored by Dietrich von Choltitz, the commander of the Paris garrison, and General Leclerc's troops were able to liberate a city that was substantially intact.

SOUTHERN FRANCE AND THE ADVANCE TO SEPTEMBER 1944

The initial planning for Overlord called for an invasion of Southern France, with the aim of confronting the Germans with landings in two geographically separate parts of the country. Although the plan had been endorsed at the Tehran conference, no firm date had been fixed for this particular operation (code-named Anvil) on the grounds that it was impossible to provide enough shipping to carry out the plan alongside the Normandy landings. Eisenhower secured agreement that it should take place after the Overlord landings, and, as late as 11 June, Churchill was pressing for the landings to be abandoned in favour of landings in the Balkans.

This suggestion was rejected by Roosevelt, who told Churchill that landings in the Balkans would be deeply unpopular in the United States; as it was an election year, it was obvious that

BRUSSELS

Following the liberation of Paris, the Allied advance seemed unstoppable, with the German troops exhausted from continuous fighting and unable to establish a defensive line. The Germans were pushed back towards Belgium and the German frontier. While the coast around Calais and Dunkirk remained in German hands, the Allies had taken Brussels and Antwerp by early September, and were in control of most of France. The Allies then paused to regroup for the final push on Germany.

Churchill would not succeed, yet the British Prime Minister made desperate attempts to convince Eisenhower to modify the plan: Eisenhower refused. Churchill joked that, as he had been forced to accept the landings, the operation should be rechristened 'Dragoon' (a pun on being dragooned into agreement), but the planning staff failed to spot the joke and earnestly began referring to the operation as Anvil-Dragoon.

By 10 August, the invasion fleet had been assembled in a variety of Mediterranean ports, and the assault began with commando landings on the night of 14 August. This was followed by an air landing aimed to seize the vital intersection at Le Muy. Some of the paratroopers were dropped outside their intended landing zone, right on top of the headquarters of the German LXII Corps. The paratroops seized their opportunity, attacking the headquarters and preventing it from coordinating the defences on the beaches against the seaborne attack. Le Muy fell the next day. The main landings took place at 05:50 on 15 August, and made good progress. On 17 August, orders for the abandonment of Southern France (apart from the ports) were issued by the German high command, and the forces there began to retreat.

The Franco-American advance proceeded smoothly; Marseille surrendered on 28 August, and leading elements of General Lucian K. Truscott's VI Corps entered Lyons on 3 September.

By the time Truscott had reached Lyons, the Allied forces in the north had carried out a rapid exploitation after their breakthrough. Montgomery launched Operation Kitten, the advance to the Seine, on 16 August, forcing the Germans to conduct a skilful, phased withdrawal across the

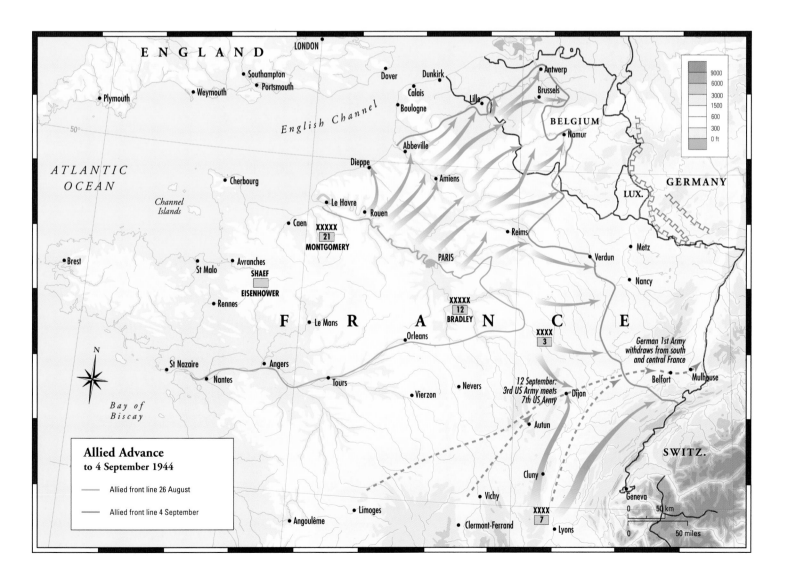

MARKET GARDEN

The decision to launch an airborne operation to capture bridges over the Lower Rhine was taken by General Eisenhower, who was impressed by the daring nature of the usually cautious Montgomery's plan. Eisenhower had chosen to follow a 'broad front' strategy against Germany, giving equal support to all his army commanders, infuriating Patton in particular. But Montgomery seemed to be offering the chance to end the war before the year's end, and Eisenhower decided to take the gamble.

The air lift in support of Operation Market Garden was enormous in its scale. When the Market Garden began on 17 September 1944, the skies over southern England and the North Sea were filled with a endless stream of aircraft – many of them the ubiquitous C-47 Dakota – and gliders carrying some 20,000 men and their equipment across the Channel to the Netherlands.

The fleet took two routes: the northern route carried the US 82nd Airborne and British 1st Airborne Divisions to their objectives at Nijmegen and Arnhem, while the southern route aircraft carried the US 101st Airborne Division to their Eindhoven drop zones. Although the southern stream suffered losses from German anti-aircraft fire, it was able to reach the drop zone, where 7000 men landed.

river to prevent being completely destroyed. The Germans continued pulling back, heading for the Belgian and German frontiers, with the Allies in pursuit. During the first days of September, the Allies began to outrun their logistics, and the advance came to a halt along a line from the Meuse to Maastricht, then south from Aachen to the Swiss border.

While plans were made for the next stage in operations, Truscott's forces linked with Patton on 11 September, trapping the last 20,000 men of the German rearguard, who surrendered. The operation in the south of France actually increased logistical problems because resources had to be diverted from Allied forces in the north; however, Anvil-Dragoon at least succeeded in ensuring stability in the south of the country, which was one of the key concerns for the Americans when they had insisted upon the operation continuing.

MONTGOMERY'S DARING PLAN

Montgomery's solution to the loss of momentum in the Allied advance was to propose a daring airborne operation designed to secure a bridge over the Rhine and to deny the Germans launch sites for V2 missiles. The plan was to land around 30,000 British and American airborne troops at key river bridges, while General Sir Brian Horrocks's XXX Corps thrust north through Holland along the 100km (60-mile) long corridor created by the landing. Montgomery argued that the operation might cause a collapse in German will to continue fighting, but, even if it did not, the Allies would at least have gained a bridgehead across the Rhine. The furthest bridge to be seized would be that at Arnhem, which the British 1st Airborne Division was to hold until the arrival of XXX Corps. The

British stretcher bearers load wounded men onto their jeep for transportation to a field hospital. By September 1944, it was clear that the war would soon be over, and many Allied soldiers became reluctant to take unnecessary risks in combat. At the same time, German resistance stiffened as the front approached Germany itself.

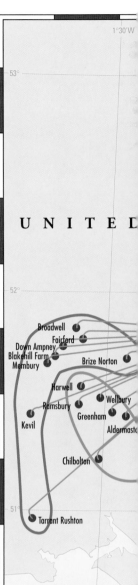

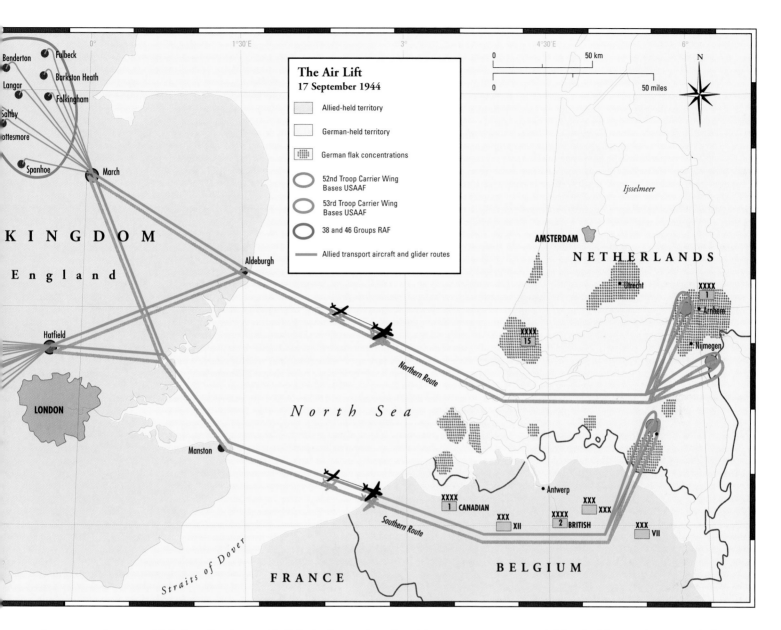

plan was code-named Market Garden, with 'Market' covering the airborne component and 'Garden' being the ground element. Eisenhower agreed to the plan, with the date being set for 17 September 1944.

While the plan was recognized as being particularly bold – in direct contrast to Montgomery's more usual careful and methodical approach – it was not without difficulties. One of the key problems was that the Allied First Airborne Army was bedevilled by the poor relationship between its commander, General Lewis Brereton, and his deputy, Lieutenant General Sir Frederick 'Boy' Browning. The two barely spoke to one another, a fact best exemplified when it transpired that the two men had planned two completely different operations for the airborne troops on 6 September, with the result that both had to be cancelled. Of equal concern was the problem of aircraft availability. Although the US Army Air Forces (USAAF) and RAF had the largest air transport fleet ever assembled, this was still not enough to transport more than a third of the army at a time.

The plans for Market Garden were duly drawn up, and envisaged the seizure of bridges at Eindhoven, Nijmegen and Arnhem. Browning made the now-immortal comment 'I think we may be going a bridge too far', but it was too late to modify the plan. On 17 September, the massed transport fleet took off from southern air bases to carry the airborne component into battle.

ARNHEM

Operation Market Garden's airborne assault began on the morning of Sunday 17 September, with the first paratroops and gliders landing shortly after lunchtime. By 14:00, some 20,000 troops, along with vehicles and equipment, had landed all along the airborne corridor, and began to prepare to move towards their objectives.

Unfortunately for the Allied plan, there were a number of problems ahead of them. The first was that the German forces in the area, particularly around Arnhem, were not as weak as had been predicted. As the 1st Airborne Division landed, Field Marshal Walther Model was already reporting news of the landings to Hitler. II SS Panzer Corps was alerted, and 9th SS Panzer Division was immediately sent to Arnhem, while the 10th SS Panzer Division was told to make all haste towards Nijmegen. This opposition was to prove a major obstacle to Allied plans.

While the Americans succeeded in capturing bridges at Eindhoven, they had to wait for XXX Corps to arrive. The XXX Corps' tanks had been advancing up a single road and had run into German opposition. German anti-tank guns inflicted some damage upon the lead elements of the advance before being silenced by a mix of air strikes and artillery. This held up XXX Corps, a portent of things to come. After pushing through this obstacle, XXX Corps then ran into more German opposition, which again took time to overcome. By the afternoon of 19 September, XXX Corps reached Nijmegen, then crossed the River Wahl. This left them only 16km (10 miles) south of Arnhem, the final objective – but German resistance was such that the advance ground to a complete halt, leaving the 1st Airborne Division cut off in Arnhem.

The 1st Airborne had been fighting in and around Arnhem for three days, and things had not gone well. The bridge in the town was meant to be captured by a surprise attack by armed jeeps, but the gliders carrying these had failed to arrive intact. Although the 2nd Battalion of the 1st Parachute Brigade reached the northern end of the bridge, reinforcements did not come.

British glider troops practise disembarking from their glider. The men of the Allied airborne divisions were all high-quality troops, and they were frustrated by their lack of participation in the campaign since the first landings on D-Day. Market Garden offered Eisenhower the opportunity to use these highly-trained men against supposedly poor-quality opposition. Unfortunately for the Allies, their intelligence was not accurate, and the lightly-armed airborne troops would find themselves fighting hard-bitten SS veterans equipped with armour and heavy weapons.

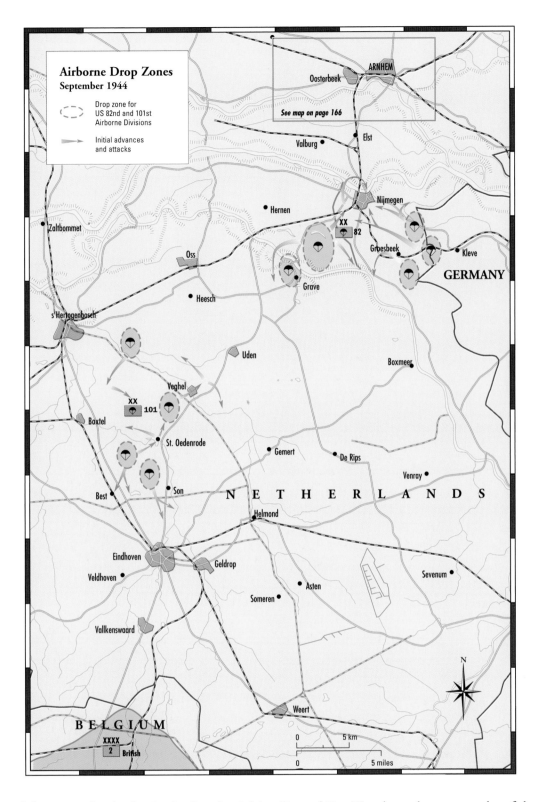

Airborne Drop Zones
September 1944

Drop zone for
US 82nd and 101st
Airborne Divisions

Initial advances
and attacks

See map on page 166

THE BRIDGE TOO FAR

By 14:00 on 17 September 1944, the first phase of Operation Market Garden's airlift was complete, and 20,000 Allied paratroops had landed. The airborne troops enjoyed initial success, taking their most of their objectives with ease, as the German defenders were taken by surprise; however, the 101st Airborne Division did suffer the mortification of seeing one of the bridges it was meant to capture being blown up as it approached it.

The British units in Arnhem faced the most difficult task, as unexpectedly a refitting SS Panzer Division attacked them almost as soon as they arrived. Nevertheless part of the bridge was soon under their control.

Meanwhile the 82nd and 101st Airborne Divisions had seized their objectives, and were ready to receive XXX Corps some time before that formation was able to break through increasingly stiff German defences. The Allied planners had miscalculated; only one good road was available for XXX Corps to follow during its offensive. It proved relatively straightforward for the German defenders to impose lengthy delays on the British troops with only a handful of men.

As a result the operation was behind schedule almost from the start, and with each hour the Germans could rush forward reinforcements to block the Allied advance towards Arnhem and the bridge that was their final objective.

The reason for this lay in the fact that Major General Roy Urquhart, the commander of the 1st Airborne Division, became detached from his headquarters and spent 36 hours hiding from German patrols until he was able to make his way back. In his absence, his subordinates had failed to agree a course of action, and devoted their attention to securing high ground outside the town rather than sending reinforcements to the bridge. The 2nd Battalion was completely isolated and, after beating off one attack, was subjected to a massive assault designed to literally blast the men from their positions. An epic stand resulted, but the task was impossible, and the Germans retook the bridge on 21 September.

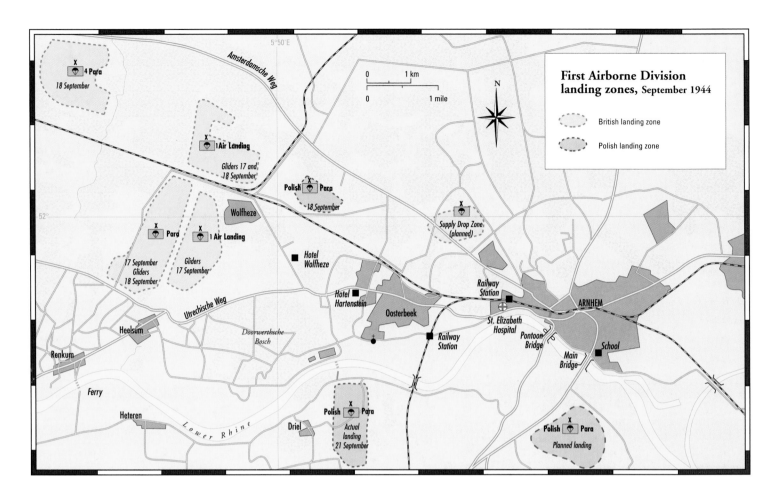

First Airborne Division landing zones, September 1944

While fighting in Arnhem continued, efforts to fly in supplies and reinforcements were made, but failed as a result of bad weather. Gradually XXX Corps battled towards Arnhem, finally reaching the south side of the Rhine on 23 September. An attempt to cross the river failed, and Montgomery decided that he had to withdraw the 1st Airborne Division. The remaining troops were evacuated across the river during the night of 25/26 September. Although Allied propaganda claims that the operation was 90 per cent successful were an exaggeration, the capture of the bridge over the Waal was to be of great utility in 1945 as a base from which to launch future operations.

BATTLE OF THE BULGE

In response to Allied successes, Hitler began to make plans for a counteroffensive which would regain the initiative for Germany. Hitler's plan was ambitious in the extreme, aiming to seize the port of Antwerp through carrying out a surprise attack in the Ardennes. Hitler's generals were aghast at his proposal, recognizing that the German army was in no state to make such a huge advance. Hitler could not be dissuaded, however, and gave orders for troops to be concentrated opposite the Ardennes, even though this would denude the Eastern Front of manpower that was desperately required there.

The offensive began on 16 December 1944. Although gains were made, they were not substantial enough for Hitler's goal of reaching Antwerp to be realized, just as his senior commanders had predicted. The northern thrust by Sixth Panzer Army stalled within a few days, while that in the centre enjoyed more success. During 18–22 December, the 101st Airborne Division was surrounded at Bastogne, and held out for some days in the face of difficult odds. Even though the Germans had pushed deep into Allied lines, once the Allies regained their footing and the weather lifted sufficiently for Allied fighter-bombers to operate, the outcome was inevitable. A counterattack began on 23 December, and Bastogne was relieved three days later. A final German effort was made on New Year's Day 1945, but this attack stalled in the face of determined Allied opposition.

On 3 January 1945, the Allies launched attacks against the northern and southern flanks of the salient created by the German advance, with the intention of reducing it once and for all. During the course of the next two weeks, the Germans were pushed back to their original starting positions. Although the offensive undoubtedly caused considerable alarm to the Allies in its early phases as the German advance made good ground, it soon became clear that German strength was inadequate to gain a major

ARNHEM LANDINGS

The air landings by the 1st Airborne Division were complicated by the fact that they occurred some distance from Arnhem itself, presenting the division with the need to move swiftly into the town to secure the bridge. As there were not enough aircraft to carry the entire airborne force in one lift, the plan was for additional troops, most notably those from the Polish Parachute Brigade and the Airborne Division's 4th Brigade, to arrive a day later, on 18 September 1944. The 4th Brigade was delayed by poor weather, however, and did not arrive until the afternoon of 18 September.

A combination of German resistance, bad luck and bad weather meant that several of the areas intended to be used for supply drops had not been secured. Other drop zones fell into German hands, and all attempts to notify the RAF of this failed. Supplies were landed as intended, and thus never reached the Allied soldiers, while alternative plans had to be made for the landing of the Polish Parachute Brigade. Part of this was dropped on 21 September, but the Germans had received early warning of the approach of the transport aircraft. Heavy anti-aircraft fire and an attack by two German fighter squadrons inflicted heavy casualties. By the time the Poles had fought their way out of the drop zone, they had been reduced to a strength of only 750 men.

RAF Dakotas drop men of the 1st Airborne Division over Arnhem during Operation Market Garden. The failure of Market Garden and a continuing supply problem, coupled with worsening weather, meant that the Allied offensive effectively stalled. Hitler saw a strategic opportunity to force the Western Allies to make peace by capturing Antwerp and driving a wedge between the British and American armies.

strategic victory. The end result was that the Germans suffered heavy losses pursuing a goal that had been unattainable from the outset.

ADVANCE TO THE RHINE

The German Ardennes offensive was a considerable shock to the Allies because it demonstrated that the Germans were still some way from being defeated. Although the ground lost during the German assault had been regained by the end of January 1945, it was clear that the Germans still posed a major challenge. Furthermore, it could be safely assumed that they would fight particularly vigorously once the war reached Germany itself.

Advancing into Germany required that the Allies cross the Rhine, which provided a natural defensive feature for the Germans; to complicate matters, the West Wall (also known as the Siegfried Line) had to be overcome prior to an advance into Germany. As if these challenges were not enough, the appalling weather meant that much of the low-lying ground near the river was under water, making it impractical for an advance.

Eisenhower's plan for crossing the Rhine involved two phases of operations. The first would see Montgomery's 21st Army Group clearing the approaches to the Rhine opposite Wesel. Under the auspices of Operation Vertiable, XXX Corps would advance from Nijmegen to the Reichswald, followed by a push by US Ninth Army through Münchengladbach. There would then be a brief pause to allow for consolidation, and 21st Army Group would prepare for a

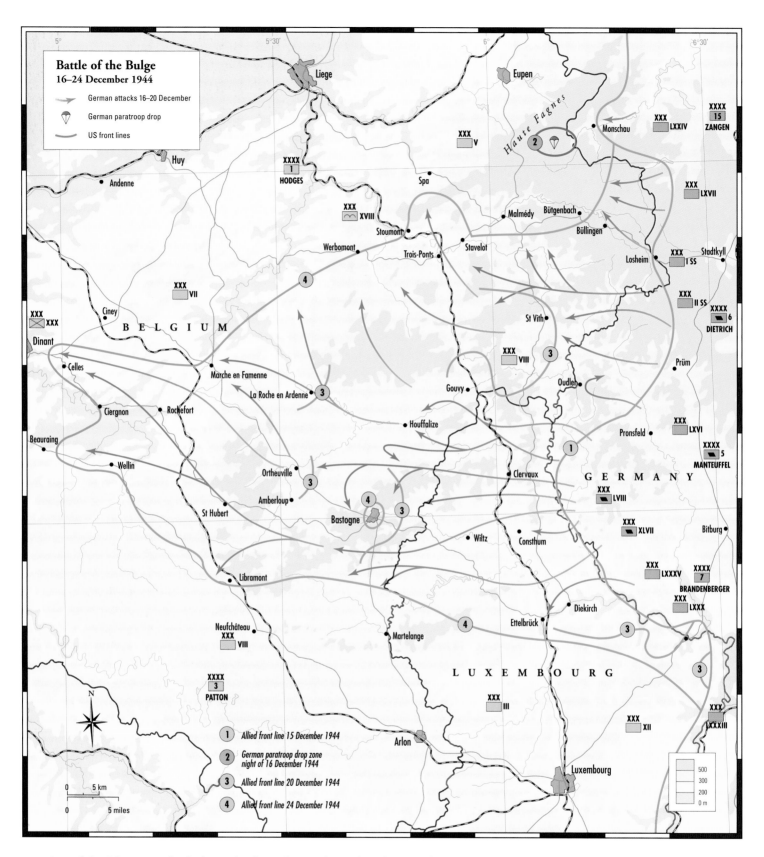

Battle of the Bulge
16–24 December 1944

German attacks 16–20 December

German paratroop drop

US front lines

HODGES

PATTON

1. Allied front line 15 December 1944

2. German paratroop drop zone
   night of 16 December 1944

3. Allied front line 20 December 1944

4. Allied front line 24 December 1944

Liege

Eupen

Haute Fagnes

Monschau

ZANGEN

LXXIV

XXX V

Spa

XXX LXVII

Huy

Andenne

XXXX 1

Malmédy Bütgenbach

Büllingen

XXX XVIII

Stoumont

Werbomont

Trois-Ponts

Stavelot

Losheim

I SS

Stadtkyll

XXX VII

Ciney

BELGIUM

St Vith

II SS

XXX
XXX

Dinant

Celles

Marche en Famenne

VIII

3

Prüm

6
DIETRICH

La Roche en Ardenne

Ciergnon

Rochefort

Houffalize

Gouvy

Oudler

Pronsfeld

LXVI

Beauraing

Wellin

Ortheuville

Amberloup

1

Clervaux

5
MANTEUFFEL

GERMANY

St Hubert

Bastogne

3

LVIII

XLVII

Bitburg

Libramont

Wiltz

Consthum

LXXXV

7
BRANDENBERGER

Neufchâteau

VIII

Diekirch

LXXX

3

PATTON

N

Martelange

Ettelbrück

LUXEMBOURG

3

Arlon

III

XII

LXXXIII

Luxembourg

500
300
200
0 m

0 5 km

0 5 miles

crossing of the Rhine, outflank the Ruhr from the north, and push on to the North German plain. If this succeeded, Montgomery would then be in a position to move on towards Berlin.

Bradley's 12th Army Group would advance to the south of Montgomery, clearing the approaches to the Rhine between Cologne and Koblenz. Patton's Third Army would swing towards Mainz and Mannheim, linking up with the US forces advancing from the Saarland. Once this was achieved, bridgeheads across the Rhine would be taken.

THE ARDENNES

The German offensive in the Ardennes was designed to change the strategic situation on the Western Front. Hitler's grand scheme envisaged seizing the port of Antwerp, driving a wedge between the British and American armies and using the advantage gained to negotiate a separate peace with the Western powers, enabling Germany to turn its attention to defeating the Soviet Union.

The plan for the offensive involved the use of commando units disguised as Americans to sow confusion as they went, misdirecting traffic and taking control of key crossing points. This idea foundered as there were too few English speakers available and also not enough captured American equipment on hand to ensure that the deception could be carried out successfully. Many commandos were shot when captured.

An airborne assault was meant to take place as well, but the paratroops were dispersed so badly after the drop that they were unable to achieve anything. Although the three German armies carrying out the offensive succeeded in driving the Americans back some distance, the success proved temporary. From 23 December, a counterattack drove the Germans back until, by the end of January, their defeat was confirmed. The Germans lost more than 120,000 men and 600 armoured vehicles in the offensive, weakening the forces available to defend against the crossing of the Rhine.

The First Canadian Army was to make the opening moves in Operation Veritable, which commenced on 8 February. German resistance was fierce, and the Allied advance proved to be far slower than expected. The defenders, drawn from the German First Parachute Army, held well-prepared defences in some depth. The terrain did not favour an attack, and the

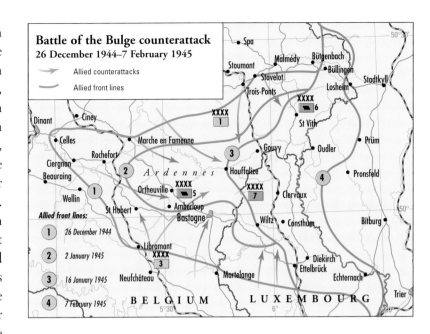

Battle of the Bulge counterattack
26 December 1944–7 February 1945

→ Allied counterattacks

Allied front lines

Allied front lines:
1 26 December 1944
2 2 January 1945
3 16 January 1945
4 7 February 1945

waterlogged ground meant that the Allies were forced to make use of narrow roads, which were far easier to defend. Further rain put the roads out of action, and the infantry was forced to slog their way across heavy ground. The US Ninth Army was unable to move after the Germans opened the Ruhr dam, and the German troops opposite them were diverted to meet the Anglo-

A German StuG assault gun during the Battle of the Bulge being camouflaged by its crew to hide the vehicle from Allied fighter-bombers. By 1944, the Allies had air superiority over the Western Front, and German troops became extremely restricted in their movements. Any significant clouds of dust or smoke would attract the attention of British Typhoons or American Thunderbolts, with their tank-killing rocket projectiles.

Canadian attack. Once the water receded, Ninth Army attacked on 23 February (two weeks after it was scheduled), meeting little resistance, as it linked with Veritable at Geldhorn on 3 March.

The American part of the operation went well. Cologne fell on 5/6 March 1945, followed by Bonn. On the evening of 6 March, a small force from Combat Command B was sent forward to close the Rhine at Remagen, to act as a shield for units moving to link up with the US Third Army. To their surprise, the bridge across the river was intact. After some fighting, American troops crossed the bridge. Once news of the surprise capture reached higher formations, American troops were out across the river. Although the bridge collapsed on 17 March, it was nonetheless the first step across the Rhine. By the end of the next day, Third Army was in control of much of the west bank of the Rhine, and ready to go across.

CROSSING THE RHINE

Although the capture of the bridge at Remagen provided the first crossing point, the first concerted effort to move across the river began on 22 March. Patton, frustrated at the fact that Remagen had been taken by First Army rather than his own, ordered his men to cross the river in boats at Nierstein and Oppenheim. Operation Plunder, Montgomery's plan for the British crossing of the Rhine, began on 23 March, with five bridgeheads established by the early

American troops try to find any available cover on their landing craft as they cross the Rhine under small arms fire. The capture of the bridge at Remagen destroyed any last hope for the Germans being able to halt the Allies at the Rhine, and the later crossing of the Rhine by Patton and Montgomery in significant numbers – the latter's operation watched by Winston Churchill – effectively sealed Germany's fate.

DRIVE TO THE RHINE

The advance towards the Rhine was particularly difficult for the Anglo-Canadian forces involved in the first phase because they faced particularly strenuous opposition while moving over difficult terrain. The first stage of the offensive, Operation Veritable, was hampered by poor weather and the fact that the British and Canadians were fighting in terrain that favoured the defender.

As a result, the advance was far slower than had been intended, and the US Ninth Army's complementary operation (Operation Grenade) had to be delayed for a fortnight after the Germans flooded the Ruhr Valley to delay the Allies' advance. The US First Army enjoyed better fortunes, and captured Cologne and Bonn. It then followed these successes with the notable capture of the Ludendorff bridge that crossed the Rhine river at Remagen.

German troops defending the bridge were meant to destroy it with explosives, and the fact that they had not done so came as a considerable surprise to the Americans who discovered this. The bridge was taken after a quick attack, and provided a useful but not vital means of getting both men and equipment across the Rhine.

Although the Ludendorff bridge collapsed on 17 March, it would not be long before the full weight of the Allied armies crossed the Rhine to drive into the heart of Germany.

morning of the next day, and the momentum of the attack was maintained by the use of an airborne assault, Operation Varsity. Varsity was designed to secure key ground ahead of the infantry, enabling them to advance with relative ease towards the banks of the river. Although a number of aircraft and gliders were lost to German flak, the operation was successful.

By 25 March, the 21st Army Group had gained a firm base on the east bank of the Rhine, consolidating the position three days later. With both sides across the Rhine, attention turned to the final phases of the war. At this point, Eisenhower changed strategy. Just as Montgomery started planning for an advance across the north German plain towards Berlin, Eisenhower decided to change the focus of operations towards the 12th Army Group, which would attack around the Elbe and Mulde rivers, with the aim of cutting the German army in two before linking with the Red Army. The 21st Army Group would move towards the Baltic coast

with the aim of reaching there before the Russians, clearing the Netherlands, seizing the north German ports and cutting off Denmark as it went. To the south of 12th Army Group, the US Sixth Army was to drive into Austria and defeat German forces remaining there, eliminating any potential last stand by the Nazi party.

In accordance with the new plan, the British Second Army broke out of its bridgehead on 28 March, crossed the River Weser and, despite some spirited German resistance around Hanover, gained 320km (200 miles) in three weeks. By 18 April on 21st Army Group's front, I Corps reached the Zuider Zee; XII Corps was well on the way to Hamburg; XXX Corps had reached Bremen; and VIII Corps had taken Lüneburg and was closing in on the Elbe.

Meanwhile, the 12th Army Group had encircled the Ruhr and carried out a methodical mopping-up operation. By the second week in April, German troops were surrendering in large numbers, often without resistance. The Ninth Army reached Hanover on 10 April, then next day advanced to the Elbe. By 18 April, while there were still some pockets of resistance to overcome, it was clear that the war did not have long to last.

THE LAST PHASE

The final phase of the Allied advance on the Western Front saw the rapid collapse of German resistance during the last days of April and the first week of May 1945. In the 21st Army Group's area, Bremen was taken on 27 April, while Lübeck and Hamburg fell on 2 May. The 12th Army Group captured Hale and Leipzig on 19

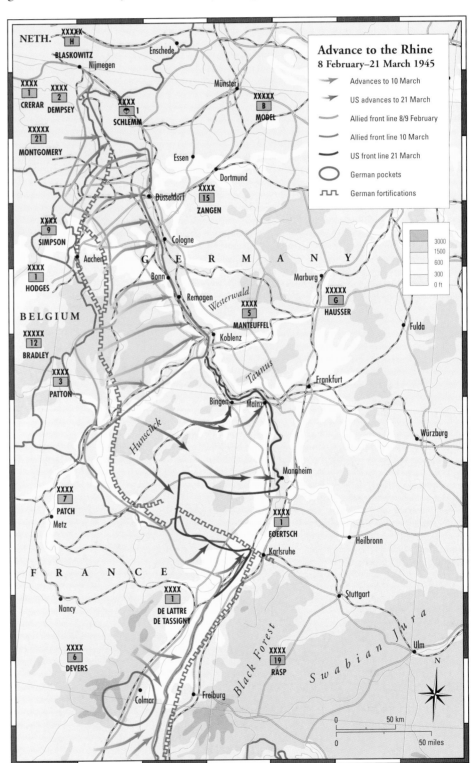

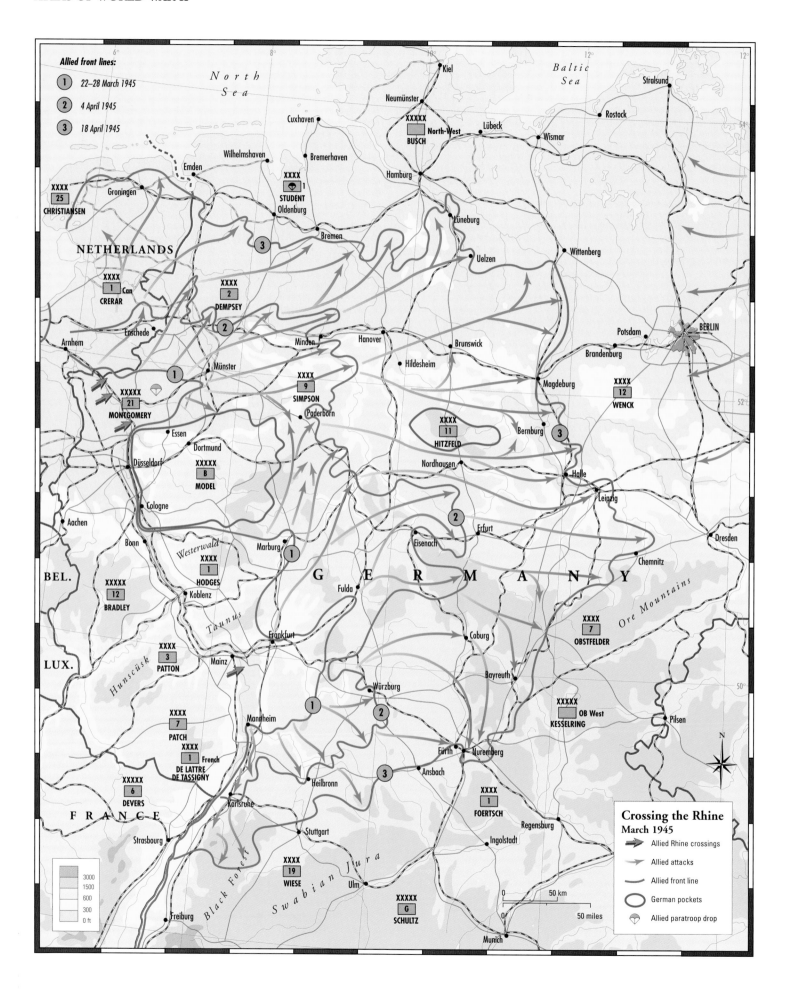

Allied front lines:
1 22–28 March 1945
2 4 April 1945
3 18 April 1945

North Sea

Baltic Sea

Stralsund

Kiel

Neumünster

Lübeck

Rostock

Wismar

Cuxhaven

Bremerhaven

XXXXX
North-West
BUSCH

Hamburg

Lüneburg

Wilhelmshaven

Emden

XXXX
1
STUDENT

Oldenburg

Bremen

Wittenberg

Uelzen

Groningen

XXXX
25
CHRISTIANSEN

NETHERLANDS

Enschede

Arnhem

XXXX
1 Can
CRERAR

XXXX
2
DEMPSEY

Münster

Minden

Hanover

Brunswick

Hildesheim

Potsdam

BERLIN

Brandenburg

Magdeburg

XXXX
12
WENCK

XXXX
9
SIMPSON

Paderborn

XXXX
11
HITZFELD

Bernburg

3

XXXXX
21
MONTGOMERY

Essen

Dortmund

Düsseldorf

XXXXX
B
MODEL

Nordhausen

Halle

Leipzig

Cologne

Aachen

Bonn

Westerwald

Marburg

1

XXXX
1
HODGES

GERMANY

Fulda

Eisenach

Erfurt

2

Chemnitz

Dresden

BEL.

XXXXX
12
BRADLEY

Koblenz

Taunus

Ore Mountains

LUX.

Hunscüsk

XXXX
3
PATTON

Mainz

Frankfurt

Würzburg

Coburg

Bayreuth

XXXX
7
OBSTFELDER

1

2

XXXXX
OB West
KESSELRING

Pilsen

XXXX
7
PATCH

Mannheim

XXXX
1 French
DE LATTRE
DE TASSIGNY

3

Heilbronn

Ansbach

Fürth Nuremberg

XXXXX
6
DEVERS

Karlsruhe

XXXX
1
FOERTSCH

Regensburg

FRANCE

Strasbourg

Stuttgart

Ingolstadt

Black Forest

XXXX
19
WIESE

Swabian Jura

Ulm

XXXXX
G
SCHULTZ

Freiburg

Munich

3000
1500
600
300
0 ft

Crossing the Rhine
March 1945

→ Allied Rhine crossings
→ Allied attacks
— Allied front line
◯ German pockets
⬙ Allied paratroop drop

0   50 km
0   50 miles

N

ENDGAME

Once the Rhine had been crossed and bridgeheads fully secured, the Allies were in a commanding position. Eisenhower's decision to change the focus of his attack away from Berlin did not cause any major planning problems, and both the 12th and 21st Army Groups were quickly able to move off for the next stage of their offensive.

In the north, the 21st Army Group enjoyed considerable success as it moved into the Netherlands and on towards the Baltic coast, and, by 18 April 1945, it was on the outskirts of Bremen, and closing in on Hamburg. To the south, the 12th Army Group advanced with similar speed, closing the Ruhr pocket during the first two weeks in April. The most notable difficulty for the Americans at this point was the sheer number of Germans surrendering to them, which presented administrative difficulties as attempts were made to process all the captives.

The Ninth Army's advance towards the Elbe also went well. On 4 April, it crossed the River Weser; four days later, it had bridged the Leine; three days after that, the Ninth Army reached the Elbe to the south of Magdeburg. Only the US Seventh Army and First French Army encountered any serious resistance, around Würzburg and Karlsruhe, respectively; even this was not enough to seriously delay the advance. By 18 April 1945, the ultimate defeat of Germany was in sight.

A smiling General Eisenhower (second from right) seen after the German surrender with senior American, British and Russian staff officers. Although VE (Victory in Europe) Day was 8 May 1945, sporadic fighting continued in Europe for another week against fanatical Hitler supporters, and the Allies still faced the potentially costly problem of defeating Japan in the Far East.

April, and Dessau three days later. On 24 April, the US First Army reached its stop line on the River Mulde and on the following day made the first link-up with Soviet forces on the Elbe near Torgau.

The US Third Army crossed the Danube on the same day, before taking Regensburg. The Third Army then moved into Austria, taking Linz on 5 May. To the Third Army's right, the US Seventh Army took Nuremberg on 20 April after a five-day battle, then crossed the Danube along with the First French Army. This finally destroyed resistance from Germany's Army Group G, leaving the way open for the French to move towards the Swiss border. Hitler's suicide was now known, and it was obvious that the end was near. By 4 May 1945, almost all German resistance had ceased. At Montgomery's headquarters on Lüneburg Heath, the Germans surrendered all their forces in the Netherlands, Denmark and North Germany; the next day, emissaries arrived at Eisenhower's headquarters and, after some attempts to delay the process, signed the armistice on 7 May at 02:40 hours. The war in Europe ended the next day.

Germany lost the war for several reasons, not least of which was the fact that it was unable to match the Allied powers in terms of industrial output and manpower. While the German army inflicted massive losses on the Red Army, the Soviet Union was easily able to sustain these; Germany, on the other hand, simply could not hope to survive while taking the losses that it suffered on the Eastern Front. On the Western Front, meanwhile, although German resistance proved troublesome at times, once the battle for Normandy was completed, the final result of World War II was never really in doubt.

The War in the Pacific

From the surprise attack on Pearl Harbor to the dropping of the two atomic bombs on Hiroshima and Nagasaki, the war in the Pacific was fought with grim determination by both sides. Although Japanese expansion was quickly stopped at the battle of Midway, it would take long, hard years of fighting before Emperor Hirohito's armies were defeated.

The origins of the 'Hawaii Operation', as Pearl Harbor was known, lay in the complex international situation in Asia during the 1930s, and the role played by Japan in those affairs. At the end of World War I, the Japanese had hoped to benefit from the peace settlements which stripped Germany of her colonies and gave them to the victorious Allies. These aspirations were not realised, and this caused considerable resentment, particularly among the fiercely nationalistic armed services. The services possessed considerable power within the Japanese political system thanks to the constitution, and in 1931, the Japanese Manchuria Army over-ran the province without reference to the government in Tokyo.

This caused international outrage, and the Japanese responded to criticism by leaving the League of Nations and increasing their armaments programme. Tension between Japan and China increased, until serious fighting started in 1937. The Japanese increased their gains in China by 1939, and once France fell, attention turned to Indo-China, as the Japanese sought to pressurise the authorities there into preventing supplies from reaching China. The French colonial government refused, prompting the Japanese occupation of Indo-China in September 1940. In response, Britain, America and the Netherlands imposed sanctions (the exiled Dutch government's instructions applying to the Netherlands East Indies). These cut off somewhere in the region of three-quarters of Japanese trade and over 90 per cent of oil supplies.

The options open to Japan were to seek compromise to secure the lifting of sanctions, or to go to war before resources ran out. With a militant nationalist military government headed by General Tojo in power, the first option was never considered.

JAPANESE PLANNING

When planning for war, it was clear that the major threat to Japan was presented by the American fleet. As a result, it was decided that the first step of the war should be to attack the American Pacific anchorage at Pearl Harbor, using carrier-borne aircraft. The Japanese had been considerably influenced by their links with the Royal Navy, and had invested heavily in carrier aviation. The dramatic success of the Royal Navy's air attack on the Italian fleet at Taranto in 1940 convinced the Japanese that a similar assault on the Americans could work, wrecking the Americans' ability to respond. Admiral Yamamoto carried out careful planning during 1941, until his final scheme of operations emerged.

Six aircraft carriers would be used to launch the attack, using over 400 aircraft. After intensive training, the carrier force assembled at an isolated anchorage in the Kurile Islands on 22 November 1941. After four days making ready, the attack force set sail, taking a circuitous route to avoid detection. Elsewhere, Japanese submarines made their way towards Hawaii independently, with the aim of providing timely intelligence, and attacking targets at anchor if possible.

While the fleet made its way into position, Japanese diplomats were tasked with conducting negotiations with the Americans: the idea was that when these broke down, an ultimatum would be issued, followed by the attack. The aim of maintaining at least

Left: An American fleet steams through the South Pacific led by USS *Essex*. From the very start of the war in the Pacific it became clear that the aircraft carrier would be the key strategic asset, and each side's fortunes ebbed and flowed with the number of carriers available to them. With the clear Japanese superiority at the outbreak of the war both in terms of aircraft carriers and in overall naval terms – particularly against the almost-obsolete British fleet – their initial dramatic success is understandable.

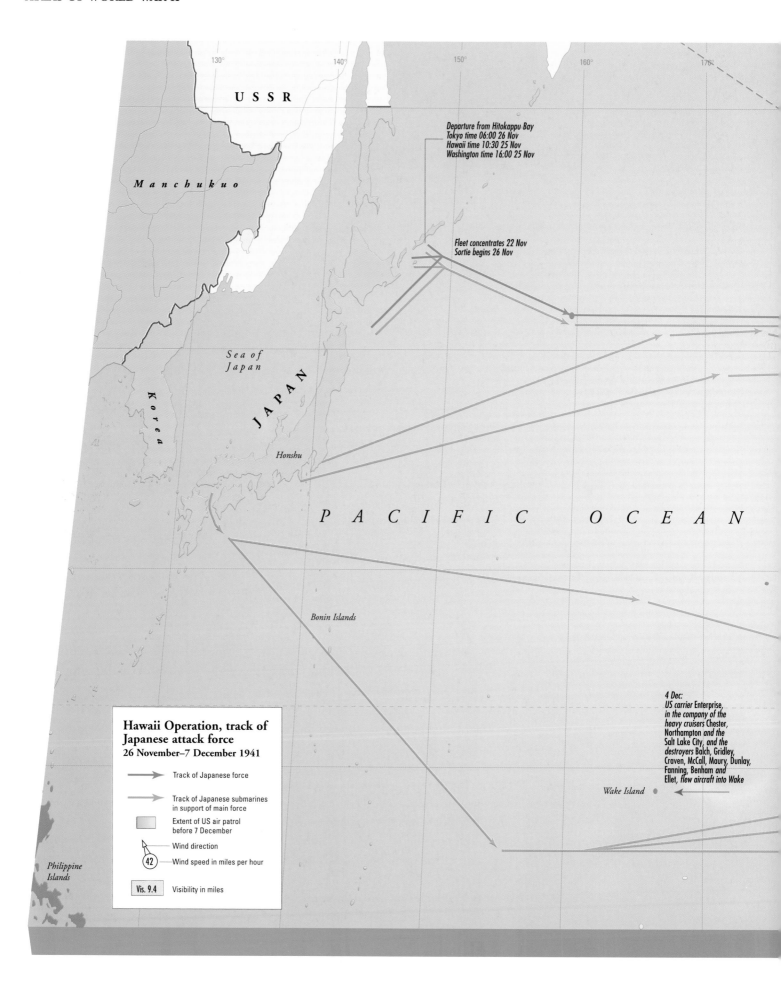

130° 140° 150° 160° 170°

USSR

Manchukuo

Departure from Hitokappu Bay
Tokyo time 06:00 26 Nov
Hawaii time 10:30 25 Nov
Washington time 16:00 25 Nov

Fleet concentrates 22 Nov
Sortie begins 26 Nov

*Sea of
Japan*

Korea

JAPAN

Honshu

PACIFIC OCEAN

Bonin Islands

4 Dec:
US carrier Enterprise,
in the company of the
heavy cruisers Chester,
Northampton and the
Salt Lake City, and the
destroyers Balch, Gridley,
Craven, McCall, Maury, Dunlay,
Fanning, Benham and
Ellet, flew aircraft into Wake

Wake Island

*Philippine
Islands*

**Hawaii Operation, track of
Japanese attack force**
26 November–7 December 1941

———▶ Track of Japanese force

———▶ Track of Japanese submarines
in support of main force

☐ Extent of US air patrol
before 7 December

⚐ Wind direction

㊷ Wind speed in miles per hour

Vis. 9.4 Visibility in miles

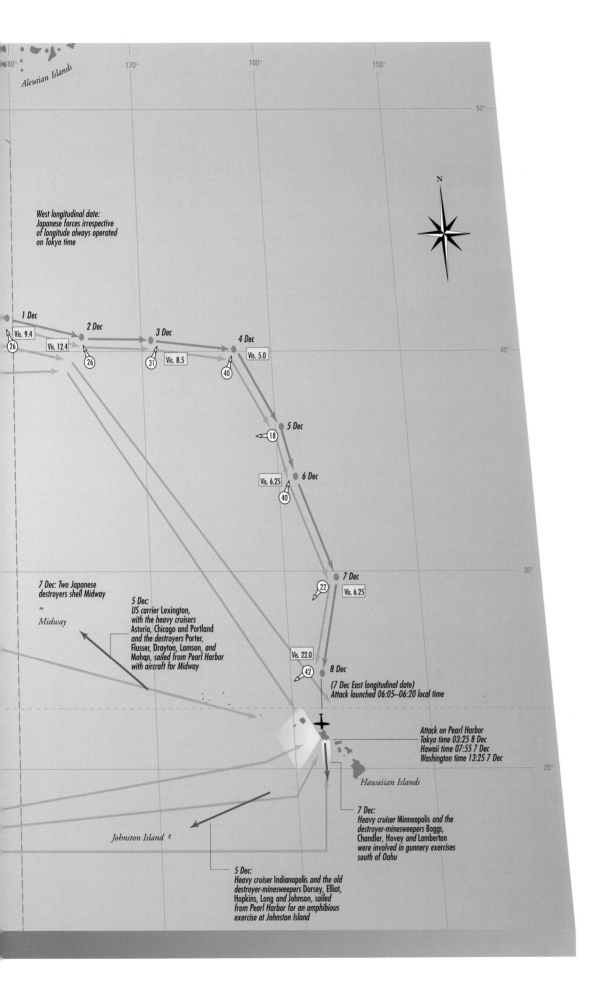

PEARL HARBOR

After the decision to launch a decisive blow against the American fleet was taken, the Japanese attack fleet of six aircraft carriers (*Akagi, Kaga, Soryu, Hiryu, Shokaku* and *Zuikaku*) assembled in secrecy on 22 December 1941. To ensure security, the fleet set off on a course that was unlikely to place it in any danger of detection. Not only was the course well beyond the radius of American flying boats operating from Hawaii or Midway Island, the route was also covered by poor weather, which would further reduce the chance of the attack fleet being compromised.

As the Japanese approached the point for launching their aircraft, submarines taking a southerly course closed in on Hawaii with the aim of conducting reconnaissance. Their information, coupled with that from agents in Hawaii, brought the disappointing news that there were no American aircraft carriers at Pearl Harbor, while other ships were carrying out exercises elsewhere. Nonetheless, there were still over 80 US Navy ships at anchor, oblivious to the approach of the Japanese fleet.

Just after 06:00 on 7 December 1941, the first wave of aircraft left the decks of the Japanese carriers, heading for their objectives on Hawaii. At Pearl Harbor, the majority of sailors slept peacefully, little aware of the carnage that was shortly to come.

The map contains the following labels:

Aleutian Islands

West longitudinal date: Japanese forces irrespective of longitude always operated on Tokyo time

1 Dec — Vis. 9.4 — 26
2 Dec — Vis. 12.4 — 26
3 Dec — Vis. 8.5 — 31
4 Dec — Vis. 5.0 — 40
5 Dec — 18
6 Dec — Vis. 6.25 — 40
7 Dec — 22 — Vis. 6.25
Vis. 22.0 — 42 — 8 Dec

(7 Dec East longitudinal date)
Attack launched 06:05–06:20 local time

7 Dec: Two Japanese destroyers shell Midway

Midway

5 Dec:
US carrier Lexington, with the heavy cruisers Astoria, Chicago and Portland and the destroyers Porter, Flusser, Drayton, Lamson, and Mahan, sailed from Pearl Harbor with aircraft for Midway

Attack on Pearl Harbor
Tokyo time 03:25 8 Dec
Hawaii time 07:55 7 Dec
Washington time 13:25 7 Dec

Hawaiian Islands

7 Dec:
Heavy cruiser Minneapolis and the destroyer-minesweepers Boggs, Chandler, Hovey and Lamberton were involved in gunnery exercises south of Oahu

Johnston Island

5 Dec:
Heavy cruiser Indianapolis and the old destroyer-minesweepers Dorsey, Elliot, Hopkins, Long and Johnson, sailed from Pearl Harbor for an amphibious exercise at Johnston Island

THE ATTACK

The raid against Pearl Harbor was carefully co-ordinated, with the different elements of the attacking waves approaching from varying heights and directions so as to confuse the defences. The high-level bombing wave did particularly well: it had been realised that no Japanese bombs were powerful enough to deal with battleships, so 355mm (14in.) shells were fitted with fins and appropriate attachment points to turn them into armour-piercing bombs that proved to be very effective on the day.

Rigorous training meant that the Japanese were well-prepared for the task in hand, and their bomb and torpedo attacks proved particularly effective against Battleship Row.

As well as attacks against the vessels in the anchorage, attacks were made against Hawaiian airfields, with the intention of destroying American fighter aircraft, so that they would be unable to interfere with the raid. As well as a large number of fighters, the Japanese managed to destroy a number of navy patrol aircraft and some of a flight of B-17 bombers that had the misfortune to arrive in the middle of the attack.

A few American fighters did manage to launch, and these shot down a handful of Japanese aircraft. Anti-aircraft fire and accidents inflicted some more losses, but when the attack was over, the Japanese had scored a significant success against the American fleet for the cost of only 29 aircraft lost.

some diplomatic legitimacy would fall apart when the Japanese ambassador was unable to deliver the ultimatum in time. While he was waiting to do this, the first wave of aircraft was on its way, and Japan was about to go to war.

PEARL HARBOR

The Japanese attack on Pearl Harbor began with the launch of the first wave of attacking carrier aircraft at 06:00 hours on 7 December 1941. At about 07:55 hours, the first aircraft arrived at Pearl Harbor, and caught the fleet totally off-guard. The Japanese aircraft split into separate formations, some heading to the nearby airfields to prevent fighters from taking off to intercept, others lining up to attack the ships.

The airfield attacks were an outstanding success, and nearly 200 aircraft were destroyed, with another 160 damaged. Only a few aircraft were left undamaged, and the threat of interference with the attacks against the ships was greatly diminished.

Those aircraft detailed to attack the ships found an array of tempting targets before them. At the centre of the harbour sat Ford Island, off which was 'Battleship Row'. The first attack was put in by high-level bombers, and then followed by lower level strikes by torpedo aircraft approaching from the opposite direction. With the ships so tightly packed, it was not difficult for the Japanese airmen to score hits as long as they timed the release of their weapons correctly.

Within ten minutes of the start of the attack, the USS *Arizona* had been struck by a torpedo and a single bomb. The latter penetrated her forward magazine and blew the ship apart. USS *West Virginia*, next to *Arizona*, took six torpedo hits and settled on the bottom, while *California* was hit by two torpedoes and started to flood. The captain of the *Nevada* managed to get under way, with the intention of escaping, but had no time to make any meaningful progress before the second wave of aircraft attacked. *California* was hit again and settled to the bottom, while the *Nevada* had to be beached to prevent her from sinking in the middle of the channel and blocking it. However, the second wave of attackers discovered that the defences were now fully alerted, and this made their task considerably more difficult.

Admiral Nagumo decided as a result that he would not launch the planned third wave of aircraft, and the last Japanese aircraft was recovered by mid-day. Nagumo then began a high-speed withdrawal.

Although the attack on Pearl Harbor was devastating, it did not serve the Japanese as well as they might have hoped. Despite the success of the raid in sinking several major ships, no aircraft carriers were caught at anchor, and it was to be these vessels that proved decisive. Furthermore,

1	Tender *Whitney* and destroyers *Tucker, Conyngham, Reid, Case* and *Selfridge*	15	Light cruiser *Raleigh*	36	Gunboat *Sacramento*
2	Destroyer *Blue*	16	Target battleship *Utah*	37	Destroyer *Jarvis*
3	Light cruiser *Phoenix*	17	Seaplane tender *Tangier*	38	Destroyer *Mugford*
4	Destroyers *Aylwin, Farragut, Dale* and *Monaghan*	18	Battleship *Nevada*	39	Seaplane tender *Swan*
5	Destroyers *Patterson, Ralph Talbot* and *Henley*	19	Battleship *Arizona*	40	Repair vessel *Rigel*
6	Tender *Dobbin* and destroyers *Worden, Hull, Dewey, Phelps* and *Macdough*	20	Repair vessel *Vestal*	41	Oiler *Ramapo*
7	Hospital Ship *Solace*	21	Battleship *Tennessee*	42	Heavy cruiser *New Orleans*
8	Destroyer *Allen*	22	Battleship *West Virginia*	43	Destroyer *Cummings* and light-minelayers *Preble* and *Tracy*
9	Destroyer *Chew*	23	Battleship *Maryland*	44	Heavy cruiser *San Francisco*
10	Destroyer-minesweepers *Gamble* and *Montgomery* and light-minelayer *Ramsey*	24	Battleship *Oklahoma*	45	Destroyer-minesweeper *Grebe*, destroyer *Schley* and light-minelayers *Pruitt* and *Sicard*
11	Destroyer-minesweepers *Trever, Breese, Zane, Perry* and *Wasmuth*	25	Oiler *Neosho*	46	Light cruiser *Honolulu*
12	Repair vessel *Medusa*	26	Battleship *California*	47	Light cruiser *St. Louis*
13	Seaplane tender *Curtiss*	27	Seaplane tender *Avocet*	48	Destroyer *Bagley*
14	Light cruiser *Detroit*	28	Destroyer *Shaw*	49	Submarines *Narwhal, Dolphin* and *Tautog* and tenders *Thornton* and *Hulbert*
		29	Destroyer *Downes*	50	Submarine tender *Pelias*
		30	Destroyer *Cassin*	51	Auxiliary vessel *Sumner*
		31	Battleship *Pennsylvania*	52	Auxiliary vessel *Castor*
		32	Submarine *Cachalot*		
		33	Minelayer *Oglala*		
		34	Light cruiser *Helena*		
		35	Auxiliary vessel *Aragonne*		

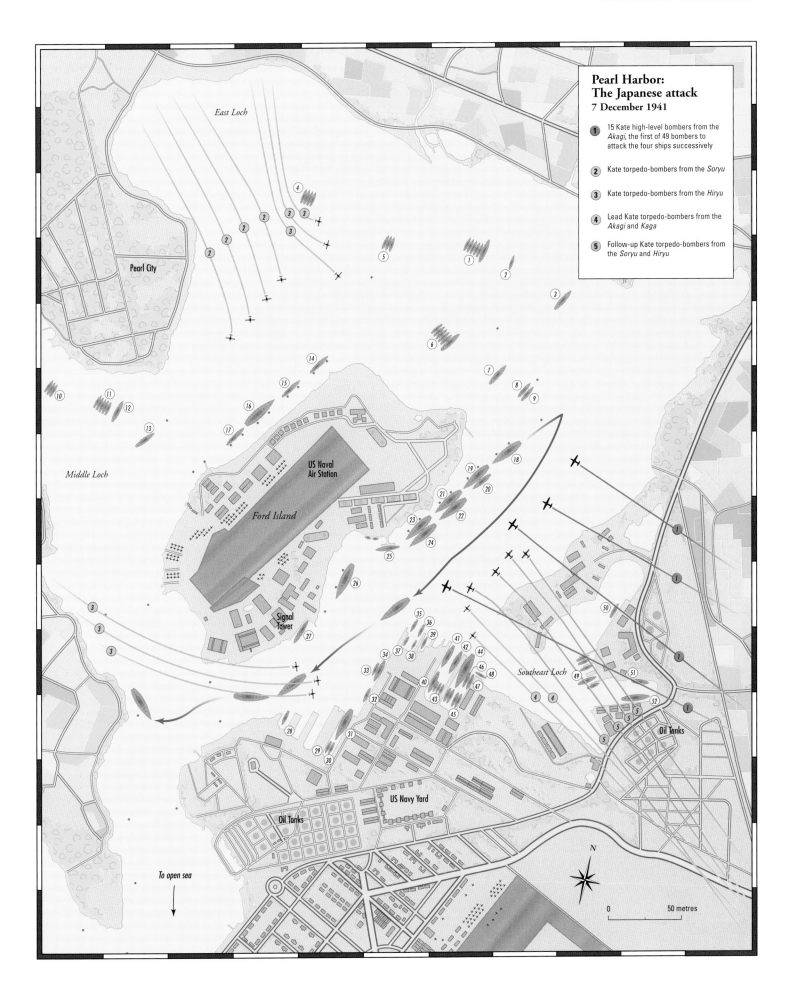

**Pearl Harbor:
The Japanese attack**
7 December 1941

1. 15 Kate high-level bombers from the *Akagi*, the first of 49 bombers to attack the four ships successively

2. Kate torpedo-bombers from the *Soryu*

3. Kate torpedo-bombers from the *Hiryu*

4. Lead Kate torpedo-bombers from the *Akagi* and *Kaga*

5. Follow-up Kate torpedo-bombers from the *Soryu* and *Hiryu*

East Loch

Pearl City

Middle Loch

US Naval Air Station

Ford Island

Signal Tower

Southeast Loch

Oil Tanks

US Navy Yard

Oil Tanks

To open sea

N

0   50 metres

Japanese Expansion
December 1941–July 1942

Japanese Empire early 1941

Occupied by Japan
December 1941–July 1942

China

Aircraft carrier attack on
Pearl Harbor

Japanese offensive operations
December 1941–March 1942

Approximate limit of Japanese
advance July 1942

Colonial possessions 1941

British (Commonwealth)

Dutch

French

Portuguese

by concentrating on sinking ships rather than destroying the shore facilities, the Japanese missed an opportunity to cripple American naval operations in the Pacific for many months to come. Once the grim tasks of salvage and recovery were completed, the Americans were able to bring Pearl Harbor back to operational status with speed.

As Yamamoto had feared, rather than strike a crippling blow to the Americans, Pearl Harbor served only to rouse them, and set Japan on course for a shattering defeat.

JAPANESE EXPANSION

The attack on Pearl Harbor marked the start of the next phase in Japanese plans for expansion. Vulnerable to western trading sanctions, the government had concluded that the only way in which Japan could ensure that its supplies were unaffected by the decisions of others was to go and acquire the territory from which these vital raw materials were sourced. While the American

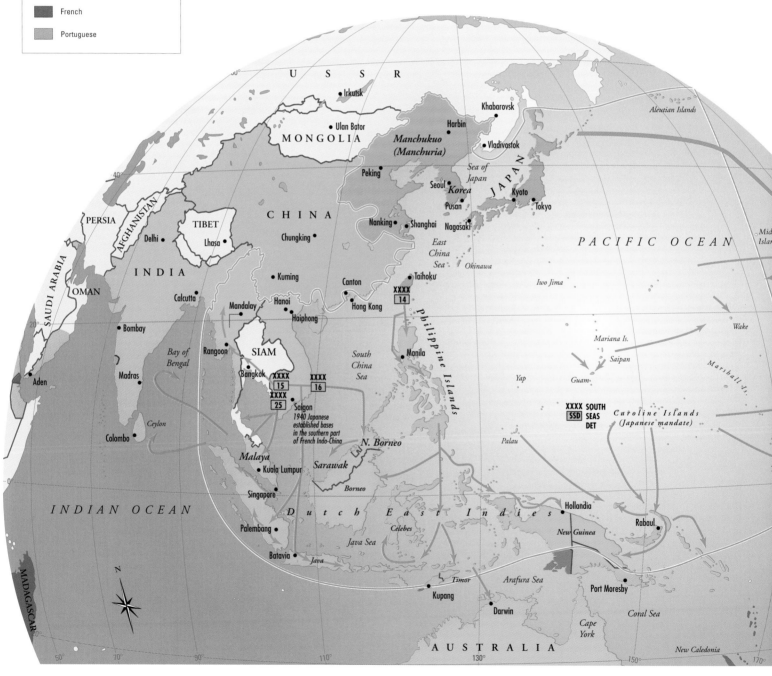

Above: The battleship USS *Arizona* explodes after a direct hit during the attack on Pearl Harbor. While the attack on Pearl Harbor gave the Japanese the initiative in the Pacific campaign that followed, the Japanese failure to locate and sink any of the American carriers – all out of port during the attack on 7 December – was to prove crucial in eventually halting the Japanese expansion.

RAPID PROGRESS

The Japanese expansion through the Pacific in early 1942 was remarkable in both its scope and speed. Resistance to Japanese attacks proved utterly ineffective as their army swept all before them. With these successes came a reputation of Japanese invincibility that would take a great deal of time to destroy.

Although facing two major world powers in the British and Americans, the Japanese were able to invade Malaya, Singapore, Burma and the Philippines with relative ease, ruthlessly crushing the resistance they encountered: by the early summer of 1942, it appeared that India and Australia might be under threat of a Japanese invasion, while the Dutch empire in the East Indies had been broken once and for all as the Japanese sought to exploit the nascent nationalist movement in Java for its own ends.

As well as taking these major possessions, the Japanese advance expanded to include many small islands and atolls, significant only for their position in the vast expanse of the Pacific Ocean, and from where the Japanese intended to operate ships and aircraft to assert their new-found hegemony over the seas.

By the middle of 1942, the picture appeared bleak for the Allies – but in fact, the turning point was not far away.

fleet was recognized as the major obstacle to the prosecution of a campaign of conquest in Asia, removing it was not the only act that needed to be carried out.

The British and Dutch both held colonies with large sources of raw material; the Dutch East Indies were a major source of oil, while Malaya's rubber production was also of considerable importance. As well as the importance of the raw materials, the Japanese government was influenced by nationalism and pride in Japan: one of the key tenets of these sentiments was that Japan should be recognized as the leading power in the Pacific. Ensuring that supplies of raw material were readily accessible was one matter, but the removal of colonial administration was another key driving force in Japanese considerations: driving the Americans, British and Dutch from the territories they controlled would be a clear articulation of Japanese strength and martial prowess. As a result, it was not just the countries with natural resources that were targeted by the Japanese, but also those of geographical significance for allowing the Pacific to be readily controlled by the Imperial Japanese Navy, and the many small islands that were controlled by their opponents.

As a result, Pearl Harbor did not mark a single blow struck against the western powers, but the start of what was intended to be a brief war of conquest. The theory underpinning this idea appeared to be solid. The British, still battling alone against the Germans and Italians in Europe, the Mediterranean and North Africa were likely to be over-stretched in attempting to deal with a Japanese attack, while the Dutch authorities appeared to be in no position to counter any threat to their territories. As a consequence, the aftermath of Pearl Harbor was marked by rapid and seemingly unstoppable Japanese conquests.

Even as Nagumo's aircraft were being recovered aboard the carriers, other Japanese units were attacking Luzon as the opening salvo in the planned conquest of the

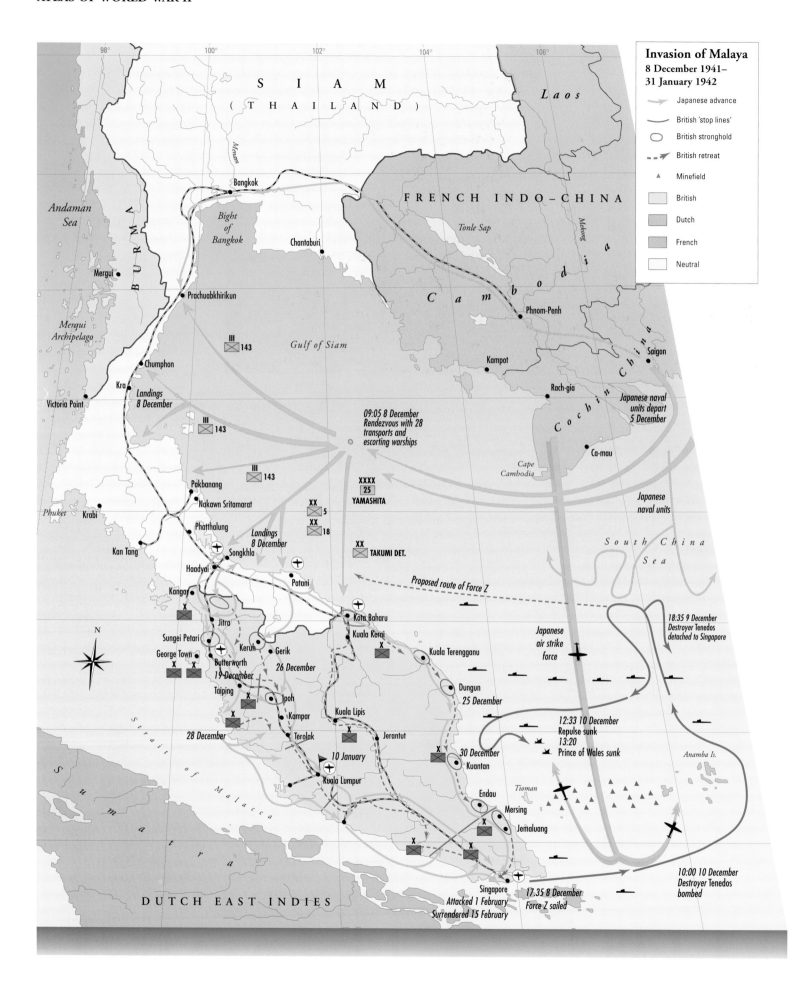

Invasion of Malaya
8 December 1941–
31 January 1942

→ Japanese advance

⌢ British 'stop lines'

◯ British stronghold

⌁ British retreat

▲ Minefield

British

Dutch

French

Neutral

Andaman
Sea

S I A M

(T H A I L A N D)

Mnam

Bangkok

Bight of Bangkok

Chantaburi

L a o s

F R E N C H   I N D O – C H I N A

Tonle Sap

Phnom-Penh

Saigon

C a m b o d i a

Mergui

Prachuabkhirikun

Gulf of Siam

III 143

Kampot

Rach-gia

Japanese naval units depart 5 December

Cochin China

Merqui Archipelago

Chumphon

Kra

Victoria Point

Landings 8 December

III 143

09:05 8 December
Rendezvous with 28 transports and escorting warships

Ca-mau

Cape Cambodia

Japanese naval units

Pakbanang

III 143

Phuket

Krabi

Nakawn Sritamarat

XXXX 25 YAMASHITA

South China Sea

Phatthalung

XX 5

XX 18

Kan Tang

Landings 8 December

Songkhla

XX TAKUMI DET.

Haadyai

Kangar

Patani

Proposed route of Force Z

X

Jitra

Kota Baharu

Kuala Kerai

18:35 9 December
Destroyer Tenedos detached to Singapore

Sungei Petari

Keruh

Gerik

X

Kuala Terengganu

Japanese air strike force

George Town

X X

Butterworth

19 December

26 December

N

Taiping

Ipoh

Kuala Lipis

Dungun

25 December

12:33 10 December
Repulse sunk
13:20
Prince of Wales sunk

X

Kampar

Anamba Is.

28 December

Terolak

X

Jerantut

X

30 December

S t r a i t   o f   M a l a c c a

10 January

Kuala Lumpur

Kuantan

Tioman

Endau

X

Mersing

Jemaluang

X

X

S u m a t r a

Singapore
Attacked 1 February
Surrendered 15 February

17.35 8 December
Force Z sailed

10:00 10 December
Destroyer Tenedos bombed

D U T C H   E A S T   I N D I E S

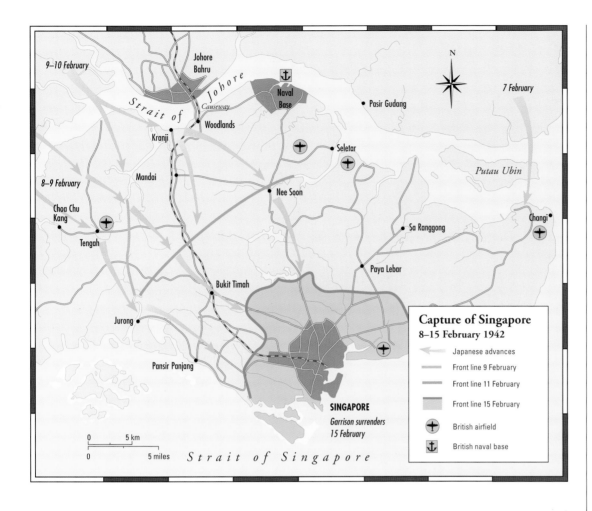

Capture of Singapore
8–15 February 1942

→ Japanese advances

— Front line 9 February

— Front line 11 February

▨ Front line 15 February

⊕ British airfield

⚓ British naval base

SINGAPORE
*Garrison surrenders
15 February*

BRITISH DISASTER

The Japanese invasion of Malaya and Singapore was greatly assisted by complacency upon the part of the British. The Japanese had been largely under-rated as a potential opponent, with little real consideration given to actual Japanese capabilities. As a result, little preparation had been made to deal with an invasion, while forces in Malaya were not given first priority for equipment. In the case of aircraft, American Brewster Buffalo fighters were despatched on the grounds that while they were outclassed in Europe, they were still likely to be better than anything the Japanese might have – a fallacy exposed as soon as combat started in earnest.

Once the Japanese had established a strong foothold in Malaya, their advance was inexorable. The British were forced to retreat as the Japanese pushed their way down the west and east sides of the peninsula, each defensive position being outflanked by a new landing further south. To make matters worse, the Japanese gained maritime supremacy when they sank the two unprotected battleships, HMS *Prince of Wales* and *Repulse*.

The surviving British troops were driven back to Singapore, but a successful crossing of the Straits of Johore by the Japanese led to the garrison being surrounded. General Percival chose to surrender on 15 February 1941.

Philippines (to be achieved in three months); while further north, troops moved from their positions in Japanese-occupied China towards the British colony of Hong Kong. To complete the first stage of the plan, Japanese ships were ferrying an army towards Malaya with the aim of driving the British out before moving north to Burma, another British possession and a source of oil.

Everywhere the Japanese attacked, they enjoyed success. A mixture of contempt for a supposedly backward and inferior military power meant that the British, American and Dutch forces had not been equipped to the required standard, and the notion that the Japanese would prove skilled jungle fighters had simply not been entertained. The results were disastrous for the Allies. Within eight months, the Japanese had driven the British from Malaya, Singapore and Burma; the Americans had been ejected from the Philippines and their Pacific territories and the Dutch had been utterly defeated in the Netherlands East Indies. By June 1942, it appeared almost inconceivable that the Japanese could be stopped in their goal of becoming the dominant power in the Pacific.

INVASION OF MALAYA AND SINGAPORE

Along with Burma, Malaya was the main objective of Japanese military planning at the end of 1941. Capturing Malaya would give the Japanese control of 38 per cent of the world's rubber production and nearly 60 per cent of tin output.

The Japanese invasion convoy was at sea even before the raid on Pearl Harbor began, and was sighted by a British reconnaissance aircraft on 6 December 1941. Bad weather prevented any further investigation by the British, and the invasion fleet continued, unmolested, until it landed its troops on 8 December shortly after 01:00 hours. The Japanese encountered extremely stiff

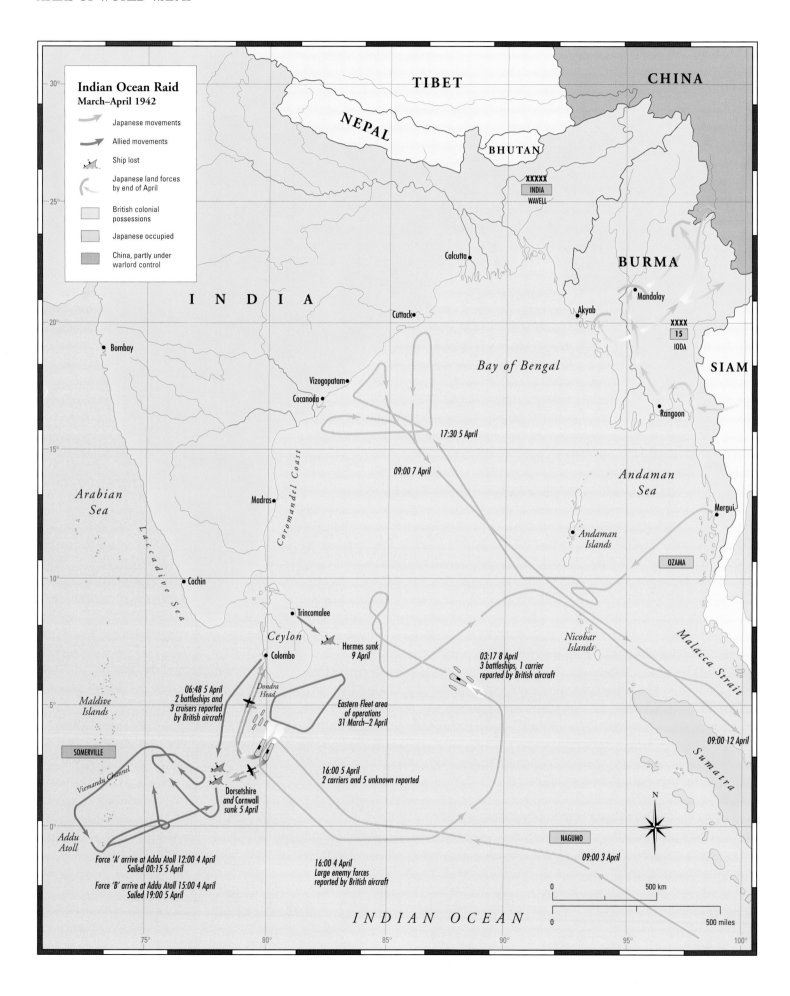

Indian Ocean Raid
March–April 1942

- Japanese movements
- Allied movements
- Ship lost
- Japanese land forces by end of April
- British colonial possessions
- Japanese occupied
- China, partly under warlord control

TIBET

CHINA

NEPAL

BHUTAN

XXXXX
INDIA
WAVELL

Calcutta

BURMA

Mandalay

Akyab

XXXX
15
IODA

INDIA

Cuttack

SIAM

Bombay

Rangoon

Vizogopatam

Cocanoda

Bay of Bengal

17:30 5 April

09:00 7 April

Andaman Sea

Arabian Sea

Madras

Coromandel Coast

Andaman Islands

Mergui

Laccadive Sea

Cochin

OZAMA

Trincomalee

Nicobar Islands

Ceylon

Hermes sunk 9 April

Malacca Strait

Colombo

03:17 8 April
3 battleships, 1 carrier
reported by British aircraft

06:48 5 April
2 battleships and
3 cruisers reported
by British aircraft

Dondra Head

Eastern Fleet area
of operations
31 March–2 April

09:00 12 April

Maldive Islands

Sumatra

16:00 5 April
2 carriers and 5 unknown reported

SOMERVILLE

Dorsetshire
and Cornwall
sunk 5 April

Viemandu Channel

N

Addu Atoll

NAGUMO

Force 'A' arrive at Addu Atoll 12:00 4 April
Sailed 00:15 5 April

16:00 4 April
Large enemy forces
reported by British aircraft

09:00 3 April

Force 'B' arrive at Addu Atoll 15:00 4 April
Sailed 19:00 5 April

0   500 km

0   500 miles

INDIAN OCEAN

INDIAN SORTIE

The Indian Ocean raid delivered a stunning blow to British naval strength in the area, and it took a great deal of time before the Royal Navy was able to operate offensively against the Japanese.

The disaster stemmed from operations by Admiral Nagumo's forces, which avoided the British ships in the vicinity and struck against Colombo and Trincomalee in Ceylon. The British were hampered by inaccurate intelligence which meant that they were refuelling several hundred miles away when the Japanese fleet appeared. The old British ships were unable to catch up with the Japanese raiders; indeed, given their age, it is debatable whether they would have been able to prevent the attacks anyway, being vulnerable to the overwhelming Japanese naval air strength on their carriers.

As a result of the raid, the old cruisers *Dorsetshire* and *Cornwall* were sunk on 5 April, while the carrier *Hermes* was sunk four days later as she sailed away from Trincomalee, without any fighter aircraft aboard. Surprised by Japanese aircraft and utterly defenceless, the carrier was sent to the bottom within a matter of minutes. Throughout the Indian Ocean raid, the Japanese consistently outmanoeuvred the Royal Navy, demonstrating the fallacy of the pre-war belief that a small force with obsolescent vessels would be enough to hold maritime superiority over the Japanese navy.

resistance, and to make matters worse, many of their troops drowned as they scrambled to the beach. As a result, the first officer to reach the beach safely gave the order to charge the British positions, which were carried in due course.

Once the Japanese had established a foothold, they began to push the British back. After the Japanese 5th Division took Singoran (Songkhla), an airfield was available, and the Japanese proceeded to win air superiority against a poorly equipped and under-strength Royal Air Force. Under the air cover, the Japanese advance continued swiftly. Once the Japanese broke through at Jitra, the situation for the British became extremely serious, even though most of Malaya still remained in their hands. As British morale declined, the Japanese surged forward, moving quickly through the Malayan jungle, until by early January 1942, the British commander, General Percival, realised that the situation was becoming untenable. By 31 January, surviving British forces had been withdrawn to Singapore.

Although Singapore was meant to be a great fortress, it was primarily built to prevent an attack from the sea rather than by land. The Japanese found it a relatively simple task to cross the narrow Straits of Johore onto the island, and the British were swiftly pushed back. By 13 February, some 80,000 men were trapped around the city, while Percival contemplated surrender. Two days later, he hoisted a white flag, and the Japanese had succeeded in inflicting the greatest humiliation in British military history upon the defending forces. British morale was severely dented by the defeat.

Below: Japanese troops land at Singora in southern Siam (Thailand) before invading northern Malaya on 8 December 1941. Although the Japanese troops were lightly equipped compared to their Allied counterparts, this lack of equipment meant that they were able to move at a rapid pace through the jungles of Malaya. At the same time, amphibious landings were used to outflank any problematic defensive positions.

Above: A mounted Japanese officer accompanies his men through scrub during the invasion of Burma, with a pagoda visible in the background. As in Malaya, the rapid advance of the Japanese caught the British and their allies off guard and unable to react in time to prevent the conquest of the country. The loss of Burma brought Japanese troops to the borders of India, the jewel of the British empire.

INDIAN OCEAN RAID

It was not only against the American fleet that Admiral Nagumo's forces scored considerable success in the early days of the war in the Pacific. Within three months of the Hawaii operation, Nagumo inflicted a similar stunning blow upon the Royal Navy in a raid into the Indian Ocean.

On 19 February 1942, four of Nagumo's carriers undertook an operation against Darwin and Broome in north-west Australia, sinking a dozen ships and inflicting serious damage to the base facilities and the towns themselves, all for the loss of just one aircraft. This was followed by four weeks' rest as the ships and crews prepared for their next mission. On 26 February, the carriers sailed for the Indian Ocean.

The Indian Ocean was a source of considerable concern for the British, since although the Royal Navy had five battleships and three aircraft carriers in the area, one of the carriers was obsolete, while four of the battleships were old and outmoded vessels that were no match for anything the Japanese were likely to use against them. The commander of the British force, Admiral Sir James Somerville, was careful to husband his resources, despite intelligence reports of a Japanese attack against Ceylon at the beginning of April. Somerville therefore kept his force together well to the west in daylight, steaming towards the expected line of approach for the Japanese at night.

Unfortunately for Somerville, his intelligence was wrong, and by the evening of 2 April 1942, most of his ships were in need of refuelling. They headed for their base at Addu Atoll, leaving two cruisers, a destroyer and the carrier *Hermes* to head for Ceylon. Just as the first of Somerville's

BURMA BOUND

The Japanese campaign in Burma simply added to the shock felt in Britain at the unexpected prowess of an enemy who had been consistently underrated in the run-up to war. Their attack exploited the lack of preparedness amongst British forces, with inadequate levels of training and inexperience combining to make the task of the defenders far more difficult.

When the invasion began on 15 January 1942, it was small in scale as the Japanese sought to capture airbases from which they could attack the Burmese capital, Rangoon.

Once Japanese forces crossed into Burma in strength, there was little that the British could do to stop them. Confusion among the high command meant that a workable defensive plan proposed by the commander in the field (Acting Major-General Sir John Smyth VC) was overruled until its sound nature was made all too clear by the enemy's actions. Once the plan was approved, however, it was too late, and the inexorable Japanese advance took Rangoon on 8 March.

By the end of April the British position in Burma was untenable, and the final soldiers withdrew to India, leaving the Japanese victorious. The failure in Burma was not only a humiliation for British prestige, but it also endowed the Japanese with a (false) aura of invincibility in jungle warfare that would take considerable time to overturn.

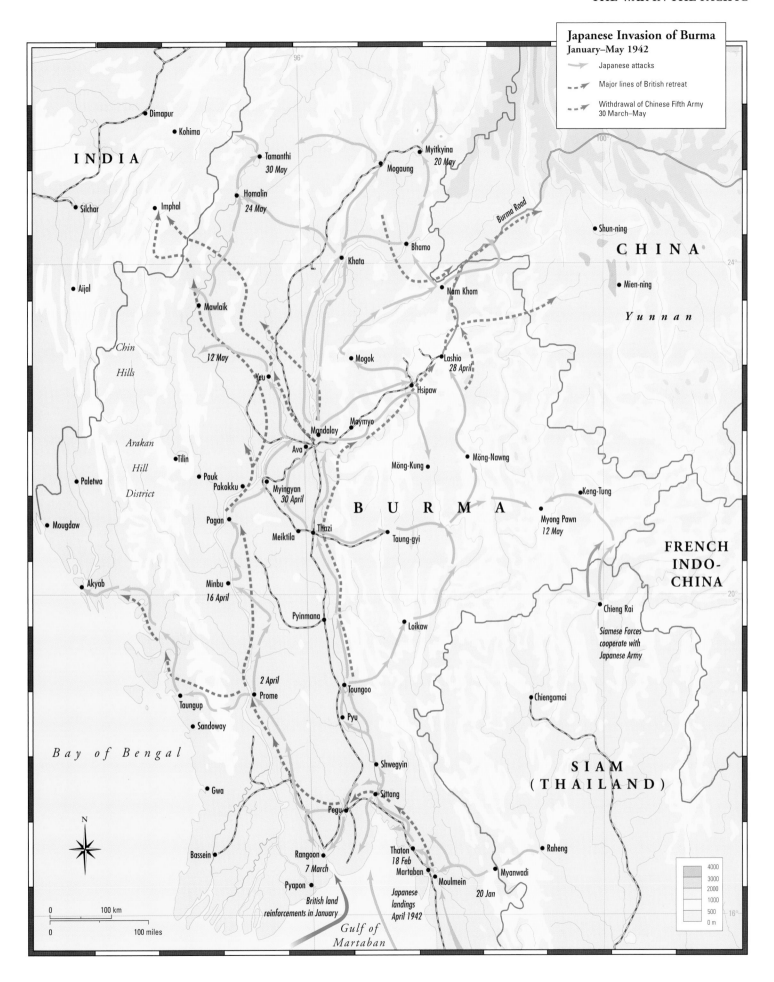

Japanese Invasion of Burma
January–May 1942

→ Japanese attacks

- - → Major lines of British retreat

- - → Withdrawal of Chinese Fifth Army
30 March–May

INDIA

Dimapur

Kohima

Tamanthi
30 May

Silchar

Imphal

Homalin
24 May

Myitkyina
20 May

Mogaung

CHINA

Shun-ning

Aijal

Mawlaik

Khata

Bhamo

Burma Road

Nam Khom

Mien-ning

Chin

Hills

12 May

Yeu

Mogok

Lashio
28 April

Hsipaw

Yunnan

Arakan

Hill

District

Maymyo

Mandalay

Ava

Möng-Kung

Möng-Nawng

Tilin

Pauk
Pakokku

Myingyan
30 April

Pagan

BURMA

Keng-Tung

Myong Pawn
12 May

FRENCH
INDO-
CHINA

Paletwa

Mougdaw

Meiktila

Thazi

Taung-gyi

Minbu
16 April

Pyinmana

Loikaw

Chieng Rai

Akyab

Siamese Forces
cooperate with
Japanese Army

2 April
Prome

Toungoo

Chiengamai

Taungup

Sandoway

Pyu

SIAM
(THAILAND)

Bay of Bengal

Gwa

Shwegyin

Raheng

N

Bassein

Rangoon
7 March

Pegu

Sittang

Thaton
18 Feb
Martaban

Moulmein

Myanwadi

Pyapon

20 Jan

*Japanese
landings
April 1942*

British land
reinforcements in January

0   100 km

0   100 miles

*Gulf of
Martaban*

4000
3000
2000
1000
500
0 m

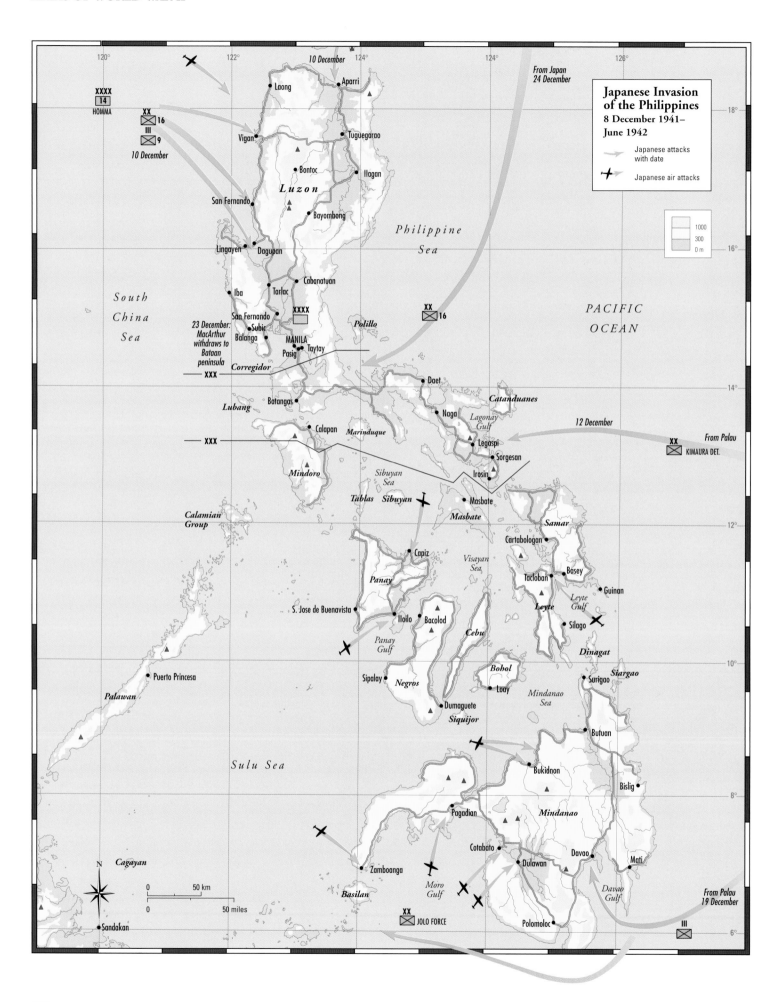

From Japan
24 December

10 December

**Japanese Invasion
of the Philippines**
8 December 1941–
June 1942

→ Japanese attacks
with date

✈ Japanese air attacks

XXXX
14
HOMMA

XX
16

III
9

10 December

Laong

Aparri

Vigan

Tuguegarao

Ilagan

Bontoc

Luzon

San Fernando

Bayombong

Lingayen

Dagupan

*South
China
Sea*

Iba

Tarlac

Cabanatuan

XXXX

23 December:
MacArthur
withdraws to
Bataan
peninsula

San Fernando

Subic

Balanga

MANILA

Pasig   Taytay

Batangas

Corregidor

XXX

Lubang

Polillo

Daet

*Philippine
Sea*

XX
16

*PACIFIC
OCEAN*

Calapan

Marinduque

Naga

*Lagonay
Gulf*

Catanduanes

XXX

Mindoro

Legaspi

Sorgesan

Irosin

12 December

From Palau

XX
KIMAURA DET.

*Sibuyan
Sea*

Masbate

Tablas   *Sibuyan*

Masbate

Samar

*Calamian
Group*

Capiz

*Visayan
Sea*

Cartabologan

Panay

Basey

Tacloban

Guinan

S. Jose de Buenavista

Iloilo   Bacolod

Cebu

Leyte

*Leyte
Gulf*

Silago

Dinagat

Bohol

Siargao

Puerto Princesa

Sipalay

Negros

Loay

Surigao

Palawan

Dumaguete

*Mindanao
Sea*

Butuan

Siquijor

Sulu Sea

Bukidnon

Bislig

Pagadian

Mindanao

Cotabato

Davao

Mati

Cagayan

N

Zamboanga

Dulawan

0   50 km

Basilan

*Moro
Gulf*

*Davao
Gulf*

*From Palau
19 December*

0   50 miles

XX
JOLO FORCE

Polomoloc

III

Sandakan

ADVANCE TO MANILA

The Japanese invasion of the Philippines was swift and ruthless, aided by the fact that the forces opposing them were relatively weak and poorly equipped. There were some 31,000 troops, of which around 19,000 were American, along with nearly 100,000 conscripts to defend the islands.

The Japanese air raids against key targets in early December meant that MacArthur could not rely upon air support to help hold out against the Japanese. A large number of aircraft had been left unprotected on Clark Field airbase and the Japanese raiders had wreaked havoc. Some of the remaining aircraft were hopelessly obsolete, and although their pilots fought bravely, they were massacred.

The first Japanese landings were small-scale affairs in the north and south to establish airbases to support the main assault, followed by the capture of the southern island of Mindanao to provide an airbase to help cover the assaults to take place against the Dutch East Indies.

The main Japanese landings on 22 December 1941 gained ground quickly against the partly-trained Philippine Army, forcing MacArthur's decision to withdraw to the Bataan peninsula and Corregidor Island or face being crushed between two Japanese pincers. He declared Manila an open city on 26 December, electing not to defend it.

Above: Japanese troops watch parts of Manila burn as they approach Luzon in their landing craft. In fact MacArthur declared Manila an open city, realising that it was effectively indefensible, and withdrew into the Bataan peninsula to conduct an extended defence in the hope of aid or reinforcements from the United States. Unfortunately for MacArthur help was not forthcoming.

ships reached Addu on 4 April, news arrived that Nagumo's ships had been sighted some 400 miles south east of the island. This left Ceylon unprotected, for although Somerville sailed immediately, there was no hope of catching Nagumo's force.

The port facilities at Ceylon were well protected by anti-aircraft guns and the RAF, and although the defending fighters suffered 50 per cent losses against the Japanese, the attack was not able to destroy the port. However, just before mid-day, a Japanese reconnaissance aircraft spotted the cruisers *Dorsetshire* and *Cornwall* and called in an attack. Ninety Japanese aircraft assailed the two ships, and sank them within 20 minutes.

Somerville's remaining ships now hurried to catch the Japanese, with the hope of intercepting them on the morning of 6 April – however, they were not swift enough to reach the enemy. The next day, worse was to follow for the British. Nagumo was spotted by a British flying boat, and once again, Somerville had returned to Addu to complete his refuelling. The Japanese struck at Trincomalee, but the advance warning at least gave time for the port to be cleared. However, a Japanese reconnaissance aircraft found HMS *Hermes* sailing close inshore. *Hermes* had sailed when the port was cleared, and had no fighters aboard to defend herself. Eighty-five Japanese aircraft set about the carrier and after sustaining 40 or so bomb hits in close succession, the old carrier capsized and sank.

Above: American prisoners on Corregidor move down to the boats waiting to transfer them to Bataan while Japanese troops move up to garrison the fortress on 7 May 1942. Many of the American prisoners would perish on the infamous 'Death March' across Bataan into captivity. Japanese warrior culture disparaged surrender as dishonour, and most Allied prisoners were therefore harshly treated.

Although Nagumo's raid marked the last time that the Japanese entered the Indian Ocean in such strength and to such effect, the raid guaranteed that there would be no immediate British response to Japanese success in the Pacific.

INVASION OF BURMA

The Japanese invasion of Burma began once it was clear that operations in Malaya were going well. The attack began on 15 January 1942, when small Japanese forces compelled the British to withdraw from the airfields at Mergui and Victoria Point. The garrison at Victoria Point had been

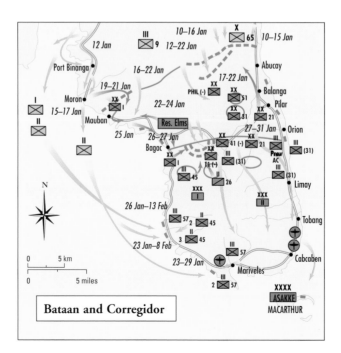

Bataan and Corregidor

After a series of Japanese attacks, the first American defensive line on Bataan was abandoned on 26 January. The Japanese attempted to outflank the second line with a series of landings in the south of the peninsula, but these were beaten back after savage fighting. Homma, the Japanese commander, then decided to wait for further reinforcements from Japan.

General Douglas MacArthur was ordered to leave by President Roosevelt, which he did reluctantly, uttering his famous promise to return on his arrival in Australia.

Meanwhile the defenders of Bataan were now on quarter rations and severely affected by disease. On 3 April the Japanese broke through, and Bataan fell swiftly, the last defenders surrendering on 9 April, leaving Corregidor and a few remaining islands to attempt to hold out.

While the other islands were being taken care of, a shattering Japanese bombardment reduced the defences on the fortress of Corregidor, and when Japanese troops were sent in to attack, the resistance was piecemeal and ineffective.

General Wainwright, who had succeeded MacArthur as commander, decided that further resistance was futile: the Americans surrendered on 6 May 1942. Many of the regular American and Filipino survivors died on the infamous 'Death March' across the Philippines into captivity.

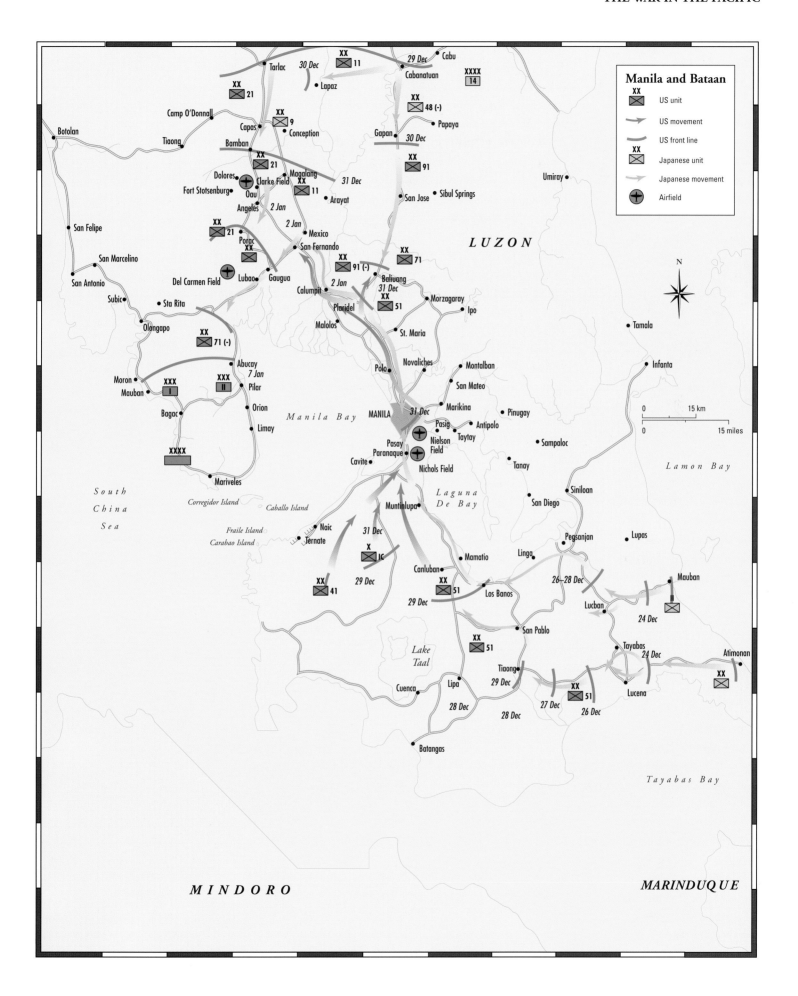

FALL OF THE DUTCH EMPIRE

The Japanese Dutch East Indies invasion force (split into Eastern and Western Forces) left the Davo anchorage on 7 January 1942. Eastern Force was to take the islands of Ceram, Ambon, Timor, Celebes, Makassar and Bali; Central Force key coastal areas in Borneo; and Western Force would take Sumatra.

The pace of the Japanese advance was startling, with Allied resistance proving almost futile in the face of overwhelming Japanese land, sea and air forces. The Dutch did not recruit the indigenous population of the East Indies as a resistance force, and thus missed the opportunity to cause more problems to the Japanese: this action was to give considerable impetus to the postwar nationalist movement in the East Indies.

Allied efforts at disrupting the operation were largely carried out at sea, but proved little threat to the Japanese. Even a surprise night attack by torpedo boats and destroyers in the Lombok Straits on 19/20 February 1942 caused no serious inconvenience to the invaders. Within a week, it was clear that the Allied position was untenable. Survivors of the Allied force made attempts to reach Australia in a variety of vessels, some enjoying success, others drowning or being captured. The Dutch Governor-General opened negotiations with the Japanese on 7 March, and surrendered the next day.

steadily reduced over the course of the previous month, while that at Mergui was surrounded three days later, before being evacuated by sea. This meant that in the space of a week, the Japanese had gained two important airfields at virtually no cost, allowing them to bomb the Burmese capital, Rangoon, with ease.

Once these airfields were taken, the Japanese Fifteenth Army (Lieutenant General Iida) drove from China and Siam towards Moulmein, with the aim of moving around the Gulf of Martaban, across the Sittan River and then into Rangoon. The Japanese planned to achieve this in eight weeks, and had a good chance of success, since there was little in their way. The British, commanded by the recently appointed Lieutenant General T J Hutton, and led in the field by Acting Major-General John Smyth VC, were poorly equipped. None of the men had any real training in jungle warfare, and many of Smyth's formations had lost their junior officers and NCOs, who had been sent to bolster the Indian Army units in North Africa. Finally, to make matters even worse, air cover was almost non-existent.

Smyth appreciated that defence would be extremely difficult with the limited forces at his disposal, and suggested that the only means of blocking the Japanese would be to face them in the open ground around the Sittan River, with the intention of stopping them there. Hutton did not agree, and refused to allow Smyth to concentrate his forces behind the barrier offered by the river. Smyth therefore did what he could, but suffered an immediate setback when the forces from 16th Indian Brigade arrived after their retreat from Tavoy and Mergui having left behind most of their support weapons and all their transport. By 26 January, the Japanese were attacking Moulmein, and two days later, another seaborne evacuation was carried out to remove the British troops. Smyth again asked to pull back across the Sittang, but permission was denied until 19 February, by which time it was too late.

Japanese pressure on the area around the bridge increased, and it was blown up on 23 February. The British forces withdrew, meaning that the number of troops available to defend Rangoon was dramatically reduced. Rangoon fell on 8 March, and the British were driven back towards India on a daily basis. Central Burma was under Japanese control by the end of April, and on 2 May, the last British troops crossed the Irrawaddy to safety. It would be some time before they would return.

INVASION OF THE PHILIPPINES

American and Filipino forces had been brought under a unified command structure in July 1941, led by General Douglas MacArthur. The main concern of the forces in the Philippines was dealing with internal unrest, so it came as something of a surprise when information about the attack on Pearl Harbor filtered through in the early morning of 9 December 1941 (since the Philippines and Pearl Harbor are separated by five time zones, this equated to the early morning of 8 December at Pearl Harbor). The commander of the American air forces in the Philippines, General Brereton, sought permission from MacArthur to bomb Japanese airfields in Formosa, but while the request was being processed, he took the eminently sensible precaution of ordering his B-17 bombers into the air so that they would not be caught on the ground by any surprise attack from Japanese raiders.

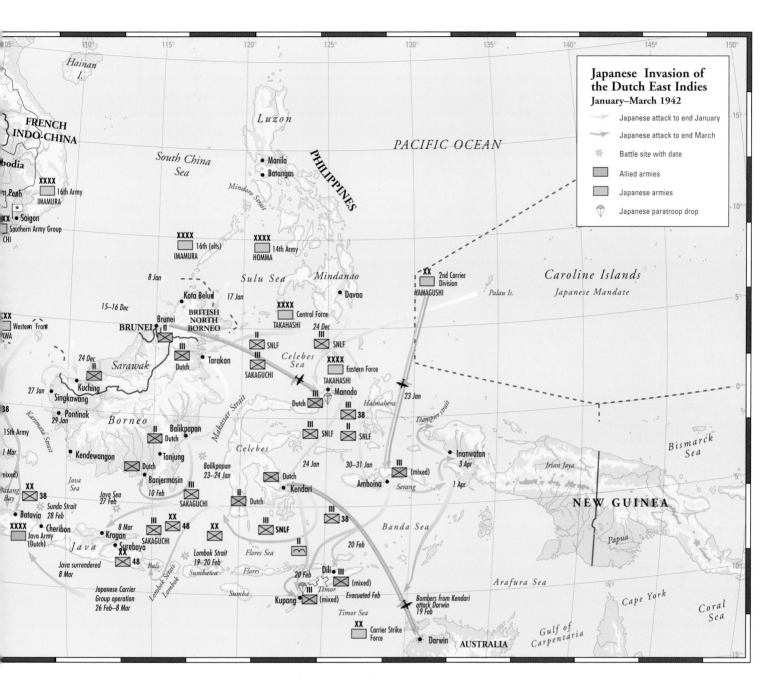

The legend of the map reads:

Japanese Invasion of the Dutch East Indies
January–March 1942

Japanese attack to end January
Japanese attack to end March
Battle site with date
Allied armies
Japanese armies
Japanese paratroop drop

Unfortunately for the Americans, the Japanese surprise attack had been prevented by fog over the airfields in Formosa, so when the B-17s returned to base to be armed for the now-approved strikes on Formosa, the Japanese air crews had taken off. Over 200 Japanese aircraft attacked the American air base at Clark Field, utterly destroying it over the course of a two-hour air raid. The B-17s, neatly lined up in the open, were easy targets, and by the afternoon of 9 December, over 100 American aircraft (including 17 bombers and over 50 fighters) had been destroyed. This was a particularly serious blow, since MacArthur's plans for defending the Philippines were based upon the premise that his forces would hold out until the US Pacific Fleet came to the rescue. With no fleet and a much-reduced air force, it was quite clear that the plan was in serious difficulties from the outset.

The first Japanese landings on Luzon took place on 10 December, with the aim of seizing airfields; these troops then pushed to the south, with the intention of meeting up with the units that were to carry out the main Japanese attack. These landings took place on 22 December, and by the following day, the invasion forces were well-established, and were moving forward, encountering very little opposition as they went. On 24 December, a further landing occurred on the isthmus south of Manila around Siain and Mauban. MacArthur began to realise that the position his forces were now in was desperate; a day before the second set of landings, he had decided that he would withdraw to Corregidor Island so that he could defend the Bataan Peninsula. He declared Manila to be an open city, and moved to Corregidor as the American and Filipino position collapsed.

TURNING POINT

The Battle of Midway was one of the most decisive battles of the Pacific War, although it was not recognised as such immediately. Japanese naval aviation suffered a grievous blow from which it was unable to recover, losing four precious carriers and – even more importantly – a large number of highly experienced pilots, many of whom had taken part in the attack on Pearl Harbor.

The key to the battle lay in the fact that American intelligence was able to provide Admiral Nimitz with a clear picture of Japanese intentions to attack Midway Island, allowing him to deploy his forces appropriately. His counterpart, Admiral Yamamoto, believed that there were no American carriers available to protect Midway, but to make sure he launched a diversionary attack against the Aleutian Islands off Alaska.

The Japanese air strikes against Midway early on 4 June 1942 marked the start of the battle. The attacks were largely successful, but Japanese attention was soon drawn to the fact that all was not as planned when American torpedo bombers from the carriers *Enterprise*, *Hornet* and *Yorktown* attacked their fleet. Although the American aircraft scored no hits on the Japanese invasion force, their presence meant that enemy carriers were in the area.

However, Japanese victory was not imminent. Many Japanese troops fell victim to tropical diseases, and this, coupled with strong American defensive positions meant that there was a lull in the fighting until April. By the time that the fighting resumed, MacArthur had been ordered to leave for the United States, departing with his memorable message 'I shall return' on 8 March. Bataan fell on 9 April, leaving just Corregidor. The Japanese took their time to reduce the defensive positions with artillery. After nearly a week of preparatory bombardment, the Japanese attacked on 5 May, and the surviving Americans surrendered the next day. The conquest of the Philippines was complete.

THE DUTCH EAST INDIES

With their array of natural resources, not least oil, the Dutch East Indies were an extremely tempting target for the Japanese. Troops landed on the Sarawak coast on 16 December, and by early January it was clear to the American, British, Dutch and Australian (ABDA) command that a full-blown invasion of the entire colony was imminent.

The Japanese divided their invasion forces into Eastern, Western and Central Forces, with the idea that these would – as their names implied – attack the east and west sides of the Dutch East Indies respectively. The concept behind the plan was elegantly simple, with the Japanese seizing ground, consolidating briefly and then moving on to their next objective. Eastern Force attacked first, seizing Celebes, then Ambon, Timor and Bali. The defenders on Timor dispersed, and carried out a guerrilla campaign against the invaders for over a year before the last of them was killed, but elsewhere the Japanese found little to stop them. An Allied naval effort in the Lombok Straits on the night of 19/20 February caught the Japanese by surprise, but was beaten off and only delayed the Japanese offensive by a few hours.

Eastern Force landed on Java on 1 March, along with Western Force, which had taken Sumatra on the way, and Central Force, which had taken key coastal areas on Borneo. The landings were preceded by the Battle of the Java Sea, in which an Allied force tried to stop the Japanese, only to be totally defeated, with the loss of all but four of its ships. The Allied forces left in Java were heavily outnumbered, and it was clear that their position was hopeless.

When the Japanese demanded talks with the local Dutch commanders on 7 March, they made it clear that they would raze the Javanese capital to the ground if a surrender was not forthcoming. With no alternative, the remaining Allied forces in the East Indies surrendered the next day.

Coral Sea

After the series of Japanese victories in the Pacific, the Americans staged a daring raid by B-25 bombers launched from the carrier USS *Hornet* on 18 April 1942. Although the raid caused little damage, it raised morale in the United States and provided a ready-made hero in the form of the attack's leader, Colonel Jimmy Doolittle. The Doolittle raid came as a rude shock to the Japanese high command,

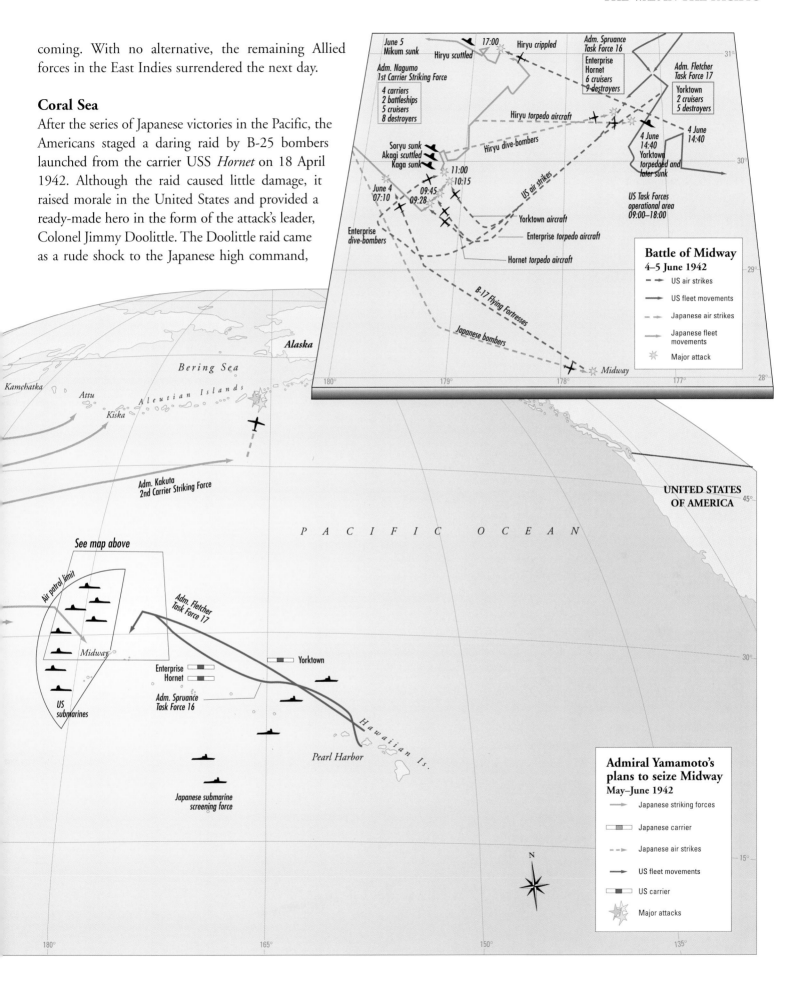

Battle of Midway
4–5 June 1942

- – ▸ US air strikes
- ──▸ US fleet movements
- – – Japanese air strikes
- ──▸ Japanese fleet movements
- ✳ Major attack

Admiral Yamamoto's plans to seize Midway
May–June 1942

- ──▸ Japanese striking forces
- ▭ Japanese carrier
- – – ▸ Japanese air strikes
- ──▸ US fleet movements
- ▭ US carrier
- ✳ Major attacks

195

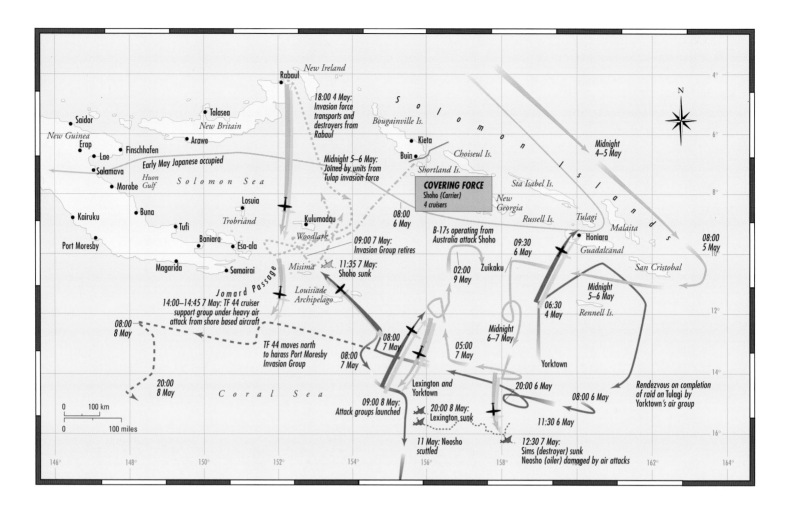

Battle of the Coral Sea
28 April–11 May 1942

→ Japanese movement

→ Allied movement

✚ Japanese air strikes

✚ Allied air strikes

🚢 Japanese sinking ship

🚢 Allied sinking ship

and they decided that they needed to extend their defensive perimeter to prevent a recurrence of the attack. To do this, they decided to carry out an amphibious assault on Port Moresby in Papua. This led to the Battle of the Coral Sea.

Forewarned after breaking Japanese naval codes, the Americans positioned two aircraft carriers against the Japanese force. The first action came when a Japanese seaplane base was attacked by aircraft from the USS *Yorktown* on 4 May 1942; three days later, an attack by US aircraft sank the Japanese carrier *Shoho*. With both sides now aware of the other's position, a major battle followed on 8 May, with the Americans losing the carrier *Lexington* and the destroyer *Sims*. The Japanese lost a number of aircraft along with their valuable crews, and were forced to call off the invasion of Port Moresby. The battle was the first strategic victory won by the Americans in the Pacific, even if it had been a draw tactically.

MIDWAY

Although the Japanese had failed in their plan to invade Port Moresby as a result of the Battle of the Coral Sea, Admiral Yamamoto was not overly concerned. The battle had seen the sinking of the US carrier *Lexington*, while the USS *Yorktown* had been damaged. Yamamoto had been given reason to believe that the *Yorktown* would be out of action for many months, while the remaining two (*Enterprise* and *Hornet*) were likely to be in the south Pacific. These factors suggested that the American fleet would be weak to the extent that drawing the remaining American ships into battle might prove decisive. Yamamoto proposed to secure this battle by

CORAL SEA

The Japanese took the decision to invade Port Moresby. The Americans had broken Japanese naval ciphers, and sent a force to block the attack. The subsequent Battle of the Coral Sea was the first naval engagement in history where the opposing fleets never saw each other, the action being carried out entirely by aircraft.

The *Shoho* was sunk on 7 May, and the next 24 hours saw further air attacks by both sides' carrier aircraft. The Japanese sank the carrier *Lexington*, along with a destroyer and an oiler, and thus sustained fewer losses than the Americans. The battle was a draw, but the invasion was off.

JAPANESE CATASTROPHE

Although these initial American strikes failed, they ensured that the Japanese fighters had to land to refuel and rearm – and it was as this was being carried out that the decisive blow was struck. The *Akagi, Soryu* and *Kaga* were all hit by bombs from American dive bombers.

As refuelling and rearming were underway, the effects of the attacks were magnified by exploding fuel and ordnance on the Japanese ships, all of which sank – *Akagi* and *Soryu* in a matter of minutes.

The sole surviving Japanese carrier, *Hiryu*, launched its aircraft to find the American carriers, successfully damaging *Yorktown,* which had only just been patched up after the Battle of Coral Sea. However, the American carrier aircraft found *Hiryu* in turn and sunk her, meaning that the entire Japanese carrier force had been lost in one day.

Yamamoto's fleet still outnumbered his American opponents, and he tried to force a surface engagement to wrest some success from the disaster. However, the American fleet, now led by Spruance as Fletcher's flagship *Yorktown* was under tow, proved to be elusive and Yamamoto was forced to give up. The Midway operation was cancelled, and the Japanese were now forced on the defensive in the Pacific. Their only consolation was the sinking of *Yorktown* by a Japanese submarine while under tow back to Pearl Harbor.

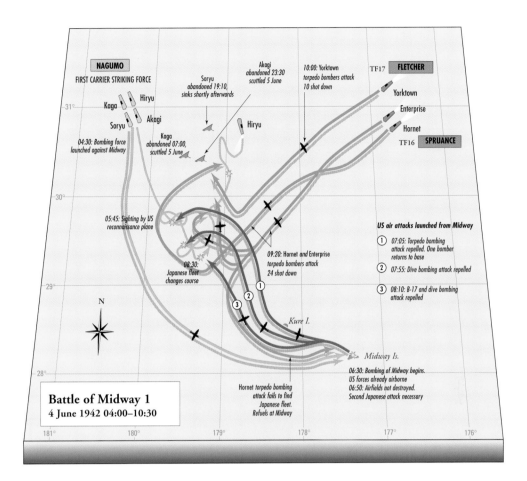

Battle of Midway 1
4 June 1942 04:00–10:30

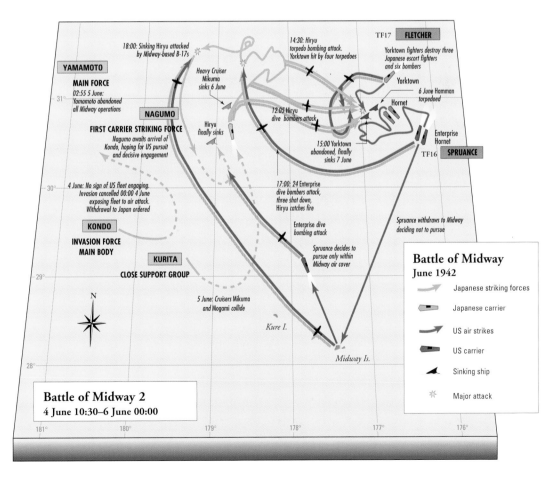

Battle of Midway 2
4 June 10:30–6 June 00:00

launching an invasion of Midway Island – he considered it impossible that the Americans would not respond, whereupon his aircraft and battleships would destroy what remained of American naval power in the Pacific.

Unfortunately for Yamamoto, the *Yorktown* was not as badly damaged as he thought; furthermore, immense efforts at Pearl Harbor meant that the carrier was ready to return to sea in a far shorter time than anyone might have thought possible. Also, code-breaking had provided the American commander, Admiral Chester Nimitz with advanced warning of Yamamoto's plan. He sent Task Force 16 (Rear-Admiral Spruance) and Task Force 17 (Rear-Admiral Fletcher) to the north of Midway, where they awaited the arrival of the Japanese. Contrary to Japanese expectations, the three carriers Yamamoto had discounted were present, waiting for their opportunity.

The Japanese began their assault on Midway on the morning of 4 June 1942. Although the raids inflicted serious damage, the Japanese were concerned when they were attacked – ineffectually – by carrier aircraft from the two American Task Forces. Japanese scout planes located some of the American ships, and plans were made to launch a strike against them once aircraft had returned from another raid on Midway. Two more American attacks against the Japanese carriers failed, but at 10:00 hours, while the Japanese were refuelling and rearming their aircraft, 35 dive bombers appeared overhead. The carriers *Akagi*, *Kaga* and *Soryu* were sunk, *Akagi* blowing up as fuel and ordnance on the main deck exploded. *Kaga* lingered until nightfall before slipping below

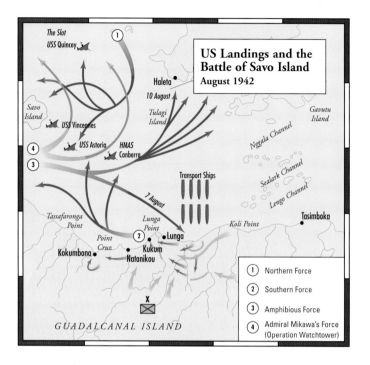

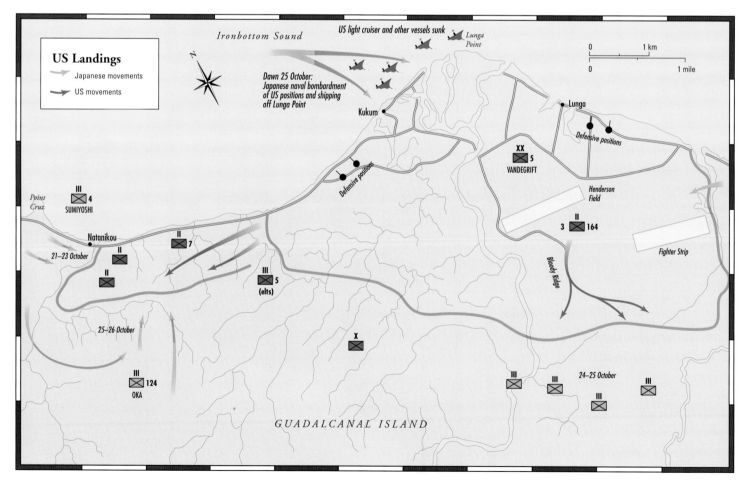

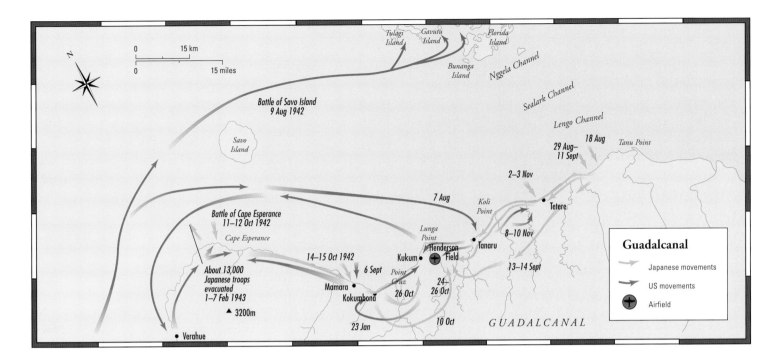

GUADALCANAL

Guadalcanal was not on the
original Allied list of objectives,
but the Japanese attempt to
build an airfield at Henderson
Field led to a hastily-
constructed plan, with the 1st
Marine Division landing on 7
August 1942 in the face of only
light resistance. The Japanese
responded swiftly, defeating the
US Navy at Savo Island.
However, the Marines remained
despite the increasing efforts of
the Japanese.

The most notable Japanese
land attacks took place on 18
August and 13 September. The
first attack was under-strength,
but the second came closer to
success. Another major Japanese
assault on Henderson Field on
24 and 25 October was repulsed
with heavy casualties,
particularly on the Japanese
side. Yet the battle remained in
the balance, and American
possession of Henderson Field
was still tenuous.

the waves, while *Soryu* sank within 20 minutes. Later in the day, the fourth Japanese carrier, *Hiryu,* was sunk. Although the *Hiryu*'s aircraft had managed to damage the *Yorktown* severly at mid-day on 4 June, it was clear that the Japanese had suffered a massive defeat. Midway marked a turning point in the war, and was the first in a series of blows from which Japan was never to recover fully.

Below: USS *Yorktown* seen during the Battle of Midway after being hit by three Japanese bombs; her damage and fire control crews are attempting to repair the damage. One bomb went down her funnel and blew all but one of her boilers. Shortly after this photograph was taken, the ship was hit by torpedoes from a second Japanese attack wave, and two days later she was sunk by *I-168*, a Japanese submarine.

BITTER STRUGGLE

The struggle for Guadalcanal continued on land and sea until early 1943, when the Japanese decided to withdraw from the island as they were unable to sustain their losses, although the Americans had in fact gained the upper hand as early as the middle of November the previous year.

However, before their decision to withdraw, the Japanese, determined to dislodge the Americans, made a number of attempts to land reinforcements from the so-called 'Tokyo Express' supply convoys, covered by powerful surface naval forces.

These convoys were vulnerable to attack however, not least from the American aircraft based at Henderson Field on the island itself, as well as the American naval forces in the area. In November 1942 the decision was made by the Japanese to make an all-out effort to defeat the Americans on Guadalcanal.

GUADALCANAL

Guadalcanal and the Solomon Islands became a key strategic objective in the South Pacific in the course on 1942. If the Japanese held them, they would serve as a base from which Allied supply lines between America and Australia could be attacked; while if they were in Allied hands, the islands would serve as a useful base from which to launch offensive action, as well as providing a shield against Japanese attacks towards Australia.

By May 1942, the Japanese had made good progress in developing the facilities on Florida Island, and reports began to reach the Americans that enemy troops were being ferried across to Guadalcanal to build an airfield. Given that this would allow the operation of Japanese bombers against shipping and possibly Australia, the decision was made to take the island. A force of 19,000 US Marines landed on 7 August 1942, and drove the Japanese into the jungle. The airfield was renamed 'Henderson Field' and completed by US engineers. Materials left by the Japanese were used to build defences around the airfield, and these were soon required.

The Japanese responded immediately, sending a force of cruisers to Guadalcanal through the passage between New Georgia and Santa Isabel, known as 'the Slot'. The Japanese soon discovered Allied ships in their way, and engaged them on the night of 9 August off Savo Island. The Japanese won a comprehensive victory, sinking four Allied cruisers, leaving the transports being escorted at their mercy. However, fearing an attack by carrier-based aircraft, the Japanese withdrew, not realising that the American carriers had been withdrawn. After missing the opportunity to cause havoc, the Japanese began to launch a series of attacks against the Marines, which degenerated into attritional fighting. The first attack on 18 August was beaten back, while the second, on 13 September came close to success – however, at dawn the next morning, a combination of American fire and air power stopped the assault in its tracks.

Further naval battles took place, the most notable being the American success at Cape Esperance on 11 October, and at Santa Cruz on 25 October, at which the Americans lost the carrier *Hornet*. By the end of October, the issue of Guadalcanal was still in doubt.

THE FINAL PHASE

The final phase in the battle for Guadalcanal and the Solomon islands came in November 1942. The Japanese decided to make one last effort to defeat the Americans, by landing their entire 38th Division on Guadalcanal, supported by all the ships in the Combined Fleet. As at Midway, American signals intelligence revealed Japanese intentions. Under the Japanese plans, while Admiral Tanaka's 'Tokyo Express' (which kept the Japanese troops on the island supplied) landed

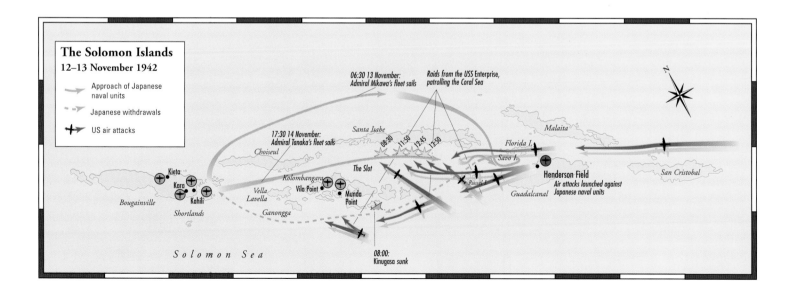

the 38th Division, while other naval forces would prevent the Americans from interfering with the landings.

On the night of 12/13 November, a fleet of two battleships, a cruiser and six destroyers under the command of Admiral Hiroaki Abe made its way along the Slot. This was countered by the Americans despatching five cruisers and eight destroyers commanded by Admiral Daniel Callaghan. The two forces met off Savo Island, and within minutes of fire being opened, Callaghan had been killed by a shell that hit the bridge of his ship, the *San Francisco*. The Americans concentrated their fire on the enemy battleships, but could do little to prevent the loss of three cruisers and two destroyers before Abe decided to withdraw to the north. Although the Japanese had won the tactical battle, they had not landed at Henderson Field. The next day, aircraft from the base found that the Japanese battleship *Hiei* had been damaged in the fighting, and showed no mercy – the ship was sent to the bottom in a savage air attack.

The 14 November saw more activity. American pilots found the troop transports and their escorts and gave them a severe mauling. Four cruisers were sunk or disabled, and six of the troop transports were sent to the bottom, killing thousands of soldiers in the process. Despite this defeat, Tanaka was ordered to make a final effort to defeat Henderson Field, by shelling the airbase with a battleship and four cruisers. This time, the US Navy was ready. Two new battleships, the *Washington* and the *South Dakota*, were waiting, along

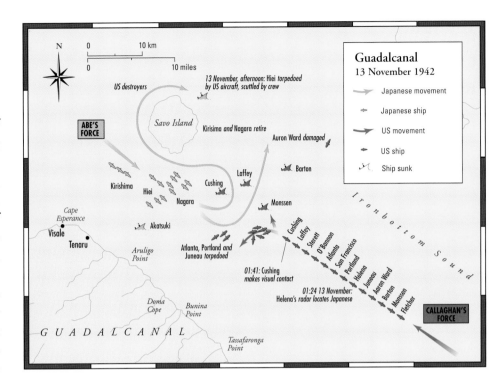

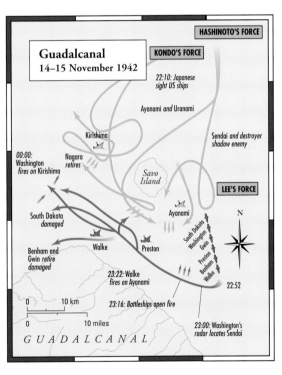

with a force of destroyers. Although *South Dakota* suffered a systems failure and took over 40 shell hits, the *Washington* used its radar-guided guns to put 54 shells into the Japanese *Kirishima*, leaving it a blazing wreck. The Japanese withdrew, leaving Tanaka with the task of landing the 38th Division in daylight against an alerted enemy. The end result was a slaughter, with the convoy under constant air attack. At the end of the day, only 2000 men from 38th Division were left alive to link up with their colleagues in the jungle. It was clear that the crisis was over for the Americans, and from early December, the Marines started to patrol aggressively beyond Henderson Field. The Japanese decided that they could not afford the continuing casualties, and began to withdraw – by 8 February 1943, the last Japanese soldier had left Guadalcanal, and the

KEY BATTLES

The decisive naval actions occurred between 13–15 November 1942 when the two sides clashed in the waters around Savo Island. On the first night, the Japanese sank three destroyers and two cruisers in the space of 20 minutes. However, the sacrifice made by the American sailors meant that the Japanese had failed in their prime objective of landing more men on Guadalcanal.

The next morning, the damaged battleship *Hiei* was sunk by aircraft from Henderson Field. During the day, four cruisers and six transports were sunk, but this disaster did not mark the end of Japanese efforts. During the night of 14–15 November the battleship *Kirishina* was sunk in less than seven minutes by the battleship *Washington*. Japanese high command decided to withdraw their men from the island.

NEW BRITAIN

Operation Cartwheel aimed to exploit the successes in New Guinea and at Guadalcanal by isolating the major Japanese base at Rabaul on New Britain. After disagreements between Admiral Nimitz and General MacArthur were resolved (limiting some of the scope originally proposed for the offensive), the operation demonstrated the classic characteristics of the later 'island hopping' campaign pursued as the Allies advanced towards Japan.

Japanese efforts at reinforcing their troops on New Guinea were dealt a savage blow at the Battle of the Bismarck Sea, when the troop convoy was annihilated by low-level bombing by American B-25 Mitchell aircraft using the newly-developed technique of 'skip bombing'. The Japanese response came in the form of the 'I-Go' air offensive, which despite its large scale did not achieve a great deal.

This was followed by the steady advance of both naval and land forces as they progressed through the chain of islands. The Allies used a mix of amphibious assault, conventional ground advances and even parachute landings to outmanoeuvre the Japanese. By November 1943, the primary aim of neutralising the threat posed by Rabaul had been achieved. The Japanese, deciding that they could not afford to embark upon an attritional battle, withdrew the bulk of their forces to Truk.

Americans had won their first and possibly most important land victory in the Pacific War.

NEW GUINEA

New Guinea, the second largest island in the world, occupied a key strategic position in the Pacific, prompting the Japanese to make plans for occupying it. Their first attempt, a direct amphibious assault on Port Moresby, was thwarted by the Battle of the Coral Sea, so an alternative option was enacted instead.

On 21 July 1942, Major General Tomatoro Horii's South Seas Detachment was landed to the east of Gona, with instructions to advance down the Kokoda Trail to Port Moresby. The plan was complicated by the fact that the Japanese believed that the Trail was a trafficable road over the Owen Stanley Mountains, only to discover that it was little more than a narrow jungle track a matter of feet wide.

Despite this setback, the Japanese skill at jungle movement and fighting was demonstrated in the course of the next two months – Kokoda was taken within a week of the landings, and by mid-September, Japanese forces were just over 48km (30 miles) from Port Moresby. They halted at this point, since Horii had orders that he was not to advance any further until he was reinforced. This suited Horri, since his supply lines were now extended. However, the fighting in Guadalcanal meant that the Japanese chose to redirect the reinforcements intended to support Horii to that campaign, while supplies were also diverted.

Below: The first American offensive of the Pacific War – American troops are transported in landing craft to Guadacanal in order to take control of the new airbase there. Unlike many of the landings undertaken subsequently, the initial landings on Guadacanal were only lightly opposed by Japanese forces.

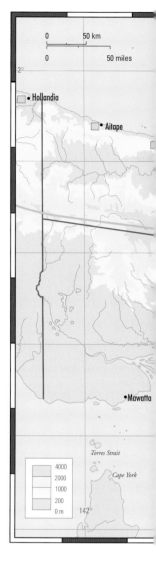

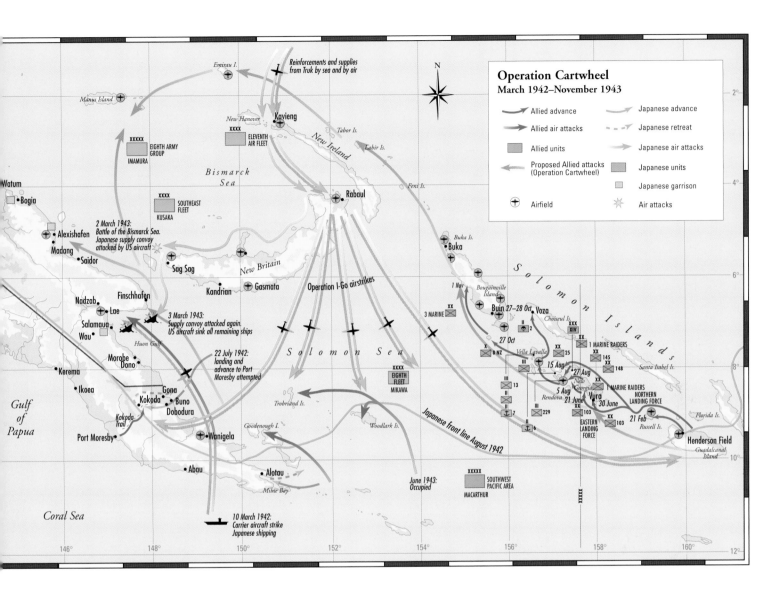

One attempt at reinforcement failed, with the Japanese force being driven back and then evacuated to Rabaul, leaving Horii in a perilous position. The Australian and American forces on the island waited, aware that Horii's position was declining with every passing day as he did not have the men or material to advance. Finally, on 24 September, Horii was ordered to withdraw to Buna and the surrounding area. The Australians counterattacked two days later, and the Japanese fell back, fighting vigorously as they did so. Horii was killed in the retreat, but survivors from his forces joined up with their colleagues holding Buna, Gona and Sanananda, where they created strong defensive positions.

THE FIRST VICTORY

At this point, General Douglas MacArthur ordered the US 32nd Division to New Guinea to assist with the Allied offensive. The 32nd Division was to take Buna, while the Australians dealt with the other two Japanese garrisons. MacArthur anticipated a swift victory, failing to appreciate that the terrain made this almost impossible. A lack of armour and heavy weapons meant that the initial attacks were thrown back with heavy losses. Several weeks of attacks achieved very little other than heavy Allied casualties, and MacArthur responded by sending General Robert Eichenberger to take over command. Eichenberger launched one attack, which failed, and then decided that he would wait until he had enough men and armour. Once these were forthcoming, the attacks went far better. The Australians took Gona on 9 December, and ten days later, the Americans launched the attack that finally removed the Japanese from Buna; Sanananda, which was now being evacuated by the Japanese, was taken on 22 January 1943. The Allies then advanced throughout New Guinea, until by September they had removed the Japanese from a large proportion of the island. Fighting continued until almost the end of the war, but the 1942–43 combat gave MacArthur his first real victory in the Pacific campaign.

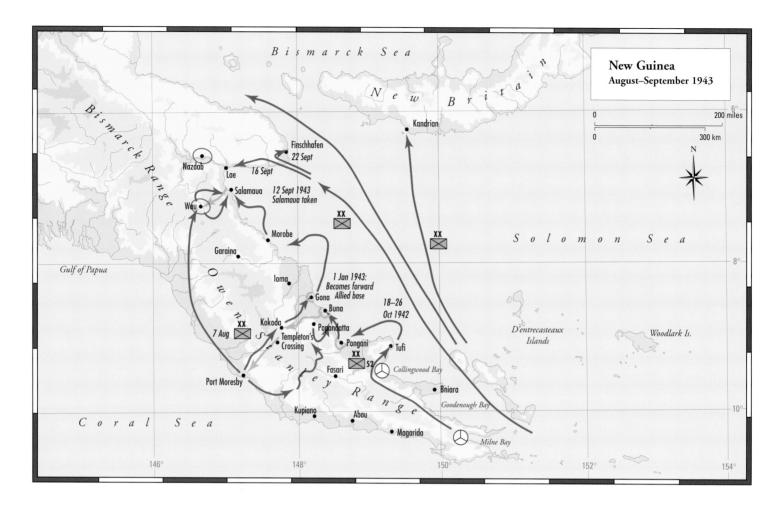

OPERATION CARTWHEEL

The success of operations in New Guinea and at Guadalcanal prompted the Allies to begin to prepare for the next phase of their operations, which was to be a push towards Rabaul. The planning was hindered by a disagreement between MacArthur and Nimitz over command and control of the operation and its intended outcome: as a compromise, the two men settled on a smaller-scale attack, codenamed 'Operation Cartwheel'. Under this scheme, the naval forces commanded by Admiral William 'Bull' Halsey would advance along the Solomon Island chain up to Bougainville, while MacArthur's land forces would conduct their offensive along the New Guinea coast, in the aftermath of their successes there at the end of 1942.

The Japanese were not slow to identify the dangers they faced in New Guinea, and made determined efforts to bolster their position. They despatched the 51st Division from Rabaul, but on 1 March 1943, their convoy was spotted by American reconnaissance aircraft. The next day, American B-25 bombers were sent out to attack the ships in what became known as the Battle of the Bismarck Sea. They caused havoc amongst the landing craft, and only 100 Japanese soldiers reached New Guinea out of the entire division despatched, as the Americans returned to bomb the remaining ships on 3 March.

The Japanese response to the series of failures since the end of 1942 took the form of an air offensive, codenamed 'I-Go', against a number of Allied bases. The problem facing the Japanese lay in the relative inexperience of their pilots, who achieved far less than they thought. Instead of the massive destruction claimed, the Japanese managed to destroy around 30 Allied aircraft, a destroyer, a corvette and two merchant ships. Japanese aircraft losses were at least the same as those of the Allies, and may have been higher. To make matters worse for the Japanese, Admiral Yamamoto decided to visit his airmen to congratulate them – but signals intercepts allowed the Americans to send P-38 fighters to shoot down his transport aircraft as he flew between bases, killing the man who planned the Pearl Harbor operation.

By the end of June, MacArthur's forces landed at Nassau Bay in New Guinea, while some 400 miles away, Halsey's men attacked New Georgia. The Japanese defended New Georgia with some vigour, and it took a month to remove them, even though they were heavily outnumbered. Halsey then bypassed the island upon which the next group of Japanese forces were based, taking Vell Lavella instead. In New Guinea, MacArthur's troops took the key Japanese bases of Lae and Salamaua. The final part of the

NEW GUINEA

The geographical location of New Guinea meant that it was of considerable strategic importance to both sides. In early 1942, the Japanese decided that they would seize the island, but their first attempt had to be postponed as a result of the Battle of the Coral Sea. An assault on the capital, Port Moresby, from the landward side was then substituted, with the first Japanese troops arriving in July.

The Japanese enjoyed some early successes, fighting their way through the jungle to take Kokoda, and then to sit atop the Owen Stanley mountains, from where they would be in a position to assault Port Moresby once reinforcements arrived. Although the Japanese came within 56km (35 miles) of the capital, they were never in a position to take it. Their supply situation was perilous, and the reinforcements that were needed for the final assault were diverted to Guadalcanal; the one attempt to land additional troops was beaten back by the defenders.

By mid-September 1942, it was clear to the Japanese high command that they would not be able to take the island, and they withdrew to the coast. A series of bitter battles then occurred as the Americans and Australians attempted to dislodge the Japanese from Gona and Buna. After initial setbacks, this was achieved in December and early January, and the Japanese were now at a serious disadvantage.

operation was the seizure of Bougainville, to allow it to be used as a base for air attacks against the Japanese outpost at Rabaul.

Landings on Bougainville started on 1 November 1943, and met little resistance. Construction of the airstrip began almost as soon as the beachhead was secured. The Japanese sent a force of 10 ships to destroy the beachhead, but this was intercepted by the US Navy, which handled the Japanese roughly. Halsey then launched a daring carrier-borne air strike against another Japanese naval thrust, risking the loss of both *Saratoga* and *Independence*, but his luck held and the Japanese were driven away. The Japanese appreciated that they had been outmanoeuvred, and withdrew their ships and aircraft to their base at Truk, bringing the battle of Rabaul to a close.

THE ALEUTIANS

The Aleutian campaign is one that received relatively little attention during the Second World War, and even less from historians. Although not decisive, it is worthy of note, since the fighting took place in some of the most extreme weather conditions encountered in the Pacific theatre, and the proximity of the islands to Alaska meant that it was important for the Americans to retain control of them.

The first fighting around the Aleutians took place in June 1942, as part the Japanese plan for the Battle of Midway. To divert the Americans' attention, two Japanese light carriers were to launch an air attack on Dutch Harbor, as a prelude to the occupation of Attu and Kiska at the western end of the island chain. Seizing these islands would neutralize any US air power there,

Below: Ordnancemen of Scouting Squadron 6 load a 227kg (500lb) bomb onto a Douglas Dauntless SBD dive bomber on board USS *Enterprise* during the fighting for Guadalcanal. Both the Americans and the Japanese used a combination of dive bombers and torpedo bombers from their aircraft carriers to attack the other fleet, with a covering screen of fighters to protect the attacking aircraft.

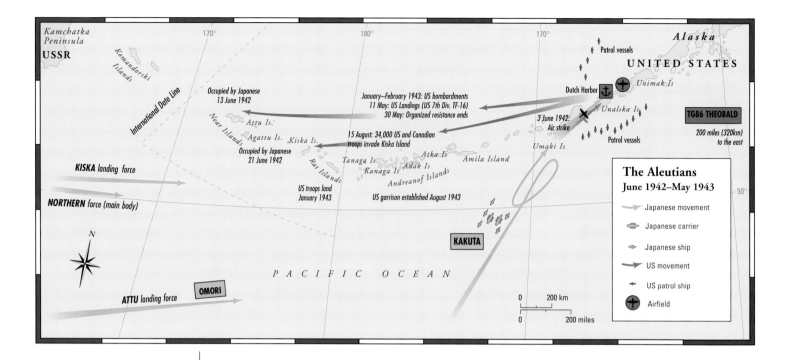

ALEUTIAN ISLANDS

The occupation of the Aleutian island chain by the Japanese at the time of the Battle of Midway appeared to suggest that they could be an important factor in the war against Japan.

Once the occupation of Attu and Kiska was detected by aerial reconnaissance, the Chiefs of Staff were greatly concerned. It appeared that the Japanese might be intending to use the islands to threaten Alaska, or perhaps Siberia.

It was not until 1943 that the forces needed to retake Attu and Kiska were ready. Aerial bombardment began in January 1943, with the landings on Attu taking place on 11 May. With fierce Japanese resistance and bad weather hampering American operations, the last resistance was crushed on 30 May. The recapture of Kiska proved far simpler, since the Japanese decided to withdraw.

and demand some American response – all of which would, according to the plan, make the operation at Midway easier. Events did not go as planned, with Midway turning into a disaster for the Japanese. The sole success from the Midway operation was that Kiska and Attu were both occupied; however, even this was limited. The air raids on Dutch Harbor had caused relatively little damage, and a 'Zero' fighter aircraft had been forced to land on Akutan Island, from where it was recovered by the Americans. This enabled a careful study of the most formidable fighter in the Japanese arsenal, and the Americans were rapidly able to develop ways to deal with it (and to build new fighters of their own that were superior to the Zero).

The appalling weather conditions in the Aleutians meant that it was nearly a week until American aircraft discovered that Kiska and Attu had been occupied (the islands were uninhabited prior to the Japanese arrival), prompting some temporary concern on the part of the Americans. Reinforcements were sent to Alaska, but the forces needed to evict the Japanese were not available in 1942. As a result, the islands were bombed and blockaded. In March 1943, a surface battle took place around the Komandorski Islands, with the Japanese commander breaking off the action too early and handing victory to the Americans.

Finally, in 1943, the reconquest of Kisa and Attu was authorised by the Chiefs of Staff. Attu was assaulted on 11 May, and after two weeks' hard fighting (made harder by the weather), was back in American hands. Ten weeks later, an invasion armada of over 100 ships assembled around Kiska. 34,000 American and Canadian troops invaded on 15 August – only to find that the Japanese, realising the futility of their position, had pulled out at the end of July.

The Aleutians did not offer the Americans a great deal in terms of territory that was useful for future operations, but it did serve to demonstrate the tenacity of the Japanese in defending island strongholds, a lesson that was to be repeated elsewhere in the Pacific as the war turned against the Japanese.

THE CHINDITS IN BURMA

The British Chindit formations owed their existence to Brigadier Orde Wingate, an unconventional officer with a background in counter-insurgency operations in Palestine. He proposed a Long Range Penetration Group to operate behind Japanese lines and supported from the air. By early 1943, the 77th Indian Brigade, or 'Chindits', was ready for operations.

On 8 February 1943, the Chindits crossed the Chindwin River into Burma, catching the Japanese by surprise. Their attacks on supply lines were very successful, and succeeded in tying down large numbers of Japanese troops, who were required to guard against attacks on their logistic chain. Unfortunately, Wingate's next step was to order his men across the Irrawaddy river, taking them into more open country. As well as leaving them vulnerable to Japanese attack, this also took the Chindits out of range of air resupply by the RAF. The constant Japanese attacks on his formation forced Wingate to order his men back across the Irrawaddy, but the Japanese had outmanoeuvred him and blocked the way: however, using their guerrilla warfare skills, the Chindits split up and made their way back into India in small groups. Despite having this advantage, the withdrawal – and sickness – took a fearful toll on the brigade, and over 30 per cent of it failed to return.

Although the First Chindit Campaign was a failure, its daring nature made Wingate and the survivors into heroes in Britain, and did not destroy the concept of long-range raids. In November, plans to seize northern Burma were laid down, and Wingate believed that a long-range penetration would facilitate operations to achieve this. The Chindits were reformed into six brigades known as Long Range Penetration Groups (LRPGs), divided into fighting columns of 400 men each with fire support and an air liaison officer to call in air support where required. Wingate planned to use half his force for the opening stages of the operation, withdrawing them to be replaced by the remainder after two months. The Second Chindit campaign enjoyed considerably more success, causing serious problems in Japanese rear areas and taking some key areas. Wingate did not live to see all of this, being killed in an air crash on 25 March 1944.

Eventually, the 77th and 111th Brigades were withdrawn after constant operations left them heavily depleted, but the remaining Chindits went on to capture Sahmaw and Taugni,

CHINDITS

The Chindits were specially-trained brigades operating deep behind Japanese lines to attack enemy lines of communication. The first Chindit operation saw fighting columns sent across the Chindwin River in mid-February 1943. They advanced deep into enemy territory, disrupting supply lines and forcing the Japanese to deploy a large number of troops on guard duties.

The decision to cross the Irrawaddy in March 1943 was a mistake. A series of battles in mid-March made it clear that the Chindits were not likely to achieve more, and a withdrawal was ordered. The raid was vital for raising British morale.

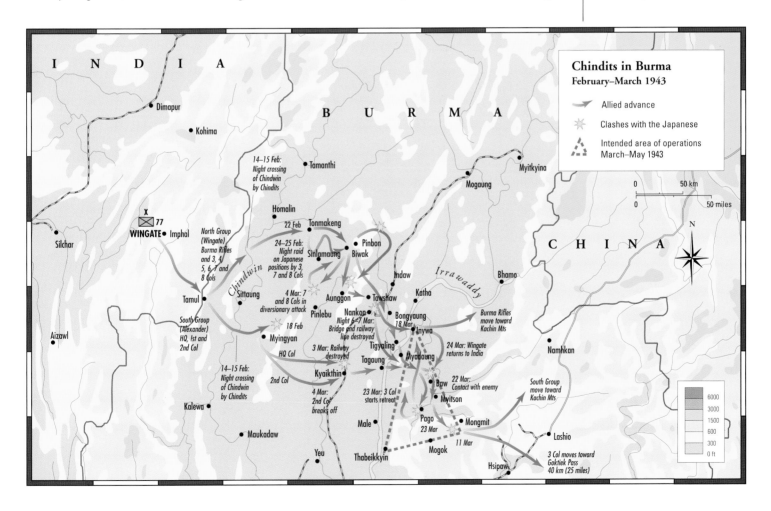

STRATEGY

The decision was made by American planners to bypass any Japanese strongholds that did not need to be eliminated immediately and concentrate on advancing on the Japanese Home Islands themselves. This island-hopping campaign would preserve American forces for the final attack on Japan that was sure to be costly in terms of both men and materiel.

contributing to wider operations in the area which left the Allies in full control of Indaw and all areas north of it by the end of 1944.

PACIFIC SITUATION

The situation in the Pacific campaign changed decisively in favour of the Allies after Midway and Guadalcanal, although it was clear that the Japanese were far from beaten. Their determined resistance against Allied offensives demonstrated that they would be hard to dislodge from the multitude of bases they had across the Pacific. It was this consideration that had led to the 'island hopping' strategy, where large Japanese garrisons on islands that were not of strategic or operational importance were left *in situ* to be dealt with later.

Although the Allies had moved to the offensive, they still had a great deal of work to do before the Japanese were finally defeated. Events in 1944 moved the Allies closer to victory (and to Japan itself), as they sought to occupy key positions. The Japanese empire remained large, though – the Dutch East Indies, Malaya, Burma and China all remained in their hands, although the strain of

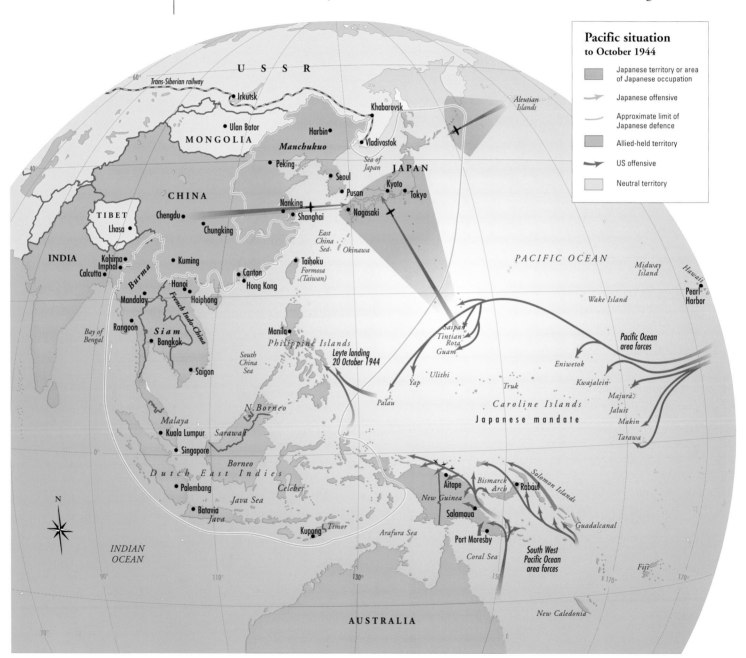

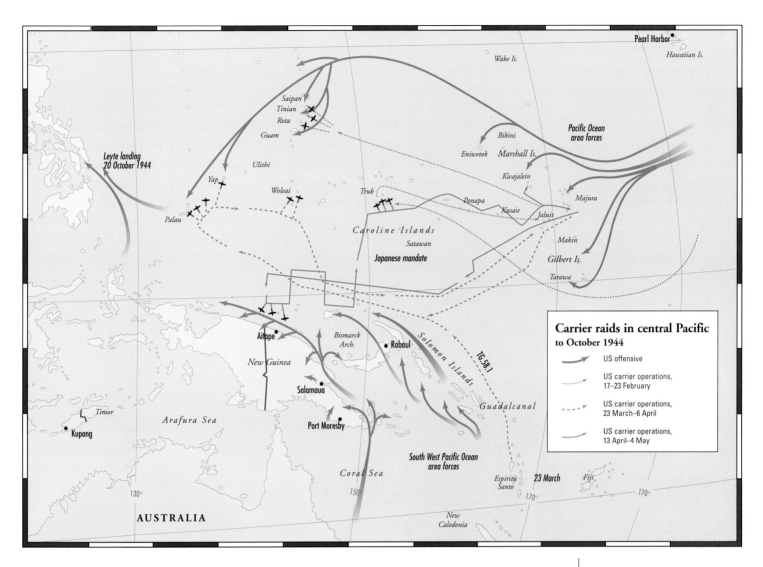

retaining these territories began to show as Allied submarines inflicted a serious toll upon the Japanese merchant marine. By October 1944, the Japanese air services only just represented a threat to the Allies, and much of their potency lay in *kamikaze* attacks, rather than any other form of air action. Operations around the Marianas had seen a wholesale slaughter of Japanese air strength, while their maritime position was increasingly precarious. The Allies were rapidly approaching the home islands of Japan, while the Philippines remained a tempting target for General MacArthur, anxious to fulfil his promise to return.

The increased proximity of the Allies to Japan increased the determination of the Japanese to resist. Fighting became ever more ferocious, with Japanese troops fighting to the last man. This in itself gave rise to concerns as to the cost of an invasion of the homeland, adding extra impetus to the development of what was then a top-secret weapon: the atomic bomb.

CARRIER RAIDS IN THE CENTRAL PACIFIC

American campaigns in 1944 were marked by a new development in the use of carrier-based aircraft, with the formation of Task Force 58, equipped with around a dozen 'Fast Carriers'. The force was under the overall command of Admiral Marc T Mitscher, who assumed control on 13 January 1944. After two weeks' final preparation, the Task Force set sail from Hawaii at the end of the month.

News of the American sortie reaching them through reconnaissance missions, the Japanese took the opportunity to withdraw a number of more important units from Truk, pulling them

CARRIER RAIDS

The early part of 1944 was marked by a number of highly successful raids by the aircraft carriers of Admiral Marc Mitscher's Task Force 58 against key Japanese targets. There were three sorties in total, encompassing two attacks against Truk, plus supporting landings in New Guinea, and raiding Palau and the Marianas.

The three carrier raids provided a clear demonstration of how aircraft had become a major maritime weapon, enabling the US Navy to remove the threat posed by Japanese island strongholds.

back to Palau. This was not the intended destination of the carriers at first, since Task Force 58 was designated to support landings on Kwajalien on 29 January. Once these had been successfully completed, the carriers headed for Majuro. They then sortied from here on 13 February, aiming to strike Truk, thereby neutralising it as an immediate threat to operations.

The first strike wave was launched just before dawn on 14 February, with a sweep by 72 Grumman F6F Hellcat fighters. Although the fighters were met by heavy (but inaccurate) anti-aircraft fire and about 80 Japanese aircraft, the Americans had little difficulty in asserting their dominance. Around 50 Japanese aircraft were shot down by the middle of the afternoon, and once air superiority had been gained, attacks against Japanese airfields began. Some 150 enemy aircraft were destroyed or damaged by these raids, while other aircraft sank over 100,000 tons of Japanese shipping around the island. Further strikes continued over the next three days, and after a final attack on 18 February, the Task Force withdrew, having destroyed over 250 Japanese aircraft and nearly 200,000 tons of shipping.

The Task Force refuelled, and then headed west towards the Marianas. It was located by Japanese aircraft on the night of 21/22 February, and an attack was authorised. The Japanese aircraft failed to score any hits on the carriers, allowing the carriers to launch a full strike the next morning. Airfields were strafed and bombed, along with any shipping that was found. Some Japanese ships escaped from their anchorages into the open sea, only to discover that American

Below: Australian troops on the Kokoda Trail in New Guinea, moving towards Buna. So much rain has fallen that the track has turned into a mudstream. With the Japanese defeat in New Guinea, the immediate threat to Australia receded, although the naval defeats suffered by Japan over the course of 1942 meant that an invasion was not likely due to the lack of protection for an invading fleet.

BLOODY TARAWA

The attacks on the Gilbert and the Marshall Islands pointed to the how the island-hopping campaign would develop. Certain key islands had to be taken, but others, where the Japanese garrison would be isolated by the loss of their supply line, could be allowed to 'wither on the vine'.

The campaigns were notable for the particularly fierce fighting that occurred. Tarawa was difficult to attack, since landing craft proved unable to cross the coral reef in front of the invasion beaches, while the nature of the terrain meant that the American force had to land opposite the Japanese defensive positions, rather than make any attempt to land elsewhere on the atoll and outflank the defenders. While Roi was relatively simple to deal with because of the success of the preliminary bombardment, heavily-wooded terrain and well-built defensive bunkers on Namur and Kwajalein meant that much of the ferocity of the American shell fire was mitigated, enabling the Japanese to put up stiff resistance against the attackers.

As well as their strategic value, the Gilbert and Marshall Island chains provided many valuable lessons for future operations against Japanese-held islands. With the fall of the entire Marshall group on 23 February 1944, the scene was set for the Battle of the Philippine Sea and operations against the Marianas.

submarines had been carefully placed there to intercept them. Once the strikes were completed, the Task Force retired to Majuro, reaching there on 23 February. There was then a break of a month before an attack against Palau was undertaken. Although the Task Force tried to stay out of range of Japanese aircraft on the approach, this failed, and another night attack had to be beaten off; again, the Japanese aircraft failed to cause any damage. The American assault began on 30 March, with the fighter sweep shooting down over 30 Japanese aircraft that attempted to intercept them. Merchant shipping was attacked, while mines were laid to confine some vessels to harbour, where they were easier targets. Once again, after a successful mission, the carriers retired to refuel.

A further sortie took place on 13 April, in support of the landings on the New Guinea coast. The landings took place on 21 April, and Japanese resistance was light. The Task Force's aircraft provided air support to the landings, and then withdrew to replenish; it then headed back to Truk. The Japanese had repaired much of the damage, and had flown in replacement aircraft. Task Force 58 started air strikes against the island on 29 April, and rapidly gained control of the air. The usual pattern of attacks on airfields was repeated, with around 90 Japanese aircraft succumbing to these raids. Having once again neutralised the threat from Truk, Task Force 58 headed for a new anchorage at Eniwetok, with its accompanying force of cruisers shelling Ponape on the way.

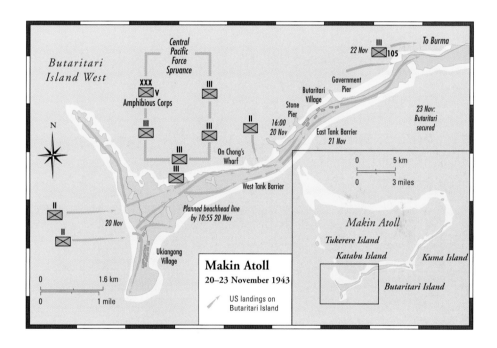

Tarawa Atoll
20–23 November 1943

Japanese pockets of resistance

Landings on Betio Island

Makin Atoll
20–23 November 1943

US landings on Butaritari Island

THE GILBERTS

After clearing the Aleutians of Japanese forces in mid-1943, American attention turned to the Central Pacific area, and the Gilbert Islands. The capture of the islands was given the codename 'Operation Galvanic', and planning vested in Rear-Admiral Raymond A Spruance. Spruance decided that the two most westerly islands, Makin and Tarawa, should be taken, since taking them would neutralize the other islands, which would no longer be able to be supplied. Makin was attacked on 20 November 1943, and taken after three days of bitter fighting, in which only one of the 800-strong Japanese garrison surrendered; American casualties were 66 killed and 150 wounded. While Making was, in relative terms, an easy operation, that to take Tarawa was very different.

One of the major difficulties with attacking Tarawa was the presence of a submerged coral reef that made it extremely difficult for landing craft to approach the beaches without grounding, which would leave them vulnerable to enemy fire. It was clear that amphibious assault vehicles (AMTRACs, or 'armoured tractors') would have to be used in addition to the landing craft. When the assault began on 20 November, the landing craft beached on the coral reef, since the water was even lower than anticipated –

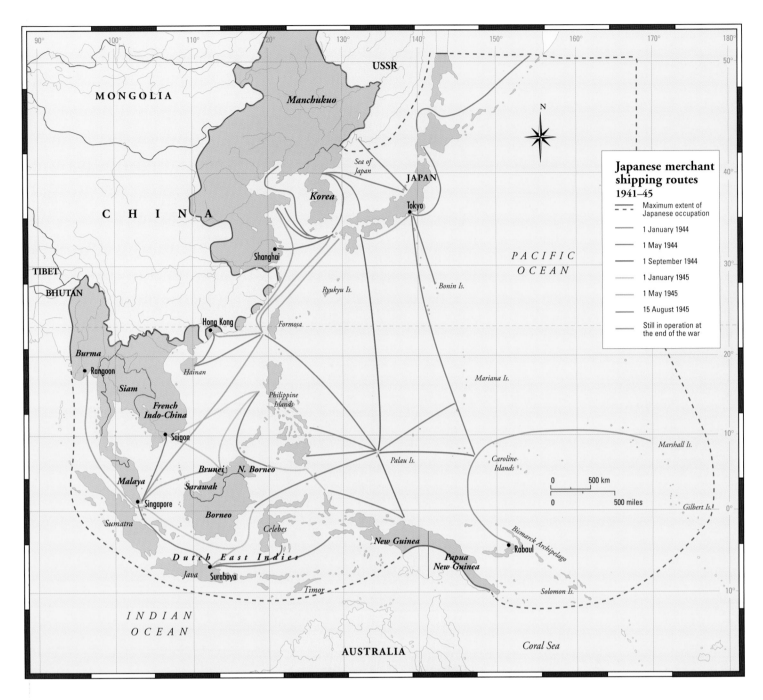

the entire landing effort was forced to depend upon tracked vehicles and the simple expedient of the troops wading ashore, often under heavy fire. At one stage, it appeared as though the Americans might not be able to make it ashore in sufficient strength, but they did so. The Japanese defenders fought to the death – out of a garrison of 4750, only 17 men surrendered. The fighting lasted for three days, and over 1000 US Marines died.

The Americans next moved on to Roi, Namur and Kwajalien in the Marshall Islands, as part of Operation Flintlock. Roi and Namur were attacked by the 4th Marine Division and Kwajalien by the 7th Infantry Division on 1 February 1944. At Roi, the Marines' greatest difficulty came from the surf conditions and the coral reef near the islands. Some of the landing craft were damaged as they approached and drifted helplessly before they were rescued. Those Marines who made it to the shore as planned found that the defenders had been stunned by the preparatory bombardment, and offered little resistance. By the evening, Roi was secured and in American hands.

SHIPPING

The Japanese relied heavily upon merchant shipping to exploit her new territories. However, after 1942, shipping losses increased substantially, and became inexorably worse. Allied submarines, coupled with effective air attack, took a heavy toll. By the end of 1944, Japan had lost control of the seas, and most of her merchant shipping.

Japanese merchant shipping losses
7 Dec 1941–31 Dec 1942

- 7 Dec 1941–30 April 1942
- 1 May–31 August 1942
- 1 Sept–31 December 1942
- Japanese territory

Total losses: 89 ships

Japanese merchant shipping losses
1943

- 1 January–30 April
- 1 May–31 August
- 1 September–31 December
- Japanese territory

Total losses: 157 ships

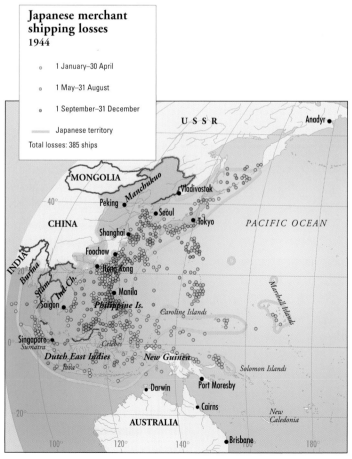

Japanese merchant shipping losses
1944

- 1 January–30 April
- 1 May–31 August
- 1 September–31 December
- Japanese territory

Total losses: 385 ships

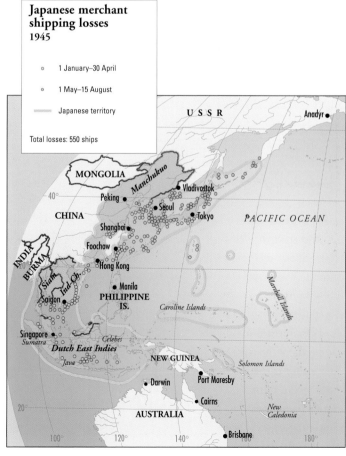

Japanese merchant shipping losses
1945

- 1 January–30 April
- 1 May–15 August
- Japanese territory

Total losses: 550 ships

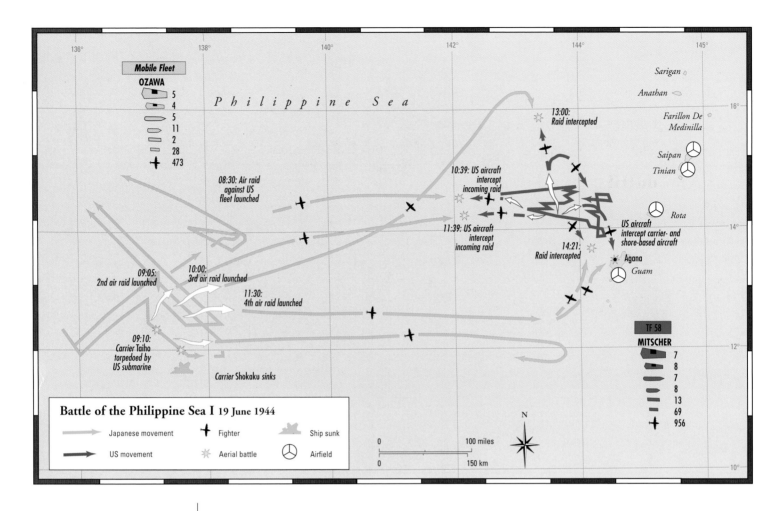

Battle of the Philippine Sea I 19 June 1944

Legend:
- → Japanese movement
- → US movement
- ✚ Fighter
- ✳ Aerial battle
- Ship sunk
- ⊘ Airfield

Map labels:
- Mobile Fleet OZAWA — 5, 4, 5, 11, 2, 28, 473
- *Philippine Sea*
- 08:30: Air raid against US fleet launched
- 09:05: 2nd air raid launched
- 10:00: 3rd air raid launched
- 11:30: 4th air raid launched
- 09:10: Carrier *Taiho* torpedoed by US submarine
- Carrier *Shokaku* sinks
- 10:39: US aircraft intercept incoming raid
- 11:39: US aircraft intercept incoming raid
- 13:00: Raid intercepted
- 14:21: Raid intercepted
- US aircraft intercept carrier- and shore-based aircraft
- Sarigan
- Anathan
- Farillon De Medinilla
- Saipan
- Tinian
- Rota
- Agana
- Guam
- TF 58 MITSCHER — 7, 8, 7, 8, 13, 69, 956

TURKEY SHOOT

The Battle of the Philippine Sea was a disaster for the Japanese. The destruction of their shore-based aircraft by Task Force 58 meant that their plan to overwhelm the Americans with massed air strength could not be realised.

When the Japanese carrier aircraft ran into the full might of the American defences, a mixture of anti-aircraft fire and defending fighters slaughtered the attackers in large numbers, dubbed 'The Great Marianas Turkey Shoot'. To make matters worse, the carrier *Taiho* was sunk by the submarine USS *Albacore*, and three hours later, the submarine USS *Cavella* sank the *Shokaku*.

Namur was more difficult, since the wooded terrain reduced the efficacy of the bombardment. The Japanese had strong defensive positions, which they defended with great tenacity. It was only when tanks came ashore that the Marines started to advance. They were checked for several hours after an ammunition bunker exploded, killing and wounding the men attacking it – momentum was lost for the rest of the day, and it was not until more tanks and men from Roi arrived that the remaining Japanese positions were carried.

Kwajalien had similarly awkward terrain, and it took until nightfall for the infantry to penetrate to the edge of the airfield in the centre of the island. Fighting over the next three days was particularly ferocious, with the Americans forced to make liberal use of tanks and flamethrowers to dislodge the defenders. Not one of the Japanese garrison survived the fighting.

JAPANESE MERCHANT SHIPPING

One of the major reasons for the Japanese embarking upon their ambitious programme of territorial expansion lay in their need for raw materials that were simply unavailable in the home islands. To ensure that Japanese industry had a steady supply of oil, rubber, tin and other key resources needed for wartime manufacture, it was essential that the Japanese control their sea lines of communication, since without this, it would be utterly impossible for them to maintain their war effort.

Upon the outbreak of war, the Japanese merchant fleet consisted of some 6 million tons of shipping, divided into three fleets. The first two were assigned specific duties in supporting the army and navy, while the third was tasked with meeting civilian requirements. This arrangement was far from efficient, and no effort was made to co-ordinate the work of the three fleets. The three-fleet arrangement ensured that the Japanese merchant marine operated substantially below

ESCAPE

The next day saw the two fleets sailing on near parallel courses for much of the day; when the Americans learned of this, they launched a strike in the late afternoon. The American aircraft managed to sink the *Hiyo* and two oilers, and damaged a number of other Japanese ships.

The surviving American aircraft returned to the carriers in darkness, almost out of fuel. Mitscher ordered his ships to turn on their lights despite the submarine risk, and this enabled over 100 aircraft to land safely, while another 80 ditched in close proximity to the fleet, allowing most of their crews to be rescued.

capacity. To compound the problems, Japanese shipyards failed to meet the requirements for routine maintenance of ships, so that by the end of the war, nearly half of the shipping that remained available to the Japanese was laid up in dock, awaiting repair.

When faced with the trial of combat, the Japanese merchant fleet sustained relatively light losses in the first months of the war, and the shipping industry provided enough new construction to offset the loss. However, the Guadalcanal campaign saw shipping losses rise dramatically. The Allies increased the rate at which they sank Japanese vessels substantially from 1943, with American submarines becoming particularly effective later in the year. American successes meant that the Japanese merchantmen were also forced to enter waters patrolled by US aircraft – if found, their chances of escaping from air attack were slim.

In November 1943, the Japanese finally made some attempts to offset the problems posed by enemy submarines, by introducing a convoy system, but this was too late. Monthly losses passed 200,000 tons, and this crippling figure was maintained for all but two of the next 14 months. The losses grew even more substantial as the Americans began offensive operations around the Dutch East Indies and the Philippines, until by the end of 1944, the Japanese merchant marine had all but collapsed. By August 1945, the Japanese had enough shipping available to guarantee just four months worth of supplies – assuming that no losses were sustained. By the end of the war, the Americans and their allies had effectively succeeded in blockading an industrial nation to the point of defeat.

Battle of the Philippine Sea

The invasion of Saipan in June 1944 compelled the Japanese to react in strength, since the loss of the Marianas would allow the Americans to base bombers in the islands, within striking range

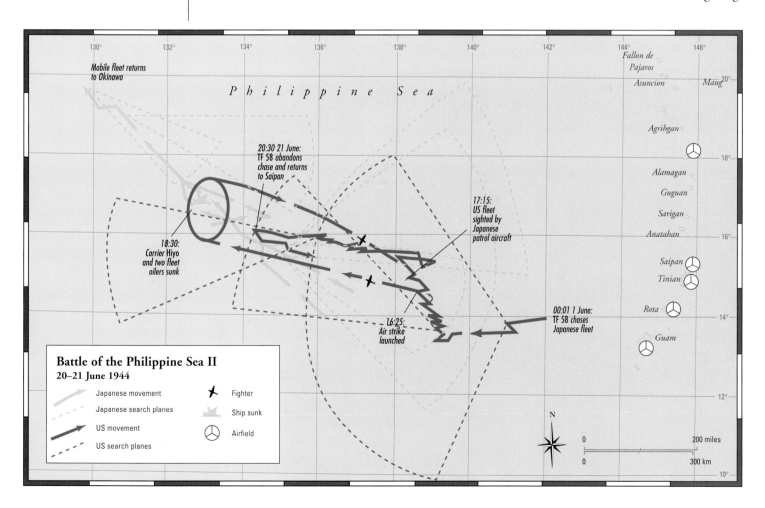

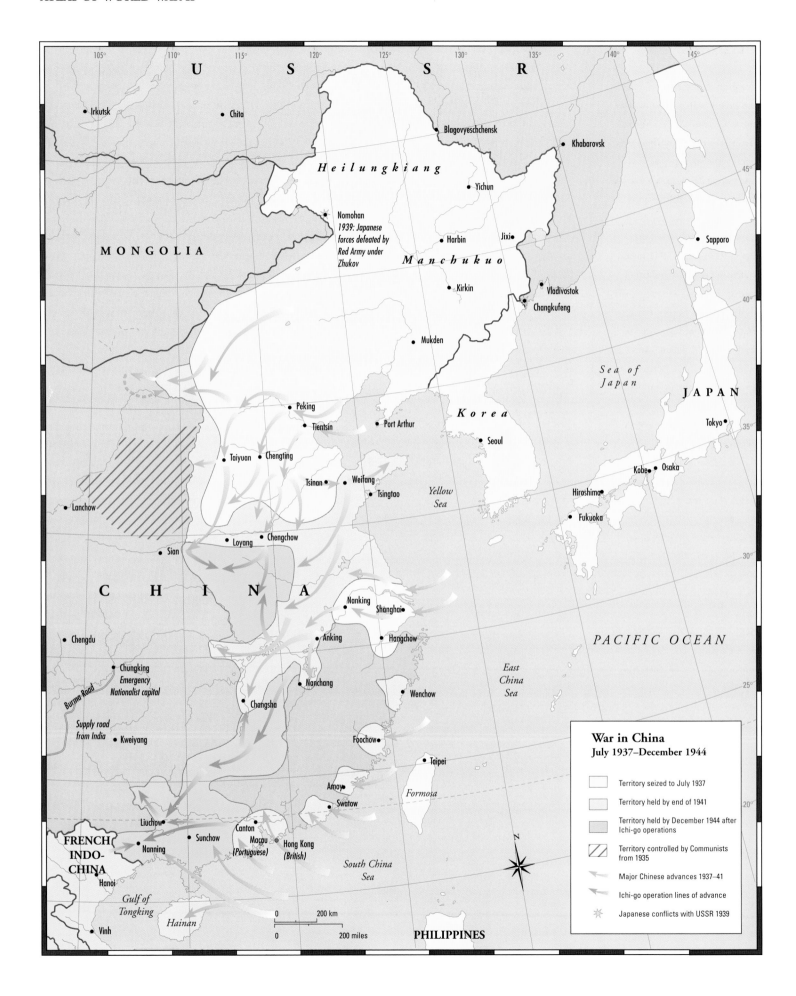

Nomohan
*1939: Japanese
forces defeated by
Red Army under
Zhukov*

Chungking
Emergency
Nationalist capital

Burma Road

Supply road
from India

**FRENCH
INDO-
CHINA**

War in China
July 1937–December 1944

Territory seized to July 1937

Territory held by end of 1941

Territory held by December 1944 after
Ichi-go operations

Territory controlled by Communists
from 1935

Major Chinese advances 1937–41

Ichi-go operation lines of advance

Japanese conflicts with USSR 1939

0   200 km

0   200 miles

PHILIPPINES

CHINA

The Sino–Japanese war from 1937 tends to be overlooked by many histories of World War II, and it is not hard to see why it can be viewed as a sideshow. The informal truces that existed between the KMT (who were concerned with the internal Communist threat) and the Japanese from late 1941 meant that there was little fighting in many areas.

Although the Americans and British were unimpressed with the behaviour of their allies in this regard, they tried to make the best of the situation, with the aim of supplying the Chinese through Burma as the war situation permitted.

The war also saw conflict between the Japanese and the USSR – in 1938 and 1939, the Soviets strengthened their border garrisons with China, and this prompted clashed at Changkufen and Nomohan Bridge; at the latter, the Red Army, under Zhukov, scored a victory, and the Japanese turned their attention to other, easier-to-conquer parts of China.

The last major Japanese offensive action in China occurred in 1944, with the Ichi-Go operation, designed to deny the Americans access to Chinese airbases. While the offensive succeeded in taking the airfields, thus preventing their use for the bombing of the Japanese Home Islands, the campaign was largely irrelevant, since the airbases had been rendered surplus to American requirements by the capture of the Marianas Islands.

Above: Douglas SBD Dauntless dive bombers during an attack on Param Island in the Truk atoll. Smoke rising from bombs dropped on buildings can clearly be seen on the island. The Japanese established a major base at Truk in the Caroline Islands that was attacked several times by American aircraft, but bypassed by the main American drive towards Japan, and the base only surrendered at the end of the war in September 1945.

of Japan itself. To prevent this possibility, the Japanese decided that they would commit their remaining carriers to the fight to remove the Americans.

The Japanese intended to base large numbers of aircraft in Guam, from where they would attack the American carriers, safe in the knowledge that they were just beyond the range of enemy carrier aircraft. The theory was fine, but in practice the operation went badly wrong. Task Force 58 had manoeuvred into position to attack the airfields on the Marianas, and almost completely wiped out the aircraft based there, so that there was little threat to the carriers when the invasion of the Marianas began.

The Japanese sent nine carriers (six light and three fleet) with five battleships, 12 cruisers, 27 destroyers and 24 submarines – an impressive force until it was compared with the 15 carriers of Task Force 58 (eight light and seven fleet), and the seven battleships, 21 cruisers, 62 destroyers and 25 submarines accompanying them.

On 19 June, the main Japanese force launched its first attack on the American carriers, only for the anti-aircraft fire and defending fighters to shoot down 42 of the 69 aircraft taking part. In return, the Japanese managed to slightly damage the battleship *South Dakota*. A second strike followed, but only minutes after it had been launched, one of the Japanese carriers was torpedoed by an American submarine, and sank. The 110 attacking Japanese aircraft were shot to pieces by the defenders, losing 79 of their number. A third strike by 47 aircraft managed to evade the defences of the forward Battle Line, but found few targets. The final strike of the day, by 82

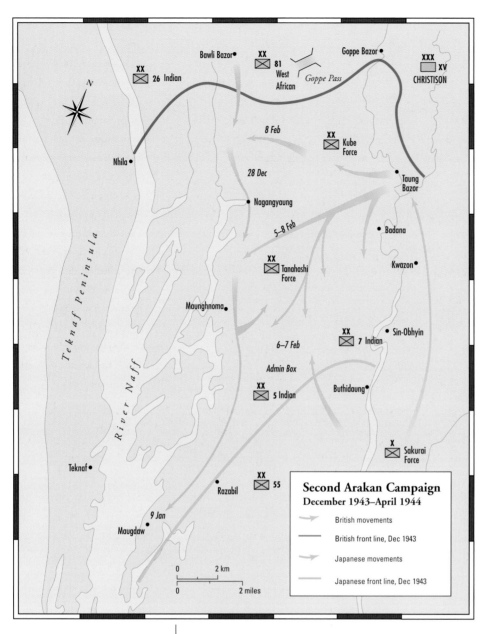

Second Arakan Campaign
December 1943–April 1944

→ British movements

━━ British front line, Dec 1943

→ Japanese movements

━━ Japanese front line, Dec 1943

0   2 km

0   2 miles

aircraft lost its way, and the 33 bombers that successfully found Task Force 58 suffered heavy losses.

At 12:22 hours, the carrier *Shokaku* was torpedoed by an American submarine, blowing up and sinking just under three hours later. The Japanese commander, Admiral Ozawa, believed reports that the land-based aircraft had inflicted serious damage on the Americans, and resolved to continue the assault the next day, a fatal error. The Americans discovered the position of the Japanese fleet late on the afternoon of 20 June, and despite the risks that would face aircrew landing on carriers at night, Admiral Spruance ordered Admiral Mitscher to launch a strike by over 200 aircraft. The attack overwhelmed the Japanese, and one carrier was sunk, and three others badly damaged, along with a number of other ships. The American aircraft returned to the fleet in darkness; in a move that endeared him to his pilots, Mitscher ordered every ship in his force to turn on its lights. As a result, 116 American aircraft landed safely and the remaining 80 survivors ditched nearby, with the majority of the crews being saved by the fleet.

The Battle of the Philippine Sea marked the effective end of Japanese carrier aviation, and with the failure to defeat the landings in the Marianas, ensured that American bombers would soon be seen over Japan in large numbers.

ARAKAN

The Second Arakan campaign used 5th Indian and 7th Indian Divisions to launch an offensive into the Arakan by XV Corps. They enjoyed some initial successes but were cut off by General Hanaya's 55th Japanese Division in an area known as the 'Admin Box' near Sinzweya. The divisions were sustained by air supply until the siege was lifted on 25 February. The Japanese then withdrew, with the two divisions in pursuit.

CHINA 1937–44

Japanese involvement in China began in 1931, with the seizure of Manchuria. This met with little resistance, since the Chinese were in the midst of a civil war. By 1937, the Japanese began to suspect that the Chinese nationalists and communists had reached an accommodation (the Sian agreement of December 1936) with the aim of challenging the Japanese. As a result, the Japanese launched a full-scale invasion of northern and central China, taking large amounts of territory with considerable brutality to Chinese civilians. The Japanese continued their expansion in 1938, and although they did not have the manpower to control all the areas they held, they made one further step in taking control of the major cities south of the Yangtze in 1941.

The Kuomintang (KMT) government of Chiang Kai-shek and Mao Zedong's communist forces spent much of the next three years fighting both the Japanese and each other. In many places, the KMT, while supposedly at war with the Japanese, was quite happy to trade with them. Chiang's reasoning for this lay in his belief that the Allies would defeat the Japanese, and that he would do better in preserving his forces for the fight against the Communists after the war was over. The Americans (Chiang's official allies) decided that they could not rely fully on KMT forces, and limited offensive action from China to the establishment of air bases from which to bomb Japan. This prompted the Ichi-Go offensives in southern China between May and December 1944. The Japanese succeeded in taking the territory in which the air bases were located, but by this time, the Americans had taken the Marianas, and did not require Chinese airfields for their bombers. Although the Japanese ended 1944 in what appeared to be an even stronger position than before in China, this was of little importance to the Pacific War.

THE SECOND ARAKAN CAMPAIGN

The Allied command structure in Burma was subjected to alteration in 1943 following the failure of the first Arakan campaign. General Sir Archibald Wavell was appointed Viceroy of India (and made a Lord), his role as supreme commander of British forces being taken by General Sir Claude Auchinleck. Auchinleck's command was now made part of Lord Louis Mountbatten's South East Asia Command, and within this new structure, substantial reorganisation took place to prepare for future operations. 11th Army Group was set up, containing 14th Army, commanded by Lieutenant-General William Slim. Slim nominated Lieutenant-General Philip Christison's XV Corps as the formation responsible for a second campaign in the Arakan, as part of renewed operations against the Japanese.

The Allied campaign plan for Burma for 1944 envisaged the reoccupation of the north of the country, and re-establishing communications with China along the Burma Road, making it possible for supplies to be sent to the Chinese. Lines of communication in India were improved, with a major logistics base being established at Kohima, ready for the forthcoming offensive, and it was as a preliminary to this goal that saw the opening of the second Arakan campaign in early January 1944. 5th and 7th Indian Divisions of XV Corps drove down into the Arakan, one on each side of the Mayu Range, with Maungdaw and Buthidaung as their objectives. The Japanese, meanwhile, had decided to launch a counter-offensive into India. To lessen the British defences, it was deemed prudent to try to draw as many British units into the Arakan, and operations to this end began in February 1944.

By 4 February, 5th Indian Division had been outflanked by the Japanese, and they then attacked XV Corps's administrative

INDIA

The Japanese decided to strike against India while the Second Arakan Campaign was in progess, targeting the two border towns of Kohima and Imphal. However, resistance was unexpectedly fierce, and a steady supply of reinforcements successfully held off the Japanese attacks for months.

Eventually the Japanese 15th Army called off the attacks after losing over 30,000 men killed. The attack had failed to ignite the anti-British rising in India that the Japanese had hoped for, and had left the defences of Burma weakened.

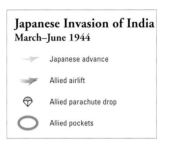

Japanese Invasion of India
March–June 1944

→ Japanese advance
⇒ Allied airlift
⊕ Allied parachute drop
◯ Allied pockets

area at Sinzweya. Air supply by the RAF and USAAF ensured that the British and Indian troops held their ground, until 26th Indian and 36th British Divisions were sent to raise the siege; by the middle of February, the Japanese were convinced that besieging Sinzweya was pointless, and withdrew. The Japanese now wished to concentrate upon an attack on Imphal. As this began, 5th Indian Division captured Razabil, and 7th Indian Division took Buthidaung. This was the last action for both divisions in the second Arakan campaign, since they were withdrawn to assist at Imphal on 22 March. They were replaced by 26th Indian and 36th British Divisions, which moved forward to capture Maungdaw and Point 551. With this ground taken, the second

Below: Japanese troops advancing through the Burmese jungle towards Kohima and Imphal, carrying their own artillery with them. The attack on India was an attempt to incite rebellion there by Indian nationalists, which would have occupied most British troops in the region and thus giving Japan valuable breathing space in which to concentrate on the Americans in the Pacific. Unfortunately for them Kohima and Imphal held out.

NEW OFFENSIVE

Once the Japanese assault at Imphal had been defeated, the Allies were in a position to drive the enemy out of Burma. After a reorganisation of his forces, General Sir William Slim, the commander of the Anglo–Indian Fourteenth Army, made plans for the invasion of Burma, aiming to defeat the Japanese once and for all.

The major part of Slim's scheme involved attacking towards Meiktila and Mandalay, with the aim of trapping the Japanese Fifteenth and Thirty-third Armies in a pincer movement and cutting off their supply route from Rangoon in the south. The Japanese plan was to retreat to the Irrawaddy river, and strongly counter-attack any attempt to cross, using their superior logistics to throw back the Allied troops.

Slim instructed the 19th Indian Division and XXXIII Corps to move directly towards the crossing near Mandalay as expected by the Japanese. At the same time he left a dummy IV Corps headquarters broadcasting as normal to fool the Japanese while sending the 7th and 17th Divisions south to cross the Irrawaddy below Mandalay and cut off the Japanese to the north.

The crossings in the north were fiercely opposed, the 19th Division clinging on to its bridgehead from 14 January, while XXXIII Corps did the same on 12 February. However the crossings of the 7th and 17th Divisions in the south were virtually unopposed.

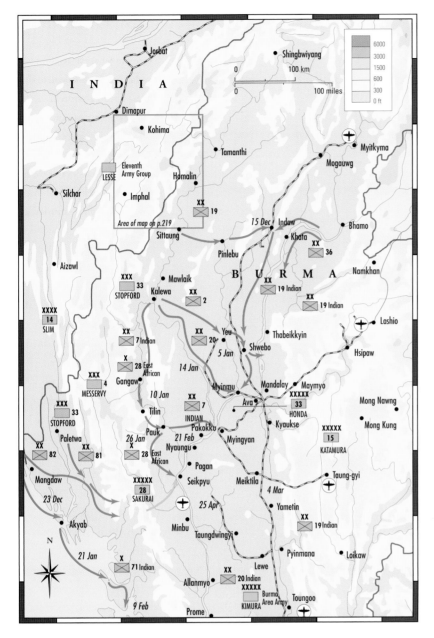

Allied Recapture of Burma
December 1944–February 1945

→ Allied advances with dates

→ Japanese counterattacks

campaign effectively ended, as plans were made to exploit the gains made.

ALLIED OFFENSIVE IN BURMA

Once the Japanese offensive against Kohima and Imphal had been seen off, the British sought to return to the offensive. Once Imphal had been relieved, General Slim reorganised his forces, sending IV Corps and 50th Parachute Brigade to the rear for a rest period, and despatching XXXIII Corps in pursuit of the Japanese 33rd Division. Meanwhile, the 36th British Division advanced to within 100 miles of Mandalay. Slim's plan for the reconquest of Burma, 'Operation Extended Capital', also called for the 19th Indian Division to cross the Irrawaddy and head for the same objective, while IV Corps was to advance through the Gangaw Valley, heading for the communications centre at Meiktila, located 80 miles south of Mandalay.

The supply lines from Imphal to the forward units were in danger of being stretched by the advance, so XV Corps was used to seize airfields for use by RAF cargo aircraft. An amphibious assault by the Corps' 3 Commando Brigade on the island of Akyab was followed by another by 71st Brigade of the 25th Division on Myebon. 71st Brigade seized the top of Ramree Island, and established a bridgehead; the rest of the division followed and expelled the Japanese, enabling the RAF to move in to make use of the airstrip to supply Allied forces in country.

SAIPAN, GUAM AND TINIAN

By early 1944, the Americans were looking to establish bases from which they could achieve several highly desirable objectives. They wishes to take territory which would allow them to bisect Japanese sea and air routes; to neutralize the Japanese base at Truk; to support further offensive action against the Philippines and to begin direct aerial bombardment of Japan. The Marianas islands matched these criteria almost perfectly, and the Joint Chiefs of Staff authorised the capture of the southern Marianas (Saipan, Guam and Tinian) under the auspices of 'Operation Forager'.

Four days prior to the assault, Admiral Marc Mitscher's Task Force 58 undertook a heavy bombardment of the Marianas, beginning with air attacks. The fighter sweep launched by TF 58's carriers destroyed over 150 Japanese aircraft, marking the opening salvo of the 'Marianas Turkey Shoot' inflicted upon the enemy's air forces. Shelling of Saipan and Tinian began on 13 June, and the bombardment reduced many of the Japanese shore positions to tangled wreckage, but, significantly, did not manage to destroy some of the better-built positions. This was noted by members of Underwater Demolition Teams carrying out beach reconnaissance missions, and the Americans were made grimly aware of the fact that the landing would be opposed.

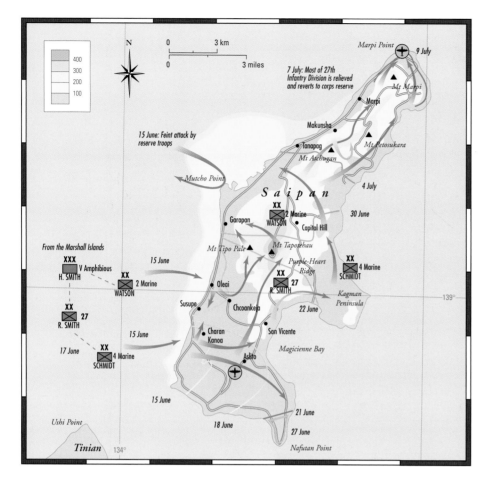

The Saipan Landings
15 June–9 July 1944

US movement

US front lines

Japanese positions, 27 June

Last Japanese counterattacks, 7 July

Airfield

The first marines went ashore early on the morning of 15 June 1944, and by nightfall they had managed to establish two beachheads in the face of heavy resistance. An enemy counterattack was driven off by naval gunfire. In the face of the resistance, the 27th Infantry Division was put ashore to help maintain momentum. Fierce fighting continued, but after a week, the Americans were in possession of most of the southern part of the island; after 10 days, they held almost all of the island's key features. This did not stop the Japanese from continuing to fight, since it took another three weeks to secure the island.

The second landing came on Guam. The invasion here had been planned to follow that on Saipan, but the Battle of the Philippine Sea diverted the navy's attention, while the need to commit the whole 27th Infantry Division to Saipan meant that there was no reserve, and the landings had to be delayed until 21 July. As at Saipan, Japanese resistance was fierce but unable to hold off the attack. A major Japanese counterattack on the night of 25/26 July was defeated, and by the end of the month the Americans controlled most of the island. Organised resistance ceased on 10 August, but the last Japanese soldiers on Guam did not finally surrender until 1960, totally unaware that the war had in fact ended some 15 years earlier.

Tinian was the final target, and Marines landed on 24 July 1944. The landings were particularly successful – by nightfall, over 15,000 men were ashore, and there had been only 15 fatalities. The island was secured within nine days, with 394 American deaths, in contrast to the loss of the entire Japanese garrison of 9000. With the Marianas secure, the Americans could move on to strike against Japan itself.

PACIFIC SITUATION IN LATE 1944 AND SPRING 1945

By late 1944, the Allies were advancing inexorably across the Pacific theatre. Although the Japanese empire still covered a large geographical area, it was steadily being reduced in size, while Allied submarines and aircraft interdicted the lines of communication linking the disparate parts of Japanese territory.

The most significant conquest between September 1944 and January 1945 was of the Philippines, liberated after particularly bitter fighting. General MacArthur was able to fulfil his promise to return, before diverting his attention to the last efforts needed to close in on the Japanese homeland.

In south Asia, British and Indian forces held off the attempted invasion of India by the Japanese and the sieges of Imphal and Kohima were raised. After a period of regrouping, the British drove through Burma so that by the late spring of 1945, the country was almost entirely cleared of Japanese troops, with only isolated pockets of resistance remaining. The next obvious target for the Anglo-Indian advance was the reconquest of Malaya and Singapore, a task planned for the late summer or early autumn. The Dutch East Indies posed something of a problem for recapture, given the size of the territories involved, but the principle of 'island hopping' – bypassing those areas which did not need to be taken to impose defeat on the Japanese applied: the Japanese forces in the islands were no threat to Australia or any other Allied territory, and could be left alone.

THE MARIANAS

The Marianas offered many strategic benefits to the Americans, not least the fact that they would serve as an excellent base for long-range bombing raids against Japan. The decision to take the islands, beginning with Saipan, was not a difficult one for the Joint Chiefs of Staff to make, and preparations began with a heavy air and sea bombardment of Saipan, Tinian, Guam and Rota on 11 June 1944. The invasion force was put ashore on 15 June, and despite resistance, the beachhead was firmly established by the end of the day; the island was conquered on 9 July.

Attention was diverted from the fighting on the islands by the arrival of the Japanese fleet. This compelled the US Navy to leave to engage the enemy in the Battle of the Philippine Sea. Once this had been successfully completed, the ships returned to provide further support, although their absence meant that the assault on Guam had to be postponed. Guam was attacked on 21 July, and although there was considerable Japanese resistance, the Americans were able to take the island within ten days.

Finally, Tinian was assaulted on 24 July, perhaps the most successful of all three operations. American casualty figures were low in comparison with the attacks on Saipan and Guam, with most of the island falling into American hands in four days; the island was declared secure on 1 August.

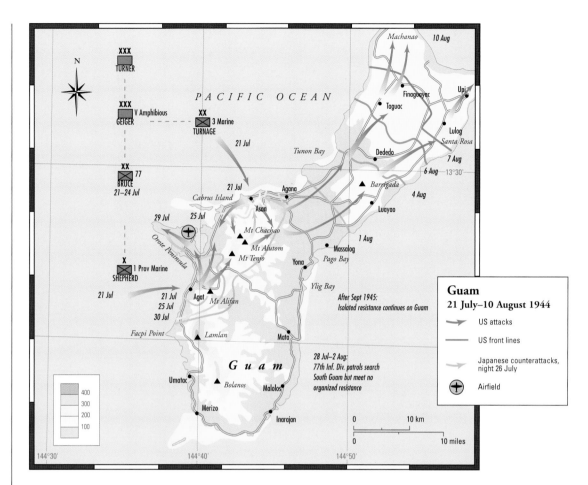

Guam
21 July–10 August 1944

US attacks

US front lines

Japanese counterattacks, night 26 July

Airfield

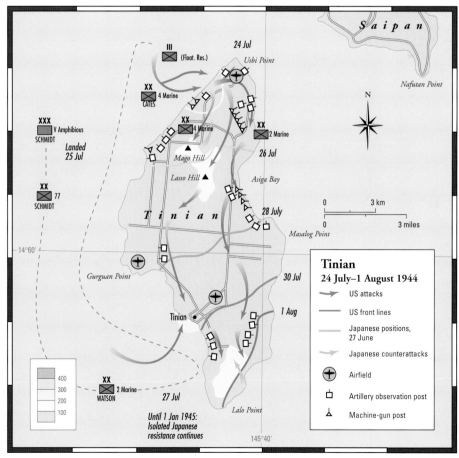

Tinian
24 July–1 August 1944

US attacks

US front lines

Japanese positions, 27 June

Japanese counterattacks

Airfield

Artillery observation post

Machine-gun post

TIGHTENING THE NOOSE

As 1945 began the situation looked desperate for Japan. Her attempt to spark a revolt in India had failed, and the Americans were dominant at sea and in the air. Worse news was to follow, with the loss of the Philippines and Burma in the first months of the year, and the initiative held by the Allies.

All that remained to do was to attack Japan itself. The next phase in operations saw the Americans come ever closer as they seized islands near to Japan to allow an invasion of the home islands to take place. Planning for landings in Japan was well under way, but concern as to the possible casualties sustained by both sides had begun to mount, since it was clear that the Japanese would fight for every inch of their homeland. This consideration was a major factor in the decision to use atomic bombs on Japanese targets with the hope of inducing surrender without invasion – but this was for the future. As the summer of 1945 arrived, it was quite clear that the defeat of Japan was near – the question was now one of how many lives would be lost before victory was delivered.

RETURN TO THE PHILIPPINES

The campaign to liberate the Philippines proved to be an extremely controversial one. US Navy leaders saw little point in attacking the islands to dislodge the Japanese, perceiving them as being

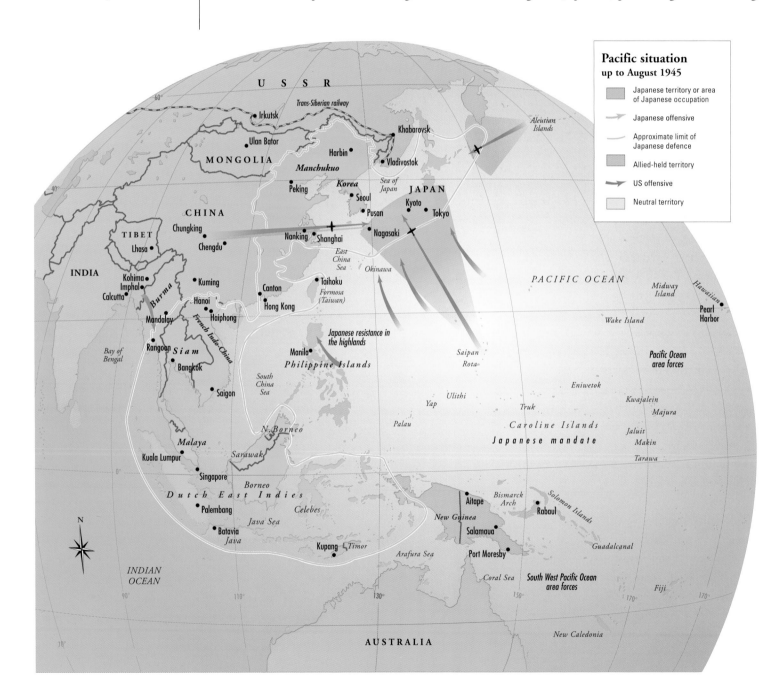

Above: British commandos landing at Akyab on 3 January 1945 as part of Operation Talon, which was intended to build a new airbase for the Royal Air Force on the Burmese coast which would allow their aircraft to resupply Slim's Fourteenth Army further in-country. The opening up of an air supply route was to prove vital for the resupply of 17th Division beseiged in Meiktila in March and later, as Slim's men moved rapidly towards Rangoon, to maintain the pace of the Allied advance.

little threat to the Allied advance. They instead proposed bypassing the islands, and attacking Formosa. General MacArthur, anxious to fulfil his promise to return, argued strongly in favour of the Philippine option.

The debate was settled once the Navy came to the conclusion that the Japanese would be compelled to throw the bulk of their remaining naval strength into defending the Philippines. A plan for invading the Philippines in December 1944 was drawn up. However, when a sortie by Task Force 38 against Mindanao encountered little opposition, the date was brought forward. A large invasion fleet was assembled, and as it approached the Philippines, Task Force 38 launched more air attacks on targets from Okinawa to the Philippine Sea, destroying the Japanese 6th Base Air Force in a huge air battle on 12 October.

On 17 October, a small force of US ships reached Leyte Gulf and shelled Sulman. The defenders managed to radio warning that an American invasion fleet was in the vicinity, prompting the Japanese to send a naval force to intervene. Admiral Takeo Kurita's First Striking Force, the surviving elements of Vice-Admiral Jisaburo Ozawa's Mobile Fleet and Admiral Teiji Nishimura's Second Striking Force, were sent to Leyte Gulf to attack the Americans. The force was still on its way when the invasion took place on 20 October 1944. The invasion was a considerable success – for the loss of only 49 men, the Americans seized control of a sizeable amount of Leyte, but resistance soon stiffened.

The Japanese First Striking Force lost some ships to American submarine attack on the way, reaching the San Bernardino Strait on 24 October, where it was engaged by the Americans. A series of air attacks by Task Force 38 badly damaged the battleship

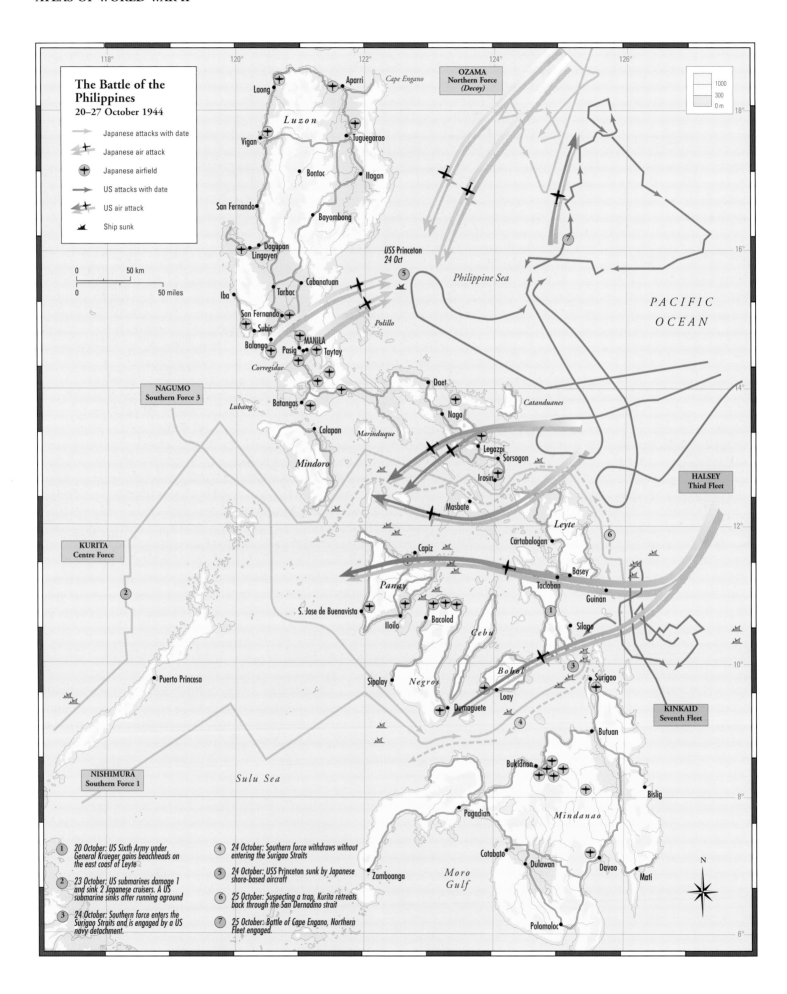

The Battle of the
Philippines
20–27 October 1944

→ Japanese attacks with date

✈ Japanese air attack

⊕ Japanese airfield

→ US attacks with date

✈ US air attack

🛥 Ship sunk

OZAMA
Northern Force
(Decoy)

Cape Engano

Luzon

Laong

Aparri

Vigan

Tuguegarao

Bontoc

Ilagan

San Fernando

Bayombong

Philippine Sea

USS Princeton
24 Oct

Dagupan
Lingayen

Cabanatuan

*PACIFIC
OCEAN*

Iba

Tarlac

San Fernando
Subic

Polillo

Balanga

MANILA

Pasig Taytay

Corregidor

Daet

NAGUMO
Southern Force 3

Lubang

Batangas

Marinduque

Naga

Catanduanes

Calapan

Legazpi
Sorsogon

HALSEY
Third Fleet

Mindoro

Irosin

KURITA
Centre Force

Masbate

Leyte

Cartabalogan

Capiz

Basey

2

Panay

Tacloban

Guinan

S. Jose de Buenavista

Bacolod

Silago

Iloilo

Cebu

1

Puerto Princesa

Negros

Bohol

3

Surigao

Sipalay

Loay

KINKAID
Seventh Fleet

Dumaguete

4

Butuan

NISHIMURA
Southern Force 1

Sulu Sea

Bukidnon

Bislig

Pagadian

Mindanao

Cotabato

Dulawan

Davao

Zamboanga

*Moro
Gulf*

Mati

N

Polomoloc

① 20 October: US Sixth Army under
General Krueger gains beachheads on
the east coast of Leyte

② 23 October: US submarines damage 1
and sink 2 Japanese cruisers. A US
submarine sinks after running aground

③ 24 October: Southern force enters the
Surigao Straits and is engaged by a US
navy detachment.

④ 24 October: Southern force withdraws without
entering the Surigao Straits

⑤ 24 October: USS Princeton sunk by Japanese
shore-based aircraft

⑥ 25 October: Suspecting a trap, Kurita retreats
back through the San Bernadino strait

⑦ 25 October: Battle of Cape Engano, Northern
Fleet engaged.

THE PHILIPPINES

In response to the approach of the American invasion fleet, the Japanese sent three naval forces under Admirals Kurita and Nishimura to Leyte Gulf, with Admiral Ozawa's formation acting as a decoy to tempt Admiral Halsey's Third Fleet away from supporting the invasion forces. This plan worked, and Halsey set off to engage Ozawa, leaving protection of Leyte Gulf to the lighter units of the American Seventh Fleet.

The Japanese suffered a number of losses in the Surigao straight, including the battleships *Fuso* and *Yamashiro*, Nishimura going down with the latter. The Americans had already suffered one loss when the carrier *Princeton* was sunk by a bombing raid.

Admiral Kurita's force surprised the small American carrier force left off Samar. Japanese cruisers overhauled the American carriers as they ran southwards, but air strikes by the Americans persuaded Kurita to retreat, missing his chance for a notable victory. The first *kamikaze* suicide attack against the fleet sank the carrier *St Lô*.

The final phase of the battle came off Cape Engano, when Halsey's Third Fleet set about Ozawa's forces, sinking four carriers by air attack. Once Halsey became aware of the danger to Seventh Fleet, he returned to Samar too late to engage Kurita. However, the US Navy was left controlling the seas around the Philippines.

Above: A Japanese *kamikaze* attack seen moments before the aircraft hit the ship. The American invasion of the Philippines saw the first use of *kamikaze* tactics by the Japanese, initially catching the Americans unawares and causing serious damage, the first attack sinking the escort carrier *St Lô* and damaging four others. However by the invasion of Okinawa the Americans had learnt successfully how to minimize the risk from *kamikaze* attacks.

Musashi, forcing the entire Japanese force to slow to the speed of the crippled battleship. A further American attack proved fatal, with the vessel sinking slowly during the course of the afternoon. The Mobile Fleet's ships approached Luzon the same afternoon, tempting the Americans to pursue it, leaving the landing beaches protected by escort carriers only. Nishimura then approached the Surigao Strait, but his ships were mauled by the US Seventh Fleet destroyer force, which sank a battleship and three destroyers, as well as damaging the battleship *Yamashiro*. The Seventh Fleet's battleships and cruisers then joined in, sending *Yamashiro* to the bottom. Kurita, meanwhile, had emerged from the San Bernardino Strait, and surprised the escort carrier force. Although the Japanese could have caused havoc amongst the carriers, the Americans gained the upper hand, and Kurita withdrew.

While the escort carriers were fending off the Japanese attacks, the rest of Task Force 38 headed north to finish off Ozawa's forces. Ozawa's ships were helpless against the American air attack, and three Japanese carriers and a destroyer were sunk before Admiral Halsey, aware of the dangers posed to the escort fleet, headed back towards Samar with the majority of his fleet. The remaining American ships sank another enemy carrier, two destroyers and a light cruiser before

RECONQUEST

After the successful capture of Leyte following the landings there on 20 October 1944 – with the staged return of MacArthur two days later, striding ashore from his landing craft – and the subsequent capture of Mindoro as a forward airbase, American attention turned to Luzon, the main island of the Philippines.

On 9 January 1945 the first American assault landed at Lingayen against minimal opposition, and pushed quickly inland. At the end of the month landings took place north and south of Manila, capturing the Bataan peninsula and isolating the Filipino capital. Resistance was fierce, however, and the city was devastated in the month's fighting before its eventual fall on 4 March.

Meanwhile Corregidor was taken by an air assault on 16 February followed up by an amphibious landing. The Japanese defenders resisted to (almost) the last man, only 19 prisoners being taken.

After the fall of Manila the Japanese defenders left on the island retreated into pockets of resistance in inaccessible areas, led by General Yamashita, who led his still-substantial forces against the Americans until complying with the general Japanese surrender on 15 August 1945.

The remainder of the Philippine Islands were retaken by the American Eighth Army, undertaking 50 separate amphibious landings during their campaign.

the Japanese survivors withdrew. The battle of Leyte Gulf was one of the largest naval battles in history, and proved a decisive victory for the Americans.

MACARTHUR'S VICTORY

Taking place alongside the Battle of Leyte Gulf, the invasion of the Philippines began with an assault on Leyte island on 20 October 1944. After an initial period of success for the Americans, fierce resistance by the Japanese 35th Army slowed the offensive down to the point where it delayed American plans for the invasion of Luzon, which was put back to 9 January 1945. The impasse on Leyte was finally settled when Lieutenant-General Walter Krueger landed a division from his 6th Army on the western side of Leyte, cutting the Japanese forces in two. Once the division was ashore, Japanese resistance became disjointed, and then collapsed, so that the island was brought under control by the middle of December 1944, although isolated pockets of Japanese resistance continued their fight for some time.

The assault on Luzon could now take place, and a week before the intended invasion, a naval force under Admiral Jesse B Oldendorf set out to bombard the island. The force came under heavy *kamikaze* attack, losing an escort carrier and three minesweepers. The Americans responded with a series of air strikes on the Japanese airfields launching the raids, and this compelled the withdrawal of enemy aircraft from the Philippines, allowing Oldendorf to carry out his bombardment.

The landing on 9 January met little opposition, and a beachhead four miles deep and seventeen miles wide was established on the first day. However, Japanese forces were waiting in strength for the Americans, and the advance slowed as the American I Corps tried to overcome the Japanese Shibu Group of some 150,000 men, in an attempt to allow US XIV Corps to advance on Manila.

By 17 January, the rate of progress was still slow, and General MacArthur ordered XIV Corps to push forward, sending his 25th and 32nd Divisions to aid I Corps in their efforts to clear the Shiba Group away from XIV Corp's line of advance. This reinforcement finally broke the Japanese resistance, and XIV Corps was able to move forwards. XIV Corps met with the Japanese Kembu Group on 23 January 1945, and fierce fighting between the two formations lasted for more than a week before the Americans managed to push the enemy back.

The US 11th Airborne Division was next to be committed to the attack, joining the advance on Manila. Fierce hand-to-hand fighting took place as the battle moved into the Philippine capital, made worse by the fact that the Japanese had refused to allow the civilian population to leave in advance of the start of the street fighting. By the end of February 1945, much of Luzon was under American control, but somewhere in the region of 172,000 Japanese troops remained on the island; this force needed to be defeated before the island could be considered ready for occupation and reconstruction. The offensive against these troops began on 6 March 1945, and continued until June, when Luzon finally came under complete control of the Americans.

BURMA RECONQUERED

General Slim's planned advance on Meiktila and Mandalay continued in February 1945, with the XV Corps preventing the Japanese 28th Army from moving to assist with the defence of Mandalay against XXXIII Corps. However this did not prevent heavy fighting when 20th Division and Japanese Fifteenth Army met at Myinmu on 12 February 1945, stopping the advance around 48km (30 miles) short of its target. IV Corps enjoyed more success thanks to its surprise crossing of the Irrawaddy, and advanced almost unopposed on Meiktila. On 1 March, 17th Division assaulted the town and took it in 48 hours. The Japanese launched a series of counterattacks, but failed to retake the town, and suffered heavy losses in the process. To the north, XXXIII Corps assaulted Mandalay, which was evacuated by its defenders on 20 March.

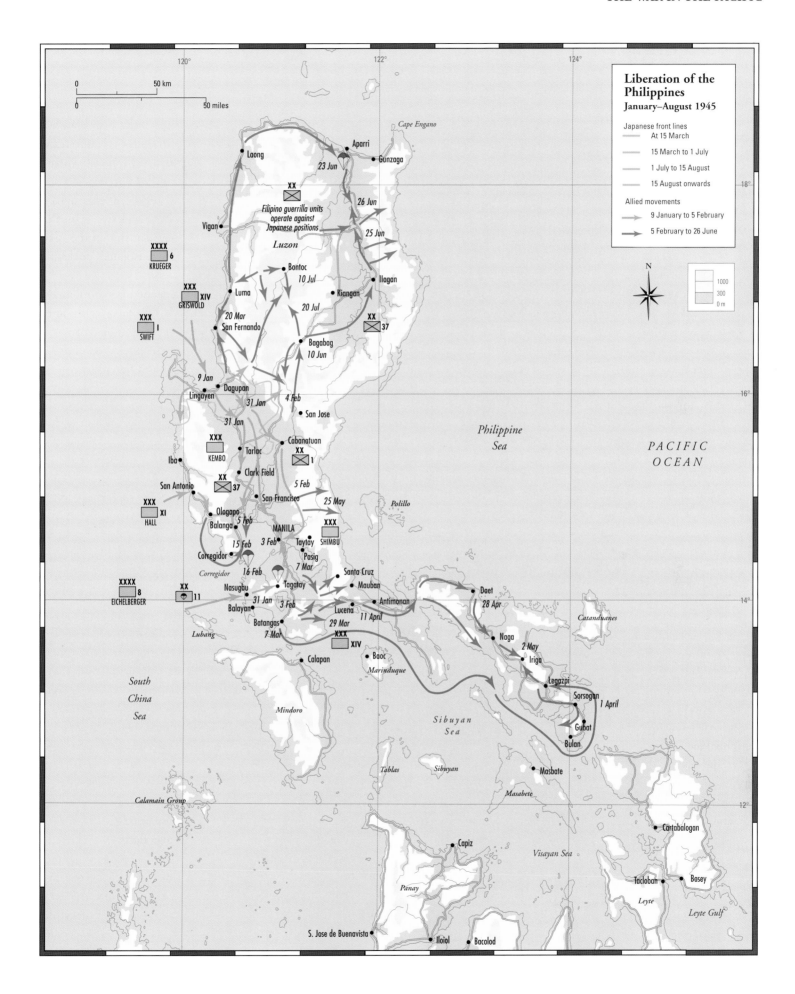

Liberation of the
Philippines
January–August 1945

Japanese front lines
    At 15 March
    15 March to 1 July
    1 July to 15 August
    15 August onwards
Allied movements
    9 January to 5 February
    5 February to 26 June

N

1000
300
0 m

Cape Engano

Aparri
Laong
Gunzaga
23 Jun

XX
Filipino guerrilla units
operate against
Japanese positions

Vigan
26 Jun

Luzon
25 Jun

XXXX 6
KRUEGER
Bontoc
10 Jul
Ilagan

XXX XIV
GRISWOLD
Luma
Kiangan
20 Jul

XXX 1
SWIFT
20 Mar
San Fernando
XX 37

9 Jan
Dagupan
Bagabag
10 Jun

Lingayen
31 Jan
4 Feb

31 Jan
San Jose

Philippine
Sea

PACIFIC
OCEAN

XXX
KEMBO
Cabanatuan
Tarlac
XX 1

Iba
Clark Field
5 Feb

San Antonio
XX 37
San Francisco
25 May
Polillo

XXX XI
HALL
Ologapo
Balanga
5 Feb

MANILA
3 Feb
Taytay
Pasig
7 Mar
XXX
SHIMBU
Santa Cruz

15 Feb
Corregidor
Mauban
Daet
28 Apr

Corregidor
16 Feb
Tagatay
7 Mar

XXXX 8
EICHELBERGER
XX 11
Nasugbu
31 Jan 3 Feb
Balayan
Antimonan
Naga
2 May
Iriga

Batangas
Lucena
11 April
Legazpi
Sorsogan

7 Mar
29 Mar
XXX XIV
Baoc
1 April

South
China
Sea

Lubang
Calapan
Marinduque
Gubat
Bulan

Mindoro
Sibuyan
Sea
Masbate

Tablas
Sibuyan
Masabete

Calamain Group

Cartabalogan

Capiz
Visayan Sea

Panay
Tacloban
Basey

S. Jose de Buenavista
Iloiol
Bacolod
Leyte
Leyte Gulf

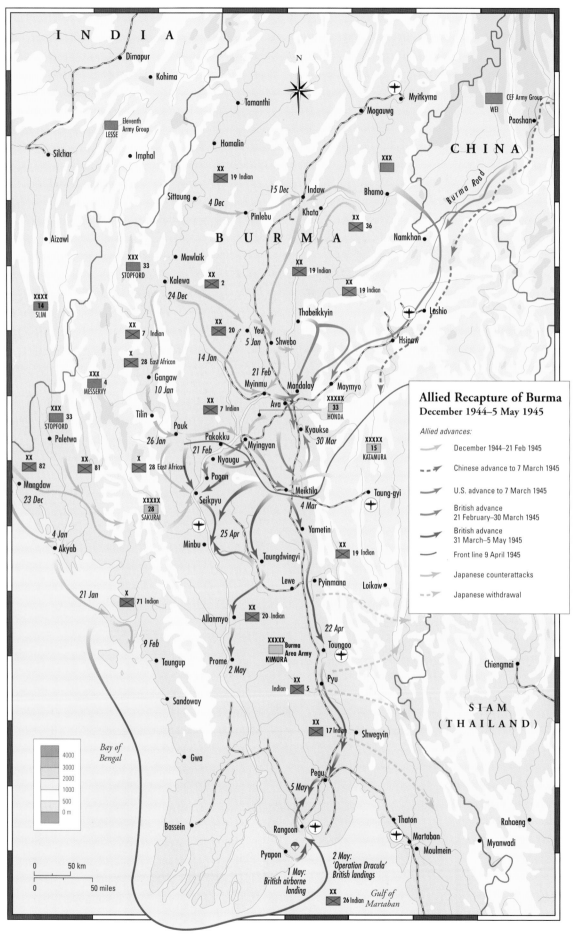

Allied Recapture of Burma
December 1944–5 May 1945

Allied advances:

→	December 1944–21 Feb 1945
⇢	Chinese advance to 7 March 1945
⟶	U.S. advance to 7 March 1945
⟹	British advance 21 February–30 March 1945
⟹	British advance 31 March–5 May 1945
—	Front line 9 April 1945
⟶	Japanese counterattacks
⇢	Japanese withdrawal

BURMA VICTORY

To ensure good logistics for the Allied offensive, XV Corps pushed along the Burmese coast to secure airfields for use by RAF cargo aircraft. A series of amphibious operations met with relatively little opposition, as the main Japanese forces withdrew into Burma, and suitable airbases were built.

Meiktila, defended only by rear area troops, was captured by the surprise attack of the 17th Division on 3 March 1945. The Japanese reacted swiftly, launching a series of attacks to recapture the vital communications hub that cut the defenders off from the rest of Fourteenth Army. Meanwhile Mandalay was taken by 19th Division after bitter hand-to-hand fighting.

By the end of March, the Japanese realised that their line of retreat was being cut off, and they began a race back to Rangoon and safety. The Allies were keen to reach Rangoon before the monsoon began at the beginning of May, as their tanks would become immobilised by the rain.

Rangoon was shelled by Royal Navy ships on 30 April. An airborne landing on 1 May secured a bridgehead for an amphibious assault (Operation Dracula) made on 2 May by XV Corps, and the landing force entered the Burmese capital (secretly evacuated by the Japanese on 1 May) the next day. Although isolated pockets of resistance remained, the war in Burma had come to an end.

Above: Marines from 1st Division watch phosphorous shells explode on the enemy ridgeline while awaiting the order to advance on Okinawa in May 1945. As at Iwo Jima, the fight for the island was a bitter struggle, and although American casualties were much lower than the Japanese, who fought almost to the last man, they were still very high. It was feared that any assault on the Japanese Home Islands would be extremely costly in terms of Allied lives, although nonetheless highly likely to succeed given the Allied superiority in equipment and fire support.

General Stillwell's Northern Combat Area Command of American and Chinese troops occupied Hsenwi and Lashio, removing the last significant opposition from the north of Burma. 36th Division then headed to Mandalay to join Slim's forces, which now prepared to move onto Rangoon.

On 30 April, a naval bombardment of Rangoon preceded an assault on the Burmese capital. The next day, an airborne battalion landed at Elephant Point, and secured a bridgehead for 26th Indian Division (from XV Corps) to land; two days later, the division was able to march into Rangoon without opposition, as the Japanese had secretly left the city on 1 May. XXXIII Corps captured Prome, which meant that all the major towns in Burma were now under Allied control. The Japanese Burma Area Army had, to all intents and purposes, ceased to exist, leaving the British and Indians with nothing more than mopping-up operations to occupy them. Burma had finally been reconquered.

IWO JIMA AND OKINAWA

By the end of 1944, American commanders had become convinced of the need to take the Japanese island of Iwo Jima. The rationale for this course of action lay in three factors. The first was that the island offered a base from which P-51 Mustang escort fighters could reach Japan, providing much-needed protection to B-29s raiding the country. Also, one of the island's two airstrips could accommodate B-29s without great difficulty, making it a perfect location for an emergency landing site for aircraft operating out of the Marianas as well as a potential location from which air raids could be launched. Another factor was that the island was regarded as part of the Japanese homeland, and capturing it could have a psychological effect upon the Japanese government and its population.

The Japanese were painfully aware of the strategic significance of Iwo Jima, and made strenuous efforts to establish effective defensive positions, sending experienced reinforcements to the islands in the latter part of 1944. By the end of the year, the defenders had dug miles of defensive tunnels that protected them from a substantial proportion of the bombardment delivered by air and sea from late November. On 19 February 1945, the invasion force was put ashore, facing little resistance. However, as the first Marines made their away a little further inshore, they were hit by heavy machine-gun fire. The Marines responded by charging the lead defensive positions, and carried them. By nightfall, some 30,000 Marines were ashore, and had isolated the highest point on the island, Mount Suribachi.

Over the next four days, the Marines fought bitterly with the Japanese until they took Mount Suribachi (which led to the famed photograph of the Stars and Stripes being raised by a Marine patrol), but this did not mark the end of the fighting. A vicious attritional battle continued for three weeks, as the Americans fought their way from bunker to bunker, clearing out the enemy. As early as the tenth day of the assault, many units were down to half strength, such was the ferocity of the fighting. On the night of 25/26 March, the remaining Japanese defenders launched a suicidal charge against the Marines and were wiped out. Some 23,000 Japanese died, and only 216 survived; the Marines lost 6,281 killed and over 18,000 wounded in the bloodiest operation in the Marine Corps' history.

Iwo Jima was followed by Okinawa, which was assaulted on 1 April 1945 by US Tenth Army. The operation ran into little opposition for the first four days, but on 5 April, skirmishes between the Americans and Japanese demonstrated that the latter had heavily fortified the southern half of the island. For the remainder of the month, the Americans attacked enemy positions, taking small areas at a time. Casualties mounted, but by the end of May it appeared that the Americans had finally gained the upper hand. Bad weather delayed their final assault, and the Japanese took the opportunity to concentrate for their last stand. After more bitter fighting, the Japanese garrison was split into three pockets and overwhelmed by the end of June.

With the end of the fighting on Okinawa, it was clear that Japan was doomed – but the stark reality of the casualties sustained by the Americans on Iwo Jima and Okinawa begged the question of how costly the final assault on Japan might be.

The end of the war was clearly approaching, with Germany defeated in Europe and resources of men and materiel from that theatre soon becoming available. However with victory so close the Allies were reluctant to suffer further unnecessary casualties. The success of the Manhattan Project in detonating an atomic device at Almagordo in July appeared to offer President Truman a new weapon with awesome destructive power that could subdue Japan at minimal cost

IWO JIMA

Iwo Jima was an island of less than 10 square miles area, but had two vital airfields that would be of considerable assistance to the American bombing effort against Japan. The Japanese had fortified the island, so when the Marines stormed ashore on 19 February 1945, they met unyielding resistance, despite the fact that there had been 75 days of preparatory bombardment from air and sea. Fighting raged for 36 days before the Marines were in control of the island – the famous picture of the American flag being raised on Mount Suribachi was taken only four days after the landings, and well before the fighting had ended.

Landings on Iwo Jima
19 February–26 March 1945

→ US advances

— US front lines

— Japanese final defensive line

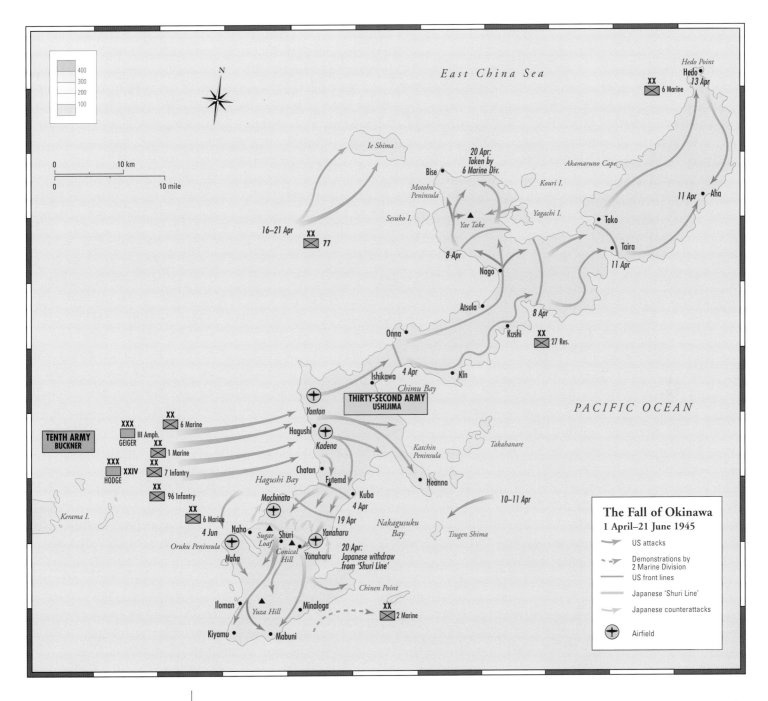

The Fall of Okinawa
1 April–21 June 1945

- US attacks
- Demonstrations by 2 Marine Division
- US front lines
- Japanese 'Shuri Line'
- Japanese counterattacks
- Airfield

OKINAWA

Okinawa was a similarly bloody experience for the Americans. The invading troops found the well-built Japanese defensive positions difficult to overcome, once they had revealed their position. The Marines fought their way through, yard by yard, against suicidal resistance. By the end of June, Okinawa was in American hands.

to the Allies. However the delay in creating a practical air-dropped weapon meant that the planning for an invasion of Japan had to continue.

SOVIET INVASION OF MANCHURIA

Although there had been clashes between Soviet and Japanese forces prior to World War II – with the Japanese coming off the worst in the encounter – neither side had wished or needed to initiate combat operations against the other. In the context of their strategic priorities between 1941 and early 1945, this made considerable sense, and both sides maintained diplomatic links. In early 1945, the Japanese government attempted to persuade the Russians to act as a neutral broker between them and the Allies to arrange peace. The Japanese were surprised when the Allies failed to respond, little realising that the Russians had not passed on the request.

The reason for this was that Stalin, once the Germans had surrendered, was eager to take control of Manchuria, Sakhalin and the Kurile Islands, something that would be facilitated by

FADED EMPIRE

The Japanese empire was still substantial shortly before the dropping of the atomic bombs. However the American campaign in the Pacific had successfully created a blockade around Japan, preventing her from resupplying or reinforcing her colonies or conquests. In effect they were 'withering on the vine', starved of food, ammunition and hope.

taking part in the war against Japan. It was not in his interests for the war to end before the Soviet Union could participate, hence his decision to make only oblique references to the development of a 'peace party' in Japan. The Allies knew better, however – signals intelligence suggested that the Japanese were eager to negotiate, and the reason for Stalin's unwillingness to tell the Americans about this lay in his aim of keeping the war going until his forces could play a role. President Truman, convinced that the post-war Soviet–American relationship anticipated by President Roosevelt was very unlikely to materialise, wished to avoid giving Stalin the chance to demand control of Japanese territory: this was a factor in his decision to use the atom bomb.

On 8 August 1945, two days after the atom bomb attack on Hiroshima, the USSR declared war on Japan, and sent 76 divisions into Manchuria. The campaign went exactly to plan. The Khorokhon Pass was taken in two days, and an advance was made into the Gobi Desert. The Russians took Changchung and Mukden on 21 August, and then Matuankiang. The Red Army then advanced towards Korea, while offshore, the Soviet navy seized the Kurile Islands in early September. The Russian victory was complete.

FIRE AND ATOMIC RAIDS

From the time of the attack on Pearl Harbor, US military planning had been predicated on the notion that bombing of the Japanese homeland would be an essential

The Japanese Empire
August 1945

Japanese territory or area of Japanese occupation

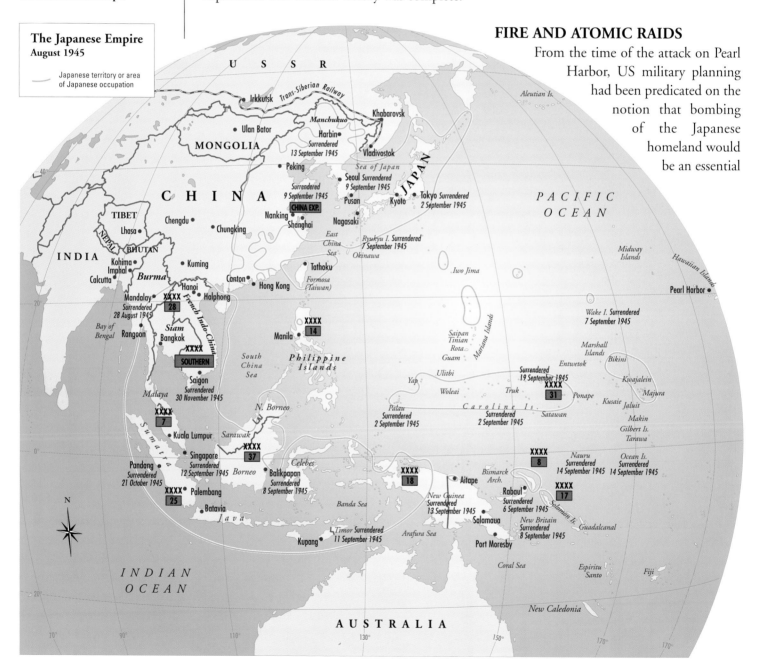

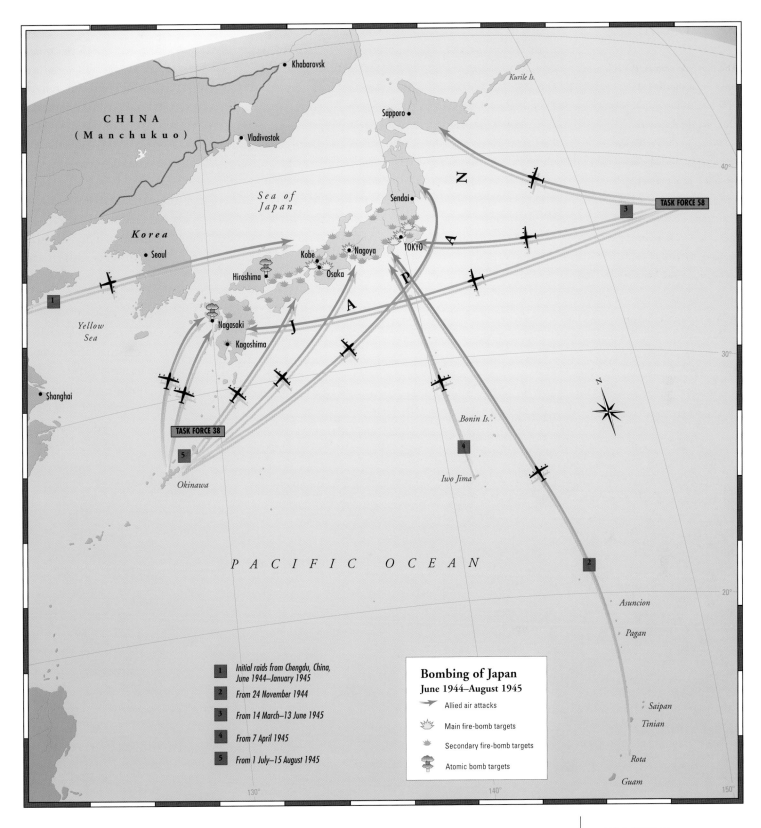

CHINA
(Manchukuo)

Khabarovsk

Kurile Is.

Sapporo

Vladivostok

Sea of
Japan

Sendai

TASK FORCE 58

Korea

Seoul

TOKYO

Kobe · Nagoya

Hiroshima

Osaka

1

Yellow
Sea

Nagasaki

Kagoshima

N

Shanghai

Bonin Is.

4

TASK FORCE 38

5

Iwo Jima

Okinawa

PACIFIC   OCEAN

2

Asuncion

Pagan

1	Initial raids from Chengdu, China, June 1944–January 1945
2	From 24 November 1944
3	From 14 March–13 June 1945
4	From 7 April 1945
5	From 1 July–15 August 1945

Bombing of Japan
June 1944–August 1945

→ Allied air attacks

Main fire-bomb targets

Secondary fire-bomb targets

Atomic bomb targets

Saipan

Tinian

Rota

Guam

component in the ultimate defeat of the enemy. The new Boeing B-29 Superfortress met the requirement for a long-range bomber with a heavy payload, and once initial teething problems had been overcome, the aircraft began entering service in large numbers. The first operations against Japan were carried out from bases in China, with the first attack taking place on 15 June 1944. Once the Marianas were captured, five airbases were built for operating B-29s, two each on Saipan and Tinian, and one on Guam. Each base could accommodate 180 B-29s.

AIR WAR

As the island hopping campaign moved closer to Japan, so the strategic bombing offensive against the Home Islands increased dramatically.

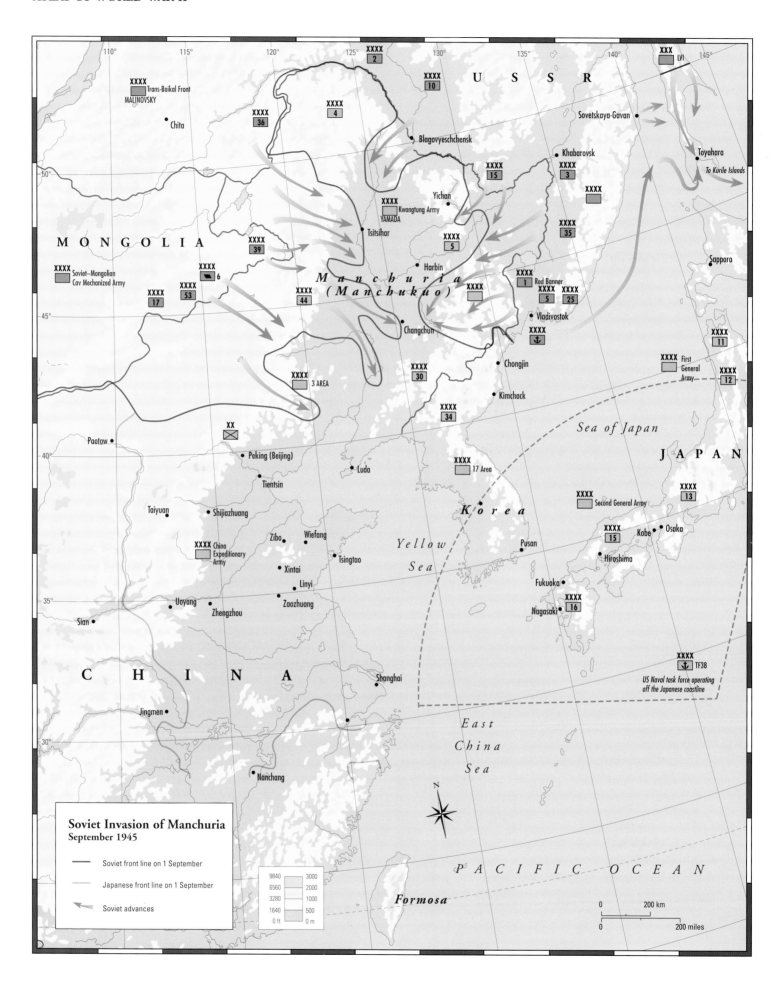

XXXX
2

XXXX
10

U S S R

XXXX
Trans-Baikal Front
MALINOVSKY

XXXX
36

XXXX
4

• Chita

• Blagovyeschchensk

Sovetskaya-Gavan •

XXXX
15

XXXX
3

• Khabarovsk

Toyahara

XXXX

To Kurile Islands

50°

M O N G O L I A

XXXX
39

XXXX
Kwangtung Army
YAMADA

• Yichan

• Tsitsihar

XXXX
5

XXXX
35

XXXX

XXXX
Soviet–Mongolian
Cav Mechanized Army

XXXX
6

• Harbin

M a n c h u r i a
(M a n c h u k u o)

XXXX
1 Red Banner

• Sapporo

XXXX
17

XXXX
53

XXXX
44

XXXX

XXXX
5

XXXX
25

45°

• Changchun

• Vladivostok

XXXX

XXXX
11

XX

XXXX
3 AREA

XXXX
30

• Chongjin

XXXX
First
General
Army

XXXX
12

• Paotow

XXXX
34

• Kimchack

S e a   o f   J a p a n

J A P A N

40°

• Peking (Beijing)

• Luda

XXXX
17 Area

• Taiyuan

• Shijiazhuang

XXXX
Second General Army

XXXX
13

• Tientsin

Zibo •

Wiefang •

K o r e a

• Pusan

• Kobe • Osaka

XXXX
15

• Zibo

• Hiroshima

XXXX
China
Expeditionary
Army

• Tsingtao

Y e l l o w
S e a

• Fukuoka

• Xintai

35°

• Uoyang

• Linyi

XXXX
16

• Nagasaki

• Sian

• Zhengzhou

Zaozhuang •

C H I N A

• Shanghai

XXXX
TF38

US Naval task force operating
off the Japanese coastline

• Jingmen

E a s t
C h i n a
S e a

30°

• Nanchang

N

Soviet Invasion of Manchuria
September 1945

———— Soviet front line on 1 September

———— Japanese front line on 1 September

⟶ Soviet advances

P A C I F I C   O C E A N

F o r m o s a

9840   3000
6560   2000
3280   1000
1640   500
0 ft   0 m

0   200 km
0   200 miles

110°   115°   120°   125°   130°   135°   140°   145°

MANCHURIA

The Soviet attack into Manchuria marked the opening of an extremely short and successful war against Japan. After prevaricating for months over approaching the Allies on Japan's behalf, Stalin declared war on the Japanese and sent his troops into Manchuria on 9 August. The Japanese were not to know that Stalin had promised the Western Allies that he would join in the Pacific War once the Germans were defeated. He transferred over 1,000,000 troops of the Red Army to the Far East in the immediate aftermath of the war in Europe, where they came up against Japanese forces that were only slightly smaller in number, but notably inferior in quality and equipment.

The Japanese were not expecting an invasion, and had not positioned their forces accordingly. As a result, the Japanese were caught off-balance, and were always struggling to respond. The Soviet assault comprised Marshal Malinovsky's Trans-Baikal Front, which was to cross the great Hingan Mountains and the Gobi Desert, while Marshal Meretskov's 1st Far Eastern Front attacked from the direction of Vladivostok. The two fronts punched through the Japanese lines, and linked up on 21 August – seven days after the Japanese had announced their capitulation. The Soviet success was completed by the seizure of the strategic Kurile Islands by their navy.

Above: Japanese fighter pilots waiting to be briefed for their next mission. By the end of the war Japan faced a shortage of skilled pilots, and the majority of her aircraft were increasingly obsolete, suitable only for conducting *kamikaze* attacks. The loss of Iwo Jima meant that American fighters could now escort B-29 bombers all the way to their targets over Japan, effectively neutralizing what remained of the Japanese air force's fighters.

The attacks by B-29s against Japan began in earnest on 24 November 1944, with an attack on an industrial target outside Tokyo. The results were disappointing, with only 24 out of 100 B-29s being able to find the factory they were aiming for. The target was attacked again, with similar results, and after the tenth mission had also failed, it was clear that a reassessment of operations was required.

On 20 January 1945, Major General Curtis E LeMay took over XXI Bomber Command, and immediately made a major change to the tactics that were to be employed by his force. Rather than continue with high-level daylight bombing, LeMay instructed that his forces would henceforth attack at night, from below 10,000 feet, and use incendiary bombs. Furthermore, since the Japanese fighter defences were far less at night, much of the B-29s' defensive armament was to be removed, saving weight.

The first of these attacks was made on 9/10 March by 300 aircraft against Tokyo and Yawata. Over 16 square miles of Tokyo was burned to the ground. This attack was followed by others on Nagoya, Osaka and Kobe; then, on 25/26 May, a major attack on Tokyo destroyed yet more of the city. Eighty-five per cent of Yokohama was razed to the ground in another fire-raid, and by July, over half a million Japanese civilians had been killed and 13 million made homeless as a result of the raids. Furthermore, from 14 March 1945, these devastating raids were accompanied by attacks launched by US Navy carrier aircraft, increasing the pressure on the beleaguered Japanese war effort. Airfields on the newly-captured islands of Iwo Jima and Okinawa were brought into action, reducing the distance that had to be flown by the bombers and especially by their escort fighters.

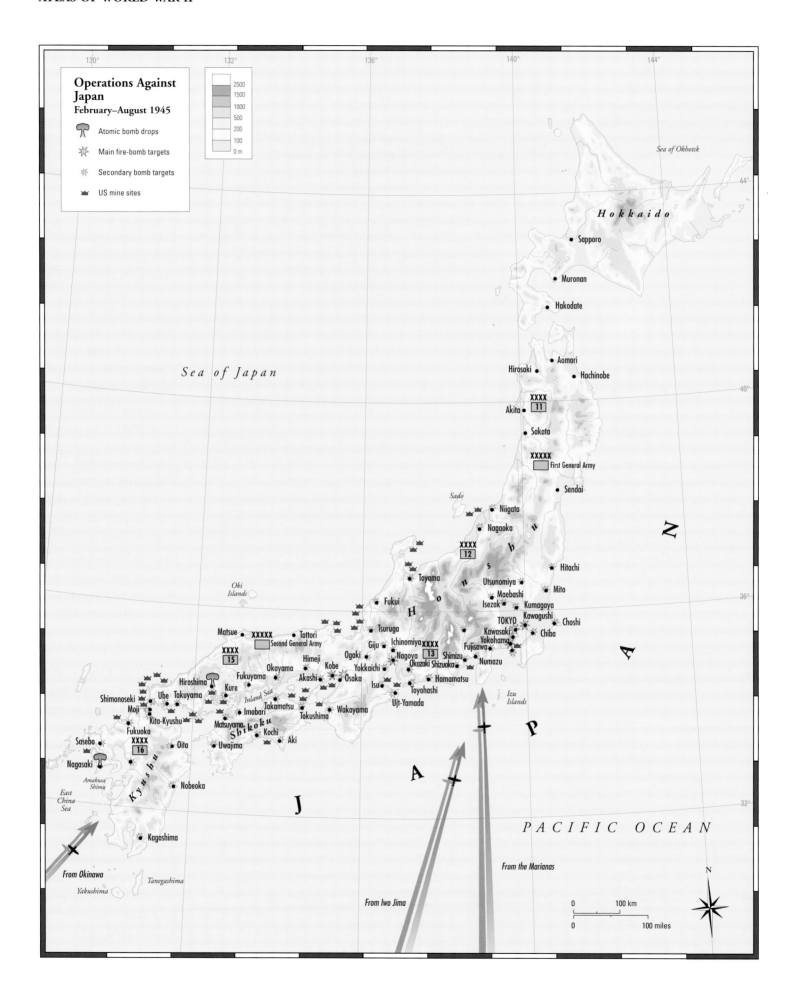

Operations Against Japan
February–August 1945

🍄 Atomic bomb drops

✳ Main fire-bomb targets

✳ Secondary bomb targets

⛀ US mine sites

2500
1500
1000
500
200
100
0 m

Sea of Okhotsk

Hokkaido

Sapporo

Muronan

Hakodate

Aomori

Hirosaki Hachinobe

XXXX 11
Akita

Sakata

XXXXX First General Army

Sendai

Sado

Niigata

Nagaoka

XXXX 12

Hitachi

Toyama

Utsunomiya Mito

Maebashi

Oki Islands

Isezak Kumagaya

Fukui H o n s h u

Tottori Tsuruga TOKYO Kawagushi

Matsue Second General Army Giju Ichinomiya XXXX 13 Kawasaki Choshi

XXXX 15 Ogaki Nagoya Shimizu Yokohama Chiba

Himeji Okozaki Shizuoka Fujisawa

Okayama Kobe Yokkaichi Numazu

Fukuyama Akashi Osaka Isu Hamamatsu

Hiroshima Kure Takamatsu Toyohashi

Ube Takuyama Imabari Ujt-Yamada

Shimonoseki *Inland Sea* Wakayama *Izu Islands*

Moji Matsuyama Tokushima

Kita-Kyushu Kochi *S h i k o k u*

Fukuoka Aki

XXXX 16 Oita

Sasebo Uwajima

Nagasaki

K y u s h u

Amakusa Shima

East China Sea

Nobeoka

Kagoshima

J A P A

N

P

Sea of Japan

From Okinawa

Yakushima *Tanegashima*

From Iwo Jima

From the Marianas

PACIFIC OCEAN

0   100 km

0   100 miles

N

Although historians have subsequently argued over whether a combination of the fire raids and the almost complete destruction of Japanese shipping would have been enough to prompt a Japanese surrender, President Truman took the view that a more dramatic demonstration of American power was required. As a result, he ordered the use of atomic bombs against Hiroshima and Nagasaki.

On 6 August 1945, Colonel Paul Tibbets, commander of the 509th Composite Group (the special unit formed for the atomic raids), took off from Tinian in a B-29 bearing the name *Enola Gay*. The aircraft reached Hiroshima to find a bright, clear early morning. At 08:15 hours, *Enola Gay* released its weapon. As *Enola Gay* turned away to avoid the blast, the bomb fell for 51 seconds, then exploded. In an instant, Hiroshima was devastated. Somewhere in the region of 70–80,000 people were killed, and another 80–100,000 injured in the raid.

The Japanese government failed to surrender instantly, and as it equivocated, the Americans carried out another raid. On 9 August, Major Charles Sweeny, flying a B-29 named *Bockscar* (a pun on the usual pilot's name) took a second bomb to Japan. It was dropped at 10:58 hours, and obliterated the city of Nagasaki. There were fewer deaths and injuries than at Hiroshima, but the numbers (35,000 dead, 50-60,000 wounded) were still horrific. The Japanese government now split into factions – one for surrender, the other for a fight to the death. The Emperor made the government's decision for it. On 14 August 1945, he broadcast to the Japanese people, telling them that the war was at an end, and that his country had been utterly defeated.

JAPANESE SURRENDER

When the Japanese capitulated in August 1945 (their formal surrender coming on 2 September), they still retained a semblance of an empire, but this was largely as a result of the fact that the

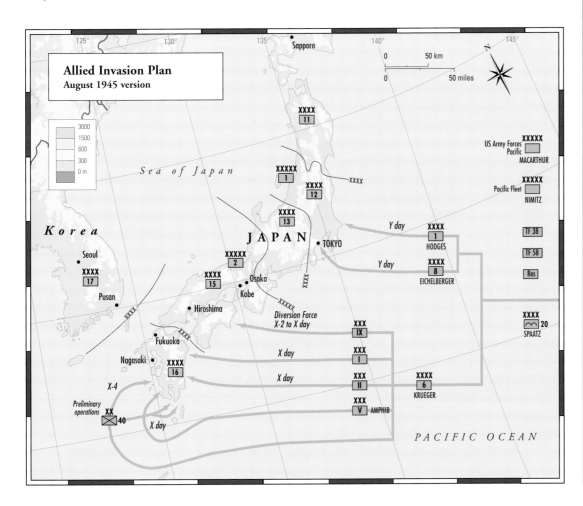

OPERATIONS AGAINST JAPAN

The fire raids on Japan have been largely overlooked in most general histories of the Pacific conflict, with the dramatic use of nuclear weapons overshadowing the earlier American raids.

After initial difficulties, General LeMay's decision to move over to fire bombing ensured that the attacks wrought absolute havoc on the Japanese cities subjected to this form of bombardment. The predominant use of flammable materials in constructing Japanese housing meant that incendiaries could quickly start a fire storm.

The fire raid on Tokyo on the night of 9/10 March 1945 killed around 84,000 civilians, a far higher toll than that exacted by either of the later atom bomb raids. The capture of Iwo Jima led to the basing of long range P-47 Thunderbolt and P-51 Mustang fighters there, and daylight raids began to complement the night raids. Such was the strength of the American air force that they had air superiority over Japan.

Over the course of the summer of 1945 the Japanese industrial base was smashed. By early August 1945, XXI Bomber Command was running out of targets for its attacks.

Meanwhile plans for the invasion of Japan were drawn up by MacArthur and Nimitz. Operation Olympic was to hit Kyushu in Novermber 1945, with Coronet to land on Honshu in March 1946.

end to hostilities preceded the planned British reconquest of Malaya. With supply lines interdicted by air and sea, the Japanese garrisons in the occupied territories had, as the 'island hopping' plan intended, begun to 'wither on the vine'. The major difficulty for the Allies came in the fact that once Japan had agreed to surrender, the garrisons in the islands that had been bypassed needed to be rounded up, disarmed and then repatriated: the risk that some of the garrisons would wish to fight to the death also remained.

This risk was substantially lower than would have been the case if the Allies had been compelled to fight their way into the Japanese heartland to enforce unconditional surrender. The invasion of the home islands was intended to be carried out in two phases. Kyushu was to be invaded in autumn 1945, followed by an assault on Honshu the following spring. To achieve this, American and British troops would have to be redeployed from Europe, while combat aircraft and shipping would also need to be brought out to the Far East to assist in the attacks. The atomic bomb attacks meant that this plan ('Operation Downfall') was not required.

Once news of the Emperor's decision reached Japanese forces, they began to lay down their arms. The British amphibious operation to retake Malaya was carried out as planned, although the landing was totally unopposed. The various Japanese outposts surrendered at different times. Japanese units on the Palau Islands and the Carolines surrendered on 2 September, simultaneous with the signature of the peace treaty between Japan and the Allies, and the remaining outposts gave up over the next few weeks. Indo-China was the last place where the Japanese occupying forces laid down their arms, with this surrender being taken on 30 November 1945.

Below: The remains of the Japanese city of Hiroshima after the explosion of the 'Little Boy' atomic bomb over the city on 6 August 1945 and the resulting firestorm which killed many thousands of civilians. The aiming point for the bomb was the bridge fourth from top in the centre. Despite the destruction, the Japanese government failed to surrender, and so a second bomb – 'Fat Man' – was dropped on Nagasaki three days later.

NAGASAKI

The atom bomb raids have historically been marked by a certain imbalance in reporting: the raid by *Enola Gay* on Hiroshima on 6 August – as the first use of a nuclear weapon – has received the most attention, and the subsequent raid on Nagasaki has been relegated to second place. However, it was the bomb dropped on Nagasaki that led directly to the Japanese decision to surrender.

When the B-29 named *Bockscar* released its 20-kiloton 'Fat Man' weapon on 9 August, the aircraft was in fact attacking its secondary target, since the original aiming point – the city of Kokura – was covered by cloud. The destruction of Nagasaki mirrored that caused by 'Little Boy' in Hiroshima, although since the countryside was less flat and the population was better off for shelters, there were more survivors.

Large areas of open water in the city meant that fires did not spread as readily, and there was no firestorm as at Hiroshima. Medical services did not collapse as they had in the aftermath of the first bombing raid, and oddly, the train network was not affected – making it easier to bring aid to the stricken city.

None of this, however, could mask the fact that the hopelessness of Japan's position had been demonstrated in the most ruthless way possible, or that a new and frightening era had been opened in world affairs. The atomic age had truly begun.

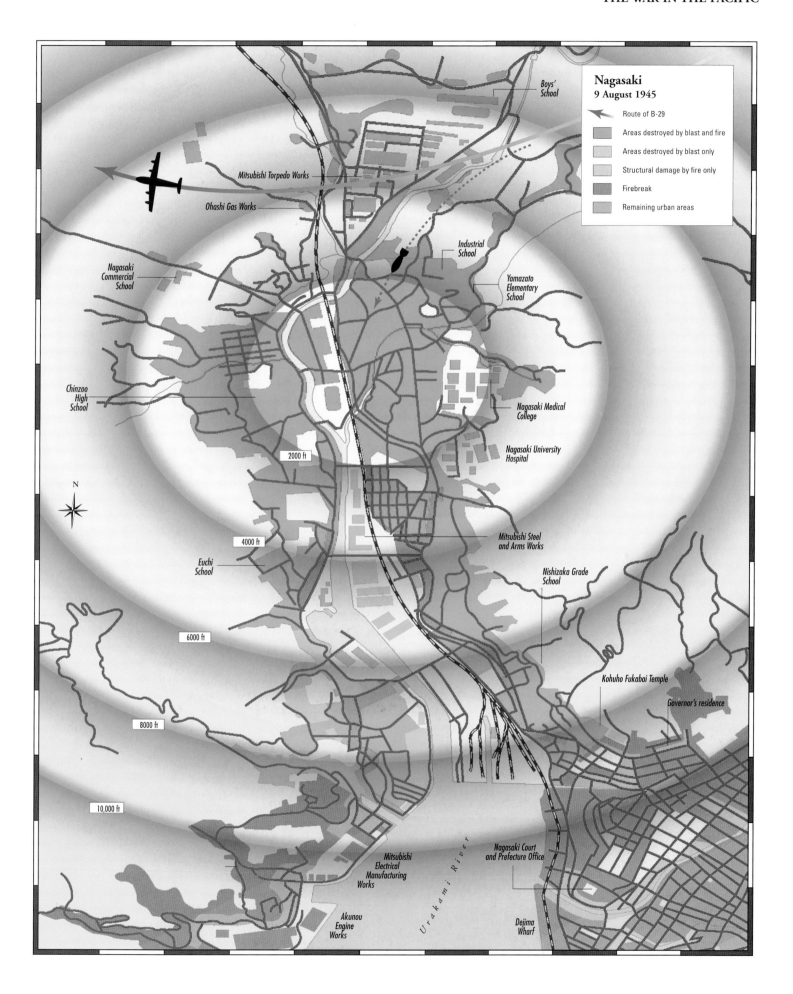

Boys'
School

Nagasaki
9 August 1945

Route of B-29

Areas destroyed by blast and fire

Areas destroyed by blast only

Structural damage by fire only

Firebreak

Remaining urban areas

Mitsubishi Torpedo Works

Ohashi Gas Works

Industrial
School

Nagasaki
Commercial
School

Yamazato
Elementary
School

Chinzoo
High
School

Nagasaki Medical
College

Nagasaki University
Hospital

2000 ft

4000 ft

Mitsubishi Steel
and Arms Works

N

Nishizaka Grade
School

Euchi
School

6000 ft

Kohuho Fukabai Temple

8000 ft

Governor's residence

10,000 ft

Mitsubishi
Electrical
Manufacturing
Works

Nagasaki Court
and Prefecture Office

Urakami River

Akunou
Engine
Works

Dejima
Wharf

Aftermath

The war left its mark on the world in several ways. Millions of men and women had served in their countries' armed forces or armaments factories; millions more had died through combat, genocide or aerial bombardment which had devastated the cities of Europe and Japan. The world was now bipolar, the Soviet Union and her former allies facing up to each other in the new atomic bomb age.

The mobilizations for war in 1939 and 1941 had differed in each nation, dependent upon the attitudes of the population, industrial capacity and financial strength of the nation and, most obviously, government policy. For France and the United Kingdom, the prospect of another major European conflict with similar levels of slaughter to World War I was appalling. The public in both nations had grown disillusioned in the aftermath of the war, as economic instability, recession and unemployment raised questions of 'was it all worth it?' By the late 1920s, Britain was firmly gripped by pacifism, and the prospect of going to war was something that nobody wished to contemplate. As a result Chamberlain's policy of appeasement won widespread support, and Churchill's warnings about Hitler saw him branded a 'warmonger'. The same pacifist attitudes could be found in France, although the latter's concerns about a resurgent Germany manifested themselves in campaigns to persuade French women to have more children (with the intention of providing a large army some 18 years later, when it was assumed that Germany might once again be a threat). The Soviet Union, after overcoming its internal strife in the revolution and subsequent civil and Polish wars, built up a professional army which in the early 1930s was one of the best in the world. However, Stalin was wary of its power, a paranoia which resulted in savage purges that decimated the Red Army high command.

MOBILIZATION FOR WAR

In Germany, attitudes were markedly different. Resentful of the terms of the Versailles settlement, the German populace suffered from economic instability, culminating in bouts of hyperinflation where life savings could be rendered valueless in 24 hours. As Germany lurched from crisis to crisis (with one brief period of stability), the radical message preached by Hitler sounded far more appealing to the German electorate. While it is a myth that Hitler won overwhelmingly in elections, he did receive enough of the vote to place him in a sufficiently strong position to be invited to become Chancellor, a fateful decision inspired by leading politicians who mistakenly thought that they could control the former army corporal.

Hitler's rise to power was swiftly followed with an aggressive foreign policy stance. Rearmament was begun in secret, and then announced to a stunned Europe in 1935. The reaction of Britain and France was initially timid. British Prime Minister Neville Chamberlain thought that Hitler was a rational statesman with whom he could do business – by the time he realised the fallacy of this point of view, it was too late. Hitler re-occupied the Rhineland (a demilitarized zone) in 1936, contrary to the terms of Versailles, and the Allies did nothing; in 1938, Austria was annexed, and again the Allies did nothing more than protest at the violation of the peace settlement.

Only once it became clear that Germany was an increasing threat did Britain and France begin to rearm. Britain's defences had to be increased in the face of public opposition, and the process was initially slow. As a result, when Hitler made demands on Czechoslovakia, the French and British governments were all too ready to accede to Hitler's scheme to avoid a war that they were

Left: The remaining senior Nazi Party figures on trial at Nuremberg after the war. In the front row, from top left, sit Hermann Göring, Rudolf Hess, Joachim von Ribbentrop and Wilhelm Keitel; all but Hess were sentenced to death. A similar war crimes trial was held for the Japanese leaders – but not Emperor Hirohito – in Tokyo. No Allied war crimes trials were held. World War II was notably different from World War I in that racially-inspired genocide occurred on a widespread basis, both in Europe and Asia.

MOBILIZATION

The mobilization process for the nations in World War II began at differing times during the 1930s. The USSR might be said to have been in a state of conflict ever since 1917, but although the command structure of the Red Army was in tatters, the armed forces would be well equipped.

Germany's mobilization began from 1934 as rearmament increased in pace and scope, until by 1939, the nation was ready for war. This was a distinct contrast to France, where political crises hampered the organization required to bolster the armed forces. Britain started rearming late, and struggled to try to catch up with Germany.

In the Pacific, the Japanese were at war with China from 1937, and World War II was simply an expansion of this conflict. The final major player was the United States. Having retreated to a position of isolation after World War I, the war in Europe saw increased US defence spending as the nation tried both to maintain neutrality and supply Britain and France. It was not until after Pearl Harbor that America was fully mobilized.

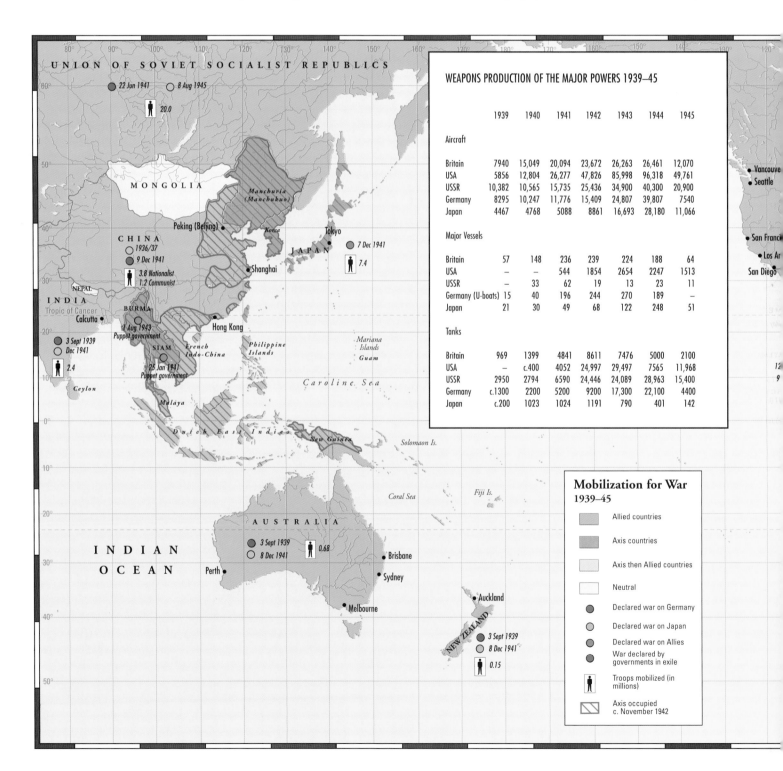

WEAPONS PRODUCTION OF THE MAJOR POWERS 1939–45

	1939	1940	1941	1942	1943	1944	1945
Aircraft							
Britain	7940	15,049	20,094	23,672	26,263	26,461	12,070
USA	5856	12,804	26,277	47,826	85,998	96,318	49,761
USSR	10,382	10,565	15,735	25,436	34,900	40,300	20,900
Germany	8295	10,247	11,776	15,409	24,807	39,807	7540
Japan	4467	4768	5088	8861	16,693	28,180	11,066
Major Vessels							
Britain	57	148	236	239	224	188	64
USA	–	–	544	1854	2654	2247	1513
USSR	–	33	62	19	13	23	11
Germany (U-boats)	15	40	196	244	270	189	–
Japan	21	30	49	68	122	248	51
Tanks							
Britain	969	1399	4841	8611	7476	5000	2100
USA	–	c.400	4052	24,997	29,497	7565	11,968
USSR	2950	2794	6590	24,446	24,089	28,963	15,400
Germany	c.1300	2200	5200	9200	17,300	22,100	4400
Japan	c.200	1023	1024	1191	790	401	142

Mobilization for War
1939–45

- Allied countries
- Axis countries
- Axis then Allied countries
- Neutral
- ● Declared war on Germany
- ○ Declared war on Japan
- ◐ Declared war on Allies
- ◑ War declared by governments in exile
- Troops mobilized (in millions)
- Axis occupied c. November 1942

clearly unprepared for. However, the fact that the crisis had brought Europe so close to war demonstrated the need for rearmament. As it became obvious that Hitler had no intention of stopping at Czechoslovakia, Britain and France increased their preparations for war.

When Poland was invaded in September 1939, Britain and France had been mobilising for war for over a year. The outbreak of war in Europe encouraged the United States to rearm, although in the face of considerable opposition from isolationists. The Japanese were already on a war footing as a result of their interventions in China, and Italy and the Soviet Union warily watched developments in the rest of Europe.

By the war's end in 1945, millions of men around the world – some 20 million in the Red Army alone – were under arms. With mass demobilisation, and the concurrent resettling of refugee populations and former prisoners of war, there were a number

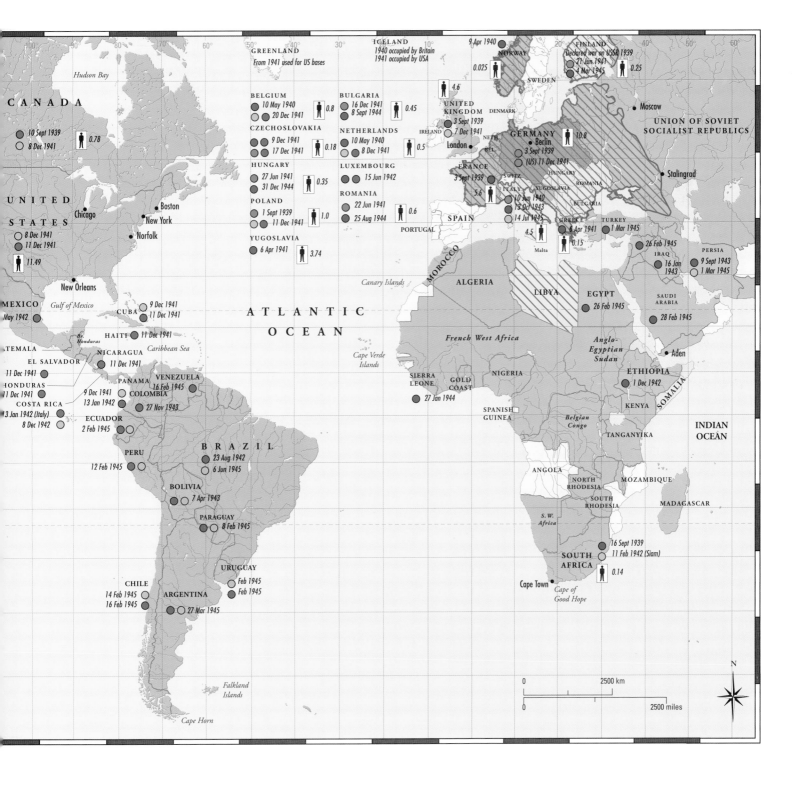

of mass migrations that took place, the most notable of these leading controversially to the foundation of Israel as a new nation state.

THE PEACE

The end of the war in Europe left Germany split in two by the invading Allied armies, with its economy and many of its cities devastated by years of Allied bombing. Poland, Bulgaria, Hungary, Romania and Czechoslovakia all had large concentrations of Soviet forces based on their territory, along with Yugoslavia. Any thoughts that these countries would soon be able to embark upon postwar reconstruction under democratically-elected governments were rapidly disabused when it became clear that Stalin wished to ensure that the Soviet Union maintained a firm grip over the direction in which all the eastern European countries progressed in order to provide a buffer from any future aggression.

The most difficult question was that of what was to happen to Germany itself. The Western Allies were anxious that the mistakes of the peace settlements at the end of World War I – which, it now appeared in retrospect, had virtually guaranteed war – were not repeated: the German population in 1919 had resented what was perceived as a dictated peace, were angered by the fact that excessive demands for reparations plunged their country into economic crisis and were horrified at what appeared to be nothing less than a deliberate attempt to humiliate Germany for all that had occurred. The end result of this process had not only allowed Hitler to become a force in politics, but had led to serious financial difficulties as the European economy, shorn of the economic power of Germany both as a producer and consumer of goods, stumbled from one problem to another. The onset of the Depression had forced Germany to adopt the politics of extremism, and Hitler had gained support he would otherwise never have had. This process encouraged the Western Allies to take a balanced approach to dealing with the defeated Germany in 1945. However the Soviet Union took a more robust line. Stalin, like the French premier Clemenceau before him, had little difficulty with the notion of preventing Germany from ever rising again (and thus becoming a potential threat), and was determined that the Soviet Union would have influence over postwar Germany – or at least the portion which the Red Army now occupied. In this way, Stalin intended to guarantee the security of the Soviet Union from future attack.

This same consideration drove Stalin's thinking regarding the rest of Europe, leading to the creation of pro-Soviet governments in Poland, Czechoslovakia, Hungary, Bulgaria and Romania in the immediate aftermath of the war, often despite the wishes of the local populations. Yugoslavia alone managed to avoid becoming a Soviet satellite thanks to the determination of its Communist leader, Tito, who broke with Stalin and pursued a policy of neutral non-alignment.

Territorially, the Soviet Union regained control of the Baltic States, and took land from eastern Poland. In exchange, the Poles were given land east of the Oder and Neisse rivers, along with the southern part of East Prussia and what had once been the international city of Danzig, now Gdansk. These alterations to the map were, initially at least, the most notable, but from 1949, the greatest sign of the legacy of the war lay in the division of Germany into two states. Although it was originally intended to reunify Germany once the reconstruction of the country was sufficiently advanced, it became clear that the victorious allies would

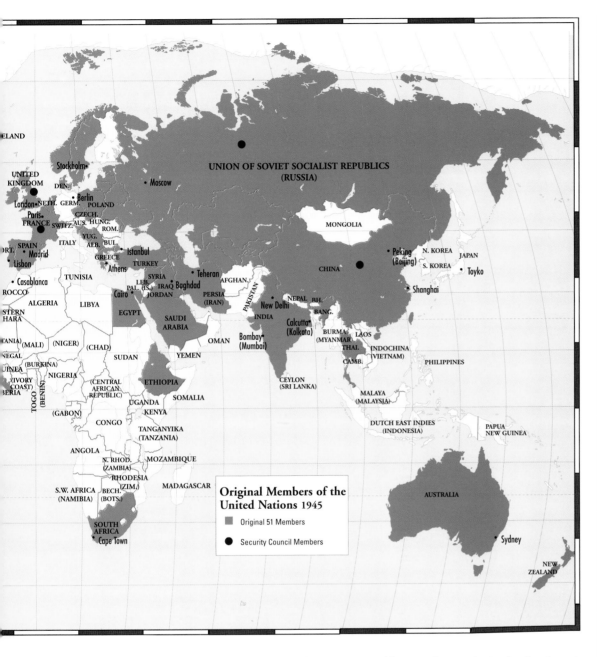

Original Members of the United Nations 1945

- Original 51 Members
- ● Security Council Members

THE UNITED NATIONS

While the war was still being fought, Allied leaders turned their attention to the postwar settlement. The failure of the League of Nations in the 1920s and 1930s dominated their considerations, and it was clear that the leading world power must be involved.

The term 'United Nations' came into use in 1942, when President Roosevelt invented it for the 'Declaration by United Nations' in which 26 nations pledged that they would fight alongside one another to defeat the Axis powers.

A declaration from an Allied summit in Moscow on 30 October 1943 saw the governments of the United States, Britain, the Soviet Union and China call for an early establishment of an international organization to maintain peace and security. That goal was reaffirmed at the Teheran conference on 1 December 1943, when Stalin, Roosevelt and Churchill met to discuss the future direction of the war effort. This drove the initial Allied planning for the United Nations.

The first outline of the UN was established at a conference at Dumbarton Oaks in Washington, D.C. between 21 September and 7 October 1944. Diplomats from the United States, Britain, the USSR and China set out the aims, proposed structure and procedures for the organisation, ready for its official launch once peace had been secured.

find agreement over the future of Germany almost impossible to achieve. Attitudes hardened, and once the Soviet blockade of Berlin in 1948 demonstrated the chasm between the two parties, it was almost inevitable that Germany would remain divided for the foreseeable future.

In strong contrast Japan was left virtually intact, with her emperor remaining as a figurehead, although reconstruction of many of Japan's cities was required thanks to the attentions of United States B-29 bombers, not least *Enola Gay* and *Bockscar*, the two aircraft that dropped the atomic bomb on Hiroshima and Nagasaki.

Casualties

The cost of World War II was immense, with the conflict being the bloodiest in the history of mankind. Unlike World War I, its successor was truly global in scope, with few parts of the world left unaffected by the fighting. The extent of casualties suffered was increased by the fact that the war saw heavy bombing of major population centres, meaning that civilians were in the front line for almost all of the war. The total number of dead is almost impossible to quantify, and estimates have altered over time. The Soviet Union is accepted to have sustained the most casualties, with the best estimates now ranging from approximately 20 million to as high as 30 million dead. Of these, many were civilians, killed in the fighting or in the brutal repression visited upon areas under Nazi occupation, where the occupiers regarded the locals as sub-human and treated them accordingly, some being shot, and others used as slave labour.

HIGH DEATH RATES

While the fighting in Europe during World War II is generally regarded from a western perspective as having been far less attritional than World War I, this is something of a misapprehension. The war on the Western Front between 1939 and 1945 was limited to two distinct periods of land combat. Between the fall of France in 1940 and the invasion of Normandy four years later, the bulk of the fighting in mainland Europe was carried out from the air – land warfare was restricted to commando raids and resistance activities. Fighting in North Africa and Italy did not lead to battles of attrition between the two sides, and when the war ended, it was possible to suggest that World War II had been far less costly. In fact, the casualty rates sustained in North West Europe were at times identical to those on the Western Front between 1914 and 1918, and on occasion were even higher. However, the relatively limited time frame in which combat between opposing armies took place meant that the losses were self-evidently lower overall.

Australian troops visit the graves of their comrades who fell in the fight for Burma. The global scale of the war saw soldiers buried thousands of miles from home on obscure battlefields. The precise casualty rates for soldiers who died in combat cannot be calculated, nor can the exact figures for the millions of civilians who died either as a result of the fighting or as part of planned genocide.

NEW CHARTER

Once the war had ended, the representatives from 50 countries met in San Francisco as part of the United Nations Conference on International Organization. The aim of the conference was to lay down the precise details for the organisation that would become the UN.

The debate was not straightforward, as Stalin argued that if the British dominions each had a seat at the UN General Assembly, then so should each of the constituent republics of the USSR. It was finally agreed that the solution was for the USSR to have three seats in the Assembly, with Ukraine and Belorussia taking the two additional places. There was also some dispute over the permanent membership of the Security Council, for although it was agreed that this was to consist of the victorious powers, some questioned whether France should be included. Also, the confused situation in China, where some parts of the country were governed by the Mao's communists, generated some discussion.

Finally, some consensus was reached. The United Nations Charter was signed on 26 June 1945 by the representatives of all 50 countries; Poland, which had not been represented at the conference, signed shortly afterwards, and did so in time to be considered one of the original Member States. The UN officially came into existence on 24 October 1945.

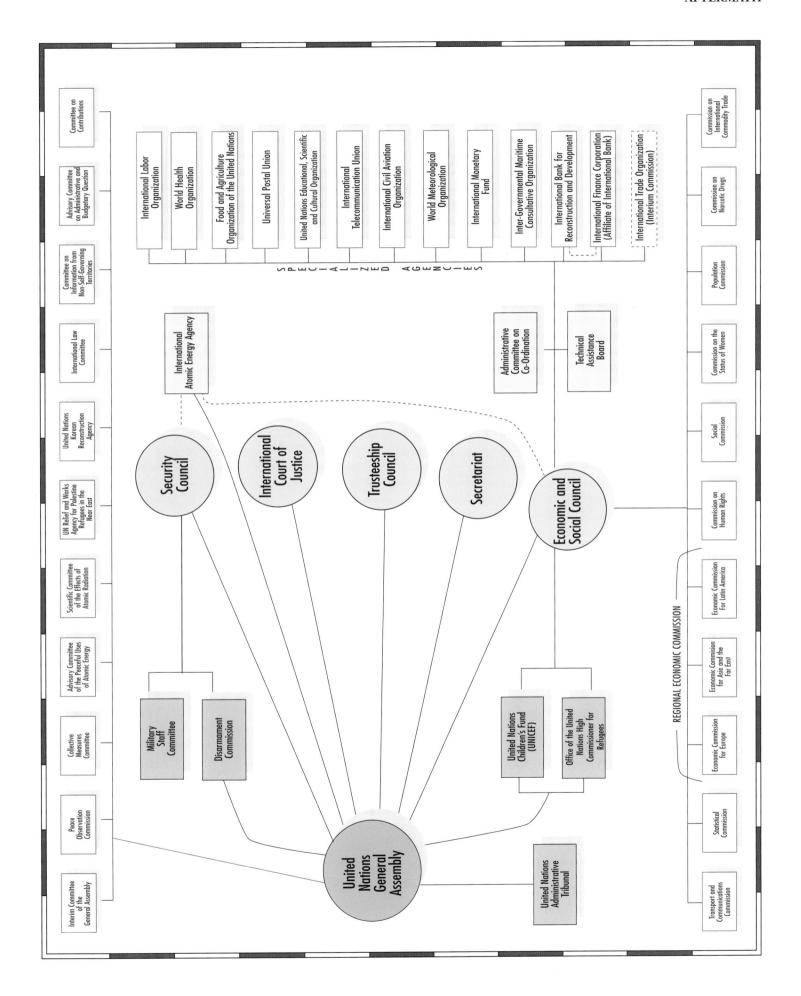

GLOBAL CASUALTIES

Quantifying the exact number of casualties in World War II is an almost impossible task, and a precise death toll will never be available. It is generally estimated that some 40 to 50 million

people died in the course of the war, with the vast bulk of these casualties coming from the USSR, which may have borne as much as 50 per cent of the total.

The number of civilian deaths was also particularly high. In Germany and Japan in particular, air attack was responsible for

inflicting severe losses amongst the civilian population, while all the other major combatants, with the exception of the United States, suffered from enemy air attacks against cities.

In occupied Europe, Jews were transported to concentration camps, where many met their

deaths, while resistance fighters also sustained losses. German reprisals for partisan activities saw whole communities massacred in retaliation. While this was a regular occurrence in the Soviet Union, it also took place in Yugoslavia, Czecho-slovakia and France.

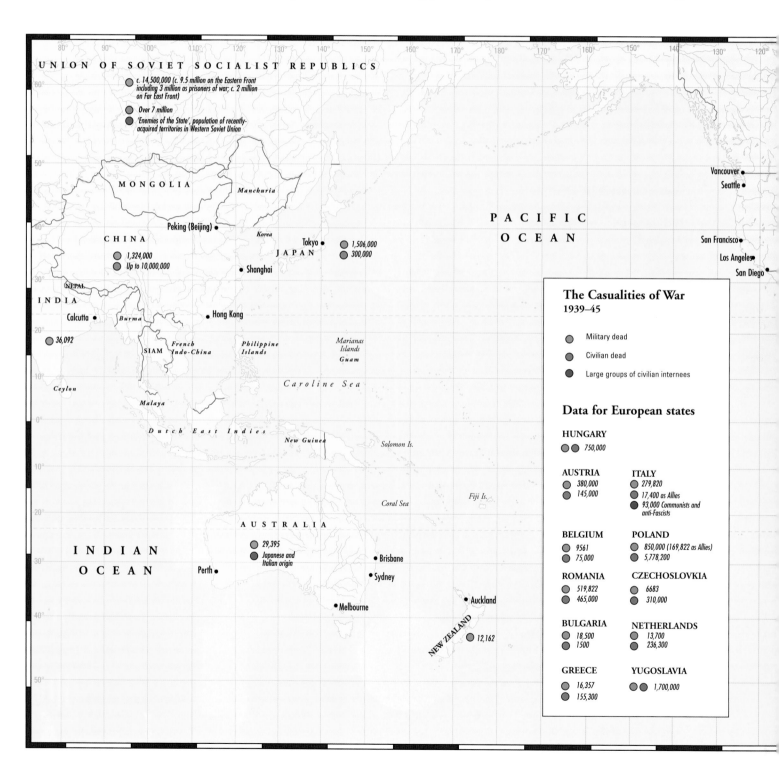

The Casualities of War
1939–45

Military dead

Civilian dead

Large groups of civilian internees

Data for European states

HUNGARY
750,000

AUSTRIA
380,000
145,000

ITALY
279,820
17,400 as Allies
93,000 Communists and anti-Fascists

BELGIUM
9561
75,000

POLAND
850,000 (169,822 as Allies)
5,778,200

ROMANIA
519,822
465,000

CZECHOSLOVKIA
6683
310,000

BULGARIA
18,500
1500

NETHERLANDS
13,700
236,300

GREECE
16,357
155,300

YUGOSLAVIA
1,700,000

The battles of attrition in the European theatre were fought on the Eastern Front. Soviet and German losses occurred on an almost inconceivable scale as the bitter conflict raged between the two sides for four years. In addition, casualties here included those taken prisoner, since neither the Germans nor the Soviets treated their captives particularly well – many prisoners never returned home as a result of this. It is estimated that four million out of five million Soviet prisoners died in German hands.

In the Pacific theatre, casualties were particularly heavy amongst the Japanese, since the belief that there was nothing more dishonourable than to surrender had wide currency. As demonstrated in the island-hopping campaigns and in Burma, Japanese soldiers generally preferred to fight to the death rather than surrender in the face of hopeless odds. Often overlooked in this theatre are the losses sustained by China in the war, which are almost impossible to quantify precisely. It is estimated that as many as 10 million civilians died, most of them in Japanese internment camps.

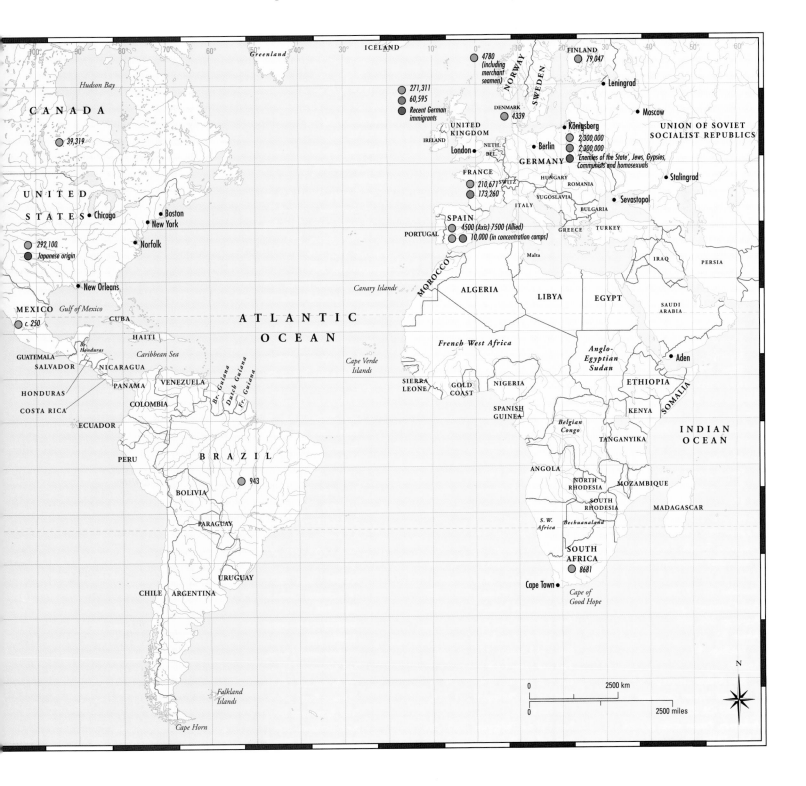

INDEX

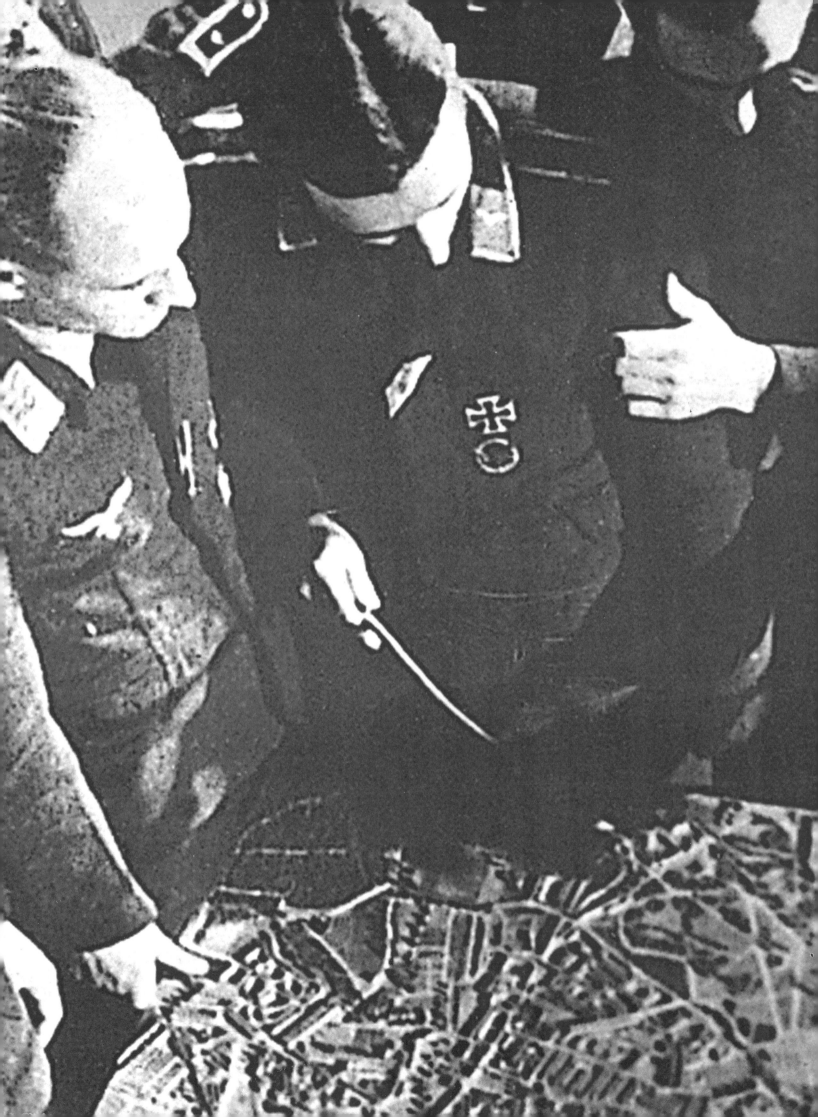